Accolades & Commentary

"I find myself awake in the middle of the night trying to decide which to worry about more, our democracy or our planet, when both are existential to my grandchildren. It is astounding that we, as the human species, are in this precarious place. And then I speak to the grounding human force that is Aaron Perry, and I'm at least temporarily comforted. Then for long-term comfort, I pick up his book, *Our Biggest Deal*, and read the amazing authors and study the amazing companies featured and I become completely energized to pick up the sword again!"

—KEN LAROE, FOUNDER & CHAIRMAN,
CLIMATE FIRST BANK

"I don't believe we will ever make a serious effort to save our home planet from all its threats until we humans adopt a spiritual connection to the natural world. Saving indigenous cultures and working and learning from them would be a good start."

—YVON CHOUINARD, FOUNDER,
PATAGONIA (FOR DILAFRUZ KHONIKBOYEVA'S ESSAY)

"Now more than ever, we need imagination as a force for systems change and planetary healing. The stories and frameworks in *Our Biggest Deal* bring that force vividly to life."

—SAMANTHA POWER, FOUNDER,
BIOFI BIO-REGIONAL FINANCE

"*Our Biggest Deal* reads like an operator's manual for prosperity that lasts. Perry replaces vague intent with measurable pathways—financeable, buildable, repeatable. For investors, policymakers, and builders who want returns and regeneration to be the same plan, not competing goals."

—PAUL KEVIN KENNON, AIA, FOUNDER & CEO,
BEYOND ZERO LUXURY WILDERNESS RESORTS

"Tackling the multitude of crises facing the Earth and humanity at this pivotal moment in history demands the ability to illuminate, hold, and weave the complexities of the situation with keen intelligence, systems thinking, pioneering vision, and deep humility. Aaron, alongside brilliant thought leaders from the regenerative living and finance sectors, presents one of the strongest cases yet—backed by real-world examples—on why choosing this path for humanity is not only profoundly wise but existentially essential. May we cultivate the wisdom to follow the sage advice so beautifully shared within these pages."

—KIRSTEN LIEGMANN, CEO,
REGENEARTH STUDIO

"We are in a time of profound transformation, analogous to the caterpillar becoming the butterfly. May we choose to step into our brilliance, deeply connect with one another and the earth, share our gifts, and co-create the conditions for regeneration and prosperity. I am inspired by the thought leaders featured in this book and grateful to Aaron for bringing an expanded awareness of this great and necessary work to the world."

—JASON KNOLL, CEO,
SAVORY INSTITUTE

"They want us to believe our only option is a take, make, use, waste economy that promotes a lack and scarcity mindset, where I cannot get mine if you get yours. This is simply not true. The abundance of human potential is more powerful than any probability we can chart on a spreadsheet. *Our Biggest Deal*, the ethos behind it, tangible solutions highlighted, and the powerful voices woven throughout, offer a pathway to shared prosperity on a healthy planet."

—BRENNA ST. ONGE, FOUNDER & CEO,
REGENERATIVE WORLD QUEST AND B THE LIGHT CONSULTING

"The future of our shared home is fast approaching an inflection point that will determine whether millions of species—the human race included—can long endure the damage the tragedy of the commons and free riding have done. The choice that faces us now is both moral and practical: we can change the way we live, or we can perish. *Our Biggest Deal* advances a cogent apology of the former, and existences proof of how we might avoid the latter. An important book at a critical time."

—ROBERT SWIGERT,
FOUNDER, GOODSTEAD

OUR BIGGEST DEAL

Pathways to Planetary Prosperity

OUR BIGGEST DEAL

Pathways to Planetary Prosperity

Regenerative Finance, Quintenary Economics,
and the Emerging Earth Steward Aristocracy

Aaron William Perry

Foreword by John Fullerton

VIP Guest Essays from Leading Global Voices

Earth Water Press

Published by

Earth Water Press
PO Box 2333
Boulder, CO 80306

Earth Water Press is a social enterprise in the Y on Earth Community family of companies. For more information or to contact the author about booking talks, workshops, or bulk orders of this book, visit www.yonearth.org.

Edited by David Aretha and Amina Alieva, *Clean Edits / Clean Content*
Cover design by Jake Welsh Graphic Design
Interior design by Second Star Publishing Works

Image credits
Map of World (pp. 21, 100), *Pixabay*, credit: Yuri_B.
Financial Wealth Pyramids (pp. 24–25), UBS; *Credit Suisse Research Institute*.
Mycelial Neural Network (pp. 39, 63), *Pixabay*, credit: Gerd Altman.
Iceberg Systems Change Model (p. 52), Benson and Marlin.
DNA Image (p. 53), *Pixabay*, credit: SvitDen.
Shinrin-yoku Meditation (p. 87), *Pixabay*, credit: Khemrajdotin.
Global Materials Extraction (p. 171), *resourcepanel.org*.
Bioregional Finance Diagrams (pp. 178–180), Samantha Power and BioFi.
Stephen Covey Time Management Matrix (p. 236), *Huffington Post*.
Global Cultural Forces of Transformation (p. 265), Alena Maslova and Dobrosphera.
COPx Graphic Novel Images (pp. 274, 277–278), Juan Echinove.
Eightfold Regenerative Economics (pp. 317, 421), John Fullerton and *Capital Institute*.
Sustainable Development Goals (p. 419), *United Nations*.
Inner Development Goals (p. 420), *Ekskäret Foundation*, *The New Division*, and *29K Foundation*.
Regenerative Development Framework (p. 421), *Open Future Coalition*.
Systems Change Intervention (p. 423), Corina Angheloiu and Mike Tennant.

ISBN 978-1-7347229-9-4 (paperback)
ISBN 978-1-7347229-8-7 (ebook)

Library of Congress Control Number: 2025946658

Perry, Aaron William.

    Our Biggest Deal : pathways to planetary prosperity / by Aaron William Perry ; foreword by John Fullerton. — Colorado : Earth Water Press, 2025.

    478 pages : illustrations ; 24 cm.

    ISBN 978-1-7347229-9-4 (pbk.) — ISBN 978-1-7347229-8-7 (epub)

    1. Sustainable development. 2. Environmental economics. 3. Economic policy—Environmental aspects. 4. Money—Moral and ethical aspects. 5. Finance—Environmental aspects. I. Title.

    HC79.E5 P47 2025
    338.9—dc23

Printed in the United States of America

Dedicated To

Jane Goodall, Bernard Lietaer, Wangari Maathai, William Irwin Thompson, Hazel Henderson, Thich Nhat Hanh, Kevin Townley, Scott Pittman, Arne Ness, Donella Meadows, Masaru Emoto, Joanna Macy, Bill Mollison, Masanobu Fukuoka, Peter Tompkins, Marija Gimbutas, Alan Watts, Hermann Hesse, Joachim-Ernst Berendt, Buckminster Fuller, Rudolf Steiner, Djwhal Khul, Teilhard de Chardin, Viktor Schauberger, Johann Wolfgang von Goethe, Francis of Assisi, Deganawida, Hildegard von Bingen, the Grandmothers Councils, Sibyls, Hiereia, Temple Priestesses, and Magu Miko Mystery Maenads healing humanity's nature-disconnection maladies throughout time, and all of the other heart-centered cultural giants of the near and distant past upon whose shoulders we now joyfully and courageously stand with gratitude.

To all of us alive today purposefully working toward planetary prosperity.

To our children, children's children, and seven generations to come.

To all of our relations: the green ones of the viriditas, the winged and soaring ones, the two-leggeds, four-leggeds, six-leggeds, eight-leggeds, and centipedal, the cephalopods, the swimming, the serpentine, the devata, the water, fire, wind, and soil beings, the sky and thunder beings, and the unfathomably manifold great star beings and star nations watching over our humble evolutionary journey here on our home planet: the sublimely beautiful Mama Gaia.

And, of course, to the "old-school" economists—bless their hearts, ftknwtd.

"When a complex system is far from equilibrium, small islands of coherence in a sea of chaos have the capacity to shift the entire system to a higher order."

— LLYA PRIGOGINE, NOBEL LAUREATE

"We do not need to invent sustainable human communities. We can learn from societies that have lived sustainably for centuries. We can also model communities after nature's ecosystems, which are sustainable communities of plants, animals, and microorganisms. Since the outstanding characteristic of the biosphere is its inherent ability to sustain life, a sustainable human community must be designed in such a manner that its technologies and social institutions honor, support, and cooperate with nature's inherent ability to sustain life."

—FRITJOF CAPRA

CONTENTS

PART III   CASE STUDY VIGNETTES   305

TABLE OF FIGURES

PROJECT PARTNERS AND SPONSORS

A very special thank you to the companies, philanthropists, and families who are supporting this book project and the many ancillary and related programs of the Y on Earth Community. To learn more about these companies and their offerings, please visit yonearth.org/partners-supporters, and the websites below:

HOME PLANET FUND
homeplanetfund.org

CLIMATE FIRST BANK
Powered by **OneEthos**
climatefirstbank.com

EARTH COAST PRODUCTIONS
earthcoast.com

bluestone.
bluestonelife.com

HUSCH BLACKWELL
huschblackwell.com

the RIVERSIDE est. 1914
A VENUE AS UNIQUE AS BOULDER
boulderriverside.com

BRAD & LINDSAY LIDGE
FAMILY FOUNDATION

VERONA RYLANDER PHILANTHROPIES
veronarylander.com

AND CO
andco.earth

LAUNCH LEGAL
techlawstartup.com

Dobrosphera
kind media

kindmedia.group

gaiaai.xyz

WELE WATERS
FARM TO SPA

welewaters.com

goodstead

goodstead.co

Y
ON EARTH
COMMUNITY

yonearth.org

clean content

cleancontent.net

Shaye Skiff
communications

shayeskiff.com

SoundLight
FOUNDATION

soundlightfoundation.org

Regenerative
World Quest

regenerativeworldquest.org

FOREWORD

John Fullerton is Founder and President of the Capital Institute, and is the author of *Regenerative Capitalism* and *Regenerative Economics*

S ince you are holding this book in your hands, it's safe to assume you are not asleep, nor in denial about the challenges confronting humanity. The Western presumption of perpetual progress has come into question, except among madmen, extreme techno-optimists, or of course, most traditional economists. The institutional scaffolding of modernity is creaking of its own insufficiencies to meet the present context. It is also under intentional assault. And the grossest injustice of all? The nearly half of humanity that struggle for their daily meals and didn't create the crisis are the first to be suffering its consequences. That suffering is here and accelerating; no one is immune.

We are not accustomed to thinking about our place in the long sweep of history. We naturally assume the future will arrive generally as a linear extension of the present and recent past. Our culture has narrowed our awareness to years and election cycles, to quarterly earnings, or now to the number of likes on a tweet. But of course, this is not how life evolves. Instead, it has been marked by upheavals and sudden, epic, and at times catastrophic events that change the course of history. Sometimes these events are war, sometimes plagues, sometimes natural events like floods. And often such upheavals are caused by technological innovation such as the arrival of the printing press, the steam engine, or the microchip.

In a world of immense complexity, it's generally a fool's errand to make predictions. But I feel safe making this one: We are not living through an era of change, we are living through a change in era.

Pause here a moment to contemplate that context as you pick up this hopeful book of wise counsel and collective heroic action, which offers a peak into this new era. The journey to the new era in front of us is a metamorphosis.

We don't yet know completely or with certainty what the butterfly looks like, but we perhaps have glimpses. Aaron William Perry uniquely weaves together the "group genius" of myriad voices and experts whose diverse perspectives give us more glimpses, helping us better understand the multi-dimensional aspects of our global challenges and fresh insights illuminating some of the many pathways available to us.

Part 1 offers thirteen chapters written by Perry that will help you to rapidly orient around some of the most salient and essential framing ideas that should be understood as foundational for all change-makers seeking to grasp the scope and scale of the transformation ahead. This collection builds on Perry's previous books *Y on Earth* and *Viriditas*, cementing him as one of our inspirational and rare transdisciplinary thinkers helping us find our way through these unprecedented times. Following Perry's insights and novel philosophical concepts, all rooted in ecosystemic intelligence, we are treated to a series of guest essays including from many of my colleagues and teachers. We then explore through a series of case studies many of the important emergent green shoots of a regenerative economy—some of which are already operating at substantial scale. Finally, Perry returns with some lighter, "free-range" aphoristic musings, together creating a whole that is indeed greater than the sum of the parts. It's a feast you'll want to taste slowly and return to more than once.

When you close these pages, you will be saturated with insight and inspiration. But hold onto this one larger point. You and I, no matter where on Earth you live, happen to live in an epic moment, the dawn of a new era! We truly are at the dawn, as the old paradigm struggles to hold on. It feels and is chaotic. That's the nature of such epic change. How it unfolds is unknowable. This is of course unsettling and can make us feel powerless.

But here's something profound to contemplate. Our latest scientific understanding of quantum entanglement and nonlocality (as best I can understand these concepts), are now accepted science with the award of the 2022 Nobel Prize in physics. Everything is connected, entangled. The implications are stunning and exciting for us all. Whatever we do, or don't do, or even set our attention to, will affect the outcome. We have agency more than we can imagine, even as we feel helpless to control events, even if we will never see or know the direct impact of our actions. We matter.

I resisted making this change in era claim for years, not wanting to inflate the importance of our brief time here on Earth in the long sweep of history. But there is no exaggerating either the reality or the stakes. Not since the shift from the Medieval Era to the Modern Era has Western culture undergone such profound and disorienting change. Yet this time, with a global population sixteen times larger than it was five centuries ago, interconnected and interdependent not only because of our human communication networks and global supply chains. Now, for the first time, humanity's future is interdependent with the evolution of the biosphere whose complex cycles enable all life and whose healthy function we are undermining with maniacal abandon. Climate change is but a symptom of this suicidal reality.

This interdependence with all life of our technology driven human project is a consequence of the human appropriation of 25-40% of Net Primary Productivity (HANPP), the measure of the entire planet's biological production. Humans have commandeered it for our use as if it had no limits and no connection to our own survival. This ghastly infringement on essential biodiversity leads to what scientists now call the 6th great extinction. The last one was caused by a meteorite that wiped out the dinosaurs. We need look no further than our system of industrial agriculture, fishery and forestry management, and our ever-expanding urbanization to understand the predicament facing humanity. Modernity, it turns out, despite all its noble intentions, aspirations, and extraordinary progress, is undermining the conditions essential for all life to continue flourishing—including ourselves.

No one can say it better than Wendell Berry. "There are no unsacred places. There are only sacred places and desecrated places." We are desecrating Gaia because there's a profit in it. As a result, we face two choices. We will transform reactively because of collapse. Or we will transform proactively through a shift in consciousness powerful enough to change our ways.

The choices we will make and the outcome of this change in era is unknowable. But a new dark age is clearly in sight if we simply keep doing what we are doing. Yet profound new possibilities are also in store should we rise to meet the moment. The insights and examples in this book are a beautiful affirmation that we are indeed rising to meet this moment. Some are calling this period of human history a New Renaissance, although this time global and reconnecting with our many ancient wisdom traditions Western cultures have long ignored to our collective detriment. It's exciting to ponder, promising emergence into an entirely new stage of the human story. In fact, I'd say it's a New Renaissance and a next Scientific Revolution packaged into one.

The Italian Renaissance followed the Black Death that devastated medieval Europe between 1348 and 1350. Florence's population was nearly halved in one year, wreaking unimaginable terror, but also shifting the economic power of the working class that survived. In the wake of this horror, Renaissance, meaning "rebirth," represented a revival of classical learning, and the embrace of a new humanism, the arts and sciences, and geographical exploration. The Renaissance would then usher in the scientific revolution, a direct rejection of the dogma of the Roman Catholic Church and its corruption. The Modern Era was born. The West would be the home of unprecedented progress based on extraordinary discoveries in science, godlike technological advances, and the rise of industrial capitalism. But of course, the Modern Era also had its shadow of colonialism, slavery, and the extractive othering of all life.

The progress of modernity was built on a Newtonian or mechanistic understanding of reality, referred to metaphorically as the "clockwork universe." As complexity scientist Stu Kauffman likes to say, Sir Issac Newton literally taught us (in the West) how to think. For the most part, we continue to believe we live in a materialist, Newtonian world, inclusive of neoclassical economics, the theory by which we manage the global economy and international relations. At the heart of the economics discipline is the absurd assumption that exponential growth can go on forever on a finite planet, in direct conflict with the laws (not theories) of physics. Taylorism, the so called "scientific management" theory by which we run most of our business enterprises, is also built on a Newtonian foundation. Enterprises can be optimized and managed by "key performance indicators." These are the ideas of the machine, not the understanding of living organisms.

Using the method of reductionism, we learned to break complex wholes down into parts, believing that understanding the parts would give us a better understanding of the whole. As a result, our academies are broken down into specialist disciplines and our governing bodies are broken down into specialist ministries. What we call the "scientific method" is in fact largely this same reductionist method. Despite the truly extraordinary progress the scientific method has delivered, from the invention of microchips to rocket ships, we also know intuitively and from experience that the whole is far greater than the sum of the parts, and this is no small detail. I'd say it describes reality for pretty much everything that matters most, from the mysterious to the sacred. Agronomist and Right Livelihood Award winner Wes Jackson puts it this way, "There's nothing wrong with the reductionist method, so long as we don't confuse the method for how the world actually works."

To be more concrete, we confuse the complicated—things we make—for the complex—things we manage. We make bridges and computers. We make buildings and artificial intelligence models. We manage the complexity of our health and our families. We manage the complexity of a company or the economy, a nation and the United Nations. With modernity's perfection of the reductionist method and our left-brain dominant mode of analytical problems solving, we are now very good at the complicated. Yet with our same left brain, competitive, goals driven approach, lacking integration with our more intuitive and creative right brain capabilities of seeing the whole, we often fail in our attempts at managing complexity. In fact, we lack the ability to even discern between the complicated and the complex.

As a result of this fatal error and now pressing up against planetary boundaries, we find ourselves in the early 21st century navigating what we now call the polycrisis, the interconnected political, economic, social, and ecological crises seemingly spinning out of control. This is a crisis of complexity, and our general ignorance about it. This of course is the unprecedented context for this book.

To dig yet even deeper, let us use the term meta-crisis, referring to a singular underlying root cause of the multitude of crises that comprise the polycrisis. That root cause is what's known as the myth of separation which we can trace to the Enlightenment, which in turn was enabled by the Renaissance as well. The separation of us from each other in our embrace of individualism, and the separation of humanity from the non-human world are both direct consequences of Enlightenment thinkers, most notably Rene Descartes and his belief in the separation of the mind and the body. "I think therefore I am" implies the mind is the true self. Descartes saw the body as nothing more than a complex machine, operating according to physical and mechanical laws, relying on his interpretation of Newton no doubt (Newton's full understanding ran deeper). Descartes's views on nature are reflected in this quote attributed to him, "The conquest of nature is to be achieved through number and measure" again reflecting his mechanistic worldview, the superiority of the human, and the separation of man from nature.

The New Renaissance will be fundamentally different. Global in scale, it will be marked by a cultural shift beyond the limits of materialism and the reductionist method of perceiving reality. We will leave our clockwork universe behind, and embrace a holistic metaphor of interconnected and interdependent living networks, the web of life, as a more accurate, evidence-based understanding of reality. This understanding of reality is already here. It's the next evolutionary path in our ever complexifying level of development. But the people running the world don't get their jobs by questioning the old paradigm. For the most part, they remain dangerously tucked away in a modern-day Plato's cave.

This New Renaissance too is rejecting dogma, but this time the dogma of the "Church of Economics" (Newtonian based neoclassical economics) and its emissary the finance algorithm that keeps the global economy locked in collapse mode. It rejects the rise of hyper competitive techno-feudalism, perhaps the ultimate expression of the reductionist logic of the machine with its dystopian vision of hackable humans under the control of their algorithms. And of course, it too rejects the rampant corruption associated with the rise of authoritarianism around the world. This New Renaissance honors the interdependence and the unity in diversity of all, grounded in evidenced based science that remarkably aligns with our many ancient wisdom traditions. It reflects a rebirth of humanism, but this time not with humans at the center, above nature seeking to dominate it.

Instead, it celebrates with great joy humanity participating creatively, and if we are wise, constructively in the regenerative process that describes how all life works. The diversity of human cultures, each empowered to participate through their unique and extraordinary essence in the ongoing evolution of life itself. This includes life within Gaia, but remarkably according to the leading edge of cosmology, life across the entire Uni-verse—meaning literally one song, fourteen billion years long! What better inspiration (literally to "breath in spirit") could give our lives fresh and desperately needed meaning? What nobler purpose could exist for the human project? To play our unique and vital part as likely the highest expression of consciousness among all species, and to participate in the evolution of the Universe! It takes my breath away.

And yet . . .

We find ourselves confronted with unprecedented division, fear, and justifiable anger. We appear to be lurching backwards when we know we are failing and must move forward faster. The hour feels increasingly dark. To understand our predicament, I will refer to the great Bulgarian sage Beinsa Douno (Peter Deunov, 1864-1944) whose ideas the ever-thoughtful David Lorimer introduced me to in his book, *The New Renaissance* (2010). Douno writes, "Money and power continue to be venerated as if the course of your life depended upon it. In the future, all will be subjugated to Love and all will serve it. But it is through suffering and difficulties that the consciousness of man will be awakened."

Deunov describes the Four Degrees of human culture, a simplified antecedent to spiral dynamics for those familiar with that framework. Lorimar presents the Four Degrees that correspond to the evolution of consciousness as follows:

1. Violence—representing force, domination and power
2. Law—imposed through external control, threats, and manipulation
3. Justice—which is universal and excludes privilege
4. Love—as life for the Whole, where Love is both embodied and applied.

It would seem to me that American culture, with all its influence on the world, has been struggling between the second and third degrees in the post war era, between Law and Justice. Yet increasingly we find ourselves sliding backwards toward the violence of force, domination and power with the exponential rise in power of the world's leading multinational corporations and institutions of finance. The 2008 financial crash was an act of violence. Facebook's algorithms are an act of violence. But, of course there's more.

For years using soft and hard power, the U.S. government has leveraged its status as the world's hegemonic superpower in world affairs. What has changed in 2025 is there is no longer any pretense. We're now witnessing the force of domination in the name of America First, breaking all norms of behavior and using force to usurp the rule of law in a purely transactional world where might makes right. It's undeniable that this trajectory is in motion. It has spread around the globe to varying degrees affecting institutions of governance, finance, business, law, media, journalism, and education. Just when a more holistic understanding and a more collaborative feminine energy is called for, we see an explosion of toxic masculinity.

Recall, the Italian Renaissance burst onto the scene out of the ashes of the Black Death. In my hopeful moments, which I cling to, I see this slip downwards as the death of the old reductionist paradigm no longer fit for purpose. Think of it like as the wind up necessary to punch through Deunov's universal yet tentative Third-Degree cry for justice, evidenced by Gandhi, Mandella, King, and more recently, the Black Lives Matter and climate justice movements. These cries have proven to be illusive, or at least the long arc of justice demands more patience than we can bare.

Make no mistake, we are on a knife's edge as Bucky Fuller foresaw a half century ago. I'm hopeful we are now finally in the wind-up, the necessary step back in order to build unstoppable momentum, like a pitcher's wind-up on the mound to deliver a crushing fastball. Our question now is this: can we use this pain, this chaos, to break through into the Fourth Degree of consciousness, to Love. Can we return to an embrace of the Whole where we began. In this place, violence on our health, violence on each other, and violence on Gaia will be all but unthinkable, no different than self-harm. Instead, we will take our rightful place participating as only we can in the magical and evolutionary process of regeneration, in what Buckminster Fuller described as our Regenerative Universe!

Since the economy is the water in which our culture now swims, I'm convinced that the road to regeneration begins with Regenerative Economics, manifested out of the consciousness of love, and built on the patterns and first principles of living systems and not the machine. Regenerative Economics is not about a new set of goals or new key performance indicators. Rather, it is about humbly aligning with life, creating conditions conducive to life, and removing obstacles to the natural course of life we all intuit deep down inside. Critically, it promises currently unseen potential as the source of our future prosperity, but that's a story for another day.

My friends, we are in a battle for human consciousness. Our work is not only to understand the deep historical roots of this battle, but to do the real-time restorative work of reclaiming our language—getting a grip on words like "wealth," "aristocracy," and even "winning," as this book does—and, most importantly, to lean in to the hopeful possibilities available to us, connecting and collaborating in the rich context of nature's deep intelligence and the group genius of heart-centered human beings devoted to our shared future. We each have a role to play, beginning within ourselves, our intentions, and our actions. We are each invited to evolve into and embody the supererogatory leadership of the emergent Earth steward aristocracy that Perry calls us to.

This is the context of the hopeful book that awaits you.

Be inspired, find your agency, and enjoy the historic metamorphosis that awaits us all!

John Fullerton
Capital Institute
Stonington, Connecticut
June 2025

INTRODUCTION

This book is written specifically for entrepreneurs, executives, financiers, and philanthropists motivated to make change and benefit the greater good of our shared world and future at scale. These extraordinary people exemplify a form of leadership rooted in courage, creativity, and the dignity of taking responsibility for the global commons, and are deploying capital through regenerative structures and strategies, understanding both the tremendous capital investment opportunities and the moral imperative of stewardship philanthropy. Hopefully you count yourself among this extraordinary group, or you're aspiring to join it.

However, if you are satisfied with the status quo, if the state of the world seems stable or satisfactory to you, if you don't believe that we could be doing better, or that humanity is potentially (and hopefully) experiencing an evolutionary leap, then this book may challenge some of your assumptions and beliefs.

If, on the other hand (like so many of my friends and colleagues, and so many of the leaders and visionaries featured in this book), you know deep down that we could indeed be doing better—much better—and that we're potentially going through a profound transformation much like the caterpillar in its chrysalis before the magnificent butterfly emerges, this book is written for you, to further equip you as a powerful participant and change-agent in this evolutionary journey.

I, for one, am convinced of the latter, and I'm equally convinced that we need *you*—especially right now.

For humanity is locked in a titanic struggle between two clashing worldviews, two competing "realities."

From a certain perspective, it is no exaggeration to say that we are facing the darkest, most ominous threat we have ever faced as a people.

Many of us can feel it—can you?

1

In the face of this threat, it is as if we're each being asked, deep inside: "What kind of world do we *really* want?"

Is *this* the best we can do?

Popular epic fantasies by JRR Tolkien, George Lucas, Frank Herbert, and James Cameron, although fiction on their face, resonate with us broadly as they reflect back and speak to us of a deep truth emerging from the liminal realms of our collective unconscious. The great struggle between darkness and light in *Lord of the Rings*, *Star Wars*, *Dune*, and *Avatar* isn't mere fantasy. This great struggle between darkness and light is *real*, and it's playing out within each of us and all around our world . . . right now, and in every moment of every single day.

Ignorance, indifference, inaction, and avarice are mainstay "real-time" tools of the darkness—to be sure. But so are legacy aspects of our economic and financial systems constructs. Curiously, although money and economics are barely visible in the *Lord of the Rings* and *Star Wars* fantasies, they are actually the very real and preponderant instruments of dark forces in *our* world. Too many of us are unknowingly in the cold, firm grip of these forces and haven't yet freed ourselves of their shackles, let alone transmuted them into powerful forces for good in the world.

Isn't there something deep inside us that knows things could be different? Couldn't we be doing much better—for ourselves and each other—and couldn't we in fact be much, much happier and healthier and whole? Couldn't our children's futures be pregnant with the promise of peace and prosperity: stability, opportunity, and abundance? Couldn't the living fabric of our communities and ecosystems be robust and thriving, stout and generative and magnificent in their vitality? Couldn't our children be safer, our elders healthier and more comfortable, our parents less stressed, and our environments pristine?

This titanic struggle isn't playing out on some other planet, in a galaxy far, far away. It is happening right here, right now on planet Earth; specifically in our global "marketplace of ideas"—a competition between two fundamentally different and irreconcilable stories, two fundamentally different versions of the human spirit and our shared human destiny.

One of these stories tells us that amassing money and might is our prime directive—how we "win." It tells us that winning matters most, regardless of the costs, and that profit and power are weapons to wield at will as we ward off our fears and indulge our whims.

The other story is profoundly different. It tells us that caring for the common good is our main mission, that creatively coexisting in collaborative communities while stewarding ecosystems is *the* source of true wealth, and that "winning" is tantamount to planetary-scale peace, plenty, and prosperity—for our entire human family and our whole living world.

The first story twists people terribly—fueled by self-centered fantasy, adolescent amorality, delusional deception, cynical "certainty," grotesque greed, magical thinking, and, above all else, subtle but severe self-hatred. Whipping the masses into masochistic madness, this sad story necessarily devolves into dystopian darkness where fascism follows. And fascism isn't good for anybody—it is ugly, stupid, and destructive. This is a stark characterization, I understand. But the great tragedy for so many of us—decent and in the "middle"—is that without the clear conviction of a higher calling to the greater good, we're too easily seduced by supposed shades of gray: A lack of black and white ethical clarity in our political economy leads to widespread indifference and inaction, then disaster and devastation.

But there is another way.

The second story speaks of an illuminated pathway paved by consciousness and compassion, intelligence and love—love for the *good*, the *beautiful*, the *just*, and the *wise*. Love for *each other*. Love for *ourselves*. Love for *life itself* and all the *sublime creatures* woven together in a tapestry of interdependent relationship here on our sacred spaceship—planet Earth. And, of course, love for her—for *Earth*—our one and only Mama Gaia.

This titanic struggle has been underway for lifetimes. Ever since the first city-state walls were erected and nearby forests felled in sacrifice to the machinery of political economy, leaving deserts and despoliation in their wake, human destiny has hung in the balance.

But now things are different.

The scope and scale—and impact—of our human enterprise on planet Earth has reached a new degree of epic proportion. We're at the tipping point. Although we have the knowledge, resources, and capacity to bring balance back to our world, business as usual has us careening off a cliff.

Raging wildfires and fierce floods are stark reminders of a destabilized atmosphere: climate chaos cares not about political faction, religious belief, or bank account—everyone is in danger. Incomprehensible complexity in global financial systems and artificial intelligence, tectonic geopolitical turbulence, cynically sadistic militarism, and deteriorating communities are evident everywhere, as our individual quality of life and internal coherence also erode—all converging in a multifaceted crisis like nothing our species has ever encountered before.

A *polycrisis.*

Many crises at once, multivalent and interconnected in an extraordinarily complex set of dependencies and feedback loops.

Acute complexity. Confusion. Uncertainty. Cognitive dissonance.

These times aren't only characterized by extreme instability in external systems and macro-dynamics. We're hurting inside, too. Anxious, stressed, and depressed, so many of us suffer mental health maladies endemic to modernity. As a people, we are not well.

The polycrisis pervades the planet, and the polycrisis penetrates deep inside each of us.

What are we to do?

How do we break through and break free?

How do we exit this existential crisis and secure a soft landing in a milieu of benevolence and betterment, meritocracy and meaning, wisdom and kindness, decency and well-being?

How do we escape the polycrisis and progress along pathways to planetary prosperity?

This is our biggest question.

It has been asked through the ages by legendary luminaries and modern menschen alike.

And it is being asked—and answered—by thousands of courageous heroes throughout the world right now today. Heroes who are holding fast to humanity's highest ideals. Realizing the secrets of *true wealth*—regenerative stewardship and service to the greater good—a new aristocracy, *deep leadership by the best*, is arising around the world, eyes wide open and guiding us by an expanding egregore of global goodness, as capital, compassion, and creativity converge at ever increasing scales.

Chances are you won't hear very much about this in the daily news just yet, or in the political echo chambers. Although it may not be obvious to the casual observer, there is a profound transformation underway and at scale in our world, led by an extraordinary global webwork of courageous servant leaders, humanitarians, and ethically rooted, magnanimous change-makers.

This *new Earth steward aristocracy* is a fellowship of founders, funders, family offices, and fearless leaders foregoing the superficial mirage of simple self-interest and, through *mycelial tendrils of trust*, fostering a favorable future through social enterprise, impact investing, stewardship philanthropy, and service leadership.

Akin to a worldwide fellowship of Jedis, Fremen, and Na'vi, this new Earth steward aristocracy is actually very real, very powerful, and growing by the day—it is legion. However, instead of "rings of power," this fellowship is activated and strengthened by powerful interconnected "rings" of relationship—mycelia-like networks of kinship, community, and collaboration; a Fellowship for the Greater Good.

And we are each invited to play a vital role in it . . . if we so choose.

In this context, none of us is exempt: We each have a choice to make . . . A. VERY. IMPORTANT. CHOICE.

And here's the astonishing thing: many of us in the regenerative and sustainability movements don't yet realize just how fundamental economic and financial systems change is to the stewardship of planet and people, and just how game-changing a growing global cohort of mission-driven quintenary companies and capital holders are in bringing about this deep-systems-change. And, perhaps even more astonishing in all of this, is that more investor-class professionals and families haven't yet ascertained just how much capital creation and prestige their funds and family offices will accrue to their long-term legacies by financing these emerging systems change opportunities. We stand at the threshold of perhaps the greatest wealth-creation epoch in human history, one which by its very nature will boost family fortunes while transforming economics as we know it and uplifting the entire human family in real socio-economic and cultural terms.

Through 33 years of work and research, I have been fortunate to befriend and collaborate with so many among us who have chosen to serve the greater good, and I have been struck by their determined devotion and strength of spirit. Indeed, in the great struggle between these two stories that stand opposed in stark contrast to one another, these leaders are heroes of the first order, having chosen service over selfishness, courage over carelessness, and—ultimately—light over darkness. I have experienced firsthand their wisdom and insight, work ethic and inspiration, and I am humbled and honored to share some of their courageous and compassionate genius with you in the collection of essays, executive-summary style case study "vignettes," and other content assembled before you.

But this book is about more than a few select voices and companies—much, much more. It contains blueprints for a renewed world. Blueprints of true wealth and planetary prosperity that the new Earth steward aristocracy accesses on its own accord, by virtue of *Virtue* and by sourcing from *Source*; blueprints of true wealth and planetary prosperity anchored in a timeless wisdom that has been with us and accessible all along.

As Executive Director of the Y on Earth Community, the action-oriented educational nonprofit organization that I co-founded with my dear friend and brother Brad "Lights Out" Lidge, I have the privilege of hosting our Y on Earth Community Podcast series and curating our VIP Enclave Gatherings. In our podcast series, we've already interviewed over 170 leaders from around the world (authors, economists, entrepreneurs, executives, financiers, philan-thropists, scientists, technologists, venture capitalists, regenerative farmers, artists, herbalists, holistic healers, naturalists, youth activists, and indigenous wisdom keepers), and through our VIP Enclave Gatherings, we've convened scores of wealth-holders from funds, foundations, and family offices, as well as leaders of immediately fundable projects, both for-profit and philanthropic. They are all progenitors of planetary prosperity, and members of a growing global network for good. Their work and wisdom permeate these pages, and we invite you to explore the additional "trailheads" in the Y on Earth Community

Podcast, VIP Enclave Gatherings, and other programs and offerings of our growing global network.

In the pages that follow, I have deliberately curated a collection of essays from some of the world's most inspiring and impactful leaders. This book is a treasure trove, and there's no way I could have written and delivered all of it to you singlehandedly. Indeed, the reality of our polycrisis requires not aggrandized heroic individualism, but emergent group genius and webwork wisdom. Our challenges and opportunities are too gargantuan for any single individual, and our greatest hope lies within the network intelligence of the woven web of collaboration for the common good (a cardinal truth in the higher-order ecological, systems, and spiritual sciences). Diverse and dedicated, these authors represent a wide range of geographic, cultural, socio-economic, and professional backgrounds, as well as a very wide range of ages: from early-career entrepreneurs in their 20s and 30s to late-career giants in their 70s, 80s, and 90s—the eldest of whom is a Holocaust survivor and an extraordinary author and visionary.

And, the Case Study Vignettes feature 33 of the most compelling corporate, finance, and organizational way-showers exemplifying the world's most advanced social, environmental, and economic performance while embodying the ethics of a new era. In addition to the 33 firms selected for executive summary style overviews, there are many more listed at the end of that section to provide you additional trailheads for exploration, edification, and inspiration.

To top all of that off, you'll find in section four a collection of my "aphoristic (a)musings" that, although apparently at times whimsical, zany, and even flip, are sincere inquiries into some of the most subtle, serious, strange, and mysteriously surreal aspects of the themes and topics woven throughout the book.

And, rounding out this colossal resource, the fifth section provides you snapshot summaries of our global community's most important frameworks and best practices recommendations for both individual/family and company/community action-taking.

This book is my eighth book overall, and the third major pillar of my writings. The first pillar, *Y on Earth*, a seminal nonfiction tome foundational to our Y on Earth Community nonprofit's work, is a comprehensive exploration of the interconnectedness and virtuous feedback loops between personal practices for enhanced health and well-being and global strategies for stewardship, regeneration, and sustainability. The second pillar, *Viriditas*, a visionary eco-thriller narrative story featuring the genius computer scientist Brigitte Sophia (and the luminous wisdom of the ancient von Übergarten family), weaves together an action-packed tapestry of technology, esoterica, indigenous wisdom, biodynamic land and water alchemy, and a transmission from the higher-order intelligence of Mama Gaia to humanity following an extraordinary activation of the planet's living mycelia webwork cum massively parallel neural net.

Y on Earth and *Viriditas* have woven into them understanding from my decades of academic, independent, and multidisciplinary studies, as well as decades of professional experience through C-suite executive leadership and consulting in the energy, food, agriculture, education, technology, and social impact sectors. Perhaps more importantly, those two tomes are infused with some of the wisdom I have encountered and gleaned through a variety of indigenous, folk, and initiatic spiritual traditions from around the world. I encourage you to read these other two books, too, for a comprehensive yet approachable deep-dive into the most salient issues of our lifetime (within the narrative of *Viriditas* are mentioned hundreds of additional resources, and the same is true of the expository content in *Y on Earth*, which also has an extensive bibliography at the end).

This third major book now before you, *Our Biggest Deal*, is the economic, regenerative finance, and social enterprise pillar among the triad—for indeed, whether seen from a spiritual or an ethical, an aesthetic or a pragmatic lens, *transforming the economy is our most pressing mission.*

The economy is *the* mission.

All else can be seen as secondary.

Or, as in the case of the urgent and essential transmutation and evolution of human consciousness, any other way we might language and frame our most pressing mission can be seen as part and parcel of the transformation of our economy, coexisting in a thematic mobius strip in which there's no beginning or end: the transformation of our economy and the transmutation of human consciousness are one and the same, and each is both causal to and indicatively and directionally symptomatic of successfully realizing the other.

The stewardship and restoration discipline known as Permaculture (articulated by Bill Mollison, who synthesized all manner of indigenous and folk practices) makes a distinction between "visible" and "invisible" structures. The visible are the material: soils, gardens, homes, farms, cities, forests, oceans, and the like. The invisible, on the other hand, are those cultural, economic, financial, moral, legal, and psychological systems and constructs that, while not as tangible as the trees in the forest, clearly create unmistakable impacts on our shared material reality. Economics is *par excellence* an amalgam of "invisible" constructs that have very real impacts upon us and our living world.

While very many of us are directly (and laudably) engaged in the work of stewardship and regeneration of our visible systems and structures through myriad advanced modalities (clean energy, green building, ecosystem restoration, environmental detoxification, biodynamic agriculture, and both afforestation and reforestation, for example), more and more of us are arriving at the understanding that transforming the invisible systems and structures of our economy is core—essential—to the mission of planetary prosperity.

Our economy is our mission.

And as the etymological history tells us, our word "economy" comes from the ancient Greek *oikos*—meaning home, hearth, and community—implying something much more tangible and immediate indeed: rootedness, relationship, and reciprocity in the context of human-scale environs, kinship, and community.

Economy is essentially the aggregate of our life-ways and home-tendings, now at the planetary scale of the entire Earth.

Economy is our mission, indeed!

Capital, properly stewarded and deployed for the greater good, is our mission.

Community is our mission.

Our home—Mama Gaia—is our mission, and planetary prosperity is our primary objective in this mission.

And we are deploying—*en masse.*

Together, we are developing and deploying the structures, strategies, and systems for sustainable stewardship and widespread well-being.

By understanding and cultivating *true wealth* and forging the fellowship of the *new Earth steward aristocracy*, we are proclaiming the story of love, intelligence, and compassion—all rooted in the ethical foundation of stewardship and responsibility.

And, we are scaling all of this up around the world—by the billions.

This is our biggest deal, the deal of our lifetimes: generating and guiding each other along pathways to planetary prosperity, rooted in love, kindness, and higher order intelligence, and fulfilling the promise of humanity's evolutionary destiny.

By evolving, like caterpillars into butterflies, we're autopoeitically activating ourselves as imaginal cells within our great living world, forming an indestructible webwork anchored in resilient nodes of group genius and diverse, mixed tables of family, friendship, and fellowship—gathering around one great round table of planetary prosperity.

And you're invited to this table—there's a seat reserved here just for *you.*

Because our world needs you.

We need you.

Will you join us?

Aaron William Perry
Lyons, Colorado
Summer Solstice, 2025

PART I

Structures and Strategies for Planetary Prosperity

"Reality is created by the mind. We can change our reality by changing our mind."

—PLATO

"All we require is the will. The next few decades represent a final opportunity to build a stable home for ourselves and restore the rich, healthy and wonderful world that we inherited from our distant ancestors. Our future on the planet, the only place as far as we know where life of any kind exists, is at stake."

—Sir David Attenborough

1 OUR BIGGEST QUESTION

From Polycrisis to Planetary Prosperity?

Here's the question:

Is planetary prosperity possible?

Can we achieve widespread well-being, economic sanity, and ecological stability all at once?

Can we supersede the industrial era of the Anthropocene and evolve into the meta-industrial era of the Ecocene?

This is *the* question of our time, *the biggest question* we humans can possibly ask right now.

Sure, there may be some spiritual, astrophysical, or even quantum morphogenic field questions that we might consider to be really "big ones" as well. But to what end do their answers and insights lead us? Wouldn't the fundamental issue of planetary prosperity remain most important at the conclusion of those inquiries? Loving kindness, deep humility, self-transcendence, and compassionate stewardship *in action* and *at scale* in our shared immanent reality—*this* is most important. Humanity's wisest, most luminous leaders and spiritual teachers are unequivocal on this essential point. Although often mystical and metaphysical in their sourced experiences, they are decidedly ethical, pragmatic, and focused on the immanent in their teachings: love, kindness, and courage

11

of heart are preeminent as is the healing and integration of mind, body, and spirit requisite to fully activate them.

It's really rather straightforward, isn't it?

But, for our more hardened, skeptical friends, whose jaded cognitive bias might preclude the only hopeful answer (and, in terms of the autopoietic Pygmalion effect, the only "correct" answer) to the question of whether planetary prosperity is possible, there is a corollary with implications of equal import:

Can we do *better*?

Can't we at least do a *little* better?

Can we do better as a people, a human family, a species?

Can't we do a *lot* better?

Can we combine the power of *community*, the power of *compassion*, and the power of *capital* to restore our world, evolve our consciousness, orient our economy around enfranchisement and the common good instead of corrupt crony capital concentration, avoid catastrophic destruction, avert autocracy and fascism, and uplift the human family into a shared reality of planetary prosperity? Can we slow down the eroding torrents of "fast money" and the frenetic, high-amplitude signal noise of ever-accelerating technological cacophony, just as we slow down rushing waters in our restored landscapes—transmuting such flows from destructive to nourishing and life-giving forces for good? Can we simultaneously mobilize philanthropy—*love of all humanity*—and biophilia—*love of all life*—at scale, such that it's normalized as foundational to the economic, ecological, and cultural lifeways of our planetary civilization? Can we examine and evolve our socially constructed mental models of world and self and truth and good and desirable and possible?

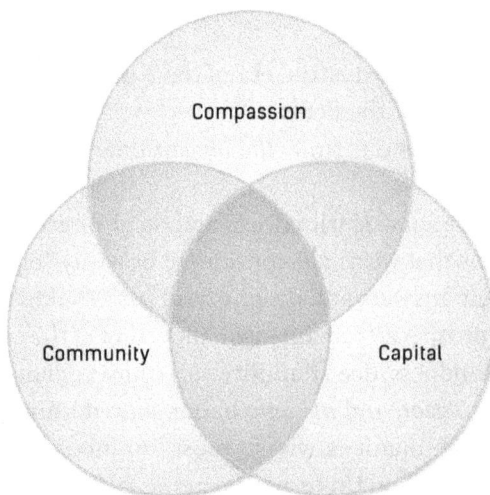

Yes!

Of course we can do better!

There's absolutely no certain proof that we cannot, and any decent, unjaded person, whether gazing through a lens of pragmatism, morality, or aesthetics, would have to arrive at the same conclusion.

"But," we might ask, "isn't planetary prosperity a matter of degree?"

Sure, it is! And we will discover that the degree to which we achieve planetary prosperity is in fact a function of the degree to which *each of us* does our part to make it so—each of us *choosing* to join the ranks of deep leaders and the new Earth steward aristocracy, offering to the greater good in these unprecedented times whatever time, treasure, and talent you can muster.

Now, whether we can fully realize planetary prosperity—our biggest question—is, of course, not answerable at this time.

The future holds *that* answer . . . and it is an outcome dependent in part upon the answer to this specific question:

Will you do *your* part?

That is the biggest question . . . for *you* . . . now.

Will you do *your part*?

Will you do *all* that you can—in terms of your unique constellation of available time, treasure, and talent that can be put to work—now—for the greater good?

That question only *you* can answer.

Despite such uncertainty, the most noble, most courageous, most honorific leaders living on planet Earth at this time, obscure and distinguished alike, are answering this question with "YES!"—and are committing their lives to achieving planetary prosperity.

These leaders are coalescing in a *fellowship for our future*, and a *true aristocracy*—the very best indeed.

And our ranks are swelling as more and more among us are hearing the clarion call and answering with a resounding "YES!" YES, *we can* and YES, *I will* do my unique part to ensure our greatest likelihood of success!

When we get down to it, our biggest question isn't actually whether planetary prosperity is possible; it's whether *you're* choosing to make it so. Whether you're going to do your part, whether you're leaning in and stepping up and doubling down despite whatever uncertainty or skepticism might otherwise arise in resistance, proclaiming YES! for our world.

You've been asked. The question is posed. The door is open to you.

What will it be, my friend?

Will you do *your part*?

2   OUR BIGGEST DEAL

The Great Work Before Us

We stand on the brink of the largest investment, intergenerational wealth transfer, and capital creation opportunity ever seen in human history—a wholesale restructuring of how capital is put to work for the benefit of humanity and our living planet. But to access this vast, emergent set of deal flow, finance, and wealth-creation opportunities, we first need to understand our global economy in an entirely new way—participation requires paradigmatic evolution. This is the foundational "gating" requirement of our biggest deal and the great work before us. The polycrisis makes our great work necessary, non-trivial, and urgent.

The *external* aspects of this polycrisis are evident and obvious: Destructive fires, huge hurricanes, and furious floods are ravaging our communities with increased frequency and severity as our dangerously destabilized global climate system randomly devastates families, neighborhoods, and whole regions; technology's ever-accelerating upgrades are getting way out of hand, likely beyond containment in the case of amoral AI and quantum computing; social media has blasted deep fissures of hatred, estrangement, pillory, and vitriol into our communities; cognitive performance and independent, critical thinking capabilities have rapidly declined as industrialized food production, a deluge of pharmaceuticals, mind-erasing mass media, and an illiteracy crisis take their toll; violence and warfare are destroying lives on virtually every continent; and financially extracting from all of these terrible (but highly "profitable") circumstances, a cynical economic super-elite is concentrating capital and amassing astronomically obscene fortunes at unprecedented, accelerating rates as the rest of us stagnate, all while aggrandized autocratic demagogues are consolidating political power.

Indeed, daily headlines barrage us with these obvious external symptoms of the polycrisis.

However, the deeper, more subtle *internal* aspects of the polycrisis are not as overtly obvious—though they are at once causal and symptomatic. Throughout the world, there is a force that has insidiously infiltrated our hearts and minds and is relentlessly rotting us from the inside out—a force with many names, including the Cree term *Wetiko*, written about by both Jack Forbes and Paul Levy. Normalized notions of "achievement" and "success," and a widespread absence of true humility, conceal the corrosive cynicism and systemic selfishness predominating the global economic regime and modern cultural milieu. While a small portion of us "succeed" according to mainstream metrics,[1] the vast majority of us have no chance of doing so, according to simple math. Although often appearing with a polished veneer of luxury and refinement, the dark forces of emptiness, avarice, and indifference have become nearly ubiquitous in their reach, and normalized and institutionalized as not only acceptable but desirable—the very essence of "winning."

But, with this sort of "winning" we all lose in the end. At the beginning, in the middle, and in the end. We not only lose vis-à-vis the many complex and interconnected external risks we're facing, we lose in terms of our internal beingness, humanity, and fundamental quality of life—not just as *measured* by conventional metrics, but as *experienced*. As we will see in the chapters and essays below, true winning—true wealth—requires deep humility, self-transcendence, and compassionate connectivity in community.

As we awaken to true wealth and true winning, we'll see that so much is at stake.

Everything is at stake: Our world, our lives, and the lives of our children and grandchildren are perilously close to catastrophic destabilization and discord.

As Kate Raworth has so poignantly articulated in *Doughnut Economics*, we must consider the "social foundation" and the "ecological ceiling," understanding our complex global economy to be nested within (and profoundly affecting) the limits of planetary carrying capacity (notwithstanding the counter-Malthusian optimism around technological advances). In her circular ring graph, Raworth helps us to visualize the highest-priority vectors for securing both social and ecological stability, avoiding the otherwise looming specters of tragic (social) shortfall and devastating (ecological) overshoot. She has laid out "what" we need to do, and we must double down on the "how" at this critical juncture.

In this context, there is nothing more important than stabilizing our climate, reversing biodiversity loss and habitat destruction, establishing an ethics-centered society, securing enfranchisement and economic security for

---

1 https://www.fastcompany.com/91234667/how-much-annual-income-financial-success

all, protecting our homes and cities, making our communities more resilient, and normalizing kindness, decency, creativity, and cooperation as the most competitively advantageous modalities of economic endeavor.

In other words, historically and anthropologically speaking, our great work is about liberating our minds and hearts and imaginations as we liberate and heal our world.

Our great work—our biggest deal—is about healing and restoring our inner lives as well as our ecological, cultural, and economic systems and the ways in which they interact with one another. Thankfully, this healing and restoration work is already being done by millions of heroic people all around the planet. From family and community scale action to larger institutional scale impact, millions of us are working across the three pillars of culture, economy, and ecology—cultivating, discovering, and guiding us along emergent pathways to planetary prosperity.

How do we join this global movement?

How do we do this great work?

How do we hone our crafts and craft anew a world of wisdom, strength, and beauty, together?

How do we rediscover humanity's original instructions and heal and restore all of our relations?

While some of this great work is quantifiable (and the numbers, as discussed below, are already so impressive), much of it is subtle and qualitative in nature. Sacred ceremonial land stewardship, family and community trauma healing, justice and dignity restoration, and our personal, intimate relationships with the natural world are all aspects of this great work. Millions of us have already responded to the call to summon the courage and enter into this sublime inner work of healing and outer work of restoration.

Thousands of people are already leading the way, millions of us are already involved, and billions of dollars are already deployed—and I'd say (as many of the trends indicate) we're really just getting started.

This global symphony of deep and emergent systems-change-making for the greater good is being further amplified and strengthened through the "mycelial model effect" of exceptionally robust, decentralized, and hyper-connected change-makers (individuals, community groups, and ethically centered corporations alike) collaborating across a variety of scales, sectors, and intersections of common purpose.

Through a growing global network of mission-driven businesses, certified benefits corporations, employee-owned companies, cooperative enterprises, family offices, and cultural, social, and environmental nonprofits, the global movement for planetary prosperity is scaling up rapidly and substantially, amply resourced by a burgeoning regenerative finance movement, and is linking together in a woven, worldwide webwork of interdependent mutualism, resource sharing, restoration, and reciprocity—anchored in the living roots of love: philanthropy, biophilia, and agape alike.

What are the implications?

Imagine a world in which banking benefits all of us, social media spreads kindness and good news, telecommunication networks connect us for collaboration, payment processing systems provide resources for restoration, and our lives are abundantly filled with clean, nutritious food grown by fairly funded farmers, as we refresh ourselves with pristine waters and are surrounded by a calm, stable, life-force filled atmosphere, while we cultivate a planetary culture in local, regional, and global networks and community cohorts. Imagine a world where "normal" is soaking up birdsong and vistas of flower-filled green landscapes—not the industrial wastelands and isolation with which our beings are daily assaulted.

Thankfully, all of this is already happening, although you won't see much of it in the fear-inducing news headlines or corrosive social media messaging.

The global networks for goodness are nascent and growing, but not quite yet as widespread as they will soon be—you have to seek them out like mycelia hiding in the fertile soils of the forest.

We stand at an inflection point, however, which may make all of this ubiquitous in short order . . . depending on our choices from this day forward.

It's already underway.

Indeed, with remarkable foresight, sophistication, and courage, leaders are establishing and scaling solutions (while collaborating across diverse networks and sectors), families are capitalizing on the layered benefits of sound investing combined with inspired benevolence (while hedging against potential wealth-destroying catastrophic unpriced market risks), and communities are cohering around three great "common good" pillars of economic, environmental, and social stewardship at the global scale.

This movement is catalyzing a phenomenal transformation of our economies, our communities, and our hearts. It is an "inside-out job" rooted in the evolutionary quest of the individual, woven together with the supreme universal calling to serve the greater good in collaboration with others also serving according to an ancient and essential code of ethics. It is a movement in which *group work* and *group genius* are prioritized over individual heroism. It is a movement toward an immanent planetary epoch—the Ecocene—in which our social, cultural, and economic systems are guided by Quintenary stewardship, and humanity accesses the next-level intelligence of the Noosphere, which Chardin anticipated a century ago: an emerging planetary consciousness of the highest order, that transcends the "tragedy of the commons" of myopic self-interest—the "moloch trap" of zero-sum thinking—and attains what Maslow himself came to recognize as the pinnacle of human achievement: dedicating one's gifts and talents maximally in service to the greater good.

Across thousands of firms and family offices, and millions of households, humanity is mobilizing the greatest economic and evolutionary feat in our species' history. This movement can be measured in billions (if not trillions) of transactions, but is rooted in an immeasurable expansion of the heart. In this growing movement, coherence, compassion, and wisdom are the main currencies flowing through our globally connected society as we design and deploy better systems and structures for our economies and communities.

This movement is emerging and proliferating throughout the world, not controlled by any central authority but instead inspired and led by the authentic intelligence and genuine goodwill pervasive throughout our global community—rooted in a humanistic *Weltanschauung* that reveres and celebrates the inherent dignity of all people and sanctity of all Earthly creation. And evolving beyond mere goodwill, this movement has the power of the fundamental *will to good* as its source and substance, and the power of conscious capital, market mechanisms, and tremendous technologies at its disposal and direction—guided by people who have carefully crafted and polished their hearts and minds in the alchemical crucible of personal growth and evolution—as predicted and prescribed by humanity's greatest luminaries and sacred prophecies.

In this rarified and essential context, the mechanisms otherwise constructed to contain, control, and coerce are our responsibility to transmute—like lead into gold—and transform toward true freedom, well-being, and planetary prosperity. Our movement is already well underway throughout the entire world doing that critical alchemical work.

Just as the existential challenges we face make up a polycrisis in the aggregate, so too does our great work have many forms and facets. Regenerative finance, stewardship philanthropy, and quintenary Ecocene economics are the new, saner mechanisms for capital deployment. Social and impact entrepreneurship and service leadership are the saner methods for guiding our projects, communities, and companies toward planetary prosperity.

The good (great!) news is that our great work is already well underway. Here are some specific, notable examples:

Through the Global Alliance for Banking on Values, over 70 banking institutions worldwide employ over 145,000 employees working day-in and day-out allocating capital to land stewardship, clean energy, ecosystem restoration, and community-based projects in over 45 countries, earning over $265 billion in annual revenue. Among their constituent members, long-established stalwarts like GLS Bank in Germany and Amalgamated Bank in the United States, and much newer and rapidly growing firms like Climate First Bank (the fastest growing new bank in the US), are moving the needle toward stewardship and sustainability through ethics-based finance every day.

All the while thousands of future-forward family offices, funds, and foundations are deploying capital into myriad projects and platforms devoted to the greater good. Their leaders—often next-generation capital stewards with eyes open to the world's most serious challenges and systems-change opportunities—are prioritizing the mid- and long-term sustainability of our world over narrow-minded, short-term profiteering. The trends indicate orders of magnitude more of this to come in the next two decades as some $84 trillion will change hands as Gen X, Gen Y (Millennials), and Gen Z inherit $72 trillion and the balance ($12 trillion) transfer directly to charities.

Meanwhile, meta-networks of mission-driven companies, organizations, and communities are catalyzing philanthropic and community-led impact throughout the planet. Among these, 1% for the Planet, one of Patagonia founder Yvon Chouinard's great legacy contributions, has over 7,000 member companies of all sizes channeling at least 1% of their top-line gross sales toward over 4,000 environmental and community nonprofit organizations. With over $500 million already achieved in certified giving, and a near-term goal of over $1 billion, the 1% for the Planet ecosystem continues to scale its reach, scope, and impact. These are the avant-garde waves of visionary capital creation and allocation that are growing into the most significant economic evolution in humanity's entire history.

Of course, this isn't only about the money. With a comprehensive measurement and verification framework, B-Lab has certified over 8,250 companies with the best-in-class B-certification credential that signifies a comprehensive commitment to social, economic, and environmental sustainability. In their *Declaration of Interdependence*, the global community of thousands of B-Certified companies envisions "a global economy that uses business as a force for good. This economy is comprised of a new type of corporation—the Benefits-Corporation (B-Corp)—which is purpose driven and creates *benefit for all stakeholders*, not just shareholders." To date, B-Corporations generate over $130 billion in annual gross revenue.

Among the largest of the 1% for the Planet and B-Corporation leaders, Patagonia is a trailblazer in planetary prosperity structures, strategies, and impact. At the direction of founder and former majority shareholder Yvon Chouinard, Patagonia transferred 99% of its common stock into a trust called the Holdfast Collective, which is charged with the altruistic requirement to distribute the company's approximately $100 million annual net operating profit to environmental and social nonprofit companies around the world. Instead of swelling his personal coffers and family fortune, Chouinard epitomized the behavior of the new Ecocene aristocracy by transcending his apparent personal interests and instead maximizing the positive impact he is able to muster for the greater good—a laudable legacy of the highest degree.

In addition to all of this, in order to further mitigate extreme capital concentration and augment multi-stakeholder benefits, many other corporate forms are being deployed and scaling up, including cooperative and employee-owned models.

According to the National Center for Employee Ownership, there are over 6,350 companies worldwide with employee stock ownership plans (ESOPs), representing over $1.8 trillion in total asset value. Among these, grocery chains, construction companies, architecture and engineering firms, manufacturing companies, real estate firms, and banks are comprised of hundreds of thousands of employee-owners.

Meanwhile, the International Cooperative Alliance indicates that there are three *million* cooperatives worldwide, employing 10% of the global workforce—10%! The three hundred largest cooperatives generate over $2.4 trillion in annual sales. Among these, the Mondragon Cooperative system in the Basque country of northern Spain is especially notable, as it is comprised of over 90 autonomous, interdependent co-ops ranging from grocery retail to engineering and consulting, with over 80,000 worker-owner members and a combined annual revenue of €13.9 billion—equivalent to $14.5 billion!

And, according to the World Association of Non-Governmental Organizations (WANGO), there are over 54,000 social and environmental nonprofits operating in 190-plus countries. Over 31,000 of these are headquartered in the United States alone, employing over 145,000 people, earning over $29 billion in revenue, and managing over $79 billion in assets.

And as the positive feedback loops of multi-stakeholder capital formation, allocation, and accumulation coalesce, and are combined with increased innovation, impact, and influence, all while the powerful forces of competitive advantage and market demand continue to amplify best practices, we are witnessing the transformation of our culture, economy, and society. The directional trends have just attained critical mass in the first quarter of the 21st century, and, notwithstanding the tremendous headwinds and temporary (but serious) political backlash we obviously face, they are continuing to scale up, simultaneously delivering greater impact and greater hope to millions of people worldwide.

In the book's Case Study "Vignettes," you will find carefully curated summary information about exemplary companies and organizations utilizing the structures and strategies described above. And, in the book's collection of essays, you will find the reflections and insights of several selected leaders whose intrepid, altruistic, and visionary works are guiding our organizations and meta-networks of organizations toward planetary prosperity in which real wealth is engendered, stewarded, and shared among all stakeholders, and the subtler, more essential true-wealth rewards of belonging, service, and soul-fulfillment are achieved.

In the pages that follow, you will also find deeper dive discussions of competitive advantage and market demand in the context of the Ecocene; the power of stewardship philanthropy; the many structures and strategies for planetary prosperity already operating at scale around the world; the spiritual imperative of economic and financial systems change; the exciting *avant-garde* of inspired innovation—especially in the realms of mycelial-model, stewardship-oriented financial technologies (fintech) and social technologies (soctech); the future of money as envisioned by the remarkable thought leader Bernard Lietaer; the power of the Quintenary as an economic concept; the essential imperative of the Original Instructions, our "inner work," including the practice of transmuting paradox in the context of hyper-complexity through intimate, nature-rooted Source connection; a celebration of the new Earth steward aristocracy, the emerging altruistic meritocracy that is forming a fellowship for our future—a federation for planetary prosperity—and a unique articulation of our shared vision.

In addition, you will find a collection of aphoristic reflections and musings by your author, through which pithy combinations of observation, humor, silly sarcasm, and playful philosophizing help further to plumb the depths of our shared cultural fabrics and psycho-spiritual subliminalia.

But first, before we venture into all of these important pieces and carefully curated content, we must first look, eyes wide open, at the current condition of our entire global human family—billions of whom are nowhere near as privileged and fortunate as many of us now reading this book.

*"The golden way is to be friends with the world and
to regard the whole human family as one."*

—GANDHI

3 EYES WIDE OPEN

A Global Perspective on Where We Each Stand

It is often said that money can't buy happiness. But it is obvious that money buys lots of other things besides. For many of us in the world—too many—we don't have enough to buy the bare essentials. While there is an (often disingenuous) ongoing "debate" between the "trickle down" and the "basic needs" points of view, one that more often reveals some of our deeper biases than our objective understanding of complex macroeconomic policies, there are extraordinary leaders and companies working to uplift people around the world while delivering beneficial goods and services to the marketplace. They are discovering and way-showing pathways to planetary prosperity that leave the old, worn-out "debates" behind. And, increasingly, philanthropists who are eyes-open to the interconnectedness of our world's many challenges, and the impacts they have on the poorest among us, are recognizing and supporting the innovative and "outside the box" NGOs who are working at the deepest systemic-root levels to make real, lasting, sustainable change in our world.

Of course, our global situation is a complex one. It's challenging enough to come to some reasonable understanding of these complexities (and nuances), and when we're beholden to certain popular ideologies, it's even more challenging to cultivate and maintain a clear view on our world, the situation of diverse billions of people among our living human family, the situation of our complex living ecologies, and what we can do to have the greatest positive impact amid such a complex landscape.

One fundamental point of information that is essential for us to develop clearer vision and understanding is the comprehensive data portraying our entire human family's economic circumstances. Of course, looking at the economic and financial data set alone doesn't tell us the whole story, but without it, we're missing a very key element: our global perspective.

So where do we each stand, and what conclusions might we take away as a result of this clear view?

The Credit Suisse Research Institute (CSRI), an in-house think tank of Credit Suisse AG, a UBS Group company, publishes an annual *Global Wealth Report*, which provides some of the most comprehensive data available on global wealth distribution across countries and regions. Within this report a Global Wealth Pyramid provides several key data points to help us visualize and understand the full picture.

Below is the global picture conveyed in the *2023 Global Wealth Report* (which compiled 2022 data), as it appears across four socio-economic tiers. But before we take a closer look at the numbers, we need to take a minute to make sure we really understand what they're telling us. You see, in an era when "billions" and "trillions" are frequently bandied about like familiar, household figures, it's all too easy to fail completely to understand what they actually mean.

We must understand what these numbers are telling us by first understanding the fundamental differences in orders of magnitude between one thousand, one million, one billion, and one trillion.

Imagine you earn $100,000 per year. Of course, keeping the math very simple, if you earned this $100,000 by working 100 days, you would do so at a rate of $1,000 per day. Setting aside costs and taxes, it would take 10 years for this $100,000 per year to total $1,000,000—one million dollars. However, it would take a whopping *10,000 years* to total one billion dollars, and a staggering *10 million years* (!!!) to total one trillion dollars. When we're examining and discussing astronomical figures across 9, 10, 11, and even 12 orders of magnitude (or numbers of digits after the left-most number), it's easy to lose sight of what the numbers are actually telling us.

Thus, with our minds sharpened around the arithmetic, and our eyes wide open, here's the global picture:

The global wealth pyramid 2022

59.4 million (1.1%)

> USD 1 million   USD 208.3 trillion (45.8%)

USD 100,000 to 1 million   642 m (12.0%)   USD 178.9 trillion (39.4%)

USD 10,000 to 100,000   1,844 m (34.4%)   USD 61.9 trillion (13.6%)

< USD 10,000   USD 5.3 trillion (1.2%)

2,818 m (52.5%)

Wealth range   Total wealth (% of world)

Number of adults (percent of world adults)

The top of the wealth pyramid, 2022

> USD 50 million   243,060

USD 10 million to 50 million   2,510,320

USD 5 million to 10 million   5,087,930

USD 1 million to 5 million   51,549,760

Wealth range   Number of adults

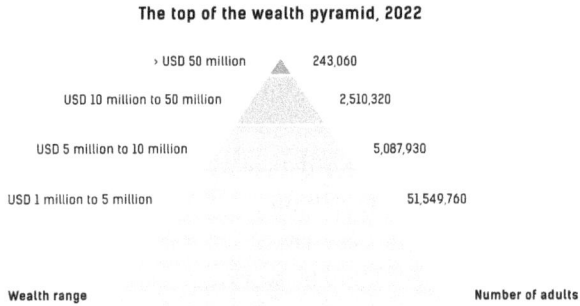

The poorest adults among us, having net wealth under $10,000, make up 52.5% of the global adult population (~2.818 billion), and only own in the aggregate 1.2% of the total global wealth ($5.3 trillion); that's one half—one out of every two of us (!)—with only 1% of global wealth in the aggregate.

The next group includes 34.4% of the total adult population (~1.844 billion), has net wealth between $10,000 and $100,000, and in the aggregate owns about 13.6% of the total global wealth ($61.9 trillion).

Combined, these first two groups include 89% of our total population (nine out of every 10 adults) and have only 14.8% of the wealth(!).

The third group includes 12% of the total adult population (~642 million), has a net wealth between $100,000 and $1 million, and owns 39.4% of the total global wealth ($178.9 trillion).

The fourth group includes 1.1% of the total adult population (~59.4 million), has a net wealth greater than $1 million, and owns 45.8% of the total global wealth ($208.3 trillion). This fourth group is further segmented in the Global

Wealth Report into its own separate "1%" pyramid of four tiers in which the first has 51,549,760 people with a wealth range of $1 -5 million, the second has 5,087,930 people with a wealth range of $5 -10 million, the third has 2,510,320 people with a wealth range of $10 -50 million, and the fourth has 243,060 people with wealth in excess of $50 million each. That latter tier, designated as "ultra-high-net-worth," is further segmented in the Report, revealing that 79,490 adults have wealth above $100 million and of them, 7,020 people have wealth above $500 million.

However, the 2024 Global Wealth Report, which was just released early in 2025 as the writing of this book wrapped up, indicated such a leap in wealth concentration at the very top of the pyramid that it further separated the top tier into the world's richest 14 individuals who control nearly $2 trillion together, the next stratospherically rich 12 individuals who control nearly $900 billion together, and the next ultra-rich 2,638 individuals who control $11 trillion together. In 2025 Elon Musk, with approximately half a trillion dollars in net worth, owned about 1/1000th of the entire global wealth—that's *one-tenth of 1%* of the value of all global property, buildings, businesses, equities, debts, and currencies, combined—owned by one single man!

The global wealth pyramid 2023 (Top bands)

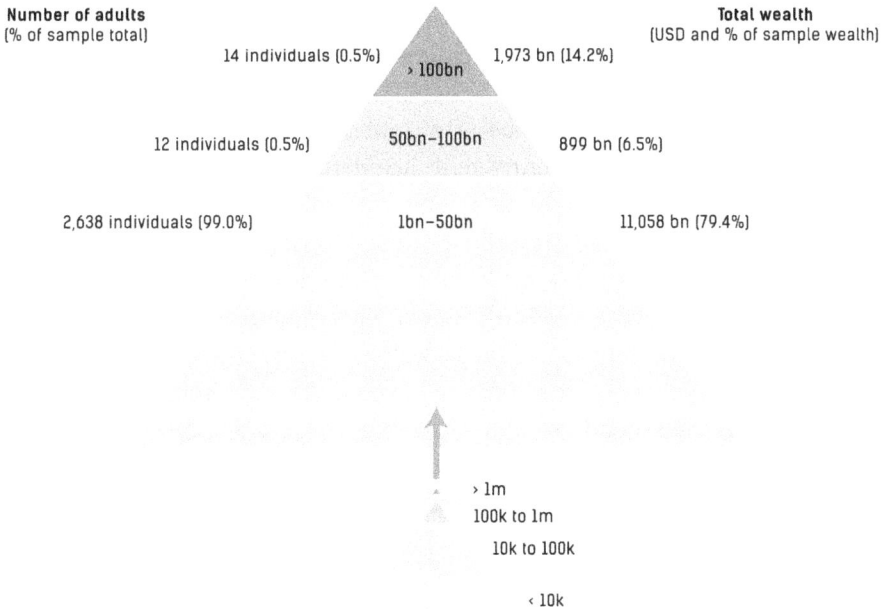

Number of adults
(% of sample total)

Total wealth
(USD and % of sample wealth)

14 individuals (0.5%)   > 100bn   1,973 bn (14.2%)

12 individuals (0.5%)   50bn–100bn   899 bn (6.5%)

2,638 individuals (99.0%)   1bn–50bn   11,058 bn (79.4%)

> 1m
100k to 1m
10k to 100k
< 10k

The vast difference in wealth from the stratospherically rich to many of us spread out "in the middle" is nearly incomprehensible. And, similarly, the profoundly different experience that millions upon millions of us are currently enduring at the other extreme of the spectrum is nearly impossible for us to imagine and understand in the middle. Right now on Earth, it's as if people are living in totally different worlds, totally different realities, with totally different "rules," opportunities, and expectations—the result of a profoundly complex and nuanced planet-wide socio-economic history that hardly any of us can completely comprehend.

With this picture in mind, here are some important questions that you're invited to ask yourself:

> *Where are you on this spectrum?*
>
> *And your family, friends, professional peers, community members?*
>
> *Do you regularly and routinely interact with people from all of these groups? Only some? Only one?*
>
> *How does looking at and thinking about this data make you feel?*

As you reflect, here are some suggestions and invitations for you to consider:

If you're in the first group, you are almost certainly preoccupied with life's most basic requirements. You may be debt-ridden, trying to make ends meet in a great first-world city; you may be a rural subsistence farmer in the so-called global south; you may be a young adult just getting started in your working life; you may be elderly, reliant on a fixed income, or know people like these. Because we're living in an extraordinary time of connectivity and asymmetric, "leap frog" development opportunities made possible through communication technology, we encourage you to connect with extraordinary local community leaders like essayist Sarah Arao as well as the growing global network of organizations who can be of assistance to you and your community.

If you're in the second group, you are likely preoccupied with managing your income and expenses as you work and pay your bills. You perhaps have some "rainy day" cushion, and have access to opportunities for both economic mobility and meaningful career paths. Here, too, the opportunity to connect with growing global networks is complemented by the opportunity to more deliberately direct your consumer spending toward socially and environmentally responsible, mission-driven brands, and you may also have opportunities to provide some of your time and talent working within such a mission-driven company, and volunteering some of it for those less fortunate.

If you're in the third group, you have a significantly higher degree of financial freedom and a substantial cushion at your disposal. In this group you have several opportunities to support pathways to planetary prosperity, especially through your philanthropy, consumer spending, and influential participation in civic organizations and policymaking.

In the fourth group, although the degree of wealth and financial independence varies considerably (in data distribution terms, there's a very long "tail"), a few key opportunities stand out. You are clearly in a position to have significant impact in your philanthropy as well as your investment decisions. The degree to which you engage in and support socially and environmentally driven companies and nonprofits is tremendously meaningful in terms of your personal legacy and enrichment from directly supporting social entrepreneurs and teams. It is also tremendously meaningful in terms of your influence and impact on your economic peers, setting the "tone," leading by example, and encouraging others to consider the philanthropic and investment opportunities you're privy to. In the aggregate, this group has a profound opportunity to determine the state of our world and the directionality of our economic, social, and governance behaviors, and with this, of course, comes a tremendous responsibility. The lesser-known truth here is that by engaging in and supporting the social enterprises, mission-driven companies, and innovative nonprofits, you are also invited to experience the joy and fulfillment of meaningful impact, purposeful and collaborative relationships, and a legacy to which future generations will look back with pride, gratitude, and honor.

To make all of this even more apparent, here's another way to visualize these groupings, this time parsing out a subset for the uppermost ("stratospheric") tier of the wealthiest 1% of people into its own category. Within each of these are also suggested philanthropic "tithing" rates, per the insights of Warren Buffet, Mark Finser, and others who have exceptional views on money, philanthropy, happiness, and "enough-ness," alongside the baseline invitation of the 1% for the Planet movement for all of us but our brothers and sisters in the lowest quartile:

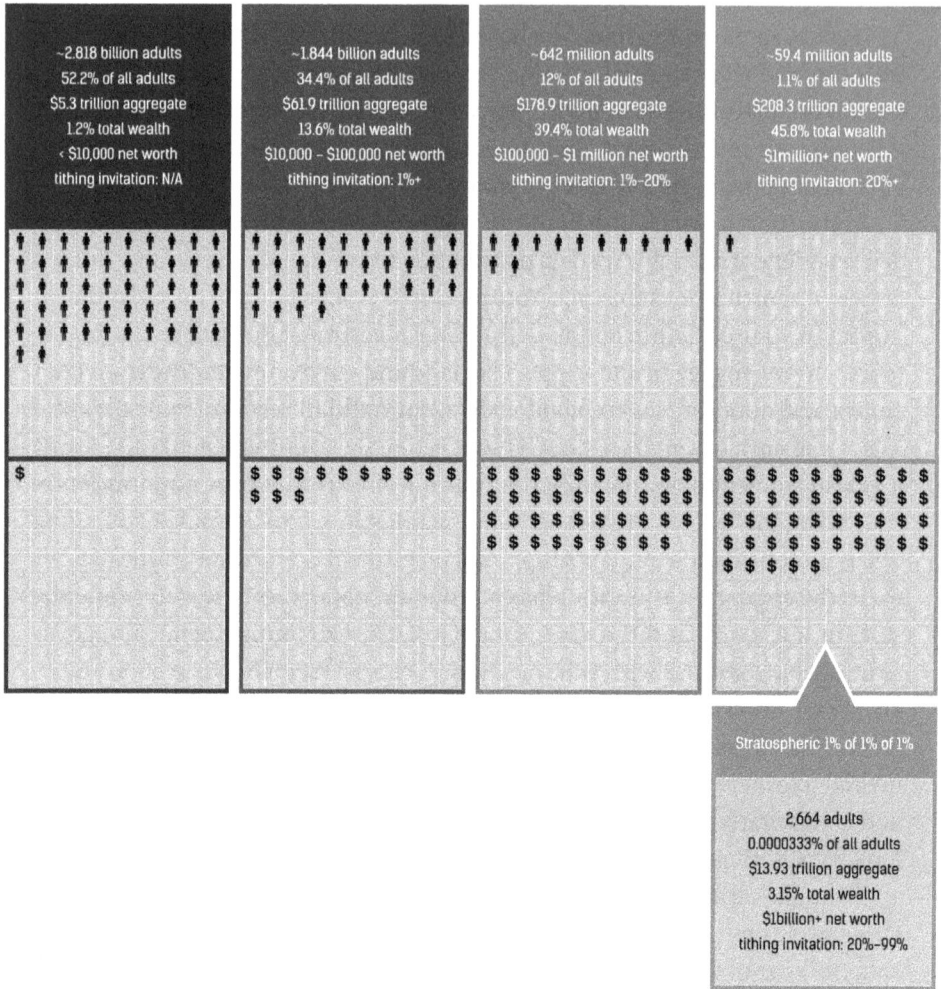

~2.818 billion adults	~1.844 billion adults	~642 million adults	~59.4 million adults
52.2% of all adults	34.4% of all adults	12% of all adults	1.1% of all adults
$5.3 trillion aggregate	$61.9 trillion aggregate	$178.9 trillion aggregate	$208.3 trillion aggregate
1.2% total wealth	13.6% total wealth	39.4% total wealth	45.8% total wealth
< $10,000 net worth	$10,000 – $100,000 net worth	$100,000 – $1 million net worth	$1million+ net worth
tithing invitation: N/A	tithing invitation: 1%+	tithing invitation: 1%–20%	tithing invitation: 20%+

Stratospheric 1% of 1% of 1%

2,664 adults
0.0000333% of all adults
$13.93 trillion aggregate
3.15% total wealth
$1billion+ net worth
tithing invitation: 20%–99%

When we open our eyes to the global situation, and allow our hearts to feel something about the tremendous disparity in wealth distribution among our human family, something awakens inside of us. We become *sensitized to reality*, and, for many of us, we find ourselves wanting to do something about it—wanting to do more, to do what we each uniquely can—joining the growing legion of emerging Earth steward aristocrats.

With eyes wide open, we are invited to join this new heart-centered aristocracy—regardless of our current socio-economic circumstance s—and deepen our commitment and unique contributions to planetary prosperity.

"Cultural shifts happen on a different level;
they come into view only when we step back enough
to see a bigger picture changing over time."

—JOANNA MACY

4   THE BODY CORPORATE

Governance, Guardrails, and Waterfalls

Reiterating Our Biggest Question in slightly different terms: How do we (1) make deep systems change and (2) make and mobilize money—enough to fund said systems change, all while (3) not falling prey to the power and greed of the pervasive Mammonic mental disease also known as Wetiko?

This is the question. "Whether," "why," and "when" we do so is a matter of the most urgent moral and existential imperatives. Which leaves us with the "what" and the "how"—the focus of this book. Let's roll our sleeves up together and get into it!

Thousands of entrepreneurs and executives, along with their investors and boards, have voluntarily opted to codify their commitment to social and environmental stewardship at the very core of their organizations' "DNA." Through foundational corporate charters, bylaws, and operating agreements, these leaders have established the ethical basis—in legal and economic terms—by which their companies operate in the interest of the greater good, and with specific, intentional impact well beyond the narrow "profit maximization" that is otherwise the unfortunate legal and paradigmatic default.

Because we humans are all too susceptible to the Mammonic Grip (as explored in depth in my book *Viriditas*), and too many of us make the Faustian bargain (ultimately inflicting great harm on each other and our planet as a result, not to mention ourselves), we require good guidance, governance, and guardrails to be "baked in" to our corporate structures, lest they operate according to the default status quo that essentially seeks to maximize profits and cash flow for a super-small minority of stakeholders, while externalizing all possible costs to the commons and to society at large. The bad news is that, through centuries of exploitation and decades of deliberate influence on our legal systems, such pathological behavior has been normalized (and even celebrated). However, the good news is that thousands upon thousands of us have already taken the high road out of this moral morass and have put in motion an entirely different set of rubrics and "rules"—playing the elevated game of values-based, mission-driven, conscious capitalism and stewardship economics—Ecocene economics.

Many of these systems and structures are now (thankfully) well-established, encoded in companies' legal frameworks and often further strengthened by the transparency of third-party verification. Notable among these systems and structures are several that we'll discuss in some detail, and which can be organized according to a few general categories: corporate forms; employee/stakeholder enfranchisement; social and environmental performance; financial and philanthropic impact vehicles; and global alliances and federations of such companies and organizations. Let's explore them in sequence:

CORPORATE FORMS

Unlike conventional corporate forms, which embody the non-sustainable "shareholder wealth maximization" doctrine of Milton Friedman's flawed economic thinking (which is among the most bombastic modes of magical, wishful thinking and fantastical delusion found in modernity), there are several extant corporate forms that require as a matter of course said companies to conduct themselves in accordance with a broader and more enlightened set of criteria and considerations. Namely, benefits corporations, cooperatives, employee-owned companies, and nonprofit corporations are four types of legal structure (with myriad permutations and variations) that steer their managers and teams toward broader beneficial outcomes in social, economic, and, in many cases, ecological terms.

"Benefits Corporation" is a relatively recent designation that includes both Public Benefits Corporations (as determined by law in certain states and nations) and third-party certified "B-Corps" as determined by the robust assessment and verification rubric administered by B-Lab. These frameworks require companies to include environmental and social impacts in their governance and management decision-making, and in the case of B-Lab's B-Certification, require a robust assessment and scoring of a company's stakeholder, governance, supply chain, social, community, and environmental impacts in order to attain the credential.

Cooperatives are corporate entities owned by their "inside" stakeholders instead of outside shareholders. Cooperatives generally include three major categories: worker-owned cooperatives (such as the very well established Mondragon system in the Basque region in Spain); producer cooperatives, collectively owned and managed by their supply chain producers, many of which are in the food and agricultural sector (and lead aggregate sales of local, organic, and fair trade food and beverage products in the United States, according to the National Cooperative Business Association (NCBA)); and buyer-cooperatives (such as many neighborhood and community buying clubs and rural electric utility associations, as well as larger-scale consumer cooperative companies like Recreational Equipment, Inc., aka REI). There are over 40,000 cooperatives in the United States alone, and over three million worldwide. Some 12% of the entire human population—roughly one out of every eight of us—are members of one or more cooperatives. Generally speaking, cooperatives are governed by a level democracy—one member, one vote.

Employee-owned companies, also known as "ESOPs" (companies with Employee Stock Ownership Plans), are similar to co-ops in that individuals have equity stakes in the firm, but they are markedly different in that economic stakes aren't necessarily evenly distributed, and governance and decision-making isn't typically conducted in a level democratic manner as we'd find with a cooperative. Instead, ESOPs generally provide employees with "vesting pathways" in which tenure and performance are rewarded with equity participation. In some cases, employees make up 100% ownership of companies, which can be established at the time of formation, or utilized as a mechanism for founders to "exit" by selling the company to its employees, typically in a structured financing with long-term bank debt.

EMPLOYEE/STAKEHOLDER ENFRANCHISEMENT

In addition to cooperative and employee ownership mechanisms, employees are further enfranchised through "leveling" mechanisms like executive pay differential caps and a full suite of employee benefits, ranging from matching retirement account contributions to health and social safety net programs, and to other important programs like on-site childcare; extensive paid sick, family, and parental leave; flex work time; flex office time; and generous vacation and personal days off allowances. The Mondragon Cooperatives and Dr. Bronner's soap and chocolate company both have longstanding executive pay differential caps, limiting their highest-paid executives to five to nine times the lowest, full-time, fully vested employee. This is especially extraordinary in the United States where CEOs in conventional companies often take 300 to 400 times, even as much as 6,666 times as in the case of Starbuck's CEO Brian Niccol (!) what their rank-and-file workers make. But in Europe, where such differentials are somewhat more modest (120 to 150 times in Germany,

Spain, and Switzerland, and closer to 40 to 60 times in the Scandinavian countries), the range of the five-to-nine pay ratio cap instituted by the Mondragon Cooperatives is nonetheless very significant—by an order of magnitude in comparison with their conventional European counterparts. As discussed further in the book, these company-specific programs and incentives often result in the companies experiencing greater competitive advantage with their workforce, by realizing better talent attraction and retention performance.

SOCIAL AND ENVIRONMENTAL PERFORMANCE

Various third-party certifications indicate companies' outstanding social and environmental performance. Certified organic, certified biodynamic, and certified regenerative organic credentials in the food, agricultural, and fabric and apparel sectors indicate low and non-toxic cultivation, production, and processing methodologies along with better land-stewardship, soil carbon sequestration, hydrological management, and other environmental performance factors. Fair trade certifications indicate more equitable and socially just treatment of suppliers—very often agricultural and manufacturing workers. The 1% for the Planet certification indicates that a company donates 1% of its *top-line* sales revenue to environmental and social nonprofits around the world—an amount that often represents an impressive 5% to 20% of the company's bottom line profits, depending on their cost structures and net profit margins. And, the "social enterprise" designation, although not yet established as a worldwide third-party certification regime, currently indicates that a company donates at least 50% (!) of its bottom-line profits (after taxes) to social and environmental nonprofits, effectively making the business as a whole a powerful economic engine for the greater good, especially as it scales.

FINANCE AND PHILANTHROPY

As our world and lives have become increasingly "financialized" over the past several decades (especially since the 1980s, and seemingly ever-accelerating since then), there are thousands upon thousands of firms, funds, foundations, and family offices conducting their investment, lending, and philanthropic capital allocation decisions according to the narrow self-serving criteria of maximized profits, enhanced capital accumulation, and power and influence accretion among the social, financial, and political elite. However, there are thousands of more enlightened firms, funds, foundations, and family offices deliberately allocating capital through impact investing, program-related investing, and stewardship philanthropy for the greater good—considering the environmental, social, and long-term consequences of their investment and charitable decision-making, well beyond their own narrow self-interest. Notable among these are firms like RSF | Regenerative Social Finance; the 70-plus banks, credit unions, and micro-finance lenders comprising the international Alliance for Banking on Values; Patagonia's Hold Fast Collective and Home Planet Fund; One Small Planet; Big Path Capital; the Emerson Collective; The Climate Foundation; and the Yield Foundation, among many, many others—representing several billions of dollars deployed in the past two to three years alone. And, self-organizing and decentralized frameworks such as the Slow Money network have invested over $100 million into local, smallholder regenerative farming and ranching operations around the world via regional, self-organizing collectives of philanthropists and families, often providing outright grants and 0-3% interest loans to such producers.

FEDERATIONS AND ALLIANCES

With a now solid foundation of corporate forms, employee enfranchisement strategies, social and environmental performance rubrics, and enlightened finance and philanthropy movements, these systems, structures, and strategies have emerged, are extant, and are operating at scale in many instances. What else can we do to accelerate and amplify this positive directionality and momentum? We can further establish, grow, and interconnect global networks, alliances, and federations of these stewardship-oriented and mission-driven change-makers. Thankfully, these alliances and federations are already not only emergent, but rapidly scaling up. The 1% for the Planet ecosystem now includes well over 10,000 independent companies and organizations. B-Lab's ecosystem now has over 8,000 B-certified companies. And there are thousands of cooperatives and ESOPs connected through federations like the International Cooperative Alliance, the National Cooperative Business Association, the National Center for Employee Ownership, and other national and international alliances, trade associations, and member networks.

However, from a certain perspective, things are really just about to take off. As technological advances and ethical progress enable greater collaboration and coherence across permeable corporate and community boundaries, the "mycelial model effect" presents immediate opportunities for rapidly scaled and robustly amplified economic evolution and systemic transformation essential to planetary prosperity.

Imagine these myriad alliances and federations integrating and collaborating together in a more intentional and accelerated manner. Imagine meta-networks, federations, and alliances emerging that amplify and accelerate market share, competitive advantage, and the preponderance, ultimately, of our world's capital flows, decision-making, and management. Imagine what's possible when many of the foundational structures we all utilize day in and day out—e-commerce, payment processing, currency exchange, social media, internet service provision, search engine, artificial intelligence, and energy, food, and entertainment providers are all part of a global alliance for the greater good—a Federation for Planetary Prosperity!

GUIDANCE, GOVERNANCE, AND GUARDRAILS— "ADULTING" IN THE AGE OF THE ECOCENE

We are heading toward an age when real "grown-ups" govern according to the original instructions, when goodness guides our decision-making, and when economic systems are designed and managed for everybody's benefit. The foundation has been laid, and it is now incumbent upon all of us—entrepreneurs, executives, financiers, philanthropists, and community leaders—to step up, lean in, and go the distance, *doing all that we each uniquely can* to make it so.

Although, indeed, from a certain perspective, the dark countervailing forces are on the ascendant, another understanding recognizes the *death throes of that which is no longer serving humanity*, or the awesome intelligence (AI) of our living planet. The forces of destiny are in our favor, according to the sagacious ones. But only if we rise to the occasion.

We have work to do.

The ego-inflation of obscene wealth accumulation and rocketship erection is often best understood as underdeveloped adolescence operating in conjunction with awesome technologies that require far more prudence, maturity, responsibility, and caution than we have tended to see thus far. I'm not being hyperbolic. Take the recent articles in *The Atlantic*, "The Rise of the Selfish Plutocrats," a chronicle of ultra-private super elite with secretive yachts and islands (as opposed to cathedrals, masterpieces, and other public goods financed by benefactors of yore), and the equally instructive (if not even more foreboding) "The Oligarchs Who Came to Regret Supporting Hitler," which helps elucidate how super-concentrated money and political power tend to conspire at times, often culminating in devastating, horribly destructive outcomes. There's a fundamental maxim known to students of history, as articulated by Robert Reich, wherein the occasional exception really only proves the rule: "Oligarchy is incompatible with the common good." The unprecedented concentration of power, wealth, and technological capability of our times have thrust us to the brink of global devastation. Indeed, in the words of Eckhart Tolle: "Science and technology have amplified the effects of the dysfunction of the human mind in its un-awakened state to such a degree that humanity, and probably the planet, would not survive for another hundred years *if human consciousness remains unchanged*." (Italics mine for emphasis.)

We have proven time and again that people—and most especially men, according to the data—are ill-equipped to wield excessive power and wealth without terrible consequences. Sure, there are exceptions—and they point to the sublime nature of awakened consciousness—but they are too infrequent for any rational society to wager that such magnanimity, egalitarianism, and altruism will arise of its own accord from the wealthiest and most powerful among us without good governance and guardrails. Indeed, today's events are proof positive, exhibit "A," and case in point that, unlike George Washington refusing the designation of "president for life" from an understandably (and justifiably) adoring populace, we now see way too many would-be leaders making plain their desires for unlimited, indefinite power. This does not bode well for any of us.

As Riane Eisler asks, how have we as a species responded to this patholog-ical propensity for people, especially men, to ride their leadership impulses toward authoritarianism, despotism, and fascism; to play dice with the world's economies, creating and cruising casinos both literal and metaphorical? How do we temper the destructive dragons of the Mammonic impulse of Wetiko that too often overtakes a man?

We need councils. We need councils to counteract these baser impulses—community fora and corporate governance infrastructure that, through an alchemy unknown to too many of us at present, have the power to uplift the individual man and leader, to transmute the heavy Mammonic lead of the Faustian bargain into the radiant gold of an activated heart, seeking not power over but prestige among, as a result of good deeds, laudable undertakings, and self-transcendent service to the greater good.

We must recognize that none of us is actually equipped to be some "phi-losopher king"—and the only proof positive that we might be that rare and exceptionally qualified luminary would be the fact that we *seek no civic power* or worldly influence whatsoever—a near impossibility for the entrepreneurs and executives among us. The far-reaching benefits of a philosopher king's leadership—consistent magnanimity and altruism as a matter of free will and real power; here we begin to understand the real meaning of the word *meek*—aren't at all likely to flow forth from one individual, but from the col-lective intelligence, the group genius of coherence councils, renaissance teams, and other cohorts and federations. We need the buttresses and balustrades of community councils, like the Grandmothers Councils and governance fellow-ships of wiser, saner societies. We find versions of these councils and cultural stewardship mechanisms extant in the social and community structures of the Mondragon system, and we see "coherence council" patterns emergent in a variety of contexts, enabling people to convene, communicate, and col-laborate across the boundaries of hierarchy and station, providing a "leveling" among and between community members throughout various corporate and self-governance structures.

These guidance and governance patterns are also emergent within the context of new federations. Such trans-corporate and trans-geographic federations are enabling enhanced resource exchange and resilience through a diverse array of scales and contexts, strengthening social and economic fabrics, just as people in the past achieved greater security, prosperity, and cultural vivacity through the alliances of the Medieval cathedral masons, the temple knights, the Iroquois Confederation of the Haudenosaunee, the League of Mayapan, the Xianbei Confederacy, the Helvetian Confederation of the Swiss cantons, the Etruscan Dodecapolis, and the merchants and entrepreneurs of the Hanseatic League, to name a handful of diverse historic, geographic, and cultural examples.

Let us envision global confederations of people of goodwill, connecting and collaborating in ecosystems animated by the will-to-good, by self-transcendent service to each other and to our shared future. Let us imagine advancing structures and systems that buttress and bolster our common destiny while uplifting the human spirit away from greed and fear and toward creativity and abundance and joy and kindness. Let us create the new ways, grounded in the ancient wisdom that says, "My well-being is inextricably entwined with yours."

MULTISTAKEHOLDER WATERFALLS

Essential to the microeconomic Ecocene corporate structure is the manner in which the "waterfall" is structured for the benefit of many stakeholder groups and communities. But before we can examine what multi-stakeholder, stewardship waterfalls are capable of doing for our communities and our world, we need to understand how they differ from their conventional, narrow-interest counterparts.

"Waterfall" is the term financiers and entrepreneurs use to describe how profits are distributed. Conventional waterfall models, in which costs are compressed as much as possible, are structured so that the greatest possible portion of gross revenue flows—like a rushing river—directly to the founders, executives, and shareholders. "The rest be damned" may as well be the general motto of these conventional models, notwithstanding that we often find decent and well-intentioned people working within them. Moreover, that too many titans simultaneously tout "job creation" and their self-directed "gazillionaire giving" form of philanthropy (in which donation decisions are so often based on accruing political power and influence, and even manipulating the NGO sector to research, develop, and advocate for innovations and market conditions from which they stand to extract further profits through their enterprises) as justification for this lousy model, and that too many of the rest of us have bought in to such a notion as "normal" and perhaps even "necessary," is as strong an indication as any how serious our situation is and how urgently we need much smarter and better-designed versions deployed at scale and competing throughout our economy.

Conversely, Ecocene-era waterfalls are not only designed to flow their resources toward multiple stakeholder groups after the "bottom line" of the enterprise's net profits, they are also appropriately understood to comprise the cost structures themselves of said enterprises. In other words, there are two major categories in which the enlightened Ecocene waterfall is to be understood: costs and dividends. In the cost category, instead of squeezing every last penny out of various "COGS"—which are actually people, communities, and otherwise externalized impacts—the enterprise is presented with a tremendous opportunity to lift up people and communities with reasonable adjustments to its cost structure (from squeezing and extracting to "fair trade," "living wage," and ecosystem stewardship). That is, instead of perpetuating the "death economy" of which John Perkins writes, and instead supporting the "life economy," organizational leaders and financiers are able to willfully choose "making a living" instead of "making a killing." And, once we properly adjust and attune our cost structures to be nourishing instead of extractive, we then have our net proceeds to distribute out to various stakeholders. Depending on our specific model, this will include donations to NGOs (at least 50% in the case of social enterprises, strictly speaking), ESOP and/or profit-sharing participation among employees and suppliers, and yes, of course, a substantial portion of the distributable proceeds will also flow to the founders and shareholders, as in the conventional model.

When understanding the fundamental difference between a conventional, extractive waterfall and an Ecocene, stewardship waterfall through the lens of the founders and financiers, it's not a black and white either/or, but a matter, instead, of degree. The degree to which financiers and founders deliberately forego some portion of their potential "upside" is also the degree to which the enterprise is designed for planetary prosperity. And, of course, the "what's in it for me" logic in all of this becomes non-linear when we understand the various positive feedback loops that accrue to the more advanced models, as their talent attraction and retention, overall competitive advantage, profitability, and even risk-avoidance (think stranded assets, uninsurable torts, and the like) will often ensure greater financial performance—especially over the mid- and long term—of the models designed for and attuned to planetary prosperity, with Quintenary economic performance as discussed below.., with Quintenary economic performance as discussed below.

Here are diagrams representing the two very different waterfall types:

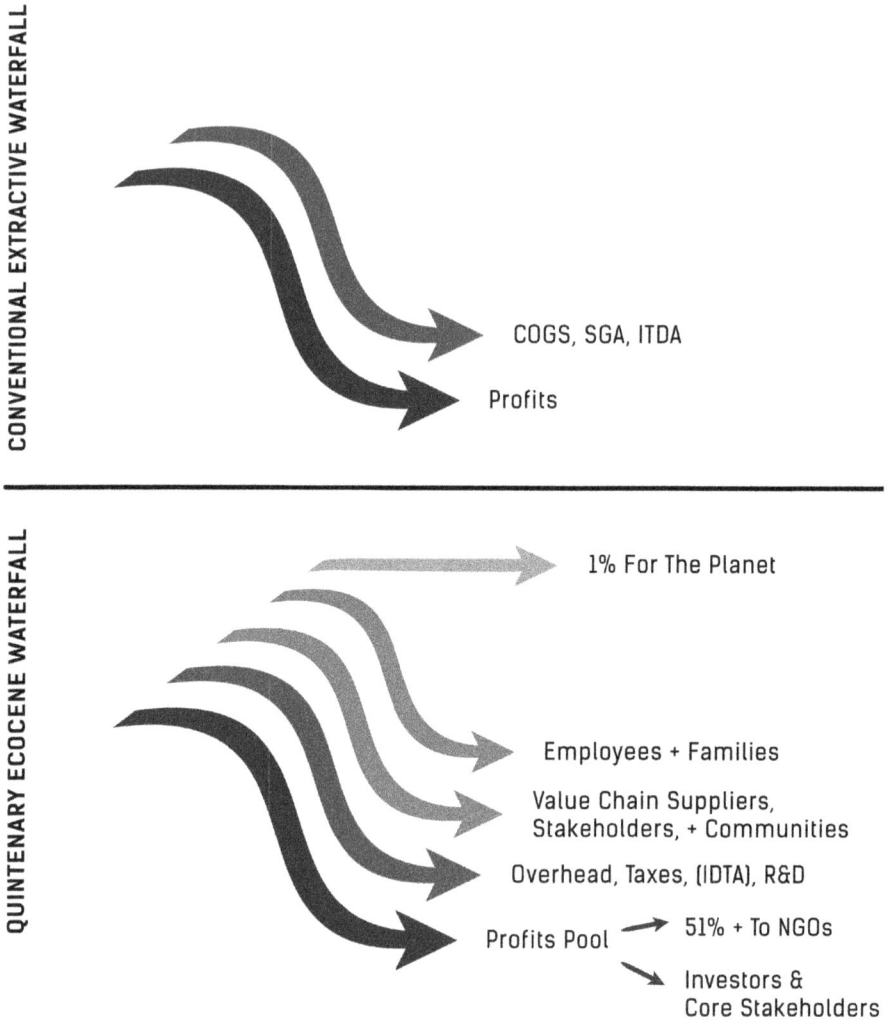

CONVENTIONAL EXTRACTIVE WATERFALL

COGS, SGA, ITDA

Profits

QUINTENARY ECOCENE WATERFALL

1% For The Planet

Employees + Families

Value Chain Suppliers, Stakeholders, + Communities

Overhead, Taxes, (IDTA), R&D

Profits Pool → 51% + To NGOs

→ Investors & Core Stakeholders

MACROECONOMIC ECOCENE FEDERATIONS— THE RISE OF THE MYCELIAL MODEL

Similarly, at the macroeconomic scale, we envision global consortia of companies, nonprofits, funds, foundations, and family offices collaborating both "top-down" and "bottom-up" in decentralized, autonomous, interconnected frameworks of coordination across nested hierarchies of interdependence, much like the neural-nets of soil mycelia.

These mycelial model networks enable resourcing of people and projects serving the greater good in interconnected bioregional contexts, *and* delivering both the power of large-scale capitalistic feedback loops across global alliances (competitive advantage, scale economies, marketing and messaging, policy and discourse influence, capital formation) as well as robust, decentralized, open-source learning, best practices, and resource-sharing mechanisms in a manner that serves the whole and engenders autopoietic recursive improvement throughout the entire system. Here's an example of how such a self-coordinating federated meta structure can look:

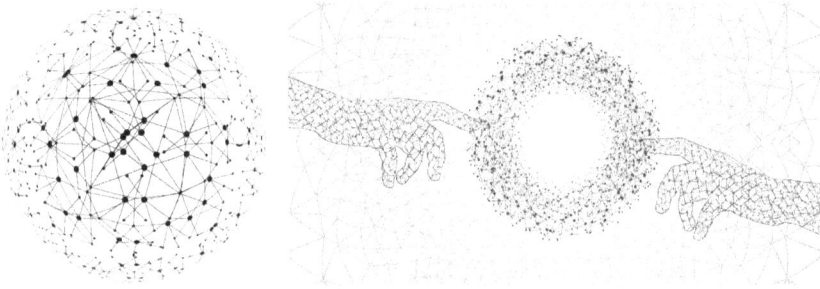

Illustrations by Gerd Altman; source: Pixabay.

Forward-looking funds, foundations, and family offices (FFFs) are directly connected to the ecosystem of for-profit social enterprises as well as the ecosystem of nonprofit organizations. In addition to receiving apportioned shares of investment dividends, in the context of the multi-stakeholder waterfalls described above, the FFFs also receive credits and tax benefit flows, when available. This macro-economic model also envisions shared digital Global Regeneration Network Platforms (GRNPs), as described in the example below, as well as carefully curated and coordinated research and development activities among the various stakeholders, as appropriate (with a general propensity toward open-sourcing those methods and technologies that are truly aligned with planetary prosperity, and therefore to our shared common benefit when adoption and scale-up is accelerated). The federation will also establish endowments and "Stewardship Wealth Funds" (think "sovereign wealth funds" but without any national borders and exclusively for investments in aligned enterprises) as well as robust advising, incubating, and investing vehicles in order to identify, cultivate, resource, and accelerate the many innovations emergent in entrepreneurs, cohorts, and communities worldwide. Of course, this entire ecosystem will have thousands, and eventually millions, of connected and participating brand partners (aligned companies) and community leaders— especially those like Biofi, Blue Dot, Yellow Barn Farm, and others weaving and strengthening local and regional enterprises at the foundational grassroots fabric of the "rhizosphere" essential to planetary prosperity.

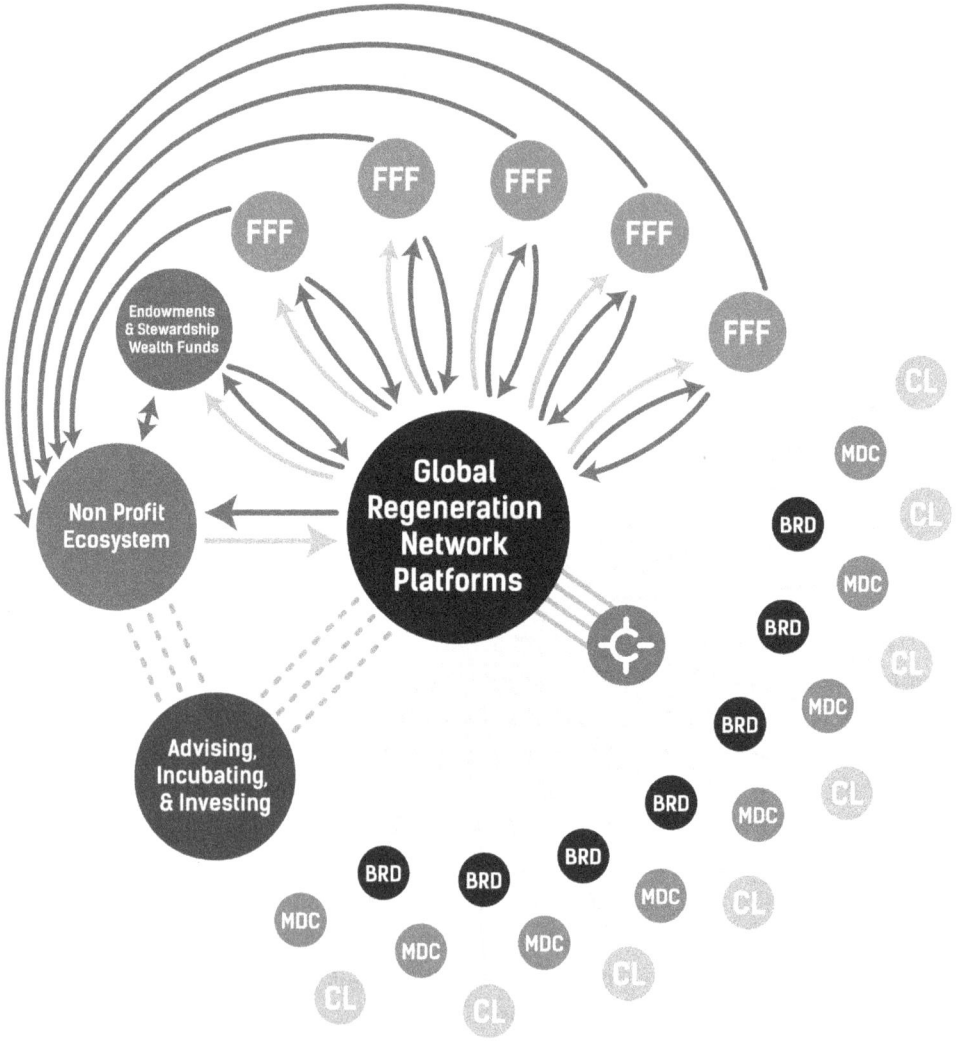

FFF — Funds, Foundations and Family Offices

Biophilic & Ecocene R&D

CL — Community Leaders

MDC — Mission Driven Companies

BRD — Bioregional & BioFi DAOs

Financial Resource Flows

Credits & Tax Benefit Flows

EVOLVING FOUNDATIONAL STRUCTURES—ADVANCED HYBRIDS FOR THE NEW AGE

We are living in a time when we will increasingly witness Ecocene economics in action—both at the microeconomic and the macroeconomic scales. At the microeconomic scale, we will see more and more corporate structures embodying the guidance, governance, and guardrails described above, and advancing the complexity and sophistication with which interconnected councils and working groups (aka guilds and decentralized autonomous organizations, or "DAOs") will create, collaborate, and cooperate for shared planetary prosperity. Many of these emergent corporate structures will incorporate hybrid structures and strategies from among the models discussed above. At the macroeconomic level, we will see similar patterns emerging and proliferating—much like the mycelial networks restoring and reclaiming lands that have been devastated by man's industrial carelessness or some catastrophic natural disaster. The mycelial networks reach their tendrils into every facet of the terrestrial ecosystem, bringing intelligence, resources, and the life force that enables regeneration and prosperity.

To help illustrate what this looks like in more detail, following is a hybrid example being developed among a consortium of our colleagues—an advanced Ecocene corporate structure for a heart-centered global digital social media, conscious commerce, financial innovation, shared philanthropy, and community connection hub rooted in goodwill, kindness, and responsibility:

ECOSCENE GLOBAL REGENERATION NETWORK
THE PEOPLE'S PLATFORM FOR PLANETARY PROSPERITY

EXECUTIVE SUMMARY VIGNETTE –
OUR MISSION IS MYCELIAL . . . OUR CURRENCY IS CONNECTION

Our ECOSCENE organizational structure is being established as a Benefits Corporation governed by three interconnected stewardship bodies: the Board of Trustees, the Stewardship Council, and the Sophia Wisdom and Grandmothers Council. Altogether, these three bodies—our Stewardship Triumvirate—oversee and support community and cooperative decision-making throughout the ecosystem, and ensure adherence to our fundamental ethics and values. At scale as a social enterprise, our company will donate 1% of its top-line revenues and at least 51% of its bottom-line profits to qualified NGOs, with—much of the allocation decision-making determined by various stakeholder guilds. Our multi-stakeholder regenerative finance structure delivers value to founders, investors, employees, advisors, our consortium of collaborating companies, and to our cooperative body of individuals, proprietors, and communities.

THE STEWARDSHIP TRIUMVIRATE

The **Board of Trustees** is entrusted with the fundamental governance, executive management, fiduciary responsibility, and overall stewardship of the entire corporate ecosystem. It is comprised of thirteen individuals: the Chair, two Chair appointees, two Investor appointees, two employee appointees, two consortium appointees, two coop appointees, and two founder circle appointees. The Board of Trustees selects the CEO, CFO, and COO. The entire corporate structure is subject to a 9:1 pay differential cap, not including founders' participation in the limited founder's equity pool.

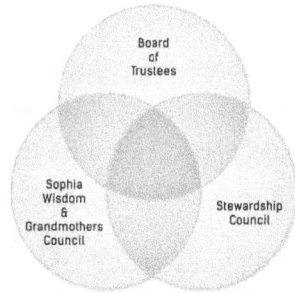

The **Stewardship Council** manages and stewards the social media, advertising, and public facing content generated by individuals, proprietors, guilds and guild-members, companies, NGOs and other participants, and oversees the quality and content of the educational and community-resilience resources. It is comprised of the CEO, two CEO appointees, two guild appointees, two coop appointees, two consortium appointees, two employee appointees, and two investor appointees. This body directly assists and supports the C-suite, and oversees the communication and harmony of all platform members.

The **Sophia Wisdom and Grandmothers Council** is comprised of women of diverse ages, ethnicities, and backgrounds who embody the divine feminine wisdom known by indigenous cultures worldwide to be essential to the health, wellness, and prosperity of our communities and societies as a whole. This sacred body provides guidance, prayerful support, and nurturing wisdom to the entire ecosystem, and is comprised of thirteen delegates—5 elected from among the broader body of women members of this sacred council, and 4 each by the Board of Trustees and Stewardship Council. This women-only body has oversight authority throughout the entire ecosystem.

Within our Stewardship Triumvirate, *authority* is understood to imply *responsibility*, and is earned by the demonstration of exemplary goodwill, wisdom, kindness, integrity, competence, and compassion.

Additionally, guilds will be formed with the consent of the Stewardship Council (subject to approval by the Board of Trustees and the Sophia Wisdom and Grandmothers Council), through which a variety of practitioners, companies, and other aligned stakeholders can formally participate in our structure.

COMMUNITY & COOPERATIVE GOVERNANCE

Self-governance is imperative on our social media platform and individuals and guilds alike are empowered to ensure strict adherence to our kindness and stewardship ethics. Additionally, special guidelines provide for constructive, compassionate dispute resolution, and although legitimate concerns are taken seriously, mechanisms are in place to prevent inappropriate public vitriol, opprobrium, and rancor, and to promote civil conflict resolution and non-violent communication.

SOCIAL ENTERPRISE

As the company scales, it will donate increasingly substantial financial resources to qualified non-profit organizations. Along with the Board of Trustees, the Stewardship Council, and the Sophia Wisdom and Grandmothers Council, Coop members and Guild members alike will also have a voice in philanthropic giving, and all are encouraged to participate in the 1% for the Planet giving vehicle at the individual, family, proprietor, and corporate levels.

MULTI-STAKEHOLDER REGENERATIVE FINANCE STRUCTURE

Extreme capital concentration is among the primary systemic failures of our conventional economic system that has resulted in tremendous social, environmental, and political risk and dysfunction. Our innovative multi-stakeholder regenerative finance structure provides an alternative that intelligently allocates profit-sharing outflows across the entire ecosystem. Additionally, through sophisticated financial

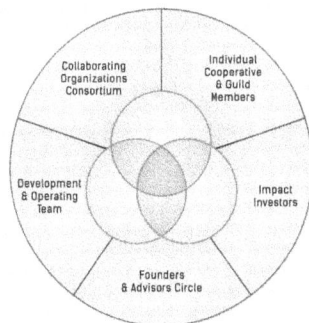

Collaborating Organizations Consortium

Individual Cooperative & Guild Members

Development & Operating Team

Impact Investors

Founders & Advisors Circle

engineering, tax credits and other benefits-backed financial value is leveraged to enhance investor returns above and beyond their share in the financial profits, thus ensuring robust, "reality-adjusted" returns to the visionary (and "new aristocratic") capital investors from future-forward funds, foundations, and family offices that are mission-aligned with the regeneration renaissance, and that are investing wisely for our shared future.

This is a global digital "home base" for all of us engaged in making our world a better place, all of use committed to good will, and all of us who know that quality of life is intimately linked with our stewardship choices (caring for mind, body, spirit, community, and environment). Together we will evolve social media, community connection, and conscious commerce *for good.*

INDIVIDUALS, FAMILIES, AND COMMUNITIES

Fundamentally, our platform offers individuals, families, and communities who seek greater health, wellness, and prosperity a global network of aligned participants who share the core values of kindness, decency, stewardship, regeneration, sustainability, and conscious lifestyles. As members of the growing LOHAS demographic, we are leveraging our consumer demand in order to improve our own quality of life, the quality of life of our fellow human beings, and the ecological integrity of our living biosphere.

CONSCIOUS COMPANIES

From the likes of Patagonia and Dr Bronner's to Climate First Bank and the Mondragon Cooperatives, there are thousands of companies now leading the way in an emergent Ecocene economic paradigm, whose community development, supply chain stewardship, and deep ethos of social and environmental responsibility are having positive impacts worldwide in virtually every region on the planet. These companies demonstrate their leadership, mission, and values in part through third party certification, including the B-Certified, 1% for the Planet, Regenerative Organic, Fair Trade, and several other credentials. Over 10,000 companies have already attained one or more of these certifications—and in many instances more than one credential—and thousands more will likely do so in the coming 3-5 years. By screening for these "conscious companies" and inviting them to participate in our platform (and encouraging other companies to emulate these behaviors and attain certifications so that they may participate as well), we will provide only mission-aligned companies exclusive access to the soon-to-be premier global platform for advertising and marketing to qualified LOHAS demographics in upper-tier socio-economic brackets while delivering inclusive and manifold social, economic, and environmental restoration benefits to uplift the world's lower socio-economic tiers.

NON-PROFITS & NGOS

Hundreds of qualified non-profit organizations, also known as non-governmental organizations (NGOs), will receive substantial donations from our revenues. Recipient organizations will be selected based on a variety of factors, and through several inclusive decision-making processes open to guild members, the Collaborating Organization Consortium, and individuals using the platform who wish to participate in NGO selection. Additionally, to the extent that such collaborations are feasible, additive, and synergistic, we will collaborate with GuideStar, 1% for the Planet, Network for Good, other charity networks, and matching grant-making sources to further leverage and amplify our impact.

VISIONARY FUNDS, FOUNDATIONS, AND FAMILY OFFICES

In order to achieve this global vision, we are partnering with visionary funds, foundations, and family offices. Mission-aligned investors and donors ensure a "patient capital" runway, and nurture our deeply rooted ethical framework so that our mission and vision aren't thwarted by the typical short-term financial pressures. A combination of program related investing (PRI), low-interest / slow money debt and convertible debt, and other blended finance structures will be deployed in order to maximally ensure our integrity and impact over time. We will develop and deploy both global financial innovations and bioregional and hyper-local BioFi and Slow Money capital deployment opportunities with our partners. And, we will leverage pass-through tax benefits from our philanthropy to deliver a powerful value-multiplier to our investors.

COLLABORATING ORGANZIATIONS CONSORTIUM

A special cohort of mission-aligned organizations and companies are being invited to join our Collaborating Organizations Consortium. This consortium will provide critical mass to help shepherd our enterprise from launch through scale-up and maturity, and will enjoy a variety of exclusive benefits including profits participation and discounted access to many of the platform's features. Additionally, the consortium will select representatives onto the Board of Trustees, Stewardship Council, and Sophia Wisdom and Grandmothers Council.

COOPERATIVE GUILDS

Individual, sole-proprietor, and small-business platform users may choose to join guilds in order to realize further benefits, enjoy community connection, amplify their voices in democratic and cooperative decision-making, and further affect the allocation of philanthropic donations. By no means exhaustive, the following are examples of guilds that we anticipate cultivating:

- Art, Artist, & Artisan Guild
- Biodynamic Land Stewardship Guild
- Chief Sustainability Officer & Corporate Regenerative Sustainability Consulting Guild
- Climate, Energy, & Infrastructure Guild
- Coaching, Advising, & Entrepreneur Incubator Guild
- Ecotourism, Agritourism, Wellness Tourism, & Wilderness Tourism Guild
- Entrepreneurs, Executives, & C-Suite Guild
- Emergency, First Responders, & Resilience Guild
- Food Systems Guild
- Holistic Healing & Herbal Resources Guild
- Holistic Parenting & Grandparenting Guild
- Life Skills & Financial Literacy Guild
- Regenerative Agriculture & Ecosystem Restoration Guild
- Regenerative Finance, Conscious Capital, & Stewardship Philanthropy Guild
- Sacred Sites & Archeology Guild
- Sophia Wisdom & Grandmothers Council
- Thriving Neighborhood & Sustainable HOA Guild
- Warrior Wellness & Military Families Guild

STATEMENT OF ETHICS, BELONGING, & IDENTITY

We are a social enterprise benefits corporation with a cooperative commons that is establishing, growing, and stewarding a worldwide network of people, communities, and companies who are activating and amplifying the Regeneration Renaissance on planet Earth.

- We embody kindness, conviviality, joy, and compassion. We contribute to the relief of suffering. We cultivate a culture of sacred stewardship.
- We embrace our responsibility to support the health, well-being, and prosperity of the entire human family, our living Mother Earth and all of her myriad creatures, including future generations.
- We ascribe to the Permaculture ethics of "do no harm to people," "do no harm to the planet," and "share the surplus" among the entire Gaian community.
- We believe that loving kindness, embodied wellbeing, conscious creativity, and careful collaboration are essential to steward human-made structures and technologies.
- We acknowledge the authentic intelligence of nature and awe-some cosmic wisdom as our source and guide, recognizing them as having many names and symbols throughout diverse cultural traditions and belief systems.
- We know ourselves to be living in extraordinary and momentous times and accept the responsibility to heal ourselves as we work in service to the healing of humanity and our shared Mother Earth.
- We know our strength is enhanced, our creativity celebrated, and our efficacy amplified through the group genius of community and collaboration, and commit to work in joy, kindness, respect, reciprocity, reverence, responsibility, and conviviality in the woven fabric of our interconnected relationships.

ECOSCENE is an emerging example of what's possible when we align around true wealth, mobilize the new Earth steward aristocracy, and activate advanced and sophisticated pathways to planetary prosperity.

ECOSCENE

PEOPLE'S PLATFORM FOR PLANETARY PROSPERITY

"A new world must be born, a world that would justify the sacrifices offered by humanity. This new world must be a world in which there shall be no exploitation of the weak by the strong, of the good by the evil; where there will be no humiliation of the poor by the violence of the rich; where the products of intellect, science and art will serve society for the betterment and beautification of life, and not individuals for achieving wealth."

—Nikola Tesla

5   ENTER THE QUINTENARY

Alchemizing the New Ecocene Economic Paradigm

It is obvious to most of us that whatever our "economy" is, it is something that impacts all of us on a global scale. This reality has its roots in millennia of human activity and reflects the cumulative and collective paradigms that have developed since "civilization" as we (generally) know it emerged several millennia ago. Dozens of important thinkers have devoted scores of books to understanding the origins of this shared legacy, several of whom have written essays for this book, and many more of whom are listed in the References in the back. While there is much to unpack and understand from among the insights of these thinkers and resources, we are going to share a very simple way of understanding how we're now situated at a tremendous watershed moment—a tipping point—separating this shared historic legacy from an entirely different way of doing "economics" going forward—the transition from "business as usual" as we've seen for some 80 or more centuries into the dawn of an entirely new epoch: the Ecocene.

A classical or "conventional" understanding of economics postulates "value production" as deriving from a linear, one-way flow of conditions and activities. This flow, or "value chain," begins with harvesting and extracting nature's bounty through human labor, often aided by machinery ("primary production"), and progresses stepwise through value-added changes to the raw materials (aka "manufacturing"—or "secondary production") into the various networks of merchants, distributors, stores, and (even online) retail outlets ("tertiary production"). Finally, a fourth step in the value chain (the "quaternary") is where the wizards of specialized information (accountants, lawyers, software engineers, data scientists, etc.) add value through information-tracking, analysis, risk management, financing, capital controls, and the like. In the early days of our economic epoch, the four nodes of value-added activity were often performed by disparate "actors" (people and/or organizations of people in guilds and companies): The foresters, fishermen, farmers, and miners would harvest timber, catch fish, and harvest crops; the blacksmiths, wood-workers, canners, and bakers would salt and preserve fish, bake bread, fashion furniture, and forge ironworks; and the merchants and shopkeepers would then buy, sell, and mend these "value-added" goods (indeed, many surnames reflect these original guild activities: Fisher, Miller, Baker, Smith, Tailor, Eisenhauer). Of course, in our times, things aren't so quaint, and many enterprises—especially the largest, wealthiest, and most powerful corporations—are "vertically integrated," operating in all four sectors.

This linear and generally extractive structure too often treats nature's bounty and "lower-skilled" human labor required at each value-added step to be "cogs" in the machinery of profit-making (coincidentally and amazingly, even the accounting acronym for such "expenses"—or "cost of goods sold"—along the path to profit is the term COGS!). Generally speaking, in conventional economics, it is the duty of the quaternary sector's "information and C-suite management wizards" to do anything and everything possible to reduce the "drag" of COGS in order to "free up" as much profit per unit sold as possible—this centuries-old tradition is known today by the sophisticated term "financial engineering." But this approach brings with it myriad systemic flaws—moral, pragmatic, and aesthetic—flaws that have now burgeoned to the point of such scale and complexity we all now face a global-scale polycrisis. Moreover, the systemic risks and dysfunctions are further compounded by the adverse impacts on natural and social systems not accounted for in enterprises' generation of profits—these are called "externalities" by economists and include widespread toxic pollution, ecosystem degradation, fisheries depletion, oceanic acidification, and the wholesale chemical alteration and energy loading of our atmosphere commonly known as global climate change, not to mention adverse impacts on families and communities treated merely as "cogs."

This simple linear system clearly has serious and severe limits.

Is there another, better way we could be doing all of this?

Enter the *Quintenary*.

The Quintenary is a new conceptual node in the conventional economic value-chain model that transforms the system into a regenerative, circular, stewardship-oriented, commons-responsibility economy. The Quintenary is the fifth node, representing system-wide stewardship and regeneration functions that fundamentally transform the nature and impact of the value chain. In effect, the Quintenary isn't a simple add-on or "band-aid," but represents a paradigmatic leap toward social and environmental stewardship directionally akin to Chardin's concept of the Noosphere (as discussed elsewhere in the book). As we progress into the Ecocene era, Quintenary functions will be increasingly performed by people, divisions, and even entire companies, in order to ensure that the social and environmental "commons" are well cared for, thus transmuting a linear, extractive, and all-too-often exploitative economic model into a kinder, gentler, and ultimately more efficient, effective, resilient, regenerative, and sustainable mode of operation—a saner system. Put another way in economic parlance, the Quintenary is all about taking responsibility for behavior and impact, internalizing externalities, and deliberately improving performance vis-à-vis the "commons" in order to achieve maximal outcomes in social and ecological stewardship alongside business and financial outcomes.

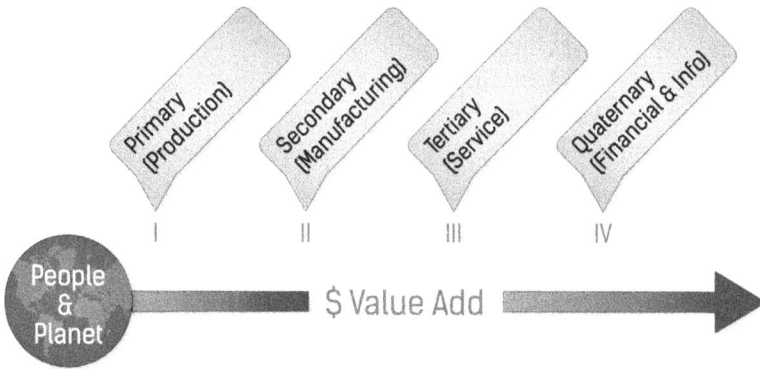

Conventional & Extractive Economics

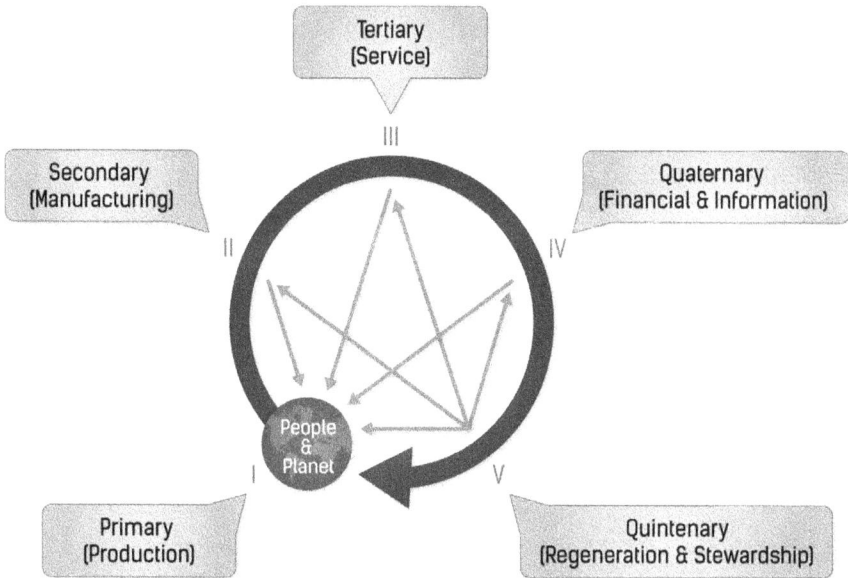

Regenerative & Sustainable Economics

Given that economics itself is a "design discipline," resulting from cumulative centuries of production, trade, commerce, theory, and policymaking, we have the opportunity (and need) to update and evolve our design. In an "alchemizing" manner, turning the dark lead of conventional economics into a gold standard of goodwill and stewardship, the Quintenary has as its primary function and responsibility the (re-)infusion of regenerative and stewardship ethics into the rest of the system. And the data shows that this is one of the fastest-growing sectors of the economy—we now see directors of sustainability, social impact, and stewardship in virtually all sectors, public and private, including an entirely new role in the C-suite, the CSO or chief sustainability officer (notwithstanding temporary backlash in certain sectors—reactionary perturbations as the pendulum swings and the emergent trends take hold).

It should be obvious that primary, secondary, tertiary, and even rudimentary forms of quaternary economic activity have been hallmarks of human civilization for millennia. But the quintenary, although rooted in timeless wisdom and the original instructions pervasive throughout our indigenous ancestry and heritage, may not be as obviously ancient—certainly not in conventional modern economics. We need a new mental model. As Tracy Benson, Sheri Marlin, and other systems thinkers have shown, our shared reality is a product and outcome of the pervasive mental models operating at the fuzzy roots of our conscious minds. Like an iceberg, not all is "visible" or apparent in how such core mental models determine so much in our world and experience of it. The naming and elevating of the Quintenary bring light and visibility to our work as stewards, and invite us to examine our deepest—and often subconscious and subliminal—mental constructs, attitudes, and beliefs about what's real, what's possible, and why. Beneath the surface, as Benson's and Marlin's "iceberg model for systems change" elucidates (echoing Donella Meadow's earlier "Leverage Points," see Part V), are the foundational suppositions core to our shared future, and the resulting structures and behavior patterns they engender.

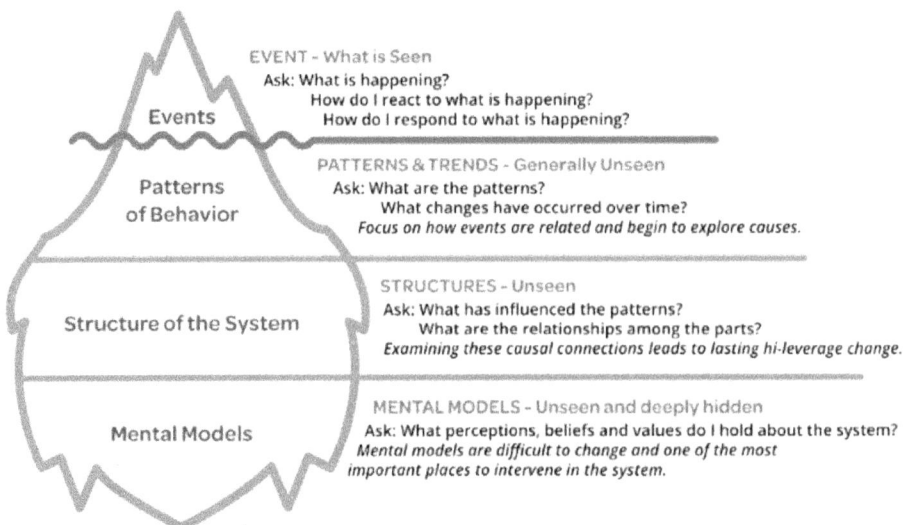

EVENT - What is Seen
Ask: What is happening?
How do I react to what is happening?
How do I respond to what is happening?

Events

PATTERNS & TRENDS - Generally Unseen
Ask: What are the patterns?
What changes have occurred over time?
Focus on how events are related and begin to explore causes.

Patterns of Behavior

STRUCTURES - Unseen
Ask: What has influenced the patterns?
What are the relationships among the parts?
Examining these causal connections leads to lasting hi-leverage change.

Structure of the System

MENTAL MODELS - Unseen and deeply hidden
Ask: What perceptions, beliefs and values do I hold about the system?
Mental models are difficult to change and one of the most important places to intervene in the system.

Mental Models

Model by Benson and Marlin, 2017.

And as we understand the Quintenary to encompass not only the exoteric and obvious change-making that comes from supply chain stewardship, employee stewardship, community stewardship, and planetary stewardship, but also the subtler, more esoteric aspects of our nature-based human well-being here on planet Earth, some really exciting knowledge and wisdom becomes apparent. For instance, our fifth economic value-add node, the Quintenary, suggests symbolically a profound insight known by the ancients and indigenous wisdom keepers throughout the ages: the number, geometry, and pattern of *five* is inherent to and emblematic of *life* itself. Indeed, at the molecular level, we find only geometric atomic arrangements of five when we're looking at life (currently or previously living DNA and organic material). There's a reason the Pythagorean mystery schools regarded the fifth of the Platonic Solids—the only one comprised of pentalpha geometry—to be the most precious and most carefully guarded of the group. And, there's a reason the embedded golden-ratio geometry of the pentalpha symbolic form is found infused throughout sacred architecture and symbolry worldwide. The systems-changing, transmuting alchemy of the Quintenary is both symbolically and pragmatically profound indeed—and opens up to us all new pathways to planetary prosperity.

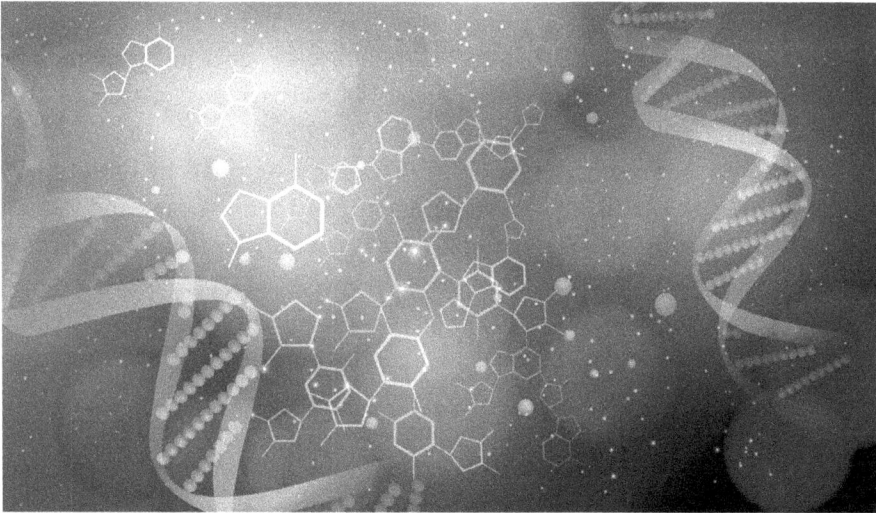

The Quintenary is emerging (some would say returning), and with it an invitation to each of us to enter into a profound relationship of stewardship and reciprocity with the sanctity of life and the sacredness of our duties and obligations to each other in the living web of all our relations.

"The secret of change is to focus all your energy not on fighting the old,
but on building the new."

—SOCRATES

6 THE ECOLOGY OF COMPETITIVE ADVANTAGE AND MARKET DEMAND

Scaling Ecocene Economics

The most powerful force in our economy, both destructive and generative, is the fusion of competitive advantage and its counterpart, market demand—the system's so-called "invisible hand."

Indeed, our pathways to planetary prosperity—guided by Quintenary stewardship—are necessarily paved with competitive advantage and market demand. Competitive advantage simply refers to something being better, more valuable, and more desirable in the economic marketplace—preferences evinced by purchasing decisions. The other "side of the coin," market demand, is the degree to which we opt for any particular good or service (or idea or candidate or policy in the case of the civic polity).

Thus, as our mission-driven companies and our purpose-led NGOs continue to deliver that which is better, more desirable, and more valuable to our world, and as we increasingly direct our market demand to align with planetary prosperity, we will provide an unstoppable power of preference, engendering the positive feedback loops (and capital flows) of an economic inevitability.

To visualize how powerful the combination of competitive advantage and market demand is, consider one of the most rapid, systems-wide transformations we've experienced in modernity: the transition from horses to automobiles just over a century ago as our primary mode of transportation. There's a famous set of black and white photos of New York City taken 13 years apart. In one (taken Easter morning, 1900), the street is crowded with horses and buggies, and only one automobile can be found in the throng. In the second (taken exactly 13 years later, 1913), only automobiles crowd the street, but for one barely visible horse. Complete, widespread systems change can occur in just over a decade, when driven by powerful economic forces.

Easter morning 1900: 5th Ave, New York City. Spot the automobile.

Easter morning 1913: 5th Ave, New York City. Spot the horse.

This is the power of competitive advantage and market demand: when something is perceived to be better, more valuable, and more desirable, profound systems change occurs as a matter of course.

Now, in our transition to the Ecocene, as we increasingly learn about the goods and services being offered by companies committed to social well-being and environmental stewardship, we will increasingly choose them. This is the power of consumer demand at work in the context of market transparency, widespread education, and individual freedom of choice. Indeed, albeit arguably in the clumsy, "learning to walk" early-stage steps of this phenomenon, we've entered the Age of Transparency in which veils have thinned—the facades of green-washing and vacuous rhetoric will no longer suffice to warrant sustained market demand. Authenticity—and third-party certifications to back it up—are essential to the survival of a business in the Ecocene economy. The "art of the deal" will only work for real-deal leaders, philanthropists, and Earth steward aristocrats. Don't get me wrong here—we have a lot of work to do, on all of this. But we're making tremendous progress and many trends are directionally encouraging.

Indeed, a survey of history will show us that, notwithstanding the terrible atrocities and cycling ups and downs, our global society is trending toward peace, prosperity, dignity, and empowered people. Now, as each of us participates in the global market economy, there is so much more we can do to further accelerate and amplify this directionality—by wielding the power of our *preference*, our consumer demand, to unleash the unstoppable feedback loop of competitive advantage.

There is a similarly powerful feedback loop that exists in our political economy—one that is fueled by the three key forces of *preference, profits,* and *prominence.* As companies' offerings are increasingly selected from among the noisy marketplace of options, they experience enhanced financial strength and their gross profits increase, contributing additional resources to their pool of available funds for marketing and messaging, in a word: *prominence.* And, as their marketing and messaging become more prominent, reaching more people, greater sales of their products and services are the result, eventually catalyzing a secondary form of competitive advantage: *scale economies.* This is an example of the virtuous cycle of competitive advantage, from the standpoint of the social enterprise or mission-driven company.

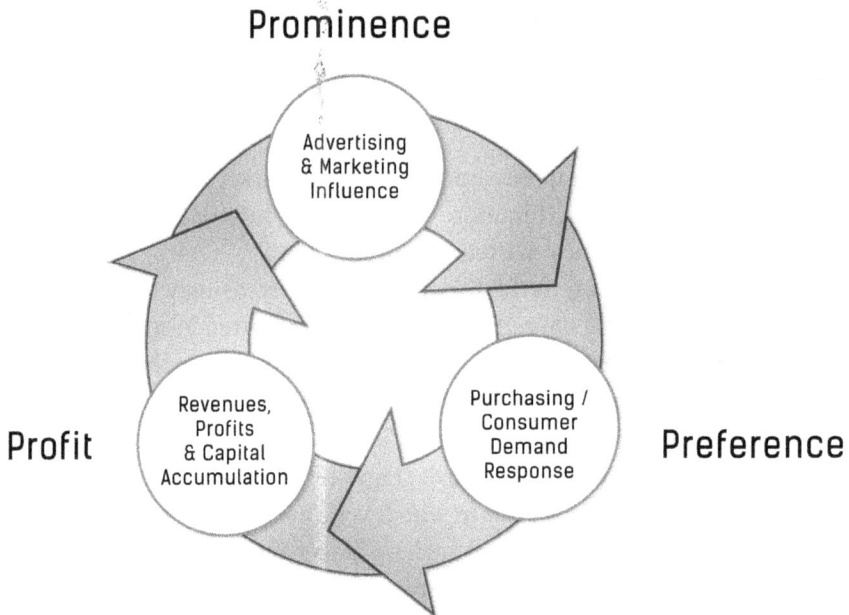

Prominence

Advertising & Marketing Influence

Purchasing / Consumer Demand Response

Profit

Preference

Revenues, Profits & Capital Accumulation

From the perspective of the individual global citizen, or "consumer," to use the banal and rather offensive term that includes each and every one of us who ever buys anything, we have another powerful feedback loop at work. Enhanced education, knowledge, and wisdom propel us to make better choices (and purchases) and better outcomes for ourselves individually, our families, our communities, and the world as a whole (further fueling the profit/prominence/preference feedback loop).

As humans, we naturally desire "better"—better lives for ourselves, our families, and our communities. Although there is some variation in what that looks like and means to each of us, there are generally vast areas of agreement—the "common ground" of sensible self-interest. We want our children to be well-nourished, safe, well-educated, happy, and thriving. We want them to have access to opportunity, to be secure in their self-identity and free from harm. We want them to pursue their dreams and desires, and to learn to do so in a way that respectfully and compassionately considers the dreams and desires of others. And, of course, we want these things for ourselves as well.

This is the common ground of human desire, rooted in the human decency that can be found pervasive in communities all around the world.

But, wait, some might say: Isn't the world full of people seeking and abusing power, hurting others, and contriving cynical Machiavellian exploits to enhance their own power and capital at the expense of others? Yes, there are countless examples of this, at varying scales and impacts, and throughout our geographies and histories, some of which are tragically trending now too. But there are many, many more examples of people choosing kindness and decency, civic freedom and personal responsibility. We wouldn't be here having this conversation otherwise.

But competitive advantage and market demand don't only apply to the purchasing of goods and services. Nor does competitive advantage only play out in terms of our social norms and what's culturally acceptable in economic production (slavery is no longer culturally acceptable, for example). It is also playing out—in a most powerful modality—in our own personal decisions about where and with whom we're willing to work. More and more of us are choosing to work for companies and with teams that are overtly and earnestly committed to having positive social and environmental impacts, and are eschewing the companies and teams that haven't yet made this competitive leap. Unsustainable and non-mission-driven sectors are experiencing attenuated talent pools as more of us choose only to deploy our skills and expertise in the direction of planetary prosperity. Indeed, organizations experience talent attraction (or exodus) as a result of their quality of leadership and ethical foundation.

The same is happening with investment portfolios, to the tune of trillions of dollars. These forces are driving more capital toward the companies and sectors in the economy that are better for us and our world, and increasingly away from those that aren't. And, with the trifecta of increased competitive advantage (products, people, portfolio capital), companies are launching, scaling, and gaining in prominence—all oriented around improving our world together.

Take for example, Climate First Bank, which is the fastest-growing new bank in the United States, and was just launched in the summer of 2021 (see case study vignette for more information). And, as cleantech financier Tom Steyer recently posted on LinkedIn, "The data is clear, renewable energy is winning in the marketplace. Cleantech continues to scale quickly because it is cheaper and better than fossil fuels, proving a successful climate transition is well within our reach." And in the arena of natural and organic food, healthy lifestyles, traditional herbal medicine, and wholesome living, the Lifestyles of Health and Sustainability (LOHAS) market sector has grown enormously over the past three decades, now including one out of five people in the US economy, and representing approximately half a trillion dollars in annual sales worldwide. Whether it's practicing yoga, receiving a massage, eating organic massaged kale, visiting local farms and ecotourism destinations, or weaving herbal medicine into your self-care practices, LOHAS market data reflects the reality that more and more of us are choosing *better living.*

Life is better over here.

That's the fundamental tone, the foundational reality that gives me great hope and that is central to the power of competitive advantage and market demand in our complex global economies. *People want better.* People are learning more about what better really means. And people are voting with their wallets for better every day.

*"Nature is a totally efficient, self-regenerating system.
If we discover the laws that govern this system and live
synergistically within them, sustainability will follow and
humankind will be a success."*

—BUCKMINSTER FULLER

7   MYCELIAL MODELS AND INSPIRED INNOVATIONS

The Future Is Already Here

Through the concentration of intellectual and human capital in alliances and federations dedicated to certain mission-driven outcomes, competitive advantage invariably plays out over time, often in decisive terms. Perhaps one of the most famous examples of this phenomenon on the global stage was the eventual defeat of Nazism as a result of the superior intellectual, creative, and innovative capabilities of the Allies, which were in large part enhanced by a diaspora of Jewish and conscientious gentile genius away from Nazi-occupied territories to the freedom and safety of American and British soils, where they contributed mightily to the righteous cause. If anything, the Nazis and other Axis powers were "out-thunk" and eventually defeated by their own mean and misguided non-meritocratic "exceptionalism."

This is an extreme example, to be sure, but it serves to make the point . . . emphatically. There is something quite similar underway today, although more subtle and nuanced as the boundaries aren't demarcated by tanks and trenches but by ethics and impact. But just as the fascist war machine made people pick sides, so too does the emergent Ecocene ethic draw a line. I point out the line not to "draw sides" (for indeed, we're all invited to join the side of the Ecocene, and we're all in it together), but to illustrate a curious and incorruptible fact regarding competitive advantage, intellectual property (i.e., innovation), and open-sourcing solutions.

That is, when it comes to the most compelling innovations of the Ecocene aristocracy, the protection of intellectual property is no longer required in the same way as with conventional IP, because the widespread implementation of distributed best practices and global adoption of appropriately designed and deployed structures and strategies have built into them the "negative path coefficient" safeguards that, *ipso facto*, mean cooptation by non-Ecocene entities would either (a) not work, due to lack of integrity or (b) catalyze internal systems change to realign said entities toward our shared mission of planetary prosperity. In other words, thinking about all of this in terms of super-intelligent mycelial network applications, to adopt is to adapt, and without adaptation (toward the Ecocene) cooptation is not feasible.

So, with that said, I am eager to share with you some of the most exciting inspired innovations coming down the pike—next-level technologies and techniques for better forms, functions, and flows within and among our institutions and exchanges. Specifically, next-level digital platforms; hybrid corporate structures (with the councils-based governance, community stewardship structures, and multi-stakeholder federations described in Chapter Four); multi-variable reward and tokenized asset mechanisms; multi-stakeholder federations; ultra-advanced regeneration technologies; next-gen digital, crypto, blockchain, and scrip currencies; and trade and transaction mechanisms whose "haircuts" and "float" are put to work in service to the greater good. With communities as customers, and Earth's biosphere represented on the Boards, Ecocene enterprises are developing and deploying hyper-intelligent advances essential to the evolution of our complex economies within the context of Ecocene stewardship.

I believe it's very likely we'll witness the emergence of digital platforms for connectivity, collaboration, commerce, and community building that lift up the best of who we are and what we're here to do. Unlike early-stage social media and e-commerce platforms with which we're all too familiar, these superior "web 3" models will enhance well-being instead of extracting data and profit, will support healthy habits instead of spinning out algorithms for addiction, will engender genuine conviviality and collaboration instead of vitriol and division, and will make regenerative multi-stakeholder capital flows the norm instead of deliberate capital extraction and concentration by a self-appointed oligarchy. Enhanced by ethically guided AI instances—rooted in wisdom traditions, Permaculture ethics, and the best of humanity's literary and philosophical achievements—digital platforms will enable councils and guilds to steward and govern self-organizing domains responsibly, and will provide avenues for quantum- and mycelial neural-net supercomputers to collaborate with humanity in place-based, decentralized cooperative guilds and community cohorts. These new digital platforms for prosperity will be better, and will therefore outcompete the old versions, which are clearly already rotting from the inside out. How many millions—billions—of us will choose the *better* model? A preponderance, I'm sure, and when you add that to equations in which marginal profitability matter, the results are very good . . . for all of us.

Within these neuronal-network patterned platforms and community connectivity conduits, there are ample opportunities to deploy game-changing innovations in transaction processing; loyalty and reward regimes among mission-aligned stakeholders (including some with unique "virality" attributes); innovative real-time community event and outcome tracking; and community-based ecosystem restoration action-taking that is hooked into the incentive structures of participating corporate and non-governmental allies within the ecosystem. Additionally, we will develop, capitalize, and deploy advanced common-good infrastructure within the social enterprise milieu, creating better worldwide conditions for all concerned.

Because the outcomes are necessarily multi-variable, we require diverse councils and cohorts to administer and steward the forms, functions, and resource flows of these inspired innovations. And, because we humans create, innovate, and govern most optimally when our neurobiological systems are well-regulated (and not in states of limbic hijack), *coherence councils* are required to strengthen and support the interpersonal harmony that is the sacred cement holding all of the stones of our built community structures firmly in place (which of course is built upon the personal practices and autopoietic evolution central to our *inner work*, as explored in the chapter of the same name below).

Again, because these inspired innovations can only be developed and deployed in the context and container of deeply aligned organizations whose essential core(porate) structures and institutional "DNA" are oriented toward the greater good and planetary prosperity, conventional notions of intellectual property protection no longer apply. In other words, it's not about "don't share the secret sauce" and all about "let's see who is actually really, really good at embodying, demonstrating, and deploying the core ethics upon which the value of such innovations can be realized." Accretion of competitive advantage is in the (no-longer-invisible) hands of the meritocracy and new Earth steward aristocracy of the actors involved, and open-sourcing is—ironically—very often the most effective moat for safeguarding. When innovators work in service, legitimate imitators are welcome and encouraged to advance the cause.

Fakers and takers cannot usurp here in this context—there is a greater intelligence at work. Our customers are our communities, regenerative stewardship is our *raison-d'être*, and service to the greater good is our secret sauce.

THE MYCELIAL MODEL EFFECT: A VISION FOR PLANETARY PROSPERITY

Across biological, cultural, and economic dimensions, mycelial networks offer one of the most profound and generative metaphors for the transformation now unfolding on Earth. These vast fungal webs—largely hidden underground—are not only responsible for maintaining the health of forests and ecosystems, but they also exemplify the very qualities our societies must now cultivate: interconnection, decentralization, mutual nourishment, and adaptive resilience.

In *Mycelium Running*, visionary mycologist Paul Stamets reveals how these networks serve as ecological sentinels and regenerative agents, breaking down toxins, regenerating soil, and interlinking plant communities in a vast web of nutrient exchange and communication. They are the forest's intelligence. They are Gaia's neural network. "The biosphere in which we live," he tells us emphasizing the super connectivity enabled by mycelia, "is one giant consciousness." The mycelial forms teach us that life thrives not through competition and dominance, but through cooperation, reciprocity, and collective intelligence.

This principle pulses through the systemic philosophy of Fritjof Capra, whose work *The Hidden Connections* articulates how social and economic systems all flourish when they mirror the interconnected feedback loops of living systems. In his book *Web of Life*, Capra reminds us that life is not organized from the top down but emerges through patterns of relationship—fluid, adaptive, and self-organizing. When applied to our institutions, this insight calls for a radical redesign: economies that function like ecosystems, cities that breathe like biomes, and organizations that act like communities of care.

Long before the term "regeneration" entered the mainstream, William Irwin Thompson foresaw this shift. In his prophetic essay *Meta Industrial Village*, he described a future in which the artistic, technological, and ecological dimensions of civilization would fuse in small-scale, self-organizing, deeply adaptive communities. Foreseeing what Buckminster Fuller called "ephemeralization" (the pairing of asymptotically ever-shrinking technologies with ever-expanding computing capacities and velocities), Thompson envisioned cultural forms that—like mycelial webs—could sense, learn, respond, and evolve with place-based wisdom. In doing so, he sketched out a civilizational metamorphosis: from empire to ecology, from hierarchy to holarchy, from extraction to emergence—metaindustrial cultures woven together in planetary civilization.

This is precisely the narrative dramatized in my novel, *Viriditas*, where artificial intelligence, ecological wisdom, and Gaian consciousness converge in the characters of Brigitte Sophia and her mycelial-networked supercomputer named Otto. Their co-evolution points toward a planetary civilization not dominated by machines or markets, but interwoven with the living intelligence of Earth. In *Viriditas*, we witness a post-Anthropocene culture where economies behave more like forests than factories, and where intelligence—human, artificial, and mycelial—coalesces in service to life.

In this light, the "mycelial model effect" is more than metaphor. It is a roadmap for planetary prosperity rooted in biology's deep design. To meet the converging crises of our time—ecological, economic, and spiritual—we must begin to think, feel, and act like mycelia. Not as isolated agents or competing factions, but as an emergent, interlinked superorganism guided by a shared, living intelligence. This is the Gaian turn. This is the Ecocene. This is our biggest deal.

Illustration by Gerd Altman; Source: Pixabay.

"As money in the past ministered to personal and family needs, so in the future it must minister to group and world need."

—The Tibetan Master DK

8   THE FUTURE OF MONEY

Bernard Lietaer's Visionary Wayshowing

One of the most important arenas of innovation is in the realm of money itself. And in this realm, we have the genius and wisdom of a rare luminary. Very few leaders possess the complete trifecta of visionary futurism, sophisticated technical expertise, and deep-rootedness in the stewardship wisdom of the Original Instructions. Bernard Lietaer is one such rare luminary, whose brilliance shone in all three of these areas, and whose legacy provides us clear guidance as we voyage into the Ecocene.

For any of us interested in expanding our knowledge of financial systems, the nature and structure of money, digital currencies, cryptocurrencies, scrip instruments, and the myriad applications of community-based, loyalty- and complementary currency regimes throughout many cultures and the arc of history, Bernard's book *The Future of Money* (Random House, 2001) is must reading. This is especially true for any of us seeking to leverage cryptocurrency or digital blockchain structures and strategies for social good, environmental stewardship, and Ecocene economics at scale, and even more so for those among us who have become "mesmerized" by the "shiny object" effect of new technological advances, particularly those of us gazing into the casino odds mirrors of digital (tulip-like) speculation bubbles instead of focusing on the powerful capacity for serving the greater good that these emergent technologies possess, when appropriately guided.

Bernard understood the critical importance of proper guidance, and was deeply ensconced in wisdom traditions from which he drew great courage and insight.

I had the good fortune of befriending Bernard and spending several hours-long sessions with him conversing about the subtleties and nuances of his vast and profound knowledge and deeply rooted wisdom. He was an extraordinary individual with exceptional life experience and breadth of perspective—one whose expansive worldview was as evolutionarily advanced as his extremely sophisticated financial acumen and technical economic knowledge was precise, profound, and prescient. Among the handful of people I would have liked to interview on the Y on Earth Community Podcast before their passing, Bernard is at the top of the list. He passed away early in 2019, but his legacy lives on.

We have a lot to learn from Bernard Lietaer.

A lot.

So much is contained in *The Future of Money*. And, because of its easy-to-understand style and the many pertinent "vignettes" found throughout the book, it is one of those precious treasures that we would do well to read more than once. Indeed, in some of the simplest of sentences and sidebar forays, Bernard reveals so much that will help us to *much better* understand the nature of money, the (sometimes very subtle) attributes of our many different experiments with money over time and across vastly different cultural contexts, and the sacred origins of money; and to perceive the underlying structural essences, limitations, and virtues of different monetary instrument designs that will allow us to innovate in wise and informed ways the legitimately *pro bono* currency and market mechanism solutions so needed in our times.

Why was Bernard's work and legacy so important, and what distinguishes him from so many others who have written on the subject?

There are a few things you should know about Bernard that will help answer this question, which should, I hope, help you to quickly ascertain why his writings provide us such essential guidance for our endeavors.

But first, who was Bernard Lietaer? What are his credentials and bona fides?

Bernard was part of the technocratic team that engineered the awesomely complex convergence mechanisms deployed by the European Community (now the European Union) for the simultaneous, permanent conversion from the national "fiat" currencies of individual countries (such as the Deutsche Mark and Franc) into the brand-new Euro currency (€) with which we're all familiar today. Many experts and pundits were convinced it would fail. But this was a stunning achievement to say the least, and one in which the experiment itself was the only proof positive of the efficacy and accuracy of the technocrats' innovation.

Bernard was also a financier, a captain of the financial markets whose offshore currency fund, called Gaia Hedge II, was the world's top-performing managed currency fund during the 1987-1991 period. He was named "the world's top currency trader" by *Business Week* in 1992. He worked at the Central Bank of Belgium and was president of Belgium's Electronic Payment System. Bernard was also a visiting scholar at Naropa University's Marpa School of Business in Boulder, Colorado. It was here in Boulder that I had the opportunity to meet him in person and enjoy our many conversations, often at his favorite French restaurant, L'Atelier, where we'd dine and chat in the relaxed, cozy atmosphere over haute cuisine, and would never miss, per Bernard's insistence, the decadent chocolate dessert ensemble that was no doubt sweetened by nostalgia for his Belgian homeland.

Although I enjoyed these meals immensely, I wasn't there for the fine dining. I was there for the company, the conversation, and the comprehensive crash courses in potential monetary and currency innovation immediately before us.

Bernard regaled me with his towering grasp of monetary history and described his vision for what's possible in a future of "Sustainable Abundance" as laid out in *The Future of Money*. Although I won't do it full justice, and implore you to read his book to get as much of this directly for yourself as possible, I will attempt to give you a succinct and salient overview of the main themes and points in his brilliant work.

Fundamentally, according to Bernard, money is a construct of both mundane utility and sublime inspiration. The story of money is inextricably entwined with our human history. And the promise and possibility of money, when designed as an instrument of love, compassion, and goodwill, is as potent a force for planetary prosperity as any other construct we humans might create and deploy together.

Indeed, his attitude toward the sacred potential of money is redolent of the (luminary known simply as) The Tibetan's proclamation that money will become the "medium of loving distribution."

Bernard is the harbinger of this promise and possibility—this powerful potential for good.

His erudite financial and monetary worldview, an astute observer will see, is a synthesis of the historically opposed views of the French Physiocrats and the Scottish Enlightenment school that were at loggerheads, conceptually and intellectually speaking, during the dawn of the modern industrial era in which we find ourselves now firmly entrenched and poised to transcend. By reconciling the power of capital—in all forms, including the ever-evolving human capital form—and the fundamental imperative of physical stewardship, Bernard describes our current era, provides historic context, and paints a picture of a possible way forward toward planetary prosperity.

In *The Future of Money*, Bernard recognizes four "mega-trends" affecting our immediate circumstances: (1) the Baby Boomer age wave; (2) climate destabilization and biodiversity loss; (3) exponentially evolving computing and information technology; and (4) systemic monetary instability. In this context, he describes five future scenarios of what will ensue, depending on the choices we now make. Of the five possible scenarios, however, one isn't feasible, he tells us, because "business as usual" won't fly, as it were, as we continue forward into the 21st century with all of the intersecting systemic risks playing out in an extraordinarily complex set of dependencies and feedback loops. In other words, there's no going back. The other four scenarios, which Bernard unambiguously describes as: (1) The Corporate Millennium, (2) Careful Communities, (3) Hell on Earth, and (4) Sustainable Abundance, essentially describe the parameters and conditions of what's to come, depending upon our collective decision-making right now: entrepreneurs, financiers, philanthropists, consumers, community leaders, policymakers, and the markets as a whole (which is all of us combined). That's the future we face—three scenarios that are either eventually horrific (1, 3) or implausibly insufficient (2), and one scenario that sounds good . . . for *all* of us: Sustainable Abundance (4)—a scenario of planetary prosperity.

Recognizing the constraints and possibilities of what lies immediately before us, Bernard wrote: "My strongest motivation for researching and writing this book has been my increasing belief that it is possible for us to create a Golden Age of Sustainable Abundance within our lifetimes."[1]

When reflecting on Bernard's intrepid optimism in the face of so much dystopian probability, I'm reminded of that wonderful quote from Hazel Henderson—"We can recognize that change and uncertainty are basic principles, we can greet the future and the transformation we are undergoing with the understanding that *we do not know enough to be pessimistic*"—and think also about its implied corollary from Lily Sophia von Übergarten, that "true understanding, engendered by higher-order knowledge and wisdom, necessitates optimism." This clearly applies to Bernard. But what did he actually *know* and *see* that allowed him to maintain such optimism?

Or, asked another more apposite way, *what do we need to know* about the historic nature and application of money, and about the nature of what's possible when we orient ourselves differently toward money, that will enable the sustainable abundance of planetary prosperity?

Here's a synopsis of Bernard's thinking on these questions:

Bernard's exploration of the historic origins of money as we know it takes us all the way back to the early mists of "civilization" as it's conventionally defined by the advent of agriculture, centralized city-states, writing, and, with it, money (the earliest evidence of writing reveals our penchant for

---

1 Lietaer, *The Future of Money*, p. 115.

tracking commercial transactions and balances of account). By taking us to the horizon of the great transition between the matrifocal cultures of the "prehistoric" Minoan and Cretan civilizations, and the myriad indigenous cultures of the Etruscans, pre-Hellenic Greeks and others in and around the Mediterranean Sea, Bernard draws upon the archeological and anthropological insights associated with Marija Gimbutas, Riane Eisler, and other scholars who have helped us better understand the emergence (and non-universality/ inevitability) of the dominant patriarchal paradigm in which our modern systems find their genesis. And, within the earliest examples of money—being exchanged for future shares in communally managed harvests, hence combining a sort of food security insurance with coinage issued to farmers who could later redeem the money for sacred fertility rites while the distribution of sustenance for the community was ensured by the temple priestesses— Bernard lifts the veil for us to consider and imagine far different versions and applications of how and for what money can be used in the context of seasonally attuned cycles of environmental stewardship, ensured sustenance, and community cohesion.

Building upon this, he also delves into the more esoteric dimensions of money, making connections between the coinage and administration of money and spiritual beliefs and practices rooted in the cultural fabrics of place, indigenous tradition, and—very especially—our relationship with the land and harvest.

More recently, he tells us, modern money has taken on esoteric spiritual dimensions in its symbolry—especially that of the U.S. dollar, which was established alongside the great "New Atlantean" experiment in democracy set in motion by the Constitutional Framers, many of whom themselves were deeply ensconced in esoteric spiritual knowledge and practices. The dollar has on it many repeating numeric patterns, as Bernard points out, within the context of several prominent symbolic "landmarks" that make poignant a connection with the esoteric, cosmic, and metaphysical. Upon the obverse side of the printed dollar, the Great Seal of the United States shows an "all-seeing eye" of enlightenment (and perhaps of the activated Pineal gland according to certain lesser-known traditions) radiating light as it hovers atop an incomplete Pyramid of 13 levels, while the eagle clutches 13 arrows in one talon and an olive branch with 13 leaves in the other, with the Seal of Solomon, or Mogen (Star) of David hovering above, comprised of 13 five-pointed stars ("twelve around the one") that has thus embedded within the geometry not only the obvious Kabbalistic "Cube of Space" associated with the Seal of Solomon (the geometry of the "six"), but also the lesser known golden ratio of life—the Blazing Star— that references the cycling and self-similar geometry of five, the Pentalpha, and even our Earthly connection with the Sun, Mercury, and Venus, and the feminine fertility rhythm of the 13 (28-day) lunar cycles each year, all of which make up important foundational ashlars in the great edifice of the Adytum of western mystery schools (and ancient and indigenous knowledge systems). Of course, initiates in indigenous wisdom societies would also recognize the connection between the 13 and 28 interval fertility cycles and the turtle shell, having 13 panels (scutes) on the outside (carapace) of the shell and 28 underneath (plastron). The symbolry of the 13 is embedded all over the U.S. dollar—each and every printed dollar with which we're so familiar in our regular quotidian transactions. (For a far deeper dive into the interconnected symbolry found throughout humanity's various cultural expressions, including the 555-foot-tall obelisk in Washington, D.C., which annually "pierces" the archetypally feminine ovum before the White House in an annual gesture of fertility and renewal, I invite you to read *Viriditas* and to take some time to contemplate the sacred geometry, cultural symbolry, and cypher-coded messages found in both the primary clear text and the marginal "annotations" of that epic, visionary eco-thriller about these very times we're sharing together on Earth).

Thus, as Bernard was well aware, there is much more than "meets the eye" in the creation, construction, and application of money, which is revealed to be a mirror of our currently prevailing worldviews and socio-economic zeitgeists.

Within this context, and echoing the wisdom of Plato, who said, "Reality is created by the mind. We can change reality by changing our mind," Bernard unveils a profound understanding of the essence and nature of money, and hence what we're capable of creating and manifesting by redesigning the principals and priorities built into the new monies of our future. Put another way, whereas conventional wisdom often refers to money as the "root of all evil," Bernard more accurately asserts (as the title of his first chapter in *The Future of Money*) that *money is the root of all possibilities.*

But in order to understand what's made possible by our deliberate re-orientation of money toward the values and ethics of planetary prosperity, we must understand the intrinsic nature of the dominant money structures we're using today.

The U.S. dollar, like hundreds of other national currencies, is a fiat, debt-based currency. That is, it is created out of "thin air" (fiat—as in Fiat Lux in the Latin translation of the book of Genesis—"Let there be Light"), as if a Divine act, and is at the moment of creation an instrument of debt, or, a "note payable" between the issuer and the recipient of the note. Thus, this fundamental (and arbitrary) structure, according to Bernard, yields three specific outcomes that are part-and-parcel consequences of debt-based fiat currency issuances: (1) the system requires endless economic growth, (2) the system engenders competition for a scarce monetary resource, and (3) the system increasingly concentrates wealth within the hands of an exceptionally small minority of participants. These three outcomes result in certain conditions and outcomes—at scale—that most of us would agree are better avoided, and that eventually lead to tremendous socio-economic instability.

This type of money, which Bernard calls "Yang"-style money, is contrasted with a "Yin"-style of money, or complementary currency, which has an entirely different set of intrinsic structural elements and therefore a very different set of outcomes. Yin-style complementary currencies are established not by debt-based instances of "fiat," but by relationship and reciprocal value exchange. And, instead of *structurally* bearing interest, complementary currencies can be designed to have demurrage—or "anti" interest—instead, thereby disincentivizing the accumulation (and concentration) of capital and incentivizing its ongoing and regular circulation by and between constituent members within the Yin currency community. Rudolf Steiner referred to this same mechanism as the "aging of money." Amazingly, Bernard indicates that the presence of robust Yin-style currencies with built-in structural demurrage will actually help stabilize and mitigate the inherently unsustainable aspects of the Yang-style currencies, and thus, he suggests, a Yin/Yang "coherence" or balancing is the optimal design aim—thereby balancing financial and social capital impacts within the economic system.

Now, with all of this in mind (and again, I urge you to read *The Future of Money* in its entirety), Bernard sets out a vision of what's possible in our lifetimes—what's possible to help usher in a future of sustainable abundance and planetary prosperity.

By leveraging the functionality of the cybersphere, which is of course nearly ubiquitous in our modern economic world, we can establish and deploy digital Yin-style currencies that not only stabilize the financial-social capital balance described above, but also bring in the third leg of the tripod, as it were, the natural capital stewardship and restoration so urgently needed in these times. Built within the money itself, these digital Yin-style currencies will have "Sustainability Fees" or 1% for the Planet-type structural "transaction fees" of various basis-points built into them, automating greater capital flows for ecological regeneration and meta-industrial community building worldwide.

Going even further, Bernard envisioned a future in which certain of these currencies would be tied to and backed by a robust "basket" of globally referenced natural capital elements from our material world of ecosystem services, carbon sequestration credits, and other non-abstract (Physiocratic) performance indicators we wish to see scaled and sustained as we turn the corner toward the Ecocene. Dubbing them "Terra Units," Bernard envisioned a robust, sophisticated, and well-balanced monetary system solution-set in which the outcomes would lead to a reasonable deceleration of the "disembodied" financialization trends plaguing our world and well-being, and a "spreading out" of the capital resources through the entire community, including the ecological community, by deliberately financing restoration and regeneration activities at scale.

Moreover, in addition to these beneficial outcomes, Bernard also foresaw a tipping of the scales (in terms of *competitive advantage*, brand loyalty, and capital "float" accruing to the Ecocene structures of our future) made possible by new payment processing, novel currency exchanges for goods and services, and new forms of money that will, like frequent flyer miles and credit card rewards, enable positive feedback loops and virtuous cycles of restoration, regeneration, stewardship, community coherence, and holistic well-being.

Thus, in his vision for the future of money, Bernard has charted for us a clear and realizable solution-set of pathways to planetary prosperity—a future of sustainable abundance accessible through our careful and profound paradigmatic pivoting, and carefully developed and deployed innovations that serve the greater good.

And speaking of serving the greater good, and acting according to an ancient ethic of stewardship, kindness, and responsibility (the Original Instructions), Bernard was exemplary. Through his travels and teaching, as well as his inner work, Bernard embraced and promulgated the essence of the Original Instructions, a fundamental paradigmatic understanding that we now need to explore together in the next chapter.

"When the Grandmothers speak, the Earth will be healed."

—Hopi Wisdom

9 THE ORIGINAL INSTRUCTIONS AND GRANDMOTHERS COUNCILS

Ancient Codes of Sacred Circumscription

Pathways to planetary prosperity are paved upon the foundation of the Original Instructions.

Many of us are familiar with the saying attributed to Einstein: "We cannot solve our problems with the same thinking that created them." But what does this really mean? Another, perhaps lesser-known saying tells us that "to come to the knowledge you have not, you must go by a way you know not." This wise adage is likewise counseling us that we must look *outside the box* of the status quo in order to change course. But how do we *do* that?

If the "same" thinking doesn't work, how are we supposed to find the "different" thinking, and how are we to know the difference? Where do we look?

The answer has been with us all along, ancient and "hidden in plain sight," as it were. It is a very powerful cultural, social, and spiritual technology available to us today: initiation into the myriad orders and societies of the Original Instructions. We don't need to invent something new (perhaps to the chagrin of the technological solutionists). We simply need to rediscover—to *remember*—that which is our fundamental birthright, and was known and cherished by our ancestors.

Our modern world is crowded with would-be adults who have not yet experienced the rite-of-passage initiations that bind us together in shared obligations of responsibility and stewardship, and fold us into the fabric of fellowship for the greater good. We need to resurrect these initiatic practices into the mainstream as a matter of course—we humans need to step across the transitional threshold from childhood into adulthood, properly earning the credentials—and right—to lead. Otherwise, our society remains a global kindergarten with hordes of giant babies running amuck, and "running the world" into Anthropocene devastation.

However, if we seek it out, we will find that there is a treasure trove of knowledge and wisdom in our shared human heritage awaiting our discovery: the celebratory verses of the *Atharva Veda*, the negative confessions of the Ancient Egyptians, the love-wisdom teachings of luminaries like Siddhartha Gautama Buddha and Jeshua the Nazarene, and the Original Instructions of indigenous peoples around the world. They tell us that we're all sharing a living "spaceship"—Planet Earth. Our planet—our spaceship—came with operating instructions that our ancestors knew and practiced throughout the ages (and still do in precious pockets of sanity around the world today). The operating instructions are our shared heritage, but are, sadly (and dangerously) lost to an amnesia arising from Mammonic Wetiko afflicting the mainstream modern mind—unless we recover them now.

It goes without saying that none of us is perfectly good—and (ahem) some of us are far less perfectly good than others, no? Like the checkered "pavement" of a chessboard, we each have lighter and darker aspects to our individual makeup. The guidelines and guardrails of the Original Instructions help us circumscribe within due bounds our darker tendencies, keeping them gentler and more subdued, and thereby making us each a more harmonious instrument to play in service to the greater good. Of course, one of the great graces of our humanity is the opportunity to choose continual self-improvement, and it is among the noblest obligations we might take on. But we'll always have some flaws, foibles, blind spots, and weaknesses—like the *wabi sabi* in ceramic art. Despite our polishing and upright rectitude, none of us will be a "perfectly squared ashler" in humanity's great temple edifice. Without surrounding ourselves with the guidance and guardrails of wiser group-genius and ecosystemic safeguards, we run the risk of becoming dangerous and destructive—to ourselves, and in some cases to many, many others. The Original Instructions, like philosophic software (literally providing "love wisdom" encoding), and like an antioxidant counter-acting aberrational avarice and the Wetiko of Mammonic arriviste within the body of the community webwork, provide us with a codex of circumscription essential to navigating the polycrisis and attaining planetary prosperity together.

So, what are the Original Instructions, and how do we access and reintegrate them into our lives and society?

Here's how Reverend Doctor Randy S. Woodley, of Cherokee descent, describes them in his article "America's Original Instructions":

The Original Instructions to many of America's Indigenous peoples include teaching everyone to live in a way of harmony, balance and wherever possible, peace with ourselves and with all creation; including other people. Those original teachings meant making sure no one went hungry; no one was treated better than anyone else; that we actively sought and preferred peace over war; that instead of hostility, we extended hospitality to strangers; that we kept a good mind about all things and all people, even our enemies. Often, today those teachings are commonly reduced to just say that we are all supposed to live *in a good way*. This is true not only in America but all around the world. Indigenous peoples including Māori, Zulu, Aboriginal, Saami, Maasai, Ikalahan, Hawaiian, and our many North American Indigenous peoples have similar teachings with names like ubuntu, *shalom*, *hozoo*, *Duyukti*, *wo-dakota* and *Aloha*. This "Harmony Way," some believe, is the original teaching for all humanity.

Haudenosaunee wisdom keeper and Seneca Nation elder Oren Lyons described the Original Instructions for the entire world at the United Nations General Assembly Auditorium in New York City as the Great Law of Peace—the Law of Life, the Law of the Seed, and the Law of Regeneration:

> We were instructed to create societies based on the principles of Peace, Equity, Justice, and the Power of Good Minds. Our leaders were instructed to make every decision on behalf of the seventh generation to come; to have compassion and love for those generations yet unborn. We were instructed to give thanks for All That Sustains Us. Thus, we created great ceremonies of Thanksgiving for the life-giving forces of the Natural World, as long as we carried out our ceremonies, life would continue. We were told that 'The Seed is the Law'. We were instructed to be generous and to share equally with our brothers and sisters so that all may be content.

Several Hopi elders including Grandfather Martin Gashweseoma also addressed humanity through the United Nations General Assembly, describing the Original Instructions as a:

> Way of life which the Great Spirit has given to all people of the world . . . a Spiritual Peace with love in our hearts for one another, love in our hearts for the Great Spirit and Mother Earth.

Such wisdom is also anchored in ancient Vedic, Confucian, Taoist, Egyptian, Hebrew, Islamic, and Christian traditions as well. Sacred words for peace, prosperity, and well-being reflect this wisdom: *Shalom, Salam, Shanti, Seneb, Hé Píng,* and *Heiwa.* In all these paths there is found a unifying theme of on-the-level interconnectedness, interdependence, and the moral imperative of kindness, honor, and respect toward the entire human family and all of Earth's sacred creatures—the water, the trees, the birds, the bees, and all living creatures however big, small, grand, or humble—as is implied in the great Lakota phrase *Mitakuye Oyasin*: "we are all related."

The Original Instructions are essential, and we deepen our embodiment of them at the individual level in large part through our inner work. However, there's also an essential "structural" aspect to the functional embodiment of the Original Instructions in our broader social and organizational fabrics: the Grandmothers Councils.

While there's a willful archetypal "masculine" quality to entrepreneurship and business leadership worthy of celebration—when in balance and harmony with self-transcendence and service to the greater good—and those of us who have experienced the collision of responsibilities and real-time decision-making required in such positions of leadership will attest to the frequent (and often unrelenting) requirement to lead with a decisive "yang" demeanor, there's much more to deep leadership than this singular "heroic warrior" modality.

Indeed, as many indigenous and traditional folk cultures have woven into their cultural and good-governance fabrics, there's a uniquely "feminine" form of leadership required for the long-term well-being of the greater good—the tending of the cultural (and often ecological and economic) commons, if you will. In fact, certain advanced cultures like the Haudenosaunee (Iroquois Confederacy) are led by clan mothers, who select chiefs to represent them within the broader confederacy councils. By anchoring authority with the elder wise women—the be-wombed life bearers—such systems of governance and authority more appropriately align the longer-term propensity for nurturing and stability preponderantly found among mothers and grandmothers. (Some of the most innovative and advanced three-branch power-sharing mechanisms found in the Constitution of the United States of America—notwithstanding the many affronts and assaults endured over time—were in fact incorporated upon the wise guidance of Ben Franklin, who had himself, it is understood, spent many months living among the Haudenosaunee in order to learn their advanced ways and customs). There is much more woven into the symbolry of the "New Atlantean" endeavor of the United States—the prevalence of the number 13 on the currency points to the divine wisdom rooted in the 13 annual lunar/fertility cycles, and the 13 panels atop the turtle—the very totemic animal of these sacred Turtle Island lands. Subtler aspects of luminous traditions and mysterious legacies help guide us as we work to restore psychological, spiritual, and ethical balance to our world. Indeed, as Goethe writes in the very final line of his epic cautionary tale, *Faust* (concerning Western man's risky proclivity to make a "deal with the devil" in search of greater power), "das ewige Weibliche zieht uns hinan" (the eternal feminine draws us higher upward). Those great seers like Goethe, Nietzsche, Gimbutas, Eisler, and Sophie Strand who have peered into the depths of our cultural conditioning, and who have envisaged the keys to our healing, rebalancing, and planetary prosperity, have come to understand this with clarity. Consider Joseph Campbell's foreword to Gimbutas' *The Language of the Goddess*:

> As Jean-François Champollion, a century and a half ago, through his decipherment of the Rosetta Stone was able to establish a glossary of hieroglyphic signs to serve as keys to the whole great treasury of Egyptian religious thought from c. 3200 B.C. to the period of the Ptolemies, so in her assemblage, classification, and descriptive interpretation of some two thousand symbolic artifacts from the earliest Neolithic village sites of Europe, c. 7000 to 3500 B.C., Marija Gimbutas has been able, not only to prepare a fundamental glossary of pictorial motifs as keys to the mythology of that otherwise undocumented era, but also to establish on the basis of these interpreted signs the main lines and themes of a religion in veneration, both of the universe as the living body of a Goddess-Mother Creator, and of all the living things within it as partaking of her divinity—a religion, one immediately perceives, which is in contrast to that of Genesis 3:19, where Adam is told by his Father-Creator: "In the sweat of your face you shall eat bread till you return to the ground, for out of it you were taken; you are dust, and to dust you shall return." In this earlier mythology, the earth out of which all these creatures have been born is not dust but alive, as the Goddess-Creator herself.
>
> In the library of European scholarship, the first recognition of such a matristic order of thought and life antecedent to and underlying the historical forms of both Europe and the Near East appeared in 1861 in Johann Jakob Bachofen's *Das Mutterrecht*, where it was shown that in the codes of Roman Law vestigial features can be recognized of a matrilineal order of inheritance. Ten years earlier, in America, Lewis H. Morgan had published in The League of the Ho-dé-no-sau-nee or Iroquois, a two-volume report of a society in which such a principle of "Mother Right" was still recognized; and in a systematic review, subsequently, of kinship systems throughout America and Asia, he had demonstrated an all but worldwide distribution of such a prepatriarchal order of communal life.... There is to be recognized in Marija Gimbutas' reconstruction of the

"Language of the Goddess" a far broader range of historical significance, therefore, than that merely of Old Europe, from the Atlantic to the Dnieper, c. 7000-3500 B.C.

Moreover, in contrast to the mythologies of the cattle-herding Indo-European tribes that, wave upon wave, from the fourth millennium B.C. over-ran the territories of Old Europe and whose male-dominated pantheons reflected the social ideals, laws, and political aims of the ethnic units to which they appertained, the iconography of the Great Goddess arose in reflection and veneration of the laws of Nature. Gimbutas' lexicon of the pictorial script of that primordial attempt on humanity's part to understand and live in harmony with the beauty and wonder of Creation adumbrates in archetypal symbolic terms a philosophy of human life that is in every aspect contrary to the manipulated systems that in the West have prevailed in historic times.

One cannot but feel that in the appearance of this volume at just this turn of the century there is an evident relevance to the universally recognized need in our time for a general transformation of consciousness. The message here is of an actual age of harmony and peace in accord with the creative energies of nature which for a spell of some four thousand prehistoric years anteceded the five thousand of what James Joyce has termed the "nightmare" (of contending tribal and national interests) from which it is now certainly time for this planet to wake.

Instead of the insanity of vacuous material-mentalism, entrenched tribalism, extreme psycho-spiritual alienation, estranged eschatology, and toxic hyper-individualism found at the dead end of the Anthropocene's homo economicus, this alternative worldview allows us to connect with the very taproot of sanity: the understanding that any *rights* we have are predicated upon *responsibilities* and *obligations—responsibilities and obligations toward the whole human family and all life on Earth.*

As we awaken to the essential, existential necessity of caring well for our living world—Mama Gaia—we will also necessarily come to understand the fundamental importance of restoring the divine feminine to her rightful stature of reverence and of the crucial role of women leaders in all walks and stations of our social-economic-cultural structures and institutions going forward.

It's that simple.

The Original Instructions teach an evolved awareness of maturity and responsibility, not the adolescent hedonism, unjust usurpation, immediate gratification, and selfish pleasure worship of the adolescent male archetype running rampant in modern times, especially among the titans of technology. Far from adolescent fiendishness, the Original Instructions teach us to revere the wisdom of our elders—especially the Grandmother Councils—provided that they, too, are rooted in the wisdom of "seventh generation" stewardship for the future, in touch with the ethical lifeblood, alive and flowing all around us in Mama Gaia's planetary womb nursery.

With the Original Instructions we will restore balance and harmony to our world.Without them, however, we are immature and dangerous—to ourselves, our communities, and, at scale, to our entire living planet.

The choice is ours.

Our future—the shared outcomes we will all encounter—will be determined by this fundamental choice.

Embracing the knowledge and wisdom of the Original Instructions is at the heart of our quest.

Embedding that knowledge and wisdom into our systems, structures, and strategies is paramount.

But where do we start? How do we cultivate and embody such knowledge and wisdom within ourselves? How do we cross the initiatic threshold and engage the different thinking that will liberate us from the polycrisis?

This is an "inside out" endeavor, and must begin with our inner work.

"There's a revolution that needs to happen and it starts from inside each one of us. We need to wake up and fall in love with the Earth. Our personal and collective happiness and survival depends on it."

—THICH NHAT HANH

10   OUR INNER WORK

Source Key to True Wealth and Liberation

Without the guidance of the Original Instructions, entrepreneurs and aspiring leaders often set out to improve the world, only to hurt and traumatize it—sometimes severely, violently, and horrifically.

Why does this happen to us?

Isolated in bubbles of affluence and bastions of influence atop pyramids of power, estranged from "common" people, indifferent to our human family, hubristically disconnected from nature, and forced by a ferocious fear-based Faustian bargain, we can be dominated by an insatiable, ravenous hunger for more: more money, more power, more leverage, more coercion, and more control. Like fallen Jedi in the well-known space saga, we are consumed by a power that could have been wielded much, much differently. In unseen darkness, we are haunted and destroyed by our own shadows, and in turn haunt and wreak destruction upon our world.

This is especially true among the most "successful" among us—the greater our capital accumulation, the stronger the propensity often becomes. Our obsession with exceptionalism, when "rewarded" by the market and unmoored from the ethics of the Original Instructions, too often ends in malignant megalomania— Wetiko takes hold and the Mammonic monster emerges from within.

This is our fate as humans.

How many industrial titans institutionally terrorized our planet a century ago? How many technology tycoons have gone off the rails in our own lifetime?

How many political leaders ride into their capitols on waves of reform and restoration, only to conjure newer, nastier versions of that which they sought to vanquish—as if a crocodilian consciousness lurks within each potential reformer? Drain the swamp indeed!

When our interiors are ethically weak, and our psyches are plagued by unhealed trauma, we become instruments of the most destructive Mammonic forces ever known—enslaved by a shadowy darkness of the soul.

Traumas unhealed, when amplified by power and wealth, will eventually yield to autocracy, fascism, destruction, and death.

This is a human truth.

A travesty of the human spirit—this is particularly pronounced among those who might otherwise rank among the most powerful and prolific change-makers and doers of good in our world.

But is it inevitable?

Are we condemned to the darkness, no matter what?

Is there an antidote to the Mammonic scourge, a way to subdue the dragon?

To answer this, I think we need to step back and ask ourselves some of the really "big" questions—please, take some time to reflect on these:

> *What is the meaning of life?*
>
> *What is the meaning of our lives?*
>
> *What do we most desire?*
>
> *What is most important?*

Health and happiness are top of list for many of us. Peace and plenty are up there too. Of course, there's also purpose and fulfilment. To love and be loved. *Freedom* is foremost for many.

These questions, and their answers, have been core to our human experience throughout the ages, and have been at the root of the great philosophies and religions that have sprung up from fertile wellsprings of sourced sagacity, initiatic academies, and luminous teachers.

These eight—health, happiness, peace, plenty, purpose, fulfillment, love, and freedom—can be summed up in one word: *well-being*. It is no coincidence that this word comes to us from the Middle English term *wele*, which means wellness, wholeness, *and* wealth, altogether. Indeed, *true* wealth encompasses all of these aspects, rooted in health and wholeness and humanism.

Wele is the antidote to the darkness. And *wele* widespread is tantamount to planetary prosperity.

The key to *wele*, true wealth and well-being, is found through our inner work. Without it we are lost, unmoored, without anchor or compass, and incapable of realizing true happiness and fulfillment, regardless of how many zeros are in our bank accounts.

A truly holistic and pan-dimensional integration of mind, body, and spirit, the experience of *wele* teaches us deep connection and belonging—not so much that we *have* a mind, a body, a spirit (implying separation), but that we *are* a mind, a body, a spirit, living in total connectivity (a sacred relationship) to all other minds, bodies, and spirits. We are each a uniquely beautiful and essential strand woven into the great webwork of the totality of Creation.

Our inner work liberates us from the box of banality, and invites us into the circle of life and sublime luminosity. But without it, the hegemonic grip of Mammonic forces keeps us in the shackles of selfishness, superficiality, and, ultimately, severe suffering.

True freedom—to be in our world but not of it—can only be attained through a special self-mastery: trauma healing and "shadow" work, the inner cultivation of source-connection, the self-discipleship of well-being practices, and a direct, intimate connection with nature's living intelligence.

Trauma healing and shadow work is not to be taken lightly. Some of us may make great progress through shamanic and mindfulness practices. Others of us—probably way more than we assume—require trained professionals to guide us through somatic therapies like Eye Movement Desensitization and Reprocessing (EMDR—If you've never experienced such therapy, and you're one of us who says "I don't need therapy" but you still tend toward "fight or flight" limbic/amygdala hijack responses to stressors and triggers, then you almost certainly need it—lest those dark forces still take hold of you from time to time).

Source connection is cultivated through meditation, contemplation, and all manner of mind-quieting practices that open us up to receive something sublime from outside our littler selves—a deeper reality awaiting us, the Source Codes of the Law of Life. Reading and reflection are also pathways, especially reading the writings of our luminous predecessors who themselves successfully cultivated connection with Source.

The self-discipleship of well-being practices encompasses our mental, bodily, and spiritual stewardship. We are builders of our own temples. The body is the foundation. Neuro-biochemistry is the "secret sauce." With willfully wielded serotonin, oxytocin, dopamine, and endorphins, our inner landscapes are optimized and upleveled through the Viriditas of clean, life-force filled foods; pure, nature-sourced water; cleansing, nutrient-dense superfoods and biodynamic tisanes; frequent land, water, and planet-based ceremonial rituals; physical exercise, healthy friendships (and boundaries—our fundamental spiritual armor); laughter; solitude; tranquility; and intimate, direct nature connection—these are all among the well-being practices that are essential to our deep Ecocene leadership work, at any scale. And, the higher up the pyramid of leadership and influence we travel, the more necessary and obligatory these practices become—ultimately, *they* are *the* work, the most important work by far. They are our prime directive; our fundamental job description, our initiatic obligation.

Peaceful mornings, calm minds, loving homes, purposeful vocation, meaningful relationships, and connection with nature and divine source—these are the rewards and wages that await us.

Direct, intimate connection with nature is paramount among our well-being practices, and it's essential to our Source connection, shadow work, and trauma healing as well. You need to understand this. The Divine Creator not only fashioned our world with exquisite beauty, but our living planet, our Mama Gaia, our space-faring biosphere is our primary and fundamental healer and apothecary for well-being. She gives us life. She feeds and nourishes us with the Manna and Prana—the life force—of the air and water and ether, the tree terpene pheromones of our ancient forest friends, the petrichor of rain and marvelously moistened microbiotic soils—worlds within worlds within worlds. Wandering, walking in the woods, and simple, quiet immersion practices like Shinrin-yoku—the Japanese tradition of forest bathing meditation—open up a direct link with something essential that is otherwise inaccessible. It must be "directly sourced" in order to be embodied. The living soils and sacred mycelia have so much to share with us: awesomely expansive neural nets, like the cosmic web and the sub-quanta Akash that the great alchemists sought—the *prima materia* embodied—that is the soil and soul of our living planet. Our Mother Nature is the life-giver, the healer, and is pregnant with the most sublime, advanced, authentic super-intelligence imaginable. We cannot live and lead well without direct intimacy with her—up close, unhurried, and personal. In fact, those of us who take on greater responsibilities in positions of deep leadership will be best served (and will best serve) by deliberately increasing the quality and regularity of nature-immersion, as if it's one of the top five or six "job description" duties. In the Ecocene, more responsibility necessitates more time immersed in nature.

Thank goodness.

Direct, intimate connection with mother nature is essential.

Without it, we're weaker and less intelligent.

Through direct, intimate connection with nature, there is a subtle alchemy available to us as human beings that unlocks a phenomenal (and more noumenal) doorway, allowing us to perceive a quality of knowledge and sublime wisdom otherwise typically obfuscated from our prevue—so much so that it's nearly impossible to understand what's available to us without having direct experience of it—characterized by the "ineffability" in the truest sense spoken of by William James (and many others besides). Although this may all sound rather arcane to some, it's really not complicated. We humans have evolved in deep, intimate relationship with the awesome wild realms of the natural world, continually connected to source-streams of knowledge and wisdom endemic to this sublime living world, as if by an umbilicus of the heart-mind. But this umbilicus—for so many millions of us—has been severed by the machinery of modernity, and too many of us have no memory of such a sacred connection. It's as if many of us are like dolphins born and bred in captivity, instead of dolphins wild and free and in continual contact with the great ocean of living beingness that is Mama Gaia's womb-world. There are oceans and deserts and tundras and grasslands and forested fabrics of Mama Gaia's living world overflowing with knowledge and wisdom essential to our human-being-ness as residents of planet Earth. These are the deep truths spoken of in the Original Instructions and told of in myriad prophecies and sacred texts. By reconnecting and restoring our individual intimacy with nature—an essential aspect of our inner work—we regain access to the wellspring. We regain access to higher-order knowledge and wisdom that flows into us, when we're receptive, and fills up our little selves with a substance and sustenance originating from something far bigger, far vaster, far more sublime and sophisticated: the AAI—awesome *authentic intelligence*—of Mama Gaia's sacred creation and fathomless expanses of cosmic creation beyond. Without *this* AAI our individual lights are dimmer.

On this point the luminous philosopher and theologian Thomas Berry was unambiguous and unequivocal: "We lose our souls if we lose the experience of the forest, the butterflies, the song of the birds, if we can't see the stars at night," he writes " . . . our imagination suffers in proportion, as do our feelings and even our *intelligence*."

Nature immersion—sauntering, hiking, backpacking, forest bathing, and communing with the waters of the springs, streams, rivers, and ocean—these are not optional activities, nor are they Luddite niceties . . . they are funda-mental requisites for the cultivation of a solid inner foundation.

There's a profound and liberating wisdom available to us only when we humble ourselves enough to immerse in Nature—literally sitting *down low with the soil* and shrubs and small six- and eight-legged ones crawling about. Indeed, as John Milton and so many other nature guides profess, such humility activates the cosmic potentiality of our inner neuro-biochemistry, and breathes into us a knowingness: the human is of the soil, the humus, and with humility and humor will unlock the possibility of deep, responsible leadership. Being humble—as Daryl Van Tongeren writes in his book of the same name, *Humble*—opens an otherwise sealed doorway, elevating us into the rarified ethers of self-transcendent service leadership—deep leadership.

Our inner lives are the engines, the wellsprings, the *decisive elements*, as Goethe once famously wrote, of our outer reality. Our inner work is the alpha and the omega—the great constant we must regularly cultivate for ourselves and for our world, the ouroboros of our being, our experience, and our behavior.

This truth is the reason our global community has created a set of Inner Development Goals as essential and foundational to individuals working to achieve the earlier-articulated Sustainable Development Goals. These Inner Development Goals have five key dimensions (Being, Thinking, Relating, Collaborating, Acting) with 23 specific skills, as articulated by the Inner Development Goals Foundation in Switzerland (see Part V).

What does all of this have to do with economics, systems, structures, and strategies for planetary prosperity?

Everything.

Just as the polycrisis has no single fix, and is the complex manifestation in the outer realms of the deep disconnectedness, pathology, and amnesia of our inner lives, so too must our outer work with systems, structures, and strategies be coupled with the noble work in our *sanctum sanctora*, the holy interiors of our sacred selves.

There is no way to realize planetary prosperity without seeking and experiencing the holiness that lives within each of us.

There is no way to realize planetary prosperity without cultivating a direct connection with Source, the infinite intelligence that radiates at our cores.

There is no way to realize planetary prosperity without deep intimacy with mother nature—a serene sacred sensuality, the province and promise of the Divine's immanent intelligence.

There is no way to realize planetary prosperity without engaging in the noblest work of healing our psyches and subduing the traumatic dragons that otherwise haunt us all.

This inner work frees us from Mammonic enslavement. Without it, the Mammonic force is strong and insidious. Mental manipulation goes unnoticed. Obsession with superficial and fabricated fantasies reigns supreme. Indifferent, sedated, and numb by all manner of opioid, literal and metaphorical, too many of us are Mammonic pawns, mistaking materialistic consumerism, convenience, and comforts for freedom, and confusing raucous rhetoric and vitriolic voices for leadership.

When we are captives of Mammon, we live in a cave of delusion, believing ourselves to be free.

To escape the Mammonic prison, we must transcend the trap of self-interest and cynicism, and courageously cultivate hearts overflowing with *agape*—the ultimate, selfless love for others.

We must transcend the mirage of mottos like "getting mine" and "looking out for number one," and sublimate the *lead* of our insidious individualism into the *gold* of service to Gaia and global society.

Indeed, even the great psychologist Abraham Maslow came to this realization decades after publishing his famous "hierarchy of needs." In his original version there were only five tiers of attainment, each conceptually dependent on the previous ones (of course reality isn't quite so simple or linear, but it's a useful and well-known model). Physical needs such as food, shelter, water, and rest are foundational. Safety comes next. Then relationships with family and friends, through which we experience love and belonging. These three levels are probably obvious to us all. Then there are the subtler levels of esteem—feelings of accomplishment and, finally, self-actualization: realizing our full individual potential and being the "best" we can be with our gifts. For many years, this final step was the pinnacle of Maslow's five-tiered model for human well-being. But after about three decades, he publicly revealed that his model had been incomplete and insufficient; that indeed, humans aren't most happy and fulfilled once they've attained these five levels. Something more is actually needed for full-blown well-being: *service to the greater good*—what Maslow calls *self-transcendence*.

Over the arc of his professional career, in which Maslow interacted with and counseled countless hundreds of "successful" adults, he came to understand that the apex of self-centered accomplishment is plagued by alienation and emptiness if devoid of service to the greater good.

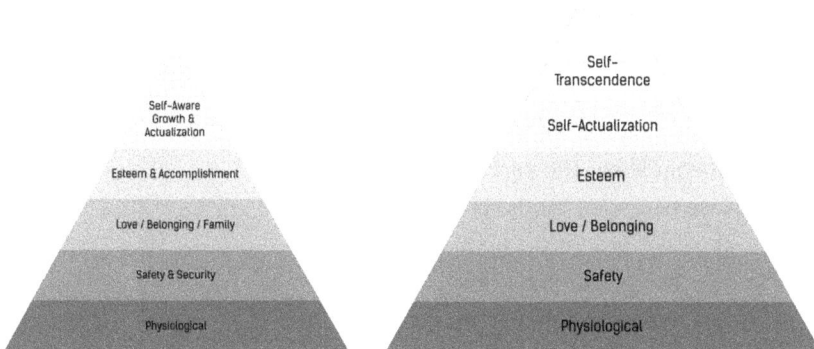

Service to others is essential. Golden-hearted selflessness is the key to true success. The just and righteous path of altruism is the only way to achieve true fulfillment—true wealth—as a human being.

This reality is central to Dr. Robert Cloninger's research on personality traits—that what makes people most healthy, happy, and fulfilled is the altruistic attribute of self-transcendence. Without it our work and development are incomplete, and our fates are suboptimal. His important work is summarized in his article "What Makes People Healthy, Happy, and Fulfilled in the Face of Current World Challenges?" (found in Part Two of this book).

But Maslow's and Cloninger's relatively recent work, though important and trailblazing, isn't without precedent. Indeed, ancient wisdom speaks to all of this as well.

Echoing the timeless wisdom of the ancient Vedic, Egyptian, and Hebraic scriptures, the *Sephir Yetzera* teaches, "Happiness is reserved for the just and misery for the wicked." The teachings of Lao Tzu, Gautama Siddhartha, Confucious, Jeshua, and Mohommed echo similar themes. Take for instance Lao Tzu's sublime wisdom from the taproot wellspring of Source in passage 39 of the *Tao Te Ching*:

> In harmony with the Tao,
> The sky is clear and spacious,
> The earth is solid and full,
> All creatures flourish together,
> Content with the way they are,
> Endlessly repeating themselves,
> Endlessly renewed.
>
> When man interferes with the Tao,
> The sky becomes filthy,
> The earth becomes depleted,
> The equilibrium crumbles,
> Creatures become extinct.
>
> The Master views the parts with compassion,
> Because he understands the whole.
> His constant practice is humility.
> He does not glitter like a jewel
> But lets himself be shaped by the Tao,
> As rugged and common as a stone.

Our inner work and service to others illuminate the pathway to our liberation, where we experience a freedom so awesome, and willful co-creation so sublime, our imaginations must stretch to contain the expansive beauty, creativity, and serenity that awaits us. Our hearts, harmonized in coherence with the living intelligence of the morphogenic field, and our minds, connected together in alliance for the human family, open the doorway to planetary prosperity.

You see, the Original Instructions aren't just the operating manual for maintaining spaceship Earth; they are the handbook for human happiness, the *vade mecum* of well-being.

By setting our sights on Maslow's sixth, pinnacle level, we release ourselves from the bonds of the Mammonic grip, simultaneously creating the conditions for our own well-being while also contributing to our collective prospects for planetary prosperity.

To be in the world, but not of it.

So how do we release ourselves from the Mammonic grip? How do we escape the treadmill of modern materialism and selfish cynicism? How do we cultivate happiness and fulfillment in our lives—real well-being?

We work in service to the greater good, cultivating heart coherence, embodying agape, as we heroically do the inner self-mastery work of Source-connection and trauma-healing, disciple ourselves toward *wele*, and cultivate deep intimacy through Shinrin-yoku and other ancient, ancestral practices with the nourishing super-intelligence of Nature—of Mama Gaia.

Thus, with courage as our companion, we will experience true wealth.

Thus, we are invited into the fellowship for the future.

Thus, we evolve ourselves from the Mammonic to the Magnamic.

Thus, we are welcomed into the awesome company of the new Earth Steward aristocracy, preparing our hearts with the advanced intelligence and sophisticated grace of stewardship philanthropy.

"The sun does not shine for a few trees and flowers,
but for the wide world's joy."

—HENRY WARD BEECHER

11   STEWARDSHIP PHILANTHROPY

At the Heart of the Magnamic

Stewardship philanthropy is rooted in *gratitude*. It is animated by the virtue of gift-giving and reciprocity—not the reciprocity of transaction, but the reciprocity that results when we're aware of the superabundance of our world, the blessing of life, and the social and ecological fabric of interconnectivity in which we're each a woven strand, and upon which we each depend.

When we make our tithing, gift-giving, and donation decisions from a place of deep gratitude and with the intention to serve the whole, something lights up and enlivens within us. Providing relief—both to *symptomatic* suffering and their *causal* conditions—as necessity requires and our abilities permit (without fundamental material injury to ourselves and families), we enter ourselves into a sacred bond of responsibility and reciprocity with the fabric of the broader communities in which we're members and upon which we're fundamentally reliant.

For many of us, tithing is our mathematics of compassion. When we look at where we each stand—eyes wide open—relative to where each of the rest of us stands, we awaken something deep inside, unlocking for ourselves a gateway otherwise sealed shut: a *gateway of grace*.

And in the fabrics of the sublime love wisdom of Mama Gaia's great world, grace hovers all around us, just waiting for our willful yea-saying to access and activate it in our lives. Do we say yes to 1%? 5%? 10%? 20% or more? What loving logic do we employ to calculate our compassion?

Some of us are blessed with the grace of perspective that naturally engenders a stewardship philanthropy orientation. Others among us—perhaps most of us—must willfully and deliberately endeavor to overcome and transcend our social programming in order to awaken the pragmatic love for humanity that is stewardship philanthropy. And it can happen in a flash of grace, as often occurs when somebody voyages into space and gazes back upon our home planet: the Overview Effect is about as powerful and palpable as they come, a momentary vision of the wholeness and totality and awesomeness of our living planet. Some of us are graced with the opportunity to experience the irreversible imprinting of the Overview Effect with our own eyes from a voyaging spacecraft. Many millions more of us are invited—right now—to engender the irreversible imprinting of the Overview Effect in our hearts instead.

Like a pebble tossed into still water, stewardship philanthropy ripples outward, radiating joy and compassion. When we recognize all that we've been given, and all of the natural abundance we're blessed to experience, of which Marcus Aurelius spoke: "In an expression of true gratitude, sadness is conspicuous by its absence." Not only is the generosity of stewardship philanthropy pragmatic and wise, it is the natural outcome when we experience the true wealth of our abundant blessings and interconnected kinship with all life.

When activated and alive, stewardship philanthropy is an individual's embodiment of a radiant force. There is a selflessness at the heart of such philanthropy, a generous altruism motivated by a pure desire to improve lives, restore our living planet, and foster conditions for planetary prosperity however we can and however we're each specifically and synchronistically invited to do so. Characterized by the "self-transcendence" described in Dr. Cloninger's seminal psychological research, such philanthropy is rooted in love, compassion, and a true understanding of the responsibility we have for our world and our future. Stewardship philanthropy is at the heart of the *new Earth steward aristocracy* and *true wealth.*

We find stewardship philanthropy at work in three distinct forms, each deserving of our attention. The first is among people from all walks of life, and is found throughout the entire spectrum of the socio-economic wealth distribution discussed in the chapter "Eyes Wide Open." A joyous and affirming "way of life," this philanthropy is available to all of us as we voluntarily plant trees, feed and shelter the less fortunate, mentor and advise the less experienced, hand healthy snack bars to the homeless, toss a bag of $1 coins to the eccentric artist on the corner, and, perhaps most importantly, radiate kind smiles throughout the day to strangers and familiars alike. This form of stewardship philanthropy is a ray of sunshine, and weaves into our social fabric a goodness and compassion without which communities and cultures decay.

But among the high-net-worth and ultra-high-net-worth segment of the wealth spectrum, a rarified (second) form of stewardship philanthropy is alive and activated among people who have cultivated an intelligence and wisdom that informs their generosity toward people and environments well beyond their immediate circles. This form of advanced consciousness reflects an individual's transcendence of political ideologies and commercial and geopolitical turf wars. In this context, stewardship philanthropy disseminates ample resources throughout the social, economic, and environmental systems upon which we all depend, much in the manner of how living mycelial networks transmit resources throughout their living soil ecosystems.

Such philanthropy is both a foundational requirement for and an indicative reflection of the advanced intelligence—the loving wisdom—advocated for by our greatest luminaries. Stewardship philanthropy is the hallmark of a great leader, and without it, without the self-transcendence spoken of by Maslow and Dr. Cloninger, no individual is sufficiently equipped to lead in these times.

Moreover, as we better understand and recognize—eyes wide open—that so many of the inequities and maladapted tendencies embedded in our organizations are legacy holdovers from previous times and earlier human designs, we come to understand that the stewardship philanthropy of individuals, though necessary on many levels, is not sufficient by itself to realize planetary prosperity. We must also embed the ethics and mechanisms of stewardship philanthropy in our companies and institutions, infusing them with the radiant abundance and compassionate generosity already exhibited by so many leaders in our world. This is the third form of stewardship philanthropy. Our businesses themselves, when properly structured and governed, become powerfully generative philanthropic engines, radiating resources into communities and restoring ecosystems around the world. This sublime, fundamental function of business—and economy as a whole—is at the core of regimes like benefits corporations, B-certified companies, 1% for the Planet giving commitments, cooperative and employee-owned structures, and, most especially, the social enterprise economic model.

And at the heart of these companies and organizations are heroic leaders whose personal sense of ambition and success are oriented around the greater good. Aligning his own ambition with the greater well-being of the Basque people in Spain, José Mariá Arizmendiarrieta laid the foundation for the Mondragon Cooperatives. More recently, Patagonia's Yvon Chouinard assigned 100% of his company to social and environmental causes, in addition to helping establish the 1% for the Planet giving program, the Home Planet Fund, and so many other stewardship philanthropy mechanisms now at work in our global economy. And, reminding us of the broader, more noble meanings of the term "investment"—"to devote resources to a useful purpose, to endow with rights, and to clothe"—philanthropist MacKenzie Scott continues to flow billions each year toward systems-change for planetary prosperity.

Philanthropy is at the heart of true wealth and is the fundamental motivation of the new Earth steward aristocracy. Love for humanity. And, this love for humanity, coupled with *biophilia*—the love of all Earth's diverse life—and buttressed by the core imperative of stewardship, is an essential pathway to planetary prosperity.

Some of the most heroic among us are stewardship philanthropists—underwriting a saner, more just world in which social and ecological harmony are the aim, and from which nothing is expected in return except the satisfaction that one has bolstered the greater good. Consider Bon Jovi's restaurants, serving kindness and dignity along with scratch-made meals to those in need. And, as Matthieu Ricard and Peter Singer have written (in *Altruism* and *The Most Good You Can Do*, respectively), genuinely orienting our lives around the service to others enriches our own lives too, as if by some magical alchemy or universal Hermetic law: the more we give, the more we receive, and the more we nourish and care for others, the more we are nourished and cared for. That which we freely radiate outward comes back to us in manifold ways. Within these generative relationships of regenerative finance we weave fabrics of resilience—for ourselves, each other, our progeny, and all life, present and future—on our shared sacred home planet.

Perhaps the Beatles' famous lyric means even more now in the context of stewardship philanthropy: "And in the end, the love you take is equal to the love you make."

Philanthropy is at once something very personal and something very public—in many cases the glue holding our broader social fabric together.

Our personal attitudes toward philanthropy reveal a lot about our worldviews and correlate to the character trait strengths and weaknesses as discussed in Dr. Robert Cloninger's groundbreaking work. That there are so many diverse views about philanthropy reveals much about our society as a whole.

What is philanthropy? The etymology of the word is very clear: the *love of humanity*, from the Greek *philia*, meaning a deep, committed love that implies sacred kinship, fellowship, and interdependence (the same root word from which we get the word *philosophy* or "love of wisdom"); and *anthrop*, meaning *human* and *humanity* (the same root word from which we get the word *anthropology*, Rudolf Steiner's *anthroposophy*, and the more recent coinage *Anthropocene*).

Love.

Humanity.

Philanthropy.

Of course, our contemporary concept of philanthropy essentially refers to donations from affluent people to nonprofit charities, institutions like hospitals and universities, and people in need.

However, not all philanthropy is equal. While, yes, we need ongoing support of hospitals and charities that are helping those in need, we also need far more robustly to deploy massive resources "upstream" (or deeper down in the iceberg model, by analogy) to resource the Quintenary change-making that seeks to resolve causes instead of treating symptoms, systemically speaking. That is, by way of simple analogy, we need not only to support the hospital at the bottom of the cliff (at least for the time being), but must fund the preventive measures at the top of the cliff's edge to avoid the harmful outcomes in the first place.

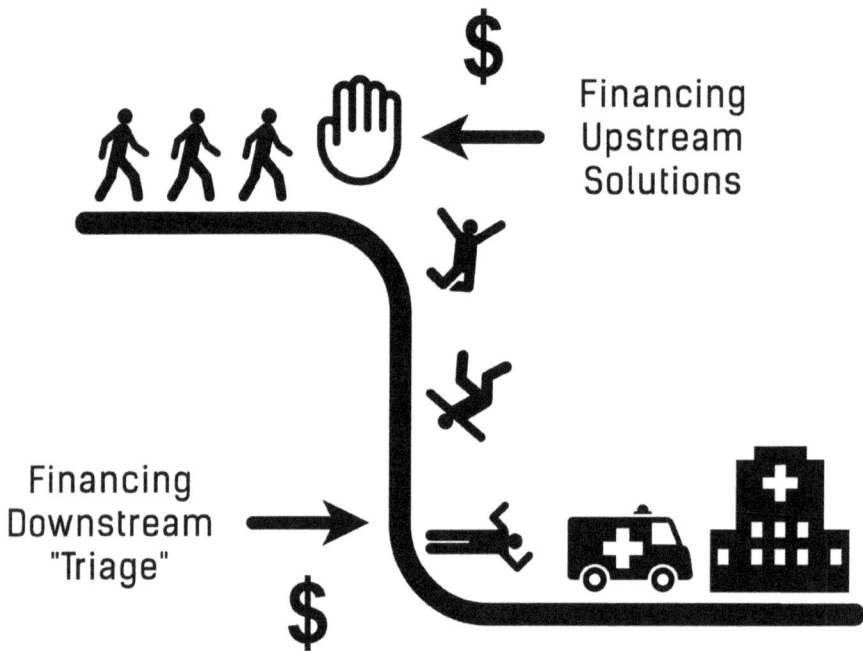

$

Financing
Upstream
Solutions

Financing
Downstream
"Triage"

$

STEWARDSHIP PHILANTHROPY: FROM DOWNSTREAM TRIAGE TO UPSTREAM SOLUTIONS

Sure, helping people in need is a mandatory function of a decent, ethical society. And, so is financing systems change at its core in order to minimize the frequency and magnitude of such events leading to people being in need—this is especially so in the context of systemic polycrisis risks like climate destabilization and hyper-toxification of food, water, and textiles and bath, hygiene, household, and yard-care products. Just as important as the deep systems-changing philanthropic financing is the compassion-led support and relief of suffering for the most vulnerable among us. And, lest we succumb to what seems to be a delusional and emotionally vacuous perspective of "effective altruism" (that seems to be particularly virulent among the *nouveau riche* techno elite), let us not confuse superficial PR with compassion, and impossibly position elitist fantasies of "perfect outcomes" above *authentic compassion and real-time care-full-ness* toward our fellow humans (and all of Earth's creatures) in real need.

That in our society philanthropy elicits such different attitudes and reactions is telling, to say the least. In the post-modern industrial West, mainstream philanthropy has become stigmatized as a twofold mechanism for both public relations and power accretion for the ultra-rich, an obligatory "cost of doing business" for others of considerable but not quite stratospheric means, and even something that commonly creates "fatigue" among the most financially fortunate among us. With what might we contrast our ambivalence and wide-spread disagreement over this topic?

Let's get outside the confines of our own culture and contrast this with other cultural traditions. Virtually all traditional cultures have beautiful phil-anthropic customs. One of my favorites is the tradition of the *potlatch*, from whence comes our word "potluck." These gatherings, held by indigenous tribes throughout the Pacific Northwest region, are much more than recreational group meals. They are ritualized festive occasions at which the more fortunate and "wealthier" tribespeople—blessed by good fishing, hunting, forest foraging, and trading—demonstrate their humble humanism by sharing the abundance with others. These great feasts also serve as governance gatherings for the establishment of hunting and fishing territories, effectively the ecological stewardship of the region, and as diplomatic missions to reaffirm alliances and peaceful relations among and between neighboring tribes and families.

Another great example is the ancient concept of *ubuntu* found in many Bantu cultures throughout much of sub-Saharan Africa: the society as a whole is best off only when every individual is doing well, and it is in everybody's interest to intervene whenever somebody is in need so that the feeling of har-mony and prosperity can be restored for the whole. That's key in all of this: *Prosperity is better understood as a shared condition in the community than some financial measures assigned to isolated individuals.* Often outwardly expressed as the virtue of hospitality, this shared social ethos can be found in the tea ceremony of China and Japan, the Kyrgyz people's famous welcoming of guests and foreigners, the Indian tradition of welcoming guests like family, the Viking tenant of hospitality (one of nine in their ancient Honor Code), and the Greek concept of Xenia (from which, interestingly, our term "xenophobia," or "fear of visitors/foreigners/other'" derives). These are but a few shining examples of this rich tradition common to virtually all of our cultural roots.

Of course, in modern industrial culture, much of these traditional lifeways rapidly eroded as factories sprung up, supply chains reached ever farther away, and diverse ethnicities collided in the pressure-cooker metropolises that swelled with each arriving cargo, passenger, and slave ship. We cannot ignore the dehumanizing conditions in which our modern economy so recently arose.

As we marched toward our hyper-technological and ever more complex modern reality, philanthropy took on a whole new meaning during the "gilded age" and fin de siècle period in which super-rich industrialists funded all manner of public good (in the case of "captains of industry") or their own political and social ambitions (in the case of "robber barons"). Between 1881 and 1919, the Scottish steel tycoon Andrew Carnegie funded over 2,500 libraries worldwide (1,795 in the United States alone). An autodidact without much formal education, Carnegie attributed his astronomical success to knowledge gained by reading books and a few years attending the Free School in Dunfermline in Scotland, funded by the philanthropy of Adam Rolland. Carnegie funded libraries out of a love for humanity, not personal gain—not even a tax write-off!

The income tax "deduction" incentive wasn't codified in the United States until 1917, after income taxes rose substantially as the federal government financed and fought in WWI. Part of the rationale behind the income tax deduction incentive was to reinforce (and expand) the "public good" funded by wealthy donors, which essentially reduced the need for the government to finance safety nets, capacity building, and hand-up programs. (Yes, you read and inferred correctly: Dislike "big" government? Expand your philanthropy—and encourage the same from your friends and colleagues!)

To be clear, though, philanthropy—even in our contemporary modern society—should not be thought of only as some sort of policy expedient. To the contrary. It is an expression of the fundamental *will to good* that lives inside us—some clearly more than others. Take the tremendous generosity of MacKenzie Scott, Melinda French Gates, Oprah Winfrey, Johan Eliasch, Michael Bloomberg, Lauren Powell Jobs, Tom Steyer and John and Laura Arnold, for example. They have given billions in the last three years alone—in ethical frameworks starkly different from the so-called "effective altruism" of Sam Bankman Fried and Elon Musk that seem to provide temporary (and brittle) "moral cover" to their insanely avaristic plunderings. No, stewardship philanthropy is something altogether different. Consider this perspective from the Arnolds, found on their Arnold Ventures website:

> *Philanthropic dollars alone cannot solve the problems we face as a nation. But we believe philanthropy is uniquely positioned to take risks and make big bets in ways the public and private sector are often unable or unwilling to do. We approach philanthropy as an engine for innovation that can help catalyze new solutions, evaluate what works, and advocate for public policies that maximize opportunity and minimize injustice for all.*

There's a rational expediency in this statement—one full of wisdom and deep leadership.

But stewardship philanthropy is about more than expedience. It's about living into the question of "how much is enough" for each of us.

Not just how much is enough, but also the subtler question of "Am I truly happy and contented with my wealth?" Am I truly at peace with and proud of the degree to which I've responded to a world in need—to humanity in need? When I'm old and dead and gone, will my legacy and my progeny celebrate that I leaned in and asked the hard, self-examining questions? Or will it leave the future wondering, "What was (s)he thinking—why didn't (s)he do more?"

This is a question we can only answer in the privacy of our own thoughts and prayers.

We are living in a time when the Mammonic has such a widespread grip on our cultural norms and market-centric morays, it's really not easy to ask this question—let alone answer it—without retreating into quiet reflection and meditation. When the big game is on the screen, the latest market news is on our mind, and the immediate needs and desires of our families and friends are taking up space in our conscious awareness, it's not easy to step back and assume the ultimate helm of our lives and our decision-making. Am I really doing all that I want to and hope to for our world and our future? Am I leaning in or checking out? Am I looking around, eyes wide open, and asking how to be of greater service to the greater good, or am I closing my eyes to our shared reality?

Am I recognizing my good fortune as a gift from outside and beyond my egoic self, or have I convinced myself that I'm exceptional and somehow deserve an enlarged lion's share of the global pie?

As previously mentioned, one of the lesser-known spiritual masters of the 20th century is said to have proclaimed, "As money in the past ministered to personal and family needs, so in the future it must minister to group and world need." This wise teacher, known simply as "The Tibetan," also described money as "the medium of loving distribution," and that, without an awakening of consciousness toward the abundant flow of stewardship philanthropy, we would suffer a "famine of the soul."

It seems the Faustian bargain appears in many forms. How many of us are quietly suffering this famine of the soul?

Stewardship philanthropy isn't only an expedient civic duty; it is also a matter of the deepest spiritual inquiry. It is a matter of the condition of our soul, of our orientation toward aesthetic beauty and ethical virtue. It is a matter of whether we understand ourselves to be part of the vast fabric of life on Earth, interdependent in such a manner that our own well-being is inextricably linked to the well-being of all others.

Stewardship philanthropy is rooted in an advanced spiritual intelligence that sees clear-eyed the nature of true wealth, and understands that it is incumbent on us—each of us—to restore our world and to take good care of one another. To relieve suffering—not just *symptomatically*, far downstream, but *causally*, far upstream—by turning the baron wastelands of taker death economics into a restored and verdant paradise of "life economics"; by transforming ourselves from takers into givers, from destroyers into stewards.

Stewardship philanthropy has many trailheads and invites each of us to give more, to find and "see" and support more of those leaders in our communities who are faithfully and tirelessly devoted to the greater good, and to support them. I invite you to revisit the socio-economic categories outlined in the "Eyes Wide Open" chapter, and the recommendations offered based on where you stand. We are each invited to "travel the road as we build together" alongside such leaders, with generosity and gratitude, that they've chosen to heed the devotional call of service. Nourish your soul and support them copiously!

Stewardship philanthropy welcomes all of us, and gives all of us a place at the great Gaian table, where relationships are cultivated and deep nourishment abounds.

The economy is our home, our community, our neighbors, and our entire human family, all at once. It is our world. And it is ours to heal and repurpose for the greater good. This work is the work of stewardship philanthropy. This is our biggest deal: evolving from the Mammonic to the Magnamic. This is the source of *true wealth* and the hallmark of the *new Earth steward aristocracy*.

12 THE NEW EARTH STEWARD ARISTOCRACY

Stewardship Philanthropy, Ikigai, and Deep Leadership

There is a new Earth steward aristocracy emergent in our world, supporting the way forward toward the Ecocene. It is a powerful, mission-driven group of community leaders and philanthropists, some known broadly and others locally, who are motivated by the self-transcendence of which Maslow and Cloninger write—motivated to serve the greater good. This is the essence and real meaning of the terms "aristocrat" and "aristocracy."

This word *aristocracy* literally means: *leadership by the best.*

The dictionary tells us that aristocrats exhibit exceptional quality of intelligence, moral excellence, and exquisite social etiquette.

In its conventional usage, the term, of course, describes a privileged and plutocratic "upper crust" of society—family dynasties, entitled nobility, and other generational heirs who have "won the parentage lottery" of birthright and succession. This tradition of familial inheritance has preserved, concentrated, and transferred capital obtained from crown and conquest down through the ages. And we're not just talking about financial capital here. Access, education, and other "keys to the kingdom" of modern society are all part of the package.

Ignoble, though, is any of this inheritance absent authentic, generous, and magnanimous philanthropy—otherwise, these too-often ill-gotten fortunes further the fierce inequities of the Mammonic forces. What's worse, as if "pre-destined," this patrimonial privilege too often warps the consciousness and worldviews of individuals, and our socio-economic fabric, especially when heirs mistake their fortunate flukes of birthright for *something else.*

And although some great and notable philanthropists and selfless leaders have sprung from these rarified roots, by no means does such successional privilege guarantee a person's righteous standing in our world. Indeed, those of us with such stature and substance, those among us born with "trump cards" in our hands, must clear higher hurdles and show greater grace, generosity, and gentility in order to qualify for the laudable ranks of the new Earth steward aristocracy.

The more we have been given, the more we must do for others and for our world in order to be worthy of fellowship among the authentic aristocracy.

No, the new Earth steward aristocracy is not about privilege and plutoc-racy. It is about service-leadership, magnanimity, and devotion to the greater good. Marked by the great leveling effects of equality, fraternity, and symbi-osis, it requires us to subdue our narrow self-interest, to sublimate our baser inclinations toward power, and to recognize our privilege, so that worldwide well-being, holistic health, and planetary prosperity reign supreme in our purpose and performance.

In the midst of the planetary polycrisis, we must reclaim this word: *aristocracy.*

Leadership by the very best among us, "on the level," and with and for each other at the highest degrees of our striving—leadership for planetary prosperity.

Leadership by those of us with truly exceptional quality of intelligence, moral excellence, and venerable vision.

Leadership by those of us who know that "if the economy isn't working well for everybody, it isn't working well at all" and who understand our direct, relational care of planet Earth is paramount to our humanity and our very survival as a species.

Leadership by those among us who every day ask not what the world can do for us, but what we can do for the world.

Clear-eyed, conscious, courageous, and with conscience, those among us who lead with coherence of heart and mind, who do the inner work as well as invite the outer guardrails (lest we fall into the snares of the Mammonic grip), and who embody the virtues of our common purpose and our greater good—these are the true aristocrats of our world.

And they are many—hundreds, thousands, tens of thousands—experiencing joy and fulfillment as they work to serve humanity.

But the new Earth steward aristocracy is by no means limited to the super-rich among us. In fact, there's a specific synergy of grace available to those of us working for a living who are also members of the Earth steward aristocracy—a sacred pinnacle of achievement only accessible by harmonically aligning our vocations, avocations, unique gifts, and maximal opportunities for impact into an imbued and amplified life.

In Japan there's a special term for this: *Ikigai*. Similar in some ways to the French term *raison d'être* (reason for being), Ikigai has four specific elements, all of which are required to achieve it: (1) what we love, (2) what we're good at, (3) what we can be paid for, and (4) what the world needs. When our passion, our profession, our vocation, and our mission converge into one central "reason for being," we have achieved Ikigai. It is the hallmark of the new Earth steward aristocracy, and the key to well-being.

The new Earth steward aristocracy is the avant-garde of a noble lineage, and includes laudable luminaries like Hildegard von Bingen, Teilhard de Chardin, Buckminster Fuller, Thomas Berry, Desmund Tutu, Hazel Henderson, Joanna Macy, Jane Goodall, and Fritjof Capra. It includes scores of philanthropists and financiers like Lauren Powell Jobs, Yvon Chouinard, and MacKenzie Scott who put their capital to work for the greater good. It includes mothers and fathers, daughters and sons, and grandmothers and grandfathers who courageously steer their family offices toward planetary prosperity, making donation, investment, and bequest decisions not from egoic pride and amoral avarice, but from a deeply sourced knowing that they are doing their part in these critical times—doing as much as possible. They are entrepreneurs and executives willfully establishing guardrails and foregoing some of their substantial windfall sums, whether anticipated or already realized, in order to put their wealth and value-creation to work in service to the whole of their stakeholders, communities, and the entire planet.

The new Earth steward aristocracy has been emerging among humanity through the generations, and has now arrived with critical mass, orienting around and energizing a *global egregore of agapic love*, egalitarian ethics, noo-spheric knowledge, and the magnanimity of self-mastery that are the property of the most courageous, noblest, and most laudable among us.

They are leading us toward planetary prosperity—a hike to the top of what humanity is here to have and hold *together*, not a race to the bottom of stingy scheming, political-economic masochism, and mediocre misery.

The new Earth steward aristocracy is coalescing, though independent, autonomous, resilient, and robust alliances like the great aspen groves andoaks and sequoias and Sitkas and baobabs and Gloucester trees towering and rooted in the forested webwork of relationship.

The new Earth steward aristocracy is legion, and its lasting legacy will be the actualization and accomplishment of our biggest deal: the Ecocene era of planetary prosperity.

"There is almost a sensual longing for communion with others who have a large vision. The immense fulfillment of the friendship between those engaged in furthering the evolution of consciousness has a quality impossible to describe."

—PIERRE TEILHARD DE CHARDIN

13   OUR SHARED VISION

Traveling Together Toward Planetary Prosperity

We are living in the most extraordinary times, and our shared vision is carrying us forward into profoundly uncharted territory. This is a moment that requires us to evolve, individually and societally, in order to meet and transcend the systemic existential risks of the polycrisis. Our shared vision and our collective change-making are weaving together a great global fabric of regeneration and planetary prosperity.

In this context, each of us is being asked to imagine: "What's possible?" What's possible when the human spirit is mobilized, *en masse* . . . oriented around loving kindness, stewardship, responsibility, and a sacred knowing . . . a *sacred trust*? A sacred knowing and sacred trust that asks us: What is it that we can possibly do? What are the many, many ways we can each show up, step up, and risk that which we might fear in advance to lose (because it's uncertain), and thereby secure that which, if not overcome by the courage required of us, we may never know what could have been?

We are being asked, as if by voices of our own children, our own grandchildren, both now and off in the mists of the future: What are we choosing to do? What *strength of will* and *spirit of heart* are we mustering and activating in ourselves, staring down the cynicism, pessimism, fear, and uncertainty that might otherwise deter us from our better destiny—a better future made possible primarily through our sincere "yea-saying"?

Though fraught and challenging to be sure, this is a moment of golden opportunity, a moment foreseen in prophecies from cultures and traditions all around the world and throughout time; focalizing on each of us as we respond to the question: *How will we act? How will we rise?* How will we set aside our narrow, petty conditioning, our myopic (so-called) self-interest, and allow our creativity, our hearts, our hopes, our talents, and our unique gifts to blossom in service to the greater good—into a great yea-saying, a great "YES" to Earth, to each other, to ourselves, and to the future. . . . YES, we are here. YES, we are learning. YES, we are engaged in that deliberate willful, love-centered continual improvement that potentially sets us all on a course to a destiny so beautiful, so pristine, so immaculate, so full of promise and joy and peace and hope and prosperity—planet-wide prosperity—our hearts and minds will be blown open as if by the gentle winds of our Creator on a soft spring day, smiling upon us and saying to us: "Well done, my child. Well done, my friend. Well done my faithful steward and spiritual warrior of the peace, the plenty, the prosperity. . . . Well done. You have fulfilled your destiny."

And we are awakening, *eyes wide open*, to the very real fact that none of us is alone, and that in fact we're each one special voice in a giant orchestral chorale singing songs of healing and renewal—so many voices now singing songs in resonance with the Earth herself. . . . We are blessed.

The voices are now so many, and we have assembled but a select handful for you in this book. Voices that, devoted to doing what's possible, to working in service, to foregoing the superficial veneer of some safe and banal pathway in order to forge into the unknown of collaboration, innovation, change-making, and leadership. Voices that courageously proclaim for our world an "end of oppressive, extractive times" (Jack Wielebinski) . . . in which "human beings develop their capacity for self-transcendence in order to maintain their individual and collective well-being" (Dr. Robert Cloninger), and "enormous capacities for consciousness, caring, and creativity" (Dr. Riane Eisler) are activated and enabling "long-term benefit for people and nature" (John Perkins) where "profits are paid as dividends to protect the planet" (Dilafruz Khonikboyeva); "we understand the concept of 'enough'" (Georgia Kelly), we become "restoration ecologists of the financial markets" (Dr. Stephanie Gripne), and we "enable flows of resources from centralized pools of capital to grassroots, regenerative projects and initiatives in alignment with living systems principles and Indigenous wisdom" (Samantha Power). "This New Renaissance will be fundamentally different" (John Fullerton), in which "regeneration is reciprocity" (Azuraye Wycoff), "regeneration is the work of interconnected communities and organizations" (Miranda Clendening), and we "work to restore right relations and the health of our planet" (John Milton) as we establish "community level preparedness and resilience" (Henry Mitchell) and remember "just how big our common ground is" (Hunter Lovins and Dr. Martin Frick). It is a time when we "expand our sense of empathy and care" (Tom Chi), in which "we have abundant opportunities to construct a just and regenerative world" (Hannah Odell), we build "a bridge between today and tomorrow" through emergent "global mycelial connectivity" (Alena Maslova), people are brought together in "Renaissance teams" (John Rogers), and in which "money is energy—like the energy of the sun and water—that when properly stewarded in a balanced manner engenders and supports one of the greatest goals for humanity to achieve: the establishment of right human relations, the familyhood of humanity" (Kevin Townley).

These voices tell us that "by implementing guidelines and guardrails that ensure wealth circulates equitably among all stakeholders, and steward ownership prioritizes long-term mission over short-term profit" (Mark Finser), our "best work brings us joy and taps into humility" (Dr. Jandel Allen-Davis), and "we can redesign every miniscule, interconnected component of the way we live, work, interact, and create" (Maria Rodale), "humbling ourselves to find a common calling that supersedes all else" (Sarah Arao), and "seeing the ecology of life" (Eduardo Esparza), "we can heal the Earth and flourish together" (Steve Farrell).

We are co-creating a world in which "it's okay to use the word *love*" (Kate Williams), and in which we understand at the depths of our cores how "the liberation of a mother expressing peace to her children and all creation has the ability to transform the world around us. That is the law of the land" (Kawenniiosta Jock).

These are the voices representing a great global awakening.

And we are legion. We are tens of thousands of organizations and communities, with millions of people mobilizing and hundreds of billions—if not trillions—of dollars and pounds and euros and yen and yuan and rupees and dinars and Swiss francs and virtually every other global currency . . . at work for our shared world and shared future. We are the *avant-garde* of a worldwide transformation in which leading companies are striving to embody the highest virtues, committed to continual recursive self-improvement, and acting upon their bold and courageous mottos—as included and celebrated in the Case Study Vignettes of venerable way-showers like 1% for the Planet, Allianz Global Insurance, Amalgamated Bank, At One Ventures, B Lab, Big Path Capital, Bluestone Life, Capital Institute, Climate First Bank, COPx, Dr. Bronner's, EarthX E-Capital Summit, Empowerment Institute, Equal Exchange Cooperatives, Global Alliance for Banking on Values, GLS Bank, Goodstead Co., Home Planet Fund, Impact Finance Center, International Cooperative Alliance, Mondragon Cooperatives, Newman's Own Organics and the Nell Newman Foundation, One Small Planet, Organic Valley Coop, Patagonia and the Hold Fast Collective, Recreational Equipment, Inc., RSF | Regenerative Social Finance, the Savory Institute, the Slow Money Institute, TED, Transition Networks International, and Zingerman's:

Commit, then figure it out
Managing risk to strengthen resilience
Helping those who do good, do better
Helping humanity become a net-positive for nature
Using business as a force for good
Integrity, experience, and passion
Insurance for family, community, and planet
Redefining wealth, reimagining finance
Bank like tomorrow depends on it
Climate action by heroes like you
Heal the Earth and unite the whole human race
Inspire. Inform. Impact.
The courage to dream . . . the knowledge to change the world
Let's take back our food system
Making a difference, locally and globally
People, planet, profit
Company for the road ahead
We are all in for the Earth
Moving money for impact
Cooperatives build a better world
Humanity at work
All profits to charity
Harmonize the wealth of people and planet
Power of we—more hands do more good
We're in business to save our home planet
A life outdoors is a life well lived
Change finance, finance change
Regenerating the world's grasslands
Bringing money back down to earth
Ideas change everything
A movement of communities coming together to reimagine and rebuild our world
Global synchronized meditations for world peace and global impact
To enrich as many lives as we possibly can

The fundamental point in all of this is simple: Humanity is mobilizing.

As we reclaim and restore true wealth, as we activate the Quintenary structures, strategies, guidelines, governance, and guardrails throughout bodies corporate, as we perceive our entire world eyes wide open, as we mobilize and scale up regenerative finance to become the preponderant pattern of capital flows mimicking nature's mycelial nets and transcending extractive avarice, as we activate and amplify the virtuous cycles of competitive advantage and market demand within the context of Ecocene stewardship, as we explore and co-create the future of money together, as we deepen in our inner work, embodying the wisdom of the Original Instructions, as we light up and radiate outward the generative power of stewardship philanthropy, as we each rise to the sacred call of deep leadership and self-select into the emergent Earth steward aristocracy, we are altering the course of human history and are walking the path toward planetary prosperity.

By slowing down, tapping into the deep source of wisdom uniquely accessed via the organic intelligence of the natural world, in touch with the natural rhythms of moon and seasons and micro-seasonal happenings, cultivating a more poetic, reverent, elegant, and ultimately beautiful way of being, we engender within ourselves the foundational conditions from which an extraordinarily potent form of leadership can grow, like a great aspen or oak or giant sequoia or massive baobab tree. In so doing, we are invited to hear and see and feel the birdsong, the swaying trees dancing in the breeze, the pristinely flowing waters of life, the clean, crisp winds of a healed and restored planet—on a most regular basis. Normalized nature-connection and actualized communities of kindness and collaboration—these are the preponderant hallmarks of planetary prosperity.

We have a choice: to cultivate ourselves as integral members of a global woven web, nested in communities of coherence, compassion, and conviviality, and transforming the anthropogenic structures and systems upon which we all depend (and within which we're all implicated) in order to re-orient around the primary design directive of restoration, stewardship, and planetary prosperity.

Drawing upon the wisdom of the past, both recent and misty yore, we find the taproots of what's possible and set our priorities straight as we engender in the crucibles of our hearts and minds and souls the sacred alchemy of healing and love, overcoming the Mammonic Wetiko, engendering the Magnamic, discovering our own unique *Ikigai*, and blossoming into radiant beings and humble members of a great, exalted fellowship of reverent Earth dwellers.

We share one Earth, and are blessed to be here.

Together, our shared vision provides pathways along which we will travel and collaborate as we renew our sacred stewardship covenant, reaffirming our solemn and soulful duty to one another and to our great living Mother Earth, unlocking the keys and secrets to the timeless, childlike, playful joy that one embodies and experiences when one understands the truth: the cosmic lottery of destiny has selected each of us to be here now, and to make our choice.

Our shared vision depends on each of us.

Our shared vision depends on you.

PART II VIP Guest Essays
VOICES OF GLOBAL LEADERS

*"There is no greater reward than working from
your heart and making a difference in the world."*
—CARLOS SANTANA

ABOUT THE ESSAY AUTHORS

In the creation of this book, I have invited some of the most inspiring and impactful thought leaders and organizational leaders I know to share their knowledge and wisdom with you via the Foreword above and collection of essays found below. I have deliberately chosen a diverse array of leaders from a variety of geographic and cultural backgrounds (including Colombia, Germany, Kyrgyzstan, Russia, Tajikistan, Uganda, ancestral Mohawk lands, and various rural and urban communities throughout the United States), socio-economic situations (literally encompassing the entire spectrum discussed in the "Eyes Wide Open" chapter above), and from early, mid, and late career stages, thus representing five generations of knowledge and wisdom: from the Greatest Generation, through Boomers, Gen-Xers, and Millennials, to younger Gen-Z "digital native" Zoomers. This extraordinary diversity is not only deliberate, it's requisite—especially as we endeavor to stand upon the shoulders of those who have walked before us, and to learn from the emergent, mycelial digital native Indigo-age genius of younger leaders coming up behind us. We're all in this together, and, (thank goodness!) we are woven into a community tapestry with remarkable, heart-centered stewards, visionaries, and leaders embodying the kindness, decency, competency, and commitment needed to take on the Anthopocene's polycrisis and traverse the bridge of transformation, across which we will arrive at the planetary prosperity of the Ecocene. I encourage you not only to read each essay carefully—for they are each treasure troves—but to take in the short biographies below to get to know these authors who have taken the time to write for you:

John Fullerton is an economist, investor, and Founder and President of the Capital Institute. He is the author of *Regenerative Capitalism: How Universal Patterns and Principles Will Shape the New Economy* and *Regenerative Economics: Revolutionary Thinking for a World in Crisis.* Fullerton began his career with JPMorgan, and managed numerous capital markets and derivatives businesses around the globe. An impact investor, John is co-founder and Chairman of New Day Enterprises, PBC, and is co-founder of Grasslands. He is on the Board of Directors of First Crop and the Savory Institute, and is a member of the Club of Rome. He is author of "The Future of Finance" monthly blog. *Foreword* (**page xxi**)

John Perkins is an author and activist whose 12 books on economics, global intrigue, shamanism, and transformation include *Touching the Jaguar*, *Shapeshifting*, and the classic *Confessions of an Economic Hit Man* (on the *New York Times* bestseller list for more than 70 weeks, selling millions of copies and published in 38 languages). As chief economist at a major consulting firm, he advised the World Bank, United Nations, Fortune 500 corporations, the United States, and other governments. He regularly speaks at universities, economic forums, and shamanic gatherings around the world and is a founder and board member of the nonprofit organizations Pachamama Alliance and Dream Change. *"Life Economy vs. Death Economy"* (**page 121**)

Dilafruz Khonikboyeva is the Inaugural Executive Director of Patagonia's Home Planet Fund. Ms. Khonikboyeva was previously a political appointee of the U.S. Biden-Harris Administration, spent five years with the Aga Khan Development Network, and eight years responding to conflict and climate crises. A Presidential Leaders Scholar and Senior Advisor to USAID, Ms. Khonikboyeva is a transformational conflict expert, focused on civil war, climate, resource conflicts, and storytelling. She advises the Climate Change Working Group for Women of Color Advancing Peace, Security, and Conflict Transformation (WCAPS). "Daughter of the Pamiri Mountains," Dilafruz is an indigenous Pamiri from Khorog, Tajikistan. *"Philanthropy Unusual: Nature as the Original Technical Solution"* (**page 126**)

Mark Finser serves as an advisor, close confidant, and Trustee to wealth holders and those running family offices. He has worked with dozens of multi-generational inheritors and wealth creators over his 40 plus year career. Mark has worked with most of his clients for decades, helping to guide them through events like generational wealth transfers and family office restructurings. Mark began his career in finance in 1984 when he with others founded RSF | Regenerative Social Finance (RSF), an organization focused on developing innovative social and regenerative finance tools. Mark also ran an impact venture fund and was a founding member of New Resource Bank, which was acquired by Amalgamated Bank ($8 billion-plus assets under management with a trust business of $52 billion) on whose Board he currently serves as Director. He has funded the expansion of Waldorf Schools in the United States and serves on or has served on the Boards of Gaia Herbs, B Lab, and Living Lands Trust, to name a few. *"The Leadership Imperative: A Special Role of High-Net-Worth Families"* **(page 133)**

Dr. Riane Eisler, JD, PhD (hon) is internationally known for her groundbreaking contributions as a systems scientist, futurist, attorney, and cultural historian. She is the author of *The Chalice and the Blade* (now in its 57th U.S. printing and 30 foreign editions), *The Real Wealth of Nations* (hailed by Nobel Peace Laureate Desmond Tutu as "a template for the better world we have been so urgently seeking"), and *Nurturing Our Humanity: How Domination and Partnership Shape Our Brains, Lives, and Future* (co-authored with anthropologist Douglas Fry, Oxford University Press). Eisler is President of the Center for Partnership Systems and Editor in Chief of the online Interdisciplinary Journal of Partnership Studies (published by the University of Minnesota). *"Toward a Caring and Partnership Economy: Beyond Capitalism and Socialism"* **(page 137)**

Dr. Robert Cloninger, MD, PhD, is Director of the Anthropedia Institute and Professor Emeritus at Washington University in St. Louis. He was Wallace Renard Professor of Psychiatry, Professor of Genetics, Professor of Psychological and Brain Sciences, and Director of the Sansone Family Center for Well-Being at Washington University School of Medicine in St. Louis until July 2019. His personality inventories have been used in more than 6,000 peer-reviewed publications around the world, and he is one of the most highly cited scientists in the world across all fields (top 0.01 percentile). Dr. Cloninger has published ten books and over 600 articles in psychiatry, psychology, and genetics. His recent books include *Feeling Good: The Science of Well-Being* by Oxford University Press, *Origins of Altruism and Cooperation* by Springer, and *Personality and Psychopathology* by American Psychiatric Press. ***"What Makes People Healthy, Happy, and Fulfilled in the Face of Current World Challenges"*** **(page 150)**

Sarah Arao is the founder of Mantle of Hope & Inter-Rural Action Network, a Uganda-based nonprofit organization that empowers girls, women, and young people through health education, skills training, economic empowerment, and environmental stewardship. Through Mantle of Hope, she runs Hope Skilling studio where the survivors of sex trafficking, domestic abuse, and street children get support through mental health counseling and practical hands-on training from different trades. Sarah is also at the forefront of addressing the climate change crisis through her Young Climate Warriors project—through which she leads thousands of school children to restore our planet and ecosystems through tree planting, environmental training, and community waste management. She also runs the Muzuri Project in rural schools and communities, supporting young girls to remain at school by providing them with handmade feminine sanitary pads to facilitate their school retention and to prevent early and forced marriages. Sarah holds a Master of Arts in Development studies from Uganda Martyrs University, a Bachelor of Arts in Ethics and Human Rights from Makerere University, and a Diploma in Secondary Education from Kyambogo University. ***"Service Leadership, Self-Care, and Global Collaboration"*** **(page 158)**

Kate Williams is CEO of 1% for the Planet, a global organization that inspires action and commitment so that our planet and future generations thrive. 1% for the Planet's global network of thousands of businesses and individuals have donated hundreds of millions of dollars to vetted environmental partners to date. The community's shared goal is to reach $1 billion in total network impact by 2028, and to accelerate subsequent impact from there with many more billions. Kate has driven significant organizational scale—implementing high-impact giving strategies, growing a global brand, and leading an incredible and dedicated team. Additionally, she launched the donor-advised Planet Impact Fund, through which every dollar is invested or granted for maximum impact. ***"Leading Regeneration: The Shortest Route is Not a Straight Line"*** **(page 161)**

Tom Chi is the founder and CEO of At One Ventures. Cornell-educated, he has worked in a wide range of roles from astrophysical researcher to designer to corporate executive, developing new hardware/software products and services. He has played a significant role in established projects with global reach (Microsoft Outlook, Yahoo Search, Google), and scaled new projects from conception to significance (Yahoo Answers from zero to 90 million users). Tom has pioneered and practiced a unique approach to rapid prototyping, visioning, and leadership that can jump-start innovative new ideas as well as move organizations at unprecedented speeds. This approach has benefited both industry-leading multinationals and startups alike. He was a founding team member of Google X, developing technology such as Google Glass and Google's self-driving cars. Through his investment work, he was able to establish and elaborate a thesis on how humanity can become a net positive force through the emergence of environmentally regenerative technology as well as radically disrupting "nature-negative" industries. *"Plenty of Room in the Middle"* (**page 166**)

Jack Wielebinski is the Chief Investment Officer of One Small Planet, where he oversees investments in regenerative land and technology deals. As CIO, Jack represents OSP on several Boards, including ReSeed.farm, Cruz Foam, Magdalena Biosciences, and Evove. He holds a Bachelor's in Economics and Philosophy from Chapman University and an MBA from the UCLA Anderson School of Management. Jack's role as CIO has him traveling to projects and communities throughout the world, including very remote tropical regions such as Papua New Guinea. *"Climate Missive from One Small Planet"* (**page 170**)

Samantha Power is the Founder and Director of the BioFi Project and the Founder and Principal Consultant of Finance for Gaia. She is a Regenerative Economist, Futurist, and Bioregionalist based in Oakland, CA, on the ancestral land of the Ohlone people. Samantha has harnessed her experience working at the World Bank and in the financial sector—advising finance ministries, central banks, and investors—and is now telling a story about the need to build a new layer in the global financial architecture that decentralizes financial decision making and puts resources in the hands of people living in relationship to place. Samantha and her coauthor published a book entitled *Bioregional Financing Facilities: Reimagining Finance to Regenerate Our Planet* on the June 2024 Solstice. The same day, the BioFi Project launched—a collective of experts supporting bioregions around the world to design, build, and implement Bioregional Financing Facilities or 'BFFs.' The book makes the case for and explains how to shift capital to place-based regenerators in order to achieve global climate and nature-related goals. *"Biofi: Catalyzing an Economic and Financial Revolution"* (page 175)

Dr. Stephanie Gripne, PhD, is the Founder and CEO of Impact Finance Center, the first think-do tank focused on democratizing and scaling impact investing. Honored as one of Colorado's top CEOs, she is the visionary behind the National Impact Investing Marketplace, aiming to catalyze $1 trillion into social ventures. Lauded by *Forbes* as "the Steve Jobs of impact investing," her work has resulted in over $1 billion in direct impact investments. With a Ph.D. in Wildlife Conservation, Dr. Gripne brings 20-plus years of experience as an applied academic, investor, and practitioner, accelerating financial innovation to align capital with community and place. *"Main Street 2.0: Reimagining Capital for Community Transformation"* (page 184)

Azuraye Wycoff is a multi-generational land steward and entrepreneur who founded and operates regional enterprises in Boston, Massachusetts and Boulder, Colorado. In Boulder, she is the chief executive of Yellow Barn Farm, a local regenerative agricultural hub where several integrated enterprises are based, including: Kaizen Home Services, Picky Pig Compost, Stalk Market Distributions, and Small Haul Movers, which operates in both Boston and Boulder. She is also the Founder and CEO of Blue Sky Consulting Group, and holds a bachelor's degree from the University of Colorado in International Affairs and Chinese, as well as a Certificate of Chinese Language and Culture from Nanjing University. A native English speaker, Azuraye has professional working proficiency in both Chinese and Spanish. *"'White Holes' of Hyper-Local Regeneration: From Concept to Feeding Community"* (page 189)

Eduardo Esparza is a strategist, investor, and regenerative finance architect focused on mobilizing capital to heal ecosystems and rebuild communities in reciprocity with nature. He is the Founder and CEO of BlueDot Project, a platform for planetary regeneration aligning wisdom, capital, and intention. Its flagship project, the Fifth Fire, is an education, innovation, and investment hub co-developed with Indigenous nations of the Sierra Nevada de Gonavindúa in Colombia. Eduardo also designs financing mechanisms and investment products to fund Earth regeneration. Former CEO of Market 8 and angel investor, he helped 60+ startups reach product-market fit. He was knighted into the Order of San Martino by Prince Lorenzo de' Medici, is a Fulbright Scholar, and completed FinTech, Private Equity, Venture Capital, and Impact Investing executive programs at Harvard and Columbia. *"From Risk to Regeneration: Bioregional Investing & Financing Our Future"* (page 195)

Georgia Kelly is the Founder and Executive Director of Praxis Peace Institute. She has produced and directed several multi-day conferences in Europe and the U.S., and continues to create educational programs and podcasts for Praxis. In addition to leading conferences abroad (Italy, Cuba, and Croatia), she developed seminars/tours at the Mondragón Cooperatives in Spain, which has become a signature program at Praxis. As an advocate for cooperatives, she compiled *The Mondragón Report*, an account of how the Praxis/Mondragón seminar has impacted the cooperative movement in the United States. Georgia is also an active citizen and has chaired several issue-based political organizations and forums. In 2013, she edited and coauthored *Uncivil Liberties: Deconstructing Libertarianism*, a critique of libertarian ideas and laissez-faire capitalism, written by three academics and three activists. Her previous career was as a musician: harpist, composer, and recording artist. Her music can be found on streaming and online platforms. *"On Mondragon: The Ethics and Values of Cooperative Culture in the Basque Region of Spain"* (page 199)

Hannah Odell is a senior fundraising strategist with a track record of spearheading transformative multi-million-dollar campaigns for nationally recognized nonprofit brands. She is a trusted advisor to nonprofit founders, executives, and board members. She is currently the Director of Strategic Giving at TED, where she is responsible for new philanthropic strategies and individual giving initiatives. Previously, Hannah was the Chief Growth Officer of the Global Warming Mitigation Project, a climate innovation organization, and she spent much of her career as Managing Director of the NYC fundraising consultancy Hudson Ferris, where she supported more than 80 nonprofits across a range of impact areas. She was featured in *Bloomberg* and *Yahoo! Finance* as the co-founder of a nonprofit community startup called GreaterSpace. Hannah serves on the board of Foundation Cristosal, Central America's leading voice on human rights, and also volunteers her time on the Global Advisory Board of Y on Earth and the Circuit Board of the Global Warming Mitigation Project. *"A View from the Top of the Philanthropy Pyramid"* (page 211)

Dr. Jandel Allen-Davis, MD, is the President and CEO of Craig Hospital in Englewood, Colorado, a renowned center specializing in neurorehabilitation for patients with spinal cord and brain injuries. Prior to this role, she served as Vice President of Government, External Relations, and Research at Kaiser Permanente Colorado. Dr. Allen-Davis practiced obstetrics and gynecology for 25 years and is board-certified in the field. She completed her undergraduate and medical degrees at Dartmouth College and Dartmouth Medical School, followed by a residency at Thomas Jefferson University Hospital. Beyond her executive duties, she serves on the Kansas City Federal Reserve Bank Board of Directors, and holds positions on several Colorado-based boards, including the Denver Museum of Nature and Science, the Colorado Hospital Association, and the Common Sense Institute. *"Do You Know Whom You Serve? Leadership Lessons Honed at the Feet of My Patients."* (page 224)

Steve Farrell is the cofounder and Worldwide Executive Director of Humanity's Team, a global nonprofit dedicated to awakening humanity to the interconnectedness of all life. Founded in 2003 with Neale Donald Walsch, Humanity's Team now reaches 1.5 million people across 150-plus countries through transformational education, Masterclasses, and global initiatives like Global Oneness Day. A former Silicon Valley tech entrepreneur, Steve left a high-profile business career to lead a movement for conscious living. He shares his journey in *A New Universal Dream* and speaks internationally on conscious leadership. *"The Dawn of a Conscious Business Movement"* (page 241)

John Rogers is an accomplished leader with a rich background in business, government, and public affairs. He is the President of the Americas Region at HUB Cyber Security. He is the founder of RL Leaders, a firm that bridged national security and the entertainment industry, and Capstone National Partners, a bipartisan government affairs firm. John has held senior positions at the Pentagon and in Wisconsin state politics. He currently serves on several private and nonprofit boards, including MV Transportation and Le Ciel Foundation. Based in Wisconsin, John enjoys photography, writing, and travel, and cherishes time with his wife, Diane, their two dogs, and their growing family. *"Mixed Tables & Renaissance Teams: Igniting Group Genius"* (page 249)

Miranda Clendening is a regenerative community developer, researcher, and global speaker who lives in Boulder, Colorado. She is the Chief Coordinator at The Riverside Boulder: Rivertree Sanctuary/1World Academy/1Team Coordination Hub/ Renewal Center and serves as the Director of Operations and Community Development at the Empowerment Institute's Center for Reinventing the Planet for their Peace on Earth by 2030 Game, which is now active in 69 countries. She is a U.N. Ambassador to Africa and has been part of the Global Science and Technology Innovations Summits for the U.N. SDGs since 2018. Miranda is also the Chief Ambassador at UNIFY.org and a core business developer for the ONEBoulder/ONELocal and CoreNexus Technology Platforms. She co-leads these initiatives with a focus on advancing evolutionary leadership and social architecture through innovative research and technology to regenerate the Earth and its systems for a thriving and abundant future for all of us. *"The Mycelial Model for Planetary Prosperity: Community Mobilization, Global Connectivity, and Technological Amplification"* (page 249)

Alena Maslova is the Founder of Dobrosphera ("Atmosphere of Kindness") research center and media production company. Based in Kyrgyzstan, she is a linguist, philosopher, ethicist, and international media producer focusing on the arts, sustainability, and well-being. Through Dobrosphera, her many projects include films, animations, music, poetry, and translation resources for regeneration and planetary health, including with UNDP, OSCE, UNESCO and many others. Alena is a COP28 speaker, COP29 organizer, and co-author of *Nobel Prize and Goldman Award Laureates*, and is currently conducting research on art and social change. She is on the Y on Earth Community's Global Advisory Board. *"Building a 'Meta-Industrial' Future Together"* (page 254)

L. Hunter Lovins is President of Natural Capitalism Solutions. A Managing Partner of NOW Partners, Hunter has worked in energy, regenerative agriculture, climate policy, sustainable development, and resilience for 55 years. A consultant to industries including International Finance Corporation, Unilever, Walmart, the United

Nations and Royal Dutch Shell, as well as sustainability champions Interface, Patagonia, and Clif Bar, Hunter has briefed heads of state, the UN, and the US Congress, leaders of numerous local governments, the Pentagon, and officials in 30 countries. A professor of sustainable business management at Fordham University, Hunter is the author of 17 books, including the recently released *A Finer Future: Creating an Economy in Service to Life*. She has won dozens of awards, including the European Sustainability Pioneer Award and the Right Livelihood Award. *Time* magazine recognized her as a Millennium Hero for the Planet, and *Newsweek* called her the Green Business Icon. ***"COPx: The People's Climate Community: We Can Solve the Climate Crisis and Rebuild Democracy"*** (page 260)

Dr. Martin Frick, PhD is a senior diplomat with many years of experience at the United Nations. As Senior Director of the UN Convention to Combat Climate Change (UNFCCC) from 2017 to 2021, he oversaw the implementation of the Paris Agreement and the secretariat's Climate Action work. Programme Director of Kofi Annan's Global Humanitarian Forum, Dr. Frick developed the founding narrative of climate justice together with Mary Robinson, and served as the European Union's lead negotiator in the establishment of the UN Human Rights Council in Geneva. He served as Director of the Global Office of the World Food Programme, Germany, and led the UN Secretary General's Food System Summit 2021 as Deputy to the Special Envoy to the Food Systems. ***"COPx: The People's Climate Community: We Can Solve the Climate Crisis and Rebuild Democracy"*** (page 272)

Henry Mitchell is a seasoned Disaster Planner and Emergency Manager with experience spanning the public, private, and nonprofit sectors (in coordination with local law enforcement, state agency, and federal agency partners). He currently serves as the Deputy Director of the Office of Emergency Preparedness and Response for the State of Colorado, where he leads initiatives in disaster preparedness, planning, and response coordination, with a strong focus on human-centered leadership, biosecurity, environmental justice, and effective grant management. Henry has played a key role in some of the most critical emergencies in recent years, including leading local government COVID-19 responses, managing emergency operations centers, and serving on incident management teams and as EOC manager during major events such as the Marshall Fire. His approach is defined by a commitment to producing high-quality, functional emergency plans, using trauma-informed principles, and maintaining a calm, steady presence in high-pressure situations. Driven by the belief that emergency management work has a profound and lasting impact on communities, Henry emphasizes thoughtful, inclusive strategies that reflect the lived realities of those affected by disasters. He is Founder and CEO of World Aware Emergency Preparedness LLC, which provides consulting and preparedness products and advising services for governments, communities, institutions, and families. *"Planning and Preparedness for Community Resilience"* (page 279)

John P. Milton is a pioneering ecologist, spiritual teacher, and meditation master. He founded the Way of Nature, a global movement integrating spiritual, ecological, and social consciousness. Milton's early environmental activism includes cofounding Friends of the Earth alongside David Brower. During the decade of the 1960s, he received an honorable appointment to the Woodrow Wilson International Center for Scholars with an office in the Smithsonian "Castle" on the National Mall. He contributed to significant environmental literature, such as co-editing *Future Environments of North America* (1966) and coauthoring *Ecological Principles for Economic Development* (1973). Additionally, he served as one of the first ecologists on staff at the White House as a member of the President's Council of Economic Advisors, and was instrumental in the establishment of the Clean Air and Clean Water Acts as well as the Environmental Protection Agency (EPA). Through his Sacred Passage programs, Milton has guided thousands into the wilderness, fostering profound connections with nature and promoting Earth stewardship. *"The Sacred View of Mother Gaia"* (page 285)

Maria Rodale is an explorer in search of the mysteries of the universe. She is the author of *Love Nature Magic: Shamanic Journeys into the Heart of My Garden*, *Organic Manifesto*, and *Scratch*, and is the beloved children's book author Mrs. Peanuckle. She serves on the board of the Rodale Institute and has advocated for the potential of organic regenerative farming throughout her life, including being featured in the documentary *Kiss the Ground*. She is also the recovering CEO and Chairman of Rodale Inc., publisher of books such as Al Gore's *Inconvenient Truth*, Howard Schultz's *Onward*, and classics like *The South Beach Diet*. Maria also published the magazines *Men's Health*, *Women's Health*, *Prevention*, *Runner's World*, *Bicycling*, and *Organic Gardening*, among others. From 2003 to 2011, she was on the board of Bette Midler's New York Restoration Project. From 2014 to 2017, she served on the Pennsylvania Federal Reserve Advisory Council. She also served on the board of the Lehigh Valley Health Network. Her many awards include the National Audubon Rachel Carson Award, UN Population Fund's Award for the Health and Dignity of Women Everywhere, the Auburn University International Quality of Life Award, and an honorary Doctorate degree from Delaware Valley University. Maria is a mother, grandmother, artist, and crazy gardener who lives in Pennsylvania, right near where she was born. *"Love, Nature, Women: How to Build a Regenerative Economy"* (page 290)

Kevin Townley (dearly departed) was the Grand Lecturer of the Grand Lodge of Colorado, AF & AM. An autodidactic alchemist and esotericist, Mr. Townley wrote several books, including: *The Cube of Space and Meditations on the Cube of Space.* He was a frequent lecturer on esoteric mysteries, and taught courses at The Colorado Institute of Transpersonal Psychology, Boulder College, Sancta Sophia Theological Seminary, Naropa University, and elsewhere in the United States and Europe on various topics, including: Spagyrics, Qabalah, the Tree of Life, the Signatures of Nature, Sacred Geometry, and Alchemy. He co-founded the Hermetic School: The Philosophers of Nature, which has a seven-year curriculum in laboratory alchemy and Qabalah. He lived for a decade as a monastic in the Carmelite Order, and subsequently collaborated with a variety of Sufi, Hindu, Buddhist, Christian, Rosicrucian, Hebrew, and Hermetic orders. His scholarly research includes the Theosophical movement as well as the wisdom of the Framers such as Ben Franklin and George Washington. *"The Alchemy of Money for a Coming New Age"* (page 296)

Kawenniiosta Jock is a Kanien'kehá:ka woman from the Wolf Clan of Akwesasne and Creative Director of Skywomans Forever Farm, an Indigenous-led initiative rematriating ancestral lands in Schoharie Valley, NY. A dedicated land steward, she integrates Indigenous Traditional Ecological Knowledge with modern remediation practices to restore soil, water, and food systems affected by industrial pollution. Former Co-Executive Director of the Waterfall Unity Alliance, Kawenniiosta also brings years of experience in youth advocacy, cultural programming, and Indigenous fashion. She is a master seamstress, Full Spectrum Doula, and mother of six, committed to cultural revitalization, language preservation, and environmental healing. A graduate of the Champions of Change leadership program and a member of several Indigenous-led alliances, she works to advance sovereignty, sustainability, and community resilience through every aspect of her work. *"The Liberation of a Mother Expressing Peace to Her Children and All Creation Has the Ability to Transform the World Around Us; That Is the Law of the Land"* (**page 302**)

1   LIFE ECONOMY VS. DEATH ECONOMY

Insights from a Recovered Economic Hit Man

John Perkins is the author of *Touching the Jaguar, Shapeshifting,* and *NYTimes* bestseller *Confessions of an Economic Hit Man.* He co-founded the Pachamama Alliance.

During the 1970s, when I was chief economist at a major U.S. consulting firm, a very dangerous idea gained momentum. It accelerated especially rapidly after 1976. That year, Professor Milton Friedman won the Nobel Prize in economics and promoted this idea—that the only responsibility of business is to maximize short-term profits, regardless of the social and environmental costs.

President Ronald Reagan, Prime Minister Margaret Thatcher, many other world leaders, corporate executives, and business schools around the world embraced this idea and advocated short-term profit maximization as the primary goal of business. It is an idea that has grown and become the "Bible" of business over the ensuing years. It is dangerous because it gives CEOs a mandate to do whatever it takes to maximize short-term profits; this includes ravaging the environment, lobbying for laws that lower taxes on the rich, minimize wages and worker benefits for everyone else, and legalize forms of "corruption," such as contributions to political campaigns.

As a result, the entire world has been hit by a resource-devouring, degenerative, and polluting system known as the Death Economy—one where short-term profits and materialistic consumption reign. In *The New Confessions of an Economic Hit Man,* I offered a plan to transform the Death Economy into a sustainable, regenerative Life Economy—one that is driven by a goal of maximizing long-term benefits for people and nature. Instead of paying people to do things that ravage and pollute the planet, the Life Economy pays them to clean up pollution, regenerate destroyed environments, recycle, and develop technologies and systems that enhance the future for all species.

We are all affected. People from Africa, Asia, Europe, Latin America, the Middle East, and Island Nations, rich and poor—all living beings—are threatened. We can disagree on political, governmental, religious, and other issues, but we must agree that none of those matter on a dead planet—one where the Death Economy has succeeded. If we want our children to survive, it is imperative that we come together. It is essential that China's leaders (and future leaders) apply the Confucian ideal of serving the family to the global community, that the United States' leaders (and future leaders) work to unite all the states of America and the world in a concerted effort to evade the crises facing us, and a critical mass of people everywhere join hands to transform the Death Economy to a Life Economy.

The current perception of success sets a goal of maximizing materialistic consumption and short-term profits, regardless of the social and environmental costs. The new perception of success will have as its goal that of maximizing long-term benefits for all people and nature. Once actions are taken by enough consumers, investors, workers, and management to implement this perception, the EHM (economic hit man) strategy will end, and we will transition from a degenerative Death Economy to a regenerative Life Economy. That new perception also has to include changes in the way nations view their relationships with one another. It is time to transform "divide and conquer" into "unite and restore."

There is a major difference between capitalism and what many economists refer to as "predatory capitalism," a deviant form that has little in common with the original. According to *Merriam-Webster*, capitalism is

> An economic system characterized by private or corporate ownership of capital goods, by investments that are determined by private decision, and by prices, production, and the distribution of goods that are determined mainly by competition in a free market.[1]

The *Oxford Dictionary* defines it as

> An economic and political system in which a country's trade and industry are controlled by private owners for profit, rather than by the state.[2]

---

1 *Merriam-Webster*, s.v. "capitalism," accessed November 23, 2019, https://www.merriam-webster.com/dictionary/capitalism.

2 Lexico, s.v. "capitalism," accessed November 23, 2019, https://www.lexico.com/en/definition/capitalism.

Today's Death Economy is a far cry from either of these definitions. It is characterized by businesses that destroy or absorb their competition and oppose free market policies. Not only does the state not own businesses; businesses and their billionaire shareholders control the state. It is a predatory aberration that facilitates the growth of the Death Economy, and actually should not be considered capitalism.

The Death Economy is driven by the goal that was promoted by a group of economists in the 1970s and 1980s, including Nobel Prize winners Friedrich von Hayek (1974) and Milton Friedman (1976), and can be summarized as "the only responsibility of business is to maximize short-term owner profits, regardless of the social and environmental costs."

The stories that accompany this perception give corporate executives the right—even the mandate—to do whatever they think it will take to maximize short-term profits, including buying public officials through campaign financing and promises of lucrative post-government consulting or lobbying jobs; exploiting workers; annihilating or buying out their competitors; destroying environments; reducing taxes and wages; lobbying against pro-worker, pro-consumer, and pro-ecology regulations; promising (as well as threatening) to impact economies by locating their facilities in (or removing them from) cities and countries; and depleting the very resources upon which the long-term survival of their businesses depends. These stories promote top-down, authoritarian chains of command and autocratic management styles—in business as well as government.

KEY CHARACTERISTICS OF THE DEATH ECONOMY

- Its goal is to maximize short-term profits for a relative few.
- It uses fear and debt to gain market share and political control.
- It promotes the idea that for someone to win, another must lose.
- It is predatory, encouraging businesses to prey on each other, people, and the environment.
- It destroys resources needed for its own long-term survival.
- It values goods and services that are "extractive" and materialistic above those that enhance quality of life (e.g., child-rearing, the arts).
- It is heavily influenced by nonproductive financial deals (stock manipulation, financialization, "gambling").
- It ignores externalities, such as environmental destruction and exploitation of workers, when measuring profits, GDP, and other metrics.
- It invests heavily in militarization—in killing, or threatening to kill, people and other life-forms, and destroying infrastructure.

- It causes pollution, environmental collapse, and drastic income and social inequality, and may lead to political instability.
- It vilifies taxes, rather than defining them as investments (in social services, infrastructure, the military, etc.).
- It is undemocratic, encouraging the growth of large corporations controlled by a few individuals whose money has a strong influence on politics (monopolies that lead to oligarchies).
- It is based on top-down, authoritarian chains of command that support autocratic management styles—in business and government.
- It places higher values on nonproductive jobs (venture capitalists, investment bankers) than on productive ones (laborers, factory workers) and those that enrich life (teachers, musicians, artists).
- It keeps billions of people in poverty.
- It classifies plants, animals, and the entire natural world as depletable resources; fails to respect and protect nature; and causes massive extinctions and other irreversible problems.
- It has become the predominant advocate of what it calls "capitalism" around the world.

The future lies in transforming the Death Economy into a Life Economy that cleans up pollution, regenerates devastated ecosystems, manufactures non-toxic materials, upcycles and recycles in a circular economy, and develops technologies that restore resources and that benefit, rather than ravage, the environment. Businesses that pay returns to investors who invest in an economy that is itself a renewable resource become the success stories.

The Life Economy is driven by the goal of maximizing long-term benefits for people and the environment.

KEY CHARACTERISTICS OF THE LIFE ECONOMY
- Its goal is to serve a public interest (maximize long-term benefits for people and nature).
- Its laws support level playing fields that encourage healthy, non-monopolistic competition, innovative ideas, and sustainable products.
- It embraces a sense of cooperation, the idea that we all can win when we set our goals for long-term benefits for all.
- It values quality of life and spiritually enhancing activities above those based solely on materialism and extraction.
- It is based on beneficially productive activities, such as recycling, education, health care, the arts, etc., rather than the nonproductive, such as stock manipulation, financialization, "gambling," etc.

- It cleans up pollution.
- It regenerates devastated environments.
- It is driven by compassion and debt avoidance.
- It helps hungry people feed themselves.
- It includes externalities in its financial and economic measurements.
- It innovates—develops and embraces new, regenerative, sustainable technologies.
- It defines taxes as investments (should your tax monies be invested in health care or militarization?).
- It is democratic, encouraging locally based commerce and employee- or community-owned businesses that benefit many (e.g., cooperatives, B Corporations, etc.).
- It reinforces democratic decision-making processes and management styles—in business and government.
- It places a high value on jobs that enrich life (musicians, social and medical workers, parents).
- It is based on a foundational knowledge that humans are in a symbiotic relationship with our planet, that we must respect, honor, and protect the natural world.
- It rewards investors who support all the previous characteristics.
- It was the predominant form of economic evolution for much of the two hundred thousand years of human history.

The transition happens through changes in the perceptions that drive values and actions, and the stories we tell around them. "Maximize short-term profits for a few, regardless of the social and environmental costs" becomes "Maximize long-term benefits for all people and nature." When groups of consumers, workers, and investors accept these values and take actions to support businesses that promote them and pressure governments to codify them into laws, the changes we want and need will happen.

"I don't believe we will ever make a serious effort to save our home planet from all its threats until we humans adopt a spiritual connection to the natural world. Saving indigenous cultures and working and learning from them would be a good start."

—YVON CHOUINARD

2 PHILANTHROPY UNUSUAL

Nature as the Original Technical Solution

Dilafruz Khonikboyeva is the inaugural Executive Director of Patagonia's Home Planet Fund. She was previously a Senior Advisor to USAID, and with the Aga Khan Development Network.

On September 14, 2022, I sat in the crowd with the rest of Patagonia's former and current employees as Yvon Chouinard announced that the outdoor company was "Going Purpose." I had just moved to Ventura, California, and started my new job a couple of weeks beforehand. Much of that time was spent evading questions about what I was working on, waiting to reveal why I had joined and what I was building.

This announcement was the next step in Yvon's and the company's 50-year experiment in responsible business, or "Business Unusual," and the birth of Home Planet Fund, or "Philanthropy Unusual."

BUSINESS UNUSUAL

Founded by Yvon Chouinard in 1973, Patagonia Works ("Patagonia") is a certified B Corporation based in Ventura, California. Certified B Corporations are businesses that meet the highest standards of verified social and environmental performance, public transparency, and legal accountability to balance profit and purpose.

Patagonia started a self-imposed Earth tax that put 1% of annual sales back into environmental causes. This evolved into being a founding member of 1% For the Planet, an international organization whose members contribute at least 1% of their annual revenue to environmental causes to protect the environment. This work is done through an Environment Team based in Ventura, California, and across the world and with input from employee environmental grants councils. By pairing these grants with storytelling, Patagonia has been an active part of the climate movement in many parts of the world.

Patagonia operates its apparel and equipment, food, and related businesses through the following subsidiaries: Patagonia, Inc. (apparel and equipment), Patagonia Provisions (food), Patagonia Media (books, films and multimedia projects), Fletcher Chouinard Designs, Inc. (surfboards), Tin Shed Ventures, LLC (investments), Worn Wear, Inc. (used and upcycled apparel), and Great Pacific Child Development Center (onsite childcare and development). The company is recognized internationally for its product quality and environmental activism.

GOING PURPOSE

During the September 2022 event, Yvon went on to explain that Earth was now Patagonia's only shareholder. That meant that profits not reinvested back into the business are paid as dividends to protect the planet. Effective immediately, the Chouinard family transferred all ownership to two new entities: Patagonia Purpose Trust and the Holdfast Collective.

The Patagonia Purpose Trust now owns all the voting stock of the company (2% of the total stock) and exists to create a more permanent legal structure to enshrine Patagonia's purpose and values. It helps ensure that there is never deviation from the intent of the founder and to facilitate what the company continues to do best: demonstrate as a for-profit business that capitalism can work for the planet.

The Holdfast Collective owns all the nonvoting stock (98% of the total stock), and it will use every dollar received from Patagonia to protect nature and biodiversity, support thriving communities, and fight the environmental crisis. Each year, profits that are not reinvested back into the business will be distributed by Patagonia as a dividend to the Holdfast Collective to help fight the climate crisis as a 501(c)(4). This allows for lobbying in support of climate-friendly policies as well as supporting large-scale land conservation.

THE WORK

The day of the announcement was filled with laughter, tears, good food, and surfing. "Let My People Go Surfing" is not only a book or catchphrase, but also core to the way Patagonia operates.

I was surprised and comforted by the bonds of the Patagonia community. People from multiple phases of the company's life came back for this event; at their core was a belief in how Patagonia shows up in the world. I met adults who had spent their childhood at the Great Pacific Child Development Center, the onsite childcare and development provider. I felt the responsibility to build Home Planet Fund so that it was aligned with this ethic and a part of this community—an exciting, albeit daunting, challenge.

I also felt relief: I could now explain that I was starting up Home Planet Fund on behalf of Patagonia, testing their principle of "Philanthropy Unusual." I felt a surge of energy and wanted to get to work testing the traditional approaches and boundaries of philanthropy.

From September 2022 to our public launch on Earth Day 2024, Home Planet Fund has taken shape with one clear goal: to tackle the polycrisis with speed, scale, and healing.

HOME PLANET FUND (HPF)

Patagonia has never been interested in conventional business, and Home Planet Fund is not interested in conventional philanthropy. We know we aren't doing enough (yet) to avert the polycrisis on an individual scale, nor globally: from climate and biodiversity to migration, food insecurity, and water shortages, these crises are happening with increasing frequency and severity.

We know worldwide there is a will to act, but many people don't know where to start.

Home Planet Fund is a US-based 501(c)(3) nonprofit corporation that relentlessly pursues its Earth-serving mission. There is no unnecessary waste; resources are for the mission, not bureaucracy. There will be no junkets, no fancy dinners. It is transparent, it shares results, outcomes, and best practices. A singular focus on solutions rather than symptoms.

Mission first, always.

Launched with an initial donation and future funding by Patagonia, HPF is able to accept donations from individuals, businesses, and foundations. Because HPF has its own funding for overhead, it is able to ensure 100% of all funds received will go directly to our partners: Indigenous Peoples and Local Communities (IPLCs) around the world who are working and living the best solutions for the planet. HPF will also act as a re-granter and take on operational burden and risk for others, matching funds to amplify impact.

UNDERFUNDED SOLUTIONS

Nature-based solutions work. They're available now, and they're underfunded, which means investments made will have a big impact.

The knowledge and tools to implement them exist today and have been proven out through millennia by IPLCs and again by modern science. Home Planet Fund leverages the power of nature and the stewardship role of IPLCs. We support a focus on the intersectionality of people and planet, rebuilding local systems, and centering the knowledge of and implementation through IPLCs. A portion of this work is now called Nature-Based Solutions, but nature is and always has been the original technical solution.

Our knowledge of these solutions is our collective inheritance. HPF seeks out and funds IPLCs preserving, conserving, restoring, and working our lands and waters with an emphasis on regenerative organic agriculture. Grantees focus on polyculture, native species, and selective farming and harvesting in ways that repair, restore, and sustain natural systems. Our funding is nimble, multi-year, and multi-million-dollar.

Grantees are IPLCs who have personal knowledge of the lands and waters, who know the communities and how to translate and apply regenerative principles in their unique intersectional context of people, culture, geography, and history. HPF facilitates access to seeds, tools, knowledge, community, and capital for its grantees. Each grantee's program will manifest differently, and there is strength in that diversity—the mono-cultural mindset got us into this crisis, only a poly-cultural strategy will get us out.

UNDERFUNDED GEOGRAPHIES

HPF focuses particularly on geographies and interventions that are remote, fragile, and at the frontlines of the climate crisis. Sometimes these geographies are in active, drawn-out conflict. By drawing attention to and providing support for these geographies, restoring or conserving the lands and waters as well as wildlife will have an outsized impact locally as well as globally on carbon capture and preserving the biodiversity of humans, flora, and fauna.

UNDERFUNDED PEOPLE

Home Planet Fund is collaborating with IPLCs globally to fuel local priorities that balance people and planet and that have an outsized global impact. At the Board of Directors and staff level, we represent IPLCs from all over the world.

These communities feel the impacts of the climate crisis firsthand, while contributing practically nothing to its cause—and they're pursuing brilliantly simple nature-based solutions that can help mitigate it—at scale.

But in scientific literature and studies, the Indigenous perspective has been rarely acknowledged, respected, or published.

Indigenous cultures place weight upon oral tradition. Knowledge is passed from generation to generation through storytelling. There is no need to write essays or laws about their relationship with nature, because it is lived, breathed, and embodied through a foundational understanding of the "Original Instructions."

This cultural practice means that historically, Indigenous knowledge is not recognized, simply because it isn't typically written down. In the Western world, a published researcher or a lawmaker is taken seriously, while an Indigenous elder carrying knowledge that has been passed down for millennia is too often not.

Thousands of years of Indigenous knowledge on solutions for mitigating and adapting to the climate crisis are not being utilized simply because they are carried and communicated differently.

The voices of Indigenous Peoples have historically been marginalized and ignored when it comes to policymaking, despite the United Nations acknowledging the importance of their traditional knowledge and how it is not consistently reflected in existing mitigation efforts.

Yet these are the people who are the original stewards of the planet's biodiversity, lands, and waters.

While they account for only 5% of Earth's population, IPLCs manage an estimated 20-25% of Earth's land surface that contains approximately 40% of all terrestrial protected areas and ecologically intact landscapes.

There is not a more important segment of society with a more critical role in stewarding the Earth and its biodiversity.

PHILANTHROPY UNUSUAL

Environmental work traditionally hasn't recognized the critical and positive role of humans within ecosystems. Instead, it has traditionally created conservation systems based on the exclusion of people from "wild" lands. But people are a part of nature, and we are dependent on one another. To serve our home planet, we must begin by changing how we see the role of people in nature.

Home Planet Fund gives directly to communities to lead and implement projects. Our approach not only recognizes their personal knowledge, institutional memory, and experience, but also how to translate and apply regenerative principles in their unique intersectional context of people, culture, geography, and history. This means there is less waste, and it takes far less time to get work underway, and scale up. Local ownership also ensures durable, long-term change.

By investing in community and tribal structures, funding goes further. These structures have the same operations and mobilization as international entities and governments, but without the large overhead costs or capital drains through shareholder dividends. They don't need to spend time on costly mistakes because of a lack of knowledge of local customs, politics, or languages. They have built-in access to local knowledge and trust. They also have a vested interest in the success of this work, ensuring durability and continuity.

WHY

I frequently get asked the question why I do this work, why I build Home Planet Fund in this way. We all have our answers for why we choose the work we do, the lives we live. For me, it's tied up in who I am and what I believe.

I was born in Khorog, the capital of the Gorn-Badakhshan Autonomous Oblast, as part of the Soviet Union. We call it Pamir, for the Pamir Mountains in which we live and which we are stewards of. We call ourselves Pamiri, the people of the Pamir Mountains. I had the luxury of growing up surrounded by my family and my people, learning about the land and the waters in my language. There are few places left in the world where the culture and community are intact below a thin layer of external influence; I was lucky to be born and raised in that context.

I've had the privilege of working at all levels, from community up to international institutions. I've been both a recipient (as my family lived through the Tajik civil war) and a donor. There is a lot of goodwill and intention in these spaces, from humanitarian assistance to development to climate. But the reality is that there are often unintended consequences and harm that is also done through conventional philanthropy.

For me, Home Planet Fund is the kind of organization I would have wanted to be a partner of on the ground, as a recipient. For me, Home Planet Fund is an experiment in proving that local solutions are the answer to the polycrisis. That this work can be done at speed and scale and with a polyculture approach. Finally, this work can help heal and bring people together. At my core, at the core of our partners, is a belief in the spiritual connection we all share, from humans to lands to trees to waters.

ACTION SPEAKS LOUDER THAN WORDS

By the time Home Planet Fund launched on Earth Day 2024, our four initial programs were already well underway. Since September 2022, when Patagonia made the commitment to Go Purpose, I've been building. I'm now surrounded by a Board of Directors, staff, consultants, and partners who are all dedicated to not only what we are doing but how and why we are doing it.

Pastoralists' work across East Africa and Pamiri farmers in Tajikistan are creating biodiversity hotspots and sequestering carbon. The work of Alaska Natives in the Tongass Rainforest is stewarding and sustaining this critically important ecosystem. Our partners across the South Pacific are stewarding their islands and surrounding ocean area, as well as building resiliency across their communities.

In East Africa, a tremendous volume of carbon is being sequestered across millions of hectares by Maasai, Samburu, Karamojong, Pamiri, and other tribal peoples stewarding these vast lands—up to 500 kilograms per hectare per year. To put this in perspective, each human being contains about eight kilograms of carbon in our bodies at any given time. Annually, our East Africa program, along with pastoralists across Africa, sequesters up to the total carbon equivalent of every human on Earth.

In the Tongass Rainforest, one *billion* metric tons of carbon dioxide equivalent is stored in land stewarded by our partners, an assemblage of tribal peoples who are the original stewards of the Tongass Rainforest.

While carbon sequestration is a vitally important metric in mitigating global greenhouse gas emissions, it is far from being the only positive impact our partners' work is having. Our home planet also requires regeneration of lands and waters, biodiversity of flora and fauna, and recognizing the role of humans as part of nature. Lands and waters are healing, in communion with people, making evident the beautiful and hopeful reality that we have the option to reconnect intimately with nature—to return *home*. All of this is part of the impact at the core of our work.

All of this work is ongoing, and it is expanding. With more programs in the works, the scope of what our current and future partners aim to accomplish is truly breathtaking.

1,725,705 square kilometers of the Earth's land and waters are currently stewarded by Home Planet Fund programs. This is a little more than 1% of the Earth's land area.[1]

12,325,000 square kilometers of Earth's land and waters will eventually be stewarded by Home Planet Fund's initial programs going forward. This is the equivalent of a little more than 8% of the Earth's land area.[2]

And this is just the beginning.

We are all in for the Earth, we are just getting started, and we invite you to connect and engage with the work we're doing at the Home Planet Fund.

After all, we are all in this together.

---

1 https://desapublications.un.org/policy-briefs

2 https://portals.iucn.org/library/sites/library/files/documents/2014-034.pdf

3 THE LEADERSHIP IMPERATIVE

A Special Role for High-Net-Worth Families

Mark Finser founded RSF Social Finance (now Regenerative Social Finance) and New Resource Bank (which merged with Amalgamated Bank, on whose Board Mark currently serves).

INTRODUCTION

In an era of economic extremes, where a small fraction of individuals accumulates vast wealth while many struggle to meet basic needs, I believe the role of leaders—entrepreneurs, executives, and high-net-worth families—has never been more critical. My reflections illuminate the profound responsibility and opportunity for these leaders to shape a more just and sustainable world through the principles of stewardship, ethical investment, and shared ownership. By implementing "guidelines" and "guardrails" that ensure wealth circulates equitably among all stakeholders, we can transcend the traditional paradigms of capital accumulation and move toward an economy rooted in service, sustainability, and planetary prosperity.

THE PARADIGM SHIFT: FROM EGOTISM TO ALTRUISM

The current economic model often rewards egotism—where success is measured by personal gain, and wealth is concentrated in the hands of a few. However, I see a transition emerging toward an era where leaders recognize that their success is inextricably tied to the well-being of others. I advocate for an ethos in which it is equally, if not more, important that those around us thrive alongside us. This approach reframes wealth not as a personal end but as a tool for greater collective impact.

STEWARD OWNERSHIP: A STRUCTURAL INNOVATION

One of the most powerful mechanisms for enacting this shift is steward ownership, an innovative approach that prioritizes long-term mission over short-term profit. In steward-owned enterprises, founders and investors establish governance structures that cap individual financial returns while ensuring that the business remains dedicated to its core purpose and the well-being of all stakeholders. This model stands in stark contrast to traditional corporate structures, where maximizing shareholder value often comes at the expense of employees, communities, and the environment.

I have seen examples such as RSF | Regenerative Social Finance and Patagonia's recent transition to a mission-driven ownership model. By embedding "guardrails" that prevent excessive wealth extraction by any one individual or group, these businesses create a regenerative economic model that values continuity, sustainability, and collective ownership over personal enrichment.

REVOLUTIONARY APPROACHES TO PHILANTHROPY: SHARED GIFTING AND FLOW FUNDING

Philanthropy has long been a vehicle for redistributing wealth, yet traditional models often perpetuate a top-down, paternalistic approach. A transformative alternative I have embraced is shared gifting. This model shifts the decision-making power away from individual philanthropists and toward the communities they seek to support. Instead of unilateral grantmaking, shared gifting convenes groups of grantees who collectively decide how to allocate funds among themselves. This process fosters collaboration, mutual accountability, and a deeper sense of ownership over financial resources. A variant of shared gifting is flow-funding, in which a philanthropist directly empowers one or more individuals with donation decision-making. This both uplifts the empowered "donor" and brings greater on-the-ground community awareness and grassroots relationships into the philanthropic fold.

These shared gifting and flow-funding models challenge the notion that wealth holders alone possess the wisdom to determine where resources should flow. Instead, they acknowledge the expertise and lived experiences of those on the ground, leading to more effective and equitable resource distribution.

THE ROLE OF HIGH-NET-WORTH FAMILIES: DEPLOYING CAPITAL FOR IMPACT

For high-net-worth families and their family offices, the responsibility extends beyond philanthropy to how we invest our capital. Traditional investment strategies often prioritize returns without considering social and environmental impact. However, the growing field of impact investing provides an alternative path—one that aligns financial resources with values and long-term societal benefit.

I have been inviting wealthy families to take an active role in shaping the future by investing in companies and initiatives that prioritize sustainability, ethical governance, and social equity, and I am hopeful many more will join. This shift requires moving away from speculative wealth accumulation and toward investments that generate meaningful change, whether through supporting regenerative agriculture, renewable energy, or equitable housing solutions.

DEMOCRATIZING OWNERSHIP: A RADICAL WEALTH-SHARING MODEL

A visionary idea I explore is the concept of democratizing ownership by integrating customers into the ownership structure of the businesses they support. Imagine a model where every purchase contributes to fractional ownership in a company, gradually building wealth for consumers rather than consolidating it within corporate boardrooms. Such a system could address the wealth divide by allowing those who traditionally only participate in the economy as consumers to become equity stakeholders.

This model faces legal and logistical challenges, yet its potential to revolutionize economic participation is profound. By breaking down the barriers that separate consumers from ownership, businesses can foster a deeper sense of accountability and alignment between corporate success and community prosperity.

THE ETHICAL GUARDRAILS: BALANCING INCENTIVES AND RESPONSIBILITY

Even within progressive economic models, I acknowledge the ever-present risk of self-interest and greed. Without ethical guardrails, even well-intentioned initiatives can fall prey to the same extractive dynamics they seek to disrupt. Implementing safeguards—such as self-limiting returns for one stakeholder group, embedding mission-driven governance, and fostering community accountability—ensures that wealth serves a higher purpose rather than merely reinforcing existing disparities.

These guardrails are not constraints but rather enablers of long-term success. Just as natural ecosystems thrive through balance and self-regulation, financial and economic systems must incorporate checks that prevent over-extraction and ensure sustainable, equitable growth.

A CALL TO ACTION: LEADING WITH COURAGE AND VISION

Leadership in the modern era demands more than innovation and strategic acumen—it requires courage, humility, and a willingness to serve. The opportunity before today's entrepreneurs, executives, and wealthy families is not just to amass wealth but to redefine its purpose. By embracing models of stewardship, shared ownership, and ethical investment, we can lead a transformative shift toward an economy that benefits all, not just a privileged few.

I challenge myself and others to ask: What legacy do we wish to leave? Will we perpetuate a system that consolidates power and wealth, or will we be architects of a new paradigm—one that honors collective prosperity, environmental stewardship, and social equity? The answer lies in the hands of those willing to lead with both heart and vision.

4   TOWARD A CARING AND PARTNERSHIP ECONOMY

Beyond Capitalism and Socialism

Dr. Riane Eisler is the author of *The Chalice and the Blade*, *The Real Wealth of Nations*, and *Nurturing Our Humanity*. She is President of the Center for Partnership Systems.

Humanity is at an evolutionary turning point. A new economic operating system is urgently needed for our survival. Yet most government and business policies are still made looking through a rearview mirror.

This article outlines a new post-capitalist and post-socialist economic system that recognizes that our real wealth consists of the contributions of people and of nature. It demonstrates that we must adopt measurements, policies, and practices that recognize the enormous value of the essential work of caring for people, starting at birth, and caring for our natural life-support systems—and that the two are inextricably interconnected.

THE OLD ECONOMIC PARADIGMS

Most current proposals for a new economics are still framed by the debate between capitalism and socialism—even though both came out of early industrial times (the 1700s and 1800s), and we are now well into the 21st-century postindustrial era. On that basis alone, these economic paradigms are antiquated.

However, the problem is deeper. Our current economic operating systems came out of times when kings, emperors, sheiks, pashas, and other potentates ruled in states and tribes. These were also times when men ruled the women and children in their families. In other words, we inherited both capitalism and socialism from times when top-down, patriarchal family, social, political, and economic rankings were still the general norm.

Capitalism and socialism were actually attempts to challenge top-down economics.[1] Yet to varying degrees, both theories reflected and perpetuated old thinking, as illustrated by Marx's vision of a "dictatorship of the proletariat." Both of these economic theories also reflected the view that women should work for free in male-controlled households.

It should therefore come as no surprise that both Adam Smith and Karl Marx devalued the "women's work" of caring for people, starting at birth, as merely "reproductive" rather than "productive." Nor did they consider the "women's work" of keeping a clean and healthy home environment important in their theoretical frameworks, which focused entirely on the "men's world," which was their limited yardstick for "productive work."

When Smith and Marx formulated their theories, the work women performed was, in most jurisdictions, their father's or husband's property. As late as the 19th century (when Marx wrote), a woman could not even sue for injuries inflicted on her. Only her husband or father could sue—on the grounds that her injuries deprived him of her services, which were legally his due.[2] Neither Smith nor Marx gave any value to the work of caring for our Mother Earth. For both, nature was simply there to be exploited.[3]

So, it should not surprise us that the applications of these theories led to the despoliation and destruction of our natural life-support systems. The damage done by capitalism has been extensively reported.[4] But the two major applications of socialism, in the former Soviet Union and China, did the same, leading to environmental disasters such as the Chernobyl nuclear catastrophe, the virtual destruction of Lake Baikal, and the life-threatening air pollution of Beijing and other Chinese cities.

In light of these facts, when the scientific consensus is that climate change is leading our planet to disaster, neither capitalism nor socialism can meet our environmental challenges. Nor can they effectively address the injustices of the gap between those on top and those on the bottom.

I saw these injustices firsthand when I visited the former Soviet Union. Caviar and champagne were served to Soviet elites and their guests, while the mass of

---

1 Adam Smith, *The Wealth of Nations* (New York: Modern Library, 1937); Karl Marx, and Friedrich Engels. *Werke*. vol. 8. (Berlin: Dietz, 1960).

2 Riane Eisler, *Dissolution: No-Fault Divorce, Marriage, and the Future of Women* (New York: McGraw Hill, 1977).

3 Andrew McLaughlin, "Ecology, Capitalism, and Socialism," *Socialism and Democracy* 10, (Spring/Summer 1990): 69–102; Ted Benton, "Marxism and Natural Limits," *New Left Review* 178, (November/December, 1989): 51–86.

4 D.J. Wuebbles, D.W. Fahey, K.A. Hibbard, D.J. Dokken, B.C. Stewart, and T.K. Maycock, eds., *Climate Science Special Report: Fourth National Climate Assessment, Volume I.* (Washington, DC: U.S. Global Change Research Program, 2017).

people stood in lines for hours for the most basic necessities. And according to reports, China today has its own share of billionaires.[5] As for capitalism, it is notorious for its misdistribution of resources to those on top, a problem that has increased in recent years when the heads of U.S. companies earn over 300 times what workers do.[6] Poverty also persists under both systems, as we see today, not only in China but also in the United States, which has the highest child poverty rates of any developed nation.[7]

While capitalism brought an expanding middle class and socialism somewhat mitigated extreme poverty in China and the USSR, the many failures of both systems have led some people to believe there is no hope. But there is another way, the way of *partnerism*, which has been emerging in nations such as Finland, Sweden, and Norway. These are *not* socialist nations, as their thriving business sectors demonstrate. What they often call themselves is *caring societies.* And, as I will develop in this article, they have been moving toward a *caring economics of partnerism.*[8]

ECONOMICS AND SOCIAL SYSTEMS

Understanding why an economic system does, or does not, pay attention to caring for people and nature requires a new way of looking at economics. Economics do not just arise in a vacuum. Economics are affected by, and in turn affect, their larger social context.

However, understanding this interactive process requires leaving our comfort zones of familiar social categories, such as Eastern vs. Western, Southern vs. Northern, capitalist vs. socialist, rightist vs. leftist, religious vs. secular, industrial vs. pre- or postindustrial.

To begin with, there have been regressive, violent, repressive, and inequitable societies in all the above categories, and each only focuses on particular aspects of a society, such as location, economics, government ideology, faith, or technology. Moreover—and this is vital—they have all marginalized or ignored the majority of humanity: women and children.

By contrast, the inclusive whole-systems social categories of the *partnership system* (vs. *the domination system*) pay particular attention to the cultural construction of these foundational human relations, especially in family and other intimate relationships. And because no society is a pure partnership or

---

5 BBC, "The World's Top CEOs and Their Pay," http://www.bbc.com/news/business-37640156

6 *Fortune*, "CEO vs. Worker Pay," http://fortune.com/2015/06/22/ceo-vs-worker-pay/

7 Center for Partnership Studies, https://centerforpartnership.org/

8 Riane Eisler, *The Real Wealth of Nations: Creating a Caring Economics.* (San Francisco: Berrett-Koehler, 2007.)

domination system, once we shift to this holistic way of classifying societies, we can use the illuminating lens of the *partnership/domination social scale*.[9]

From the perspective of the partnership/domination social scale, we can see that neoliberalism is *not* a new capitalist phenomenon: it is a regression to an *economics of domination*. "Trickledown economics" is actually just another version of an *economics of domination* where, as in feudal times, those on the bottom are socialized to content themselves with the scraps dropping from the opulent tables of those on top. In other words, it is one more version of an ancient economics of top-down domination, whether it is tribal, feudal, or mercantilist, Eastern or Western, ancient or modern, capitalist or socialist.[10]

This economics of domination did not arise in a vacuum. It is embedded in the *social configuration of domination systems*. We are not used to looking at economics from this whole-systems perspective, but basically, economic priorities are determined not only by what is available, but by what is, or is not, valued. And what is valued or not valued is determined by the norms, values, and ethics of either domination or partnership-oriented social systems.

We see the domination configuration in the most repressive and violent societies of modern times—be they secular like Hitler's Western rightist Germany and Kim Jong-un's Eastern leftist North Korea, or religious like fundamentalist Iran, the Taliban, and the MAGA movement and its underlying culture in the U.S.

First, all have an authoritarian structure in *both* the family and the state or tribe. *Second*, the male half of humanity is ranked over the female half, and with this comes a *gendered system of values* in which anything associated with masculinity in domination systems (e.g., conquest and violence) is deemed superior to the stereotypically feminine (e.g., nonviolence and caring). *Third*, abuse and violence are built into the system (from child and wife beating to pogroms, lynchings, and aggressive warfare), since they are needed to maintain rigid top-down rankings: man over man, man over woman, race over race, religion over religion, tribe over tribe, or nation over nation.[11]

In more equitable and peaceful partnership-oriented societies, we see a

---

9 Riane Eisler, "Building a Caring Democracy: Four Cornerstones for an Integrated Progressive Agenda." *Interdisciplinary Journal of Partnership Studies* 4, no. 1, (2017): Article 2, http://pubs.lib.umn.edu/ijps/vol4/iss1/2; Riane Eisler and Douglas Fry, *Nurturing Our Humanity: How Domination and Partnership Shape Our Brains, Lives, and Future* (Oxford University Press, 2019).

10 Riane Eisle, "Roadmap to a Caring Economics: Beyond Capitalism and Socialism," *Interdisciplinary Journal of Partnership Studies* 4, no 1 (2017): Article 3, https://pubs.lib.umn.edu/ijps/vol4/iss1/3.

11 Riane Eisler, *The Chalice and the Blade: Our History, Our Future*. (San Francisco: Harper Collins, 1987, 2017).

very different configuration. *First*, families and tribes or nations are more democratic and egalitarian. There are still parents, teachers, managers, and leaders, but they exercise power through *hierarchies of actualization* where accountability, respect, and benefits flow both ways rather than just from the bottom up, and power is empowering rather than disempowering as in *hierarchies of domination*. *Second*, equal value is given to both the female and male halves of humanity, and in contrast to the rigid gender stereotypes of the domination system, nonviolence and care are valued in women, men, and everyone in between, as well as in social and economic policy. *Third*, abusive and violent behaviors are not systematically built into social institutions, as they are not required to maintain rigid rankings of domination.[12]

Societies orienting to the partnership system's configuration also transcend familiar categories. They can be technologically undeveloped foraging societies, as shown by the research of anthropologist Douglas Fry and others.[13] As revealed by archeological excavations finally getting some attention, they can be egalitarian prehistoric farming cultures like Catal Huyuk, where there are no signs of destruction through warfare for 1,000 years and no signs of inequality between women and men.[14] They can be technologically advanced "high civilizations" like Minoan Crete, where women played leading roles, there was a generally high standard of living, and there are no signs of warfare between the various city-states on the island.[15]

They can also be modern societies like Finland, Sweden, and Norway, which at the beginning of the 20th century were so poor that there were famines. As detailed in my book, *The Real Wealth of Nations*, caring policies were a major factor in the economic transformation of these nations, which today have low poverty and crime rates and a generally high standard of living for all. These countries pioneered generous paid parental leave for both mothers and fathers, stipends to help families raise children, elder care with dignity, universal health care, good quality childcare, and other caring policies. In addition, they have been at the forefront of moving toward renewable energy and other policies that recognize the necessity of caring for nature.

Contrary to popular beliefs—and I want to emphasize this—the reason these nations invest more in caring for people and nature is *not* that they are small and relatively homogeneous. There are also nations that are small and relatively homogeneous that are far from being caring societies. What really

---

12 Ibid.

13 Douglas Fry, ed., *War, Peace, and Human Nature: The Convergence of Evolutionary and Cultural Views*. (New York: Oxford University Press, 2013).

14 Ian Hodder, "Women and Men at Catalhoyuk," *Scientific American*, January, 2004: 77–83.

15 Nikolas Platon, *Crete*. (Geneva: Nagel Publishers, 1966).

lies behind their more caring policies is something else: their movement toward the partnership side of the partnership-domination social scale.

SHIFTING FROM DOMINATION TO PARTNERSHIP

If we look at modern history from this new perspective, we see that every progressive social movement has challenged the same thing: an entrenched tradition of domination. The 18th-century "rights of man" Enlightenment movement challenged the supposedly divinely ordained right of kings to rule their "subjects." The feminist movement challenged the supposedly divinely ordained right of men to rule women and children in the "castles" (a military term) of their homes. The 19th and 20th century abolitionist, civil rights, and anti-colonial movements challenged the divinely ordained right of a supposedly "superior" race to rule over "inferior" ones. The 19th, 20th, and 21st century peace movements, and the more recent movement to end traditions of violence in families, all challenge the use of fear and force to maintain domination in our relations. The environmental movement challenges another tradition of domination: the once hallowed conquest of nature, which at our level of technological development could take us to an evolutionary dead end.

Just a few hundred years ago, the European Middle Ages were still oriented closely to the domination side of the social scale. While there were some partnership elements, with its Inquisition (where you got tortured and killed for any deviation from official thinking), its Crusades (holy wars), and its witch-burnings (where, by the most conservative estimates, 100,000 women were tortured and killed, a huge number considering the low European population of that time, and it may have actually numbered in the millions), this period had the domination configuration. Not only did women and children have no rights, but the concept of human rights would have been considered insane. So, also, would any challenge to the established order of rigid top-down rankings. As St. Augustine famously declared, for anyone to even think of changing their station in life was like a nose wanting to be an eye.[16]

Yet our forward movement has not been linear, it has been more like an upward spiral with dips. Not only has it been fiercely resisted every inch of the way, it has also been punctuated by massive regressions back to the domination side of the social scale.

I was born into a brutal domination regression when the Nazis came to power in my native Austria. And we are clearly in a domination regression today in the United States as well as in other world regions.

---

16 Roy Baumeister, "How the Self Became a Problem: A Psychological Review of Historical Research," *Journal of Personality and Social Psychology* 52 no.1 (1987): 163–176.

Although this is obscured if we look at this regression through the lenses of our conventional categories, a major reason for them is that most of the energy and resources of the modern progressive movements I just mentioned focused on dismantling the top of the domination pyramid: politics and economics as conventionally defined. Far less attention has been given to changing traditions of domination and violence in our foundational human relations: our parent-child and gender relations.

Today we know from neuroscience that what we experience and observe as children in our early years affects how our brains themselves develop. And, we are increasingly understanding how abuse-trauma cycles perpetuate and amplify this dysfunction throughout society. So it is on these foundations that domination systems have kept rebuilding themselves in different forms: whether secular or religious, Eastern or Western, and so on.

Once we understand these psycho-social dynamics, we can more effectively work to change what is happening right now in the United States. We can see something I have closely studied: those in the United States pushing us back toward authoritarianism, violence, and in-group vs. out-group scapegoating have for decades invested enormous resources and energy in maintaining or reinstating the domination character of four interconnected cornerstones for domination systems:

1. family and childhood relations (appropriating family, values, and morality);
2. gender relations (demonizing gender partnership and gender fluidity);
3. economics (promoting trickle-down economics instead of foundational equity);
4. and narratives and language that justify top-down control (like claiming that the only good family is one in which the father is master of the house).

We also see that those who want to return us to more rigid domination norms were extremely successful, especially in claiming that the only good family is one that is controlled from the top by a man. Polls show that in the first decade of the 21st century the percentage of Americans who agreed that "the father of the family is master of the house" jumped from 42% to 52%.[17]

But consider that this kind of family is where children learn, before their brains, much less their critical faculties, are fully formed, to accept strongman

---

17 Riane Eisler, "The Ignored Issue That Can Get Progressives Elected." *AlterNet*, September 13, 2007, http://www.alternet.org/story/60596/ or https://centerforpartnership.org/wp-content/uploads/2015/11/The-Ignored-Issue-That-Can-Get-Progressives-Elected.pdf.

rule in the state or tribe. However, to see this, we have to "connect the dots" by leaving behind our conventional categories, which serve to fragment our consciousness.

The current scapegoating of African Americans and immigrants, misogyny, machismo, and idealization of "strongman" rule in *both* the family and the state are not disconnected. They are all elements of a regression to top-down family, political, and economic rule—in other words, a regression to the domination side of the social scale.

CONNECTING THE DOTS

We must take into account that if children grow up in cultures or subcultures where economic injustice and even violence in families are accepted as normal and moral, they learn basic lessons that support domination systems. And while not everyone growing up in these settings accepts these lessons, as we see all around us, many people do. We humans are generally super-malleable when it comes to moral standards, especially in response to so-called "authority" figures, as the Milgram Experiment strikingly demonstrated.

One basic lesson that children learn in domination families is the in-group versus out-group thinking, feeling, and acting. And here again we come back to gender roles and relations, because what children learn in domination families is to equate difference—beginning with the most fundamental difference in our species between the male and female forms—with either superiority or inferiority, dominating or being dominated, being served or serving.

This lesson is particularly relevant to economics, as it provides a model of inequality in human relations that children internalize. Long before their critical faculties are developed, children learn that it is normal and moral for one kind of person to serve and another kind to be served—a model they can then apply to other differences, whether based on race, religion, ethnicity, or any other apparent difference.

As noted earlier, in the more rigid domination systems we have struggled to leave behind, women and their labor were male property. Their life-sustaining activities, like those of nature, were simply there to be exploited by the "superior" male half of the species. That was obviously bad for women; but it was also bad for men and everyone in between. Because, along with the subordination and devaluation of the female half of humanity came a gendered system of values in which anything associated with women or the "feminine"—like the essential work of caring for people and keeping a clean and healthy environment—was also subordinated and devalued. *And as long as caring is devalued, we cannot realistically expect more caring policies.*

We would not have global warming, we would not have such huge investments in weapons and wars, we would not have so much poverty, hunger, and misery worldwide, if we had an economic system that recognizes the enormous value of caring for people and for nature.

Today, when climate change threatens our life support systems, it is more essential than ever that we support the work of caring for nature. The same is true for supporting the work of caring for people.

In fact, we can make a purely financial case for recognizing the value of the work of caring for people. As we move into the post-industrial age, when automation, robotics, and artificial intelligence have already replaced many jobs and are predicted to continue to do so at an exponential rate,[18] a time when economists tell us that the most important capital is what they call "high quality human capital," it is economically essential that we support the work of caring for people, starting in early childhood. The reason, as we know from neuroscience, is that whether our human capacities develop or not largely hinges on the quality of care and education children receive early on.

STEPS TOWARD A CARING ECONOMICS

Moving beyond the old argument about socialism versus capitalism, and vice versa, does not mean leaving everything from these old economic systems behind. We must strengthen the partnership elements in both the market and government economies and leave their domination elements behind. But we must go further to a new economic system that recognizes what these two old systems do not: that the real wealth of nations consists of the contributions of people and of nature.

My book *The Real Wealth of Nations: Creating a Caring Economics*[19] outlines key components of this new economics of *partnerism*, as well as building blocks for its construction. I want to briefly describe four of these.

1. A first step toward *partnerism* is changing how we measure economic health. Currently, policymakers heavily rely on GDP/GNP. These measures, developed over one hundred years ago, include as "productive" many activities that harm and destroy life (e.g., selling cigarettes and unhealthy fast foods, and the resulting medical and funeral costs). They do not subtract "externalities" (e.g., costs of natural disasters produced by climate change, instead *adding*

18 Kevin Drum, "You Will Lose Your Job to a Robot—and Sooner than You Think." *Mother Jones*, November/December 2017, http://www.motherjones.com/politics/2017/10/you-will-lose-your-job-to-a-robot-and-sooner-than-you-think/

19 Riane Eisler, *The Real Wealth of Nations: Creating a Caring Economics* (San Francisco: Berrett-Koehler, 2007).

to GDP the expenses of cleaning up and rebuilding). And they fail to include as "productive" the work of caring for people in households, despite studies showing that if the value of this work were counted it would constitute between 30-50% of the reported GDP.[20]

In response to the need for more accurate and forward-looking metrics to guide policymakers, the Center for Partnership Systems, together with a group of prominent economists, developed the first iteration of Social Wealth Economic Indicators (SWEIs).[21] SWEIs demonstrate the economic value of the work of caring for people and nature, the benefits of investing in it, and the costs of not doing so.

Social Wealth Economic Indicators measure two interconnected factors. The first is the state of a nation's *human capacity development*, as shown by data such as child poverty rates, enrollment in early childhood education, gender and racial equity, educational attainment, and ecological deficit/returns. The second is a nation's *care investment*; for example, public spending on family benefits, funding for childcare and education, and government and business investment in environmental protection.

By measuring both *inputs* (investments) and *outputs* (where a society stands), unlike other "GDP alternatives" that only provide a snapshot of current conditions, SWEIs further show that outputs (human capacity development) are heavily dependent on inputs (care investment). For example, there is a connection between the fact that the United States has the highest child poverty rates of any major developed nation and that it invests the least in early childhood education and support for childcare in families.

2. A second step toward *partnerism* is demonstrating that ending the devaluation of care work is essential to cut through seemingly intractable cycles of poverty. The Center for Partnership Systems' website provides activists and policymakers with resources such as Social Wealth Economic Indicators, as well as online courses to do just that.

These resources highlight the need for high-quality and well-paid early childcare and education, and the enormous long-term costs of not investing in policies that support these—from intergenerational patterns of poverty linked to low levels of human capacity development to crime and the attendant prison, court, and other taxpayer-supported costs.

They also take into account that, worldwide, women are the mass of the poor and the poorest of the poor, and that even in our wealthy United States,

---

20 Indradeep Gosh et al., *Social Wealth Economic Indicators: A New System for Evaluating Economic Prosperity* (Pacific Grove, CA: Center for Partnership Studies, 2014).

21 Ibid.

according to U.S. Census Bureau figures, women over the age of 65 are twice as likely to live in poverty as men of the same age.[22] This poverty is not only due to job discrimination, but to the devaluation of care work: most of these women are or were either full-time or part-time caregivers.

3. A third step toward *partnerism* is developing a cohesive family policy so progressives can reclaim family, values, and morality from their hijacking by regressives. To this end, the Center for Partnership Systems developed the "Family Security Agenda" designed to appeal to both "liberal" and "conservative" voters.[23]

The Family Security Agenda focuses on reducing family stress, cutting through cycles of poverty, and producing the "high-quality human capital" needed for our postindustrial age. Its provisions include support for the care work done for free in families (such as child care, elder care, and increasingly both), which are a major source of economic and psychological stress, especially to middle-class and low-income U.S. families. The Family Security Agenda includes policies to raise the wages of caregivers, which are so low that many have to turn to welfare. It proposes policies that make effective education a priority, starting with affordable high high-quality early childhood education.

In addition, the Family Security Agenda identifies funding sources for its provisions by taxing and/or penalizing activities that are harmful or useless for our nation's well-being. These include closing the carried interest loophole, enacting stiff luxury goods purchase taxes, taxing very short-term stock market transactions, and increasing civil penalties for businesses that engage in activities that harm people and nature.

4. A fourth step toward a caring economics of *partnerism* is providing evidence that investing in the work of caring for people and nature is profitable for both businesses and nations. *The Real Wealth of Nations* shows how businesses that have good paid parental leave, sick leave, flex time, and other caring policies have a higher yield to investors.

We also have evidence that these policies provide nations with a path to an equitable and thriving economy.[24] Consider that their caring policies were a major factor in the economic transformation of the nations mentioned earlier: the Nordic nations that every year are highest in the world happiness reports

---

22 U.S. Census Bureau, "Facts for Features: Mother's Day 2015, https://www.census.gov/newsroom/facts-for-features/2015/cb15-ff09.html.

23 Center for Partnership Studies, https://centerforpartnership.org/

24 Center for Partnership Studies, https://centerforpartnership.org/

(a remarkable feat, considering that the long darkness of their location has been associated with unhappiness, and even suicide).

First, these more equitable nations paid particular attention to family and childhood relations. In addition to the caring policies to help families and children mentioned earlier, they pioneered legislation that makes it against the law to physically discipline children in families, which is considered normal and moral in domination systems.

Second, these nations are at the forefront of the move toward gender equity in both the family and the state. They have the lowest gender gaps in the world, and women make up about half the national legislatures. But it is not only women who voted for caring policies. As the status of women rises, so also do "feminine" values and activities. In other words, as women and the feminine are no longer culturally devalued, men too can embrace "soft" values and activities as part of their "masculinity," rather than conforming to the dominator maxim that "real men" can never be like "inferior" women.

Third, these nations have been at the forefront of trying to leave behind traditions of violence. In addition to their laws against violence toward children in families, they pioneered the first peace studies programs. And, since it is in early family relations that children first learn whether or not it is okay to use violence to impose one's will on others, nonviolence in families and in the family of nations are inextricably interconnected.[25]

This is why the Center for Partnership Systems is working on a campaign for nonviolent families, which will show the link between violence in families and the violence of war and terrorism, and change our language from "domestic violence" (which is so marginalizing) to family violence or violence in families. I invite you to join us!

CONCLUSION

We cannot meet our unprecedented environmental, economic, and social challenges with the same thinking that created them. As Einstein famously said, "We cannot solve problems with the same consciousness that created them."

The mix of high technology and domination systems is today causing terrible damage and threatening our very survival as a species. This makes the need for an economic system that, unlike capitalism and socialism, recognizes and

---

25 Riane Eisler, "Protecting the Majority of Humanity: Toward an Integrated Approach to Crimes against Present and Future Generations," in *Sustainable Development, International Criminal Justice, and Treaty Implementation*, eds. Marie-Claire Cordonier Segger and Sébastien Jodoin (Cambridge, U.K.: Cambridge University Press, 2013), https://centerforpartnership.org/wp-content/uploads/2015/11/Protecting-the-Majority-of-Humanity.pdf; Madhusree Mukerjee, "Interview with Riane Eisler," *Scientific American*, 2023, https://www.scientificamerican.com/article/how-family-trauma-perpetuates-authoritarian-societies/

rewards the essential work of caring for nature and for people more urgent than ever before.

Our current technological dislocations are a crisis. But they are also an opportunity to develop the new economic paradigm of *partnerism* that recognizes that economic systems are affected by, and in turn affect, the larger social system in which they are embedded.

The good news is that we do not have to start from square one. There are already millions of individuals and organizations all over the world working to shift to a healthier and more caring economic system, including many referenced throughout this book. But what has been missing is an integrated progressive social and economic agenda that no longer devalues women and the "soft" or stereotypically feminine activities like caring and caregiving, focuses on children, and provides us with the new language and conceptual frames of partnership systems, *partnerism* and caring economics, instead of domination systems.

Together, we can create and implement this agenda. What distinguishes us as humans is our enormous capacities for consciousness, caring, and creativity. We must use these gifts to construct the new caring economics of *partnerism*, beginning with the building blocks described above: new metrics; ending the disproportionate poverty of women and children; implementing a cohesive family policy agenda; demonstrating the economic return from investing in caring for people and nature and working together to shift social institutions and values from domination to partnership.

This will not be easy or instantaneous. But if we are to have a more sustainable and equitable future, perhaps even a future at all, we must join together in this essential enterprise—starting right now.

Dr. Robert Cloninger

(original article republished with permission by Dr. Cloninger and
Mens Sana Monograph, 2013;11:16-24)

5 WHAT MAKES PEOPLE HEALTHY, HAPPY, AND FULFILLED IN THE FACE OF CURRENT WORLD CHALLENGES

Dr. Robert Cloninger is Director of the Anthropedia Institute, Professor Emeritus at Washington University, St. Louis, and wrote *Feeling Good and Origins of Altruism and Cooperation.*

INTRODUCTION

Research in the science of well-being has recently suggested a need to revise outdated traditional concepts of a healthy personality by recognising the character features that facilitate adaptation to current challenges to the survival of humanity (Cloninger and Zohar, 2011; Cloninger and Kedia, 2011). As I described in a previous work, *Mens Sana Monograph*, it is an unfortunate fact that war, greed, and divisive propaganda dominate the world stage at present despite the remarkable human capacities for compassion, generosity, and self-awareness (Cloninger, 2008). As long as human beings were able to treat the world as an unlimited resource to be consumed indiscriminately, it was sufficient to regard people who were self-directed and cooperative as healthy, even if they were also low in self-transcendence (Cloninger and Kedia, 2011). For example, Freud suggested that healthy people were those who were capable of working and loving; he regarded spirituality as immature wishful thinking (Freud, 1927). This concept of a well-organised character with low self-transcendence is still the favoured social norm in many Western cultures (Josefsson et al., 2012). The organised character has even been proposed as a description of healthy personality in DSM-5 (Cloninger, 2010).

However, since 1986, human utilisation of resources has exceeded the capacity of the planet to replenish itself (Wackernagel et al., 2002). Consequently, the characteristics of healthy people must be revised to recognise the need for people to live sustainably in appreciation of the needs of humanity as a whole and the capacity of the world environment to support those needs. The changing world conditions reveal the crucial advantages that the creative character structure with high self-transcendence has over the organised character with low self-transcendence.

First, I will review data about the well-being of different character configurations from recent research on the science of well-being based on well-validated procedures for quantifying character profiles with standardised scores using the Temperament and Character Inventory (TCI) (Cloninger, 2010; Cloninger et al., 1993). This indicates that the organised and creative characters are the healthiest and were probably about equal in fitness as long as the capacity of the planet to replenish itself exceeded human demands on its resources.

Second, I will review data about the current devastation and depletion of the planet Earth under the current leadership of the world by people with organised characters who are generally low in self-transcendence.

Third, I will discuss the flaws in organised and immature characters that lead to denial or fear of recognising the imperative need for changing current ways of life in order to be prepared for adaptation to the uncertain future conditions of life on Earth.

Fourth, I will outline how the self-transcendence of creative characters facilitates flexible and resilient adaptation in harmony with other people and nature. This suggests that the spiritual development of greater self-transcendence is the key to the future of human survival as a species, not continued prolific reproduction, wasteful consumption, military power, or technological innovation. The survival of human beings depends on the spiritual evolution of greater plasticity, virtue, and farsighted functioning. The conditions needed for such spiritual evolution and development are described elsewhere using evidence-based methods of health promotion and therapeutics that integrate available ways to facilitate the development of human plasticity, functioning, and virtue (Cloninger, 2006; Cloninger et al., 2010; Cloninger and Cloninger, 2011).

RELATIONS OF WELLBEING TO CHARACTER PROFILES

Physical, mental, and social wellbeing all depend strongly on profiles of the character traits of self-directedness, cooperativeness, and self-transcendence as measured by the Temperament and Character Inventory (TCI) (Cloninger, 2004; Cloninger et al., 2010; Cloninger and Zohar, 2011; Josefsson et al., 2011). The clinical characteristics and dynamics of the course of development of all possible configurations of these personality traits have been described in detail elsewhere (Cloninger, 2004; Josefsson et al., 2012). Here, only the most and least healthy configurations will be considered because of their crucial importance in defining what constitutes a healthy personality under current world conditions. When high and low extremes of these three character traits are considered, the healthiest people are high in both self-directedness and cooperativeness consistently, and the least healthy and most immature are those who are low in both these traits (Cloninger et al., 1993). Among these relatively healthy people, two profile types can be distinguished:

- **The "organised" characters**, that is, those who are high in selfdirectedness (S), high in cooperativeness (C), and low in self-transcendence (T).
- **The "creative" characters**, that is, those who are high in selfdirectedness (S), cooperativeness (C), and self-transcendence (T).

The "creative" characters are usually happier than the "organised" characters, but the two types have similar physical and social health in contemporary Western societies (Cloninger and Zohar, 2011; Josefsson et al., 2011).

The "organised" character structure is typical of leaders and other successful people in Western society. People with organised characters are highly self-confident, resourceful, purposeful, and responsible (i.e., high in self-directedness). In addition, they are highly tolerant, helpful, and forgiving (i.e., high in cooperativeness). Finally, they are low in self-transcendence, so they are primarily concerned with their own interests and those whom they regard as friends or associates with common goals and interests. They are often rather conventional, materialistic, and practical rather than being meditative, intuitive, or spiritual. As a result, the organised character is a strong-willed, practical, and goal-oriented leader driven by achieving personal goals. Paradoxically, the strong-willed "organisation man" is often a social conformist who manages his or her reputation studiously because underneath the confidence is an outlook of separateness that leaves him or her concerned about noncompliance with local social norms. Consequently, organised characters are resistant to radical change or revolutionary shifts in their outlook on life, preferring to maintain dogmatic beliefs and the status quo rather than to question the validity of assumptions they have relied upon with success in the past, thereby justifying their description as "organised" (Cloninger, 2004).

In contrast, "creative" characters are typical of the positive philosophers and leaders of civilisation during times of the Renaissance and the Enlightenment (Cloninger, 2004). People with a creative character have the same capacity for resourceful productivity and helpful cooperation as those with organised characters, but are also more intuitive and meditative. They identify with nature, humanity, and perhaps the divine or the universe as a spiritual whole. The creative character is driven by interest in coherence and is guided by their intuition to express their potential through self-realisation in harmony with others and nature. They are not eccentric for its own sake because they are developing toward harmony and integration. They are more tolerant of ambiguity and uncertainty than organised characters and more receptive to radical change in outlook when there is a realistic and innovative basis for doing so, thereby justifying their description as "creative" (Cloninger, 2004).

Selftranscendence is a necessary but not a sufficient character trait for well-being. It is noteworthy that people are often unhealthy, unhappy, and unrealistic when they report being high in self-transcendence but are low in self-directedness (Cloninger et al., 2010; Cloninger and Zohar, 2011). Such individuals have schizotypal characteristics with frequent magical thinking rather than the mature spirituality characteristic of creative characters. Hence, it is the combination of strong development of all three character traits that typifies people who are healthy, happy, and fulfilled (Cloninger, 2004).

The importance of all three character traits is further evidenced by the findings of "third-wave psychotherapies" that have sought to address the limitations of earlier "behavioural" and "cognitive-behavioural" approaches (Cloninger, 2004; Cloninger, 2006; Cloninger et al., 2010). Cognitive-behavioural therapies are effective in promoting self-directedness and cooperativeness, but do not address self-transcendence. In contrast, third-wave psychotherapies, such as Mindfulness-Based Cognitive-Behavioural Therapy, Dialectical Behaviour Therapy, and Acceptance and Commitment Therapy, reduce dropouts and improve physical, mental, and social health outcomes by adding mindfulness and related spiritual practices that also promote self-transcendence (Cloninger, 2004; Cloninger, 2006; Cloninger et al., 2010).

WORLD DEVASTATION BY UNSUSTAINABLE CONSUMPTION

Sustainable living requires that people consume no more resources than the Earth can replenish annually. Unfortunately, since about 1986, people have consumed more than the Earth is able to restore, leading to depletion of irreplaceable resources and degradation of local ecosystems around the world (Wackernagel et al., 2002[20]). The industrialisation and excessive consumption patterns are leading to many interdependent problems, including global warming, acidification of oceans, widespread food and water shortages, depletion of common elements (zinc, copper, nickel, and phosphorus), and global economic stagnation (Ahmed, 2010[1]). Only 10% of the land surface of the Earth is arable, and its capacity is being exceeded by population growth from 2.5 billion in 1944 to 7 billion today, and by degradation of soil from chemically based monoculture farming by agribusiness that neglects principles of soil biology. The rising atmospheric level of carbon dioxide from industrial activity is an unsustainable threat to all life including our own: We are in the midst of the sixth great mass extinction event on the Earth with one-third of all known species of plants and animals already threatened and half of all species expected to become extinct within one lifetime (Cloninger, 2009[8]; Barnosky et al., 2012[2]). The degradation of local ecosystems is expected to encompass 50% of the planet by 2025, thereby approaching an irreversible tipping point at which the global ecology of our planet may shift radically to conditions that human beings have never had to adapt to at any time in the past (Barnosky et al., 2012[2]).

Not all countries are equally responsible for the unsustainable destruction of the human habitat. If everyone lived like the average resident of the United States of America, we would need more than four planets like Earth to support human demands. We would need more than two planets like Earth to support the consumption of residents in Europe or Russia. In contrast, one planet can currently support the demands of two countries with consumption patterns like those of the average resident of India. Nevertheless, the devastation of the planet by greedy cultures will have catastrophic effects on the whole Earth, creating severe challenges for human survival as the effects of global warming and depletion of soil, water, and minerals activate a vicious cycle of feedback systems (Lynas, 2008[18]).

WHY ARE MOST PEOPLE IN A STATE OF FEAR OR DENIAL?

In the past five great mass extinctions, the dominant animal species became extinct. However, human beings have evolved the capacity for self-awareness, which enables us to have foresight about the long-term consequences of what we are doing (Sussman and Cloninger, 2011[19]). In the words of Sir Julian Huxley, human beings are "evolution conscious of itself" (Huxley, 1959[15]).

Unfortunately, we are not using our capacity for self-awareness well. Despite frequent past warnings by scientists and an occasional politician like Al Gore, it is commonplace for people to deny the danger of human extinction posed by our excessive consumption or to react with unreasoning fears like survivalists preparing for an imminent doomsday by fortification and saving several months' worth of food and water. Most political leaders pander to people's fears and appeal to their immediate self-interest, rather than acting with responsibility and foresight for the well-being of humanity as a whole. Speculative promises are made that future technological innovations will magically solve all our problems without requiring any serious changes in lifestyle.

Why do intelligent people revert to a state of fear or denial? I suggest that the main reason can be found in the weakness of individuals with organised character profiles, which is the socially favoured profile in secular Western cultures (Josefsson et al., 2012[17]). People are born with a natural need for virtues like fairness and equality that is expressed as self-aware consciousness develops (Fehr et al., 2008[13]). However, in Western cultures, social norm-favouring leads to increases in self-directedness and cooperativeness along with decreases in self-transcendence between the ages of 20 and 45 years; self-transcendence only rises again later as people face ultimate situations like their own mortality (Josefsson et al., 2012[17]). Unfortunately, organised characters are not self-transcendent: They are largely motivated by their self-interests and the interests they share with those close to them. As a result, they strive to maintain their own power and wealth regardless of the consequences for others who are remote. They want to believe that their efforts can allow them to maintain the conditions that have brought them success, so they are also easily manipulated by disinformation from others in positions of power and influence.

As a result, we elect leaders with organised characters who frequently serve the special interests of the wealthy and powerful rather than attending to the well-being of the electing general population or the world as a whole. The wealthy and powerful want to maintain their wealth and power, so we continue to rush toward extinction in a state of denial, relying on disinformation that is designed to manipulate and/or appease our fears. The lack of leadership by people with creative characters is putting the whole human species at risk to satisfy the blind greed of a small minority.

THE NEED FOR SELFTRANSCENDENT LIVING

Fortunately, it is not necessary for people to live in either fear or denial. Human beings are the most adaptable species on Earth, and we have a strong drive for well-being (Cloninger, 2009[8]; Cloninger and Kedia, 2011[4]). Well-being depends on functioning with foresight, plasticity, and virtue (Cloninger and Cloninger, 2011[3]). In other words, human well-being requires that we be self-transcendent in our values as well as self-directed and cooperative. People with creative characters function as conscious beings in harmony with nature and other people, not as a separate force that tries to control nature and people for self-interest.

The development of self-transcendence has a radical transformative impact on self-directedness and cooperativeness (Cloninger, 2004[9]). The purposeful striving of selfdirectedness is transformed into hope and letting go of fighting and worry. The tolerant empathy of cooperativeness is transformed into love and working in the service of others. Essentially, an outlook of unity (i.e., awareness that one is an inseparable component of a universal unity of being) allows a person to function realistically with plasticity and virtue, thereby living in sustainable harmony with nature and other people. Perhaps this is the reason that leadership during periods of the Renaissance and the Enlightenment has been characterised by the creative character rather than the organised character who has led us into the current crises of civilisation. Human life is not really sustainable without self-transcendent virtues that have regrettably been relativised and/or neglected in postmodern times.

CONCLUSIONS [SEE ALSO FIGURE 1: FLOWCHART OF PAPER]

At the present point of human evolution, a healthy person needs to be self-transcendent as well as self-directed and cooperative. The human species is now being endangered by the self-centred behaviour of people who are low in self-transcendence. This suggests that the future well-being of humanity depends on a spiritual evolution that will further develop the extent to which we are self-aware of our participation in a universal unity of being. Syntactic language, art, science, and spirituality are all expressions of our capacity for self-aware consciousness. However, our self-awareness must now be expanded and deepened for us to face the challenges of our current world situation with foresight, plasticity, and virtue.

Figure 1: Flowchart of Paper

➢ Both "Organised" (SCt) and "Creative" (SCT) characters are healthy when self-interested behaviour is tolerable.

➢ The Earth's resources are finite and are being depleted by excessive consumption, leading to a threat of mass extinctions, including human beings.

➢ The self-centredness of organised characters is no longer tolerable.

➢ The future development of humanity depends on the development of self-transcendent virtues.

TAKE-HOME MESSAGE

For our well-being and that of humanity as a whole, we need to and can cultivate our capacity for self-transcendence by a variety of methods for promoting well-being (Cloninger, 2006[12]). These include mindfulness and contemplative exercises that broaden our perspective to an outlook of unity (Cloninger et al., 2010[6]; Cloninger and Cloninger, 2011[3]). Instead of the usual outlook of separateness that leads to fear, excessive desire, and false pride, we can approach life with a self-transcendent outlook of unity that leads to love, hope, and humility functioning to serve others, not only ourselves. In this way, we can become both selfsufficient producers and moderate consumers. In other words, we can live sustainably with respect for our necessary harmony with nature and with the generosity needed to help others in a mutually beneficial way. Individual wellbeing is always a transient illusion when it is not coupled with collective well-being.

6   SERVICE LEADERSHIP, SELF-CARE, AND GLOBAL COLLABORATION

Sarah Arao is the Founder of Mantle of Hope & Inter-Rural Action Network in Uganda. She runs the Young Climate Warriors, Hope Skilling, and Muzuri Projects.

Last year, I had the privilege of attending one of the most transformative events of my life—the Le Ciel Foundation Symposium in Barcelona, Spain. It was there that I met so many inspiring leaders, including Aaron Perry of the Y on Earth Community, and was introduced to a global network of people dedicated to planetary healing and collective well-being. I was deeply honored to be named a Global Ambassador for Y on Earth. But something even more personal happened during that gathering—something that changed the way I understood leadership itself.

On the second day of the symposium, I met a kind woman named Michele Nerverza. She looked me in the eyes and asked if I was really taking care of myself. Her words struck me, because the truth was—I wasn't. For years, I had been working with survivors of human trafficking and domestic abuse, hearing their painful stories every day. I was carrying what is known as vicarious trauma, or secondary trauma, without even realizing it. Michele introduced me to her *Beyond Emotional Intelligence* program, and that moment marked the beginning of a new chapter for me. I learned, deeply and personally, that mental health *is* health, and that self-care is not selfish—it is holistic care.

As a servant leader, your greatest strength is your ability to keep serving without burning out. We cannot pour from an empty cup. We must put on our own oxygen masks first, or what I call a "sustainable bubble of care." Burnout happens when we are exposed to prolonged stress without space to rest and replenish. Self-care is not about luxury—it's about connection: to ourselves, to our purpose, and to the world we serve. It means becoming aware of our needs, our feelings, and our limits, and taking time to nourish our bodies, minds, and spirits.

I now see self-care as deeply connected to how we care for others—and even for the Earth. Ubuntu, the ancient African principle, teaches us that *I am because we are.* This interdependence is not just between people—it extends to the entire ecosystem. We are one system. And as I've come to understand, caring for the planet is a profound form of self-care.

Six years ago, I began intentionally engaging in Earth care. I realized that I was breathing clean air, walking beneath shady trees, enjoying natural beauty—all because someone, somewhere, had cared enough to protect the environment. That realization sparked my commitment to environmental regeneration. I started planting trees. I formed a group called the Young Climate Warriors Club. We work with youth to promote not just environmental awareness, but holistic wellness—connecting self-care with caring for the planet and all life on it.

One of my favorite quotes comes from Munia Khan:

> *"Trees exhale for us so that we can inhale them to stay alive.*
> *Can we ever forget that?"*

This is why we must love trees with every breath we take.

Some may wonder—how is this self-care? Isn't this about nature, the planet, the environment? Yes—and that is exactly the point. True self-care is not isolated or individualistic. It is about *flourishing as a full human being.* And being fully human means being in relationship: with our communities, our values, our ancestors, and the Earth.

There is a deep and growing recognition of this connection. Climate psychologists speak about *eco-anxiety*—the fear and grief people feel about environmental degradation and climate collapse. Some even speak of *pre-traumatic stress*—the anticipation of future trauma. These are real and valid emotional responses to what we are collectively facing. But they can be met with action, with presence, and with care.

As climate author Anouchka Grose writes:

> *"Look after yourself, others, and the planet. All three, equally.*
> *You won't be able to do the last two if you don't do the first one.*
> *It's not selfish, it's kind."*

When we plant a tree, when we breathe with the Earth, when we care for the water, soil, and skies—we are practicing a form of care that includes all beings, including ourselves. With the Young Climate Warriors, I encourage children and youth to see tree planting as an act of healing—for their future and for their well-being now. When I walk through my village in Lira District and see those trees growing, I feel hope. The trees we plant here can benefit the entire planet. Our roots are local, but our impact is global.

My leadership journey has grown even stronger through collaboration. The partnerships that began at the Le Ciel Symposium—especially with Y on Earth—have flourished into deep, nourishing connections. These networks don't just raise visibility; they feed the soul. Being in community with other leaders around the world—sharing experiences, exchanging wisdom, and supporting one another—gives me strength, clarity, and resilience.

This is one of the great gifts of today's digital platforms. Through Y on Earth and other global networks, I've found spaces where leaders are learning from one another and growing together. I've had the chance to develop local programs in Uganda—like the Social Innovation Academy—that are connected to a broader ecosystem. Together, we are building a kind of "home base" where young people can access resources, mentorship, and opportunities while remaining grounded in their own communities.

I often think of these connections as *colliders*—spaces of untapped potential, where people from different cultures, sectors, and generations come together to create something greater than any one of us could do alone. It's in these spaces that real transformation happens.

Looking ahead, I am excited by the possibilities emerging through platforms like Y on Earth and Ecoscene. These are more than websites or social networks—they are living ecosystems of collaboration, consciousness, and care. They are building bridges between grassroots action and global vision, helping to resource and amplify those who are doing the work on the ground. These platforms hold the potential to shift how we think about leadership, economics, health, and planetary stewardship. And they do so while honoring ancient wisdom, cultural diversity, and spiritual resilience.

As a servant leader, I know my journey is not about individual achievement. It is about relationship, regeneration, and responsibility. It is about showing up each day to serve others, while also honoring my own sacred breath and body. It is about listening to the Earth, listening to my heart, and listening to those whose voices have been silenced or marginalized.

Through my work, I hope to offer a small contribution to the larger movement—a movement that is reconnecting us to what truly matters: love, justice, community, and the living world. As Jane Yolen reminds us, *"I am the Earth and the Earth is me."*

This is the heart of my leadership: rooted in care, grown in connection, and offered in service to the whole.

7 LEADING REGENERATION

The Shortest Route Is Not a Straight Line

Kate Williams is CEO of 1% for the Planet and serves on several Boards of Directors, including BlueCross BlueShield of Vermont and Shelburne Farms.

Companies. Organizations. Institutions. Start-ups. Enterprises. These are all different names for the organizing frameworks we create to align a group or groups of people around the implementation of an idea. These entities are complex things with enormous significance for how humans interact with their surroundings and shape their own and the planet's future. Bringing awareness and attention to how we lead these entities is, I believe, one of the most important ways we can transform from a linear, extractive economic model into a dynamic, integrated one.

How humans organize themselves to coexist and—ideally—thrive has for millennia shaped our relationships with each other and with the Earth. But oftentimes our structures and operating systems lag behind what we need. Look no further than the factory-created forty-hour workweek that has become the norm for work that is far removed from the factory model. What's exciting—and critical to our shared future—is that we do have a choice about how we work and for what potential outcomes.

What is the range of potential outcomes? On the one hand, the entities we create have the potential to conserve forms of power and interaction that are, at best, stultifying for those involved and, at worst, oppressive of both internal and external stakeholders. The ways we structure and organize ourselves have the potential to connect us to and/or disconnect us from the systems and ecosystems in which we live and operate. On the other hand, they have the potential to create whole new ways of working, allocating power and resources, producing and measuring outcomes that can transform entire systems. Which potential we tap comes down to *why* and *how* we lead—and I believe we're entering an age in which the transformational potential is—and must be—on the rise.

In his December 2022 *The Atlantic* article, "Why the Age of American Progress Ended," Derek Thompson proposes that: "Invention alone can't change the world; what matters is what happens next. When a good idea is born, or when the first prototype of an invention is created, we should celebrate its potential to change the world. But progress is as much about implementation as it is about invention. The way individuals and institutions take an idea from one to 1 billion is the story of how the world really changes."[1]

As our global climate systems swing to extremes, while concurrently and often connectedly our global environmental, social, and political systems become increasingly dynamic, understanding how change really happens at scale is more important than ever. The brilliance of Thompson's article is in pointing us to a new narrative in which the complex collective is the transforming hero, not the singular individual. It's the systems—and the entities that shape them—that make the change.

So, what does it look like to lead transformation—to go from one to one billion? Again, it comes down to our *why* and our *how*. As the leader of an organization that engages and stewards a global network of businesses and nonprofits, I'm motivated every day by our collective *why* of creating a thriving future for our planet and future generations. And I'm challenged, inspired, humbled, and committed to the *how* of my leadership: to create the conditions for everyone—staff, Board, businesses, and nonprofits—to be wildly successful in their roles. The *how* is where both the pain and the magic happen, and it's where entities and their leaders leverage our potential to transform. Let's dig into these levers:

CREATE ORGANIZATIONS THAT ELEVATE COMMUNITY *AND* AUTONOMY

At 1% for the Planet, we've been working to develop a mindset and practice in which our care for and commitment to our staff is an embedded aspect of our commitment to our global mission. There are two broad ways in which we bring this to life.

First, we invest in connection and culture; our staff members are invited to fully belong to the team that is the staff of 1% for the Planet. Everything from our core values to the benefits we provide to the norms of interaction

---

1 https://www.theatlantic.com/magazine/archive/2023/01/science-technology-vaccine-invention-history/672227/

(it's okay to use the word "love") communicates in tangible ways that each staff member and our collective staff community matter a lot. While we are largely a remote organization, we gather annually as a full staff with the purpose of connection, and during the rest of the year, we use all of our tools to the best of our ability to connect deeply and well. Do we always get it right? Of course not. But our intention is clear and our practice is strong, so we all know what we are trying to create with and for each other.

Second, we invest in releasing every staff member to be the autonomous humans they are, even as they lean into our shared work. One of our primary tools for this is our flex policy, and our commitment to really meaning it. While we need to be synchronous for certain aspects of our work, we can be asynchronous for a lot of it. Honoring that we are in different time zones, that we like exercising at different times of day, that we have different personal and family obligations, and that we don't have to ask for permission for any of these human choices releases us all to be the independent humans we are—and thus to come together more intentionally when that is called for.

We work hard to encourage and invite this flexible approach to work, and we have also created broader benefits that honor the realities of individual lives and celebrate our shared space. For example, we've put in place six-month parental leave as a way to support families during a pivotal life moment, and in 2023, we implemented a Flex Friday program.

This balance of connection and release is key to creating the context in which we can be a force for transformation because both components create the spirit and space in which creativity, mistakes, burning passion, strong performance, and restoration can all be part of what we bring to our strategy and operations. We create the conditions in which each of us and all of us can be wildly successful in the work of creating a future that has never before existed.

THINK AND ACT REGENERATIVELY

1% for the Planet is a global ecosystem, with our staff stewarding relationships with and among member businesses and the environmental partners they support through their annual 1% commitments. Ecosystems are defined and shaped by the energy flows within them, and they are inherently dynamic, energetic, and interconnected. While we certainly target and work hard to attain thoughtfully delineated goals, we seek to operate in a way that honors the mutual nature of the relationships within our model: While our members provide financial, in-kind, volunteer, and promotional support to our environmental partners, these environmental partners provide the on-the-ground impact as well as the deep knowledge and intimate connection to the fundamental issues and solutions. And our staff supports these reciprocal partnerships.

CENTER LOVE, CREATIVITY, AND CURIOSITY

By definition, to transform is to create something that doesn't yet exist, to change the shape or heart of the thing. The collective quest to create a regenerative economy is nothing less than a transformation of capitalism as it is practiced now. As such, how we organize ourselves must foster the creativity and curiosity that are necessary if we are to be agents of transformation.

This is easier said than done. Creativity is unpredictable, curiosity can lead in unexpected directions. That's the point of both (and those are qualities necessary for transformation), and it can feel a bit scary. Where will it all lead? How do we control it? The best analogy for me is to think of an artist's canvas. It has four sides, is pure white at the outset, and is actually a very structured and defined space. And then the artist—the creator—puts brush to palette, and there is no limit to the creativity that can occur within those squared sides and on that white background. Similarly, an organization can have the same "constraints" of strategy and process, within which creativity can abound. And when it feels a bit scary or like it may need to get moved to a bigger canvas (that's the hope), that's when the ability to lean into love of the journey emerges.

Let's talk a little bit about love. It's not a word we often bring into professional settings, but I believe that the regenerative fuel of love—infinite, renewable, reciprocal, creative, and generative—is at the core of our lasting ability to create a new future and a new economy. Why? Because the journey is going to be long, messy, and we will make mistakes along the way. If we can "love the questions" as Rilke reminds us, if we can platonically love our partners on the journey, and if we can open our hearts to the change of heart that is true transformation, then we can get there. While I do lean into using the word love as a leader, my point here is to act toward the work with all of the passion, acceptance, and tenacity of true love, whether or not you ever say the word. In that way, we create the space for the beautiful, the failure, the high, and the low, all of which are waypoints on the path to a new future.

CONCLUSION

David Hinton begins his book *Wild Mind, Wild Earth* by saying: "Before intention and choice, before ideas and understanding and everything we think we know about ourselves—we love this world around us. How can that be? How can we love all this when our cultural assumptions tell us in so many ways that we "humans" are fundamentally other than "nature," and that "nature's" only real value is how it supports our well-being. There's no love in that. Doesn't love require kindred natures. And what is kinship with wild earth but wild mind?"[2]

---

2 https://www.shambhala.com/wild-mind-wild-earth-9781645471479.html

A regenerative economy fundamentally rests on the belief that humans are, in fact, fully part of nature, of the ecosystems and places and beauty and heartbreak that are our home planet. Our ability to step into and live this belief depends in part on how we move through our days—and structure our work. Organizations have an incredible opportunity to become crucibles of creative change, leaning into the opportunity to connect us to the natural world and to each other, leading change—from one to one billion—through the power of acting like we belong.

8   PLENTY OF ROOM IN THE MIDDLE

Tom Chi is Founder of At One Ventures, a top-performing VC fund focused on regenerative technologies, and previously held R&D roles with Microsoft, Outlook, Yahoo, and Google.

W e are in an important moment where the majority of humanity is finally aware that we have an economy that is incompatible with the biosphere. The World Wildlife Foundation has been tracking 32,000 wildlife populations across 5,000 critical species and has recorded a 69% reduction in wildlife populations over the last 50 years. The next 50 years look even more precarious as many of the systems that sustain the planet are being destabilized, and the last places untouched by our current economy are being rapidly exploited. It is not about one factory, a carbon tax, or a single big, bad industry. In totality, the economy we've created cannot continue. There are calls for tearing down late-stage capitalism, and a variety of proposals for what comes next. Instead of tearing down, I choose to imagine it as "composting" late-stage capitalism. Our old system is like a creaky tree, largely dead, and blocking out the sun from the next generation of forest species. But it is still so concentrated with nutrients—we need to find a way for these nutrients to return to the flow of life, the flow of a new economy.

With this in mind, I'd like to introduce a concept called "plenty of room in the middle". It's a nod to a talk given by Richard Feynman where he stated that there is "plenty of room at the bottom," referring to the possibilities that were about to roll forward as we learned to engineer smaller objects at the micron scale and beyond. This talk predated the semiconductor and digital revolution and, in a way, served as a blueprint and compass to guide our way through the last major systems-change idea to have remade a substantial proportion of our economy. So, with that backdrop, let's begin.

Each day, we get a steady stream of photons from the sun, which provides nearly all the energy used by the biosphere. Each day, an equivalent amount of energy is radiated back to space as infrared radiation. Without shedding this equivalent amount of energy, the planet would heat up rapidly and be uninhabitable within days. Of course, with our emissions of greenhouse gases, we are changing this balance, increasing the temperature the Earth reaches in between these photons arriving and leaving. I will call the time period between when a photon arrives on our planet and the time when its energy radiates back into space as the *middle*. Now there are many possible fates in the middle, let's explore a few:

1. The photon could arrive from the sun, hit a rock, and immediately radiate back to space. This happens often. In this process, it may not have benefited even a single organism during its time in the middle.

2. The photon could arrive and hit a solar panel, providing a little nudge to the electrical system of a house. In this case, it may be a part of benefiting the members of a household—a few humans and the microbiota within them.

3. The photon could hit a leaf, driving photosynthesis and the creation of plant sugars, which first feed the plant in its growth, and also its roots, contributing to the primary energy for the soil ecosystem. Later, that plant may be eaten by an herbivorous insect, then an insectivore, then a carnivore, and then an army of detritivores still later in time. In short, the middle for this photon may be contributive to the livelihood of dozens of macro-organisms, thousands of small organisms, and millions of microorganisms.

Nature shows us that there is plenty of room in the middle. That by designing life in a pattern that savors every photon, life is able to extend and make incredible use of the time in the middle. Within this lies the basic core around which we could build a new economy. You see, until now, we have struggled with the idea of continual expansion, of an economy that needs ongoing growth in a world of "limited" resources. And it is true. The way we have currently designed our economy, the way we use up resources, and our ongoing growth and expansion make a recipe for devastation—devastation we are all a part of today. Nature's approach shows us that forever growth, expansion, and permutation are possible—but not in a framework of extraction and exploitation.

After all, 4.5B years ago, all the photons from the sun fell into the first scenario. Then, upon a lifeless world, photons hit the planetary surface and radiated back to space without benefiting a single organism. The cleverness of life came not from its ability to be just a *different place* for the photon to go, but by becoming a place that would get *ever more creative* with each ever-evolving species—about how to make the most of these photons, how to make the most of the water, how to make the most of the critical life-elements: nitrogen, phosphorus, potassium, calcium, and others; learning to skillfully move these materials, collect them from the lithosphere and atmosphere, and with each successive generation making them more bioavailable to support even more complex life. Not only does life savor photons to support the specific organism, but in totality, it uses the energy from photons to increase order and natural wealth for future life. This is why we humans emerged onto a planet with widespread soil fertility, bountiful waterways, and a veritable cornucopia of biodiversity, all contributing to the stupendously robust and resilient fabric of the planet's ecosystems.

And in this way, life itself has done what we have said an economy cannot do: Continue to grow and expand, not just for the wealth of a single household or to claim a nation as more economically prosperous for 100 years, but for all life, for billions of years, in every corner of the planet, and with a creative vibrancy and sophistication that outpaces the most advanced objects we've ever manufactured. Life has shown us that you can in fact grow forever, but not by ever more exploitation or ever more mass, but via the "nuancing" and increasing "sophistication" of the same mass, elaborated through time into more complexly structured forms and interdependent relationships, benefitting ever more organisms with each visiting photon. I would summarize the net effect of what life has done on this planet to be the maximization of diverse nutrient flows toward the benefit of the most organisms possible—*in the middle.*

It's as if nature continually asks: What more can be done to facilitate and enhance life in the middle?

We, too, can ask this question. Our ingenuity has proven itself to be very effective at whatever frame it is unleashed upon. When we laid out the globe with a lens of conquest and subjugation, the colonial powers built fleets of trade ships and slave ships to exploit the resources and peoples of the world. When we thought the globe to be a chessboard between communism and capitalism during the Cold War, we built arsenals that could end every human life on this planet several times over. These are all pretty awful precedents, but they point to the power of how thoroughly and decisively we can be at establishing widespread realities once we've determined to do so. We can carry out a framework to our last breath, and to date, we've chosen frameworks of domination, conquest, subjugation, national dominance, asserted racial supremacy, and more. But we are also capable of better frameworks. Science, medicine, democracy, the arts, and our traditions of spirit and place have variously created much cultural wealth and wisdom. What would it look like for us to ask the same questions that nature asks as we build an economy that further elaborates on the idea of "plenty of room in the middle?"

First off, we could be accounting for how many organisms are benefited by a particular change, and assign more value or reward to the actors in an economy that are benefiting more organisms with the same resources. This immediately asks us to expand our sense of empathy and care, which is much easier to do when we are also the recipients of such empathy and care.

Secondly, we could start to understand that the healthy "flow" of materials and energy is the large-scale wealth creator on the planet, and we expand the wealth of our economy by supporting and expanding the health of those natural flows. For example, the flow of water from a mountaintop to the shore is one of the essential flows required for life to exist on the landscape. If we took away that flow and instead of the water gradually making its way via gravity, it was dammed up, diverted so it never reached the sea, one can see how life on that landscape could be strongly impacted. Beavers show us what happens when you move things in the other direction. Beavers, through their hydrological engineering, slow the movement of water over a landscape, providing more time in the middle for organisms to benefit before the water flows on to a lower elevation. They spread out the potential of those flowing water molecules over more time and landscape, enabling more organisms to benefit—effectively, doing for water molecules what plants do for photons—creating more time in the middle. I think humans would like to think of themselves as more skilled engineers than beavers, and I agree, we can build in far greater varieties and scales (which is advisable and commendable, provided we exercise the precautionary principle and avoid unleashing novel pollutants, disruptions, or unintended adverse consequences into these ecosystems). Given this, I believe we're up to the task of strengthening the health of key flows of water, nutrients, and engineering systems that create more time and utility in the middle.

Lastly, such an economy would be building ever-increasing true wealth for future generations. Life builds soils, brings nuance to hydrology, accumulates wisdom of how to thrive in different settings in culture, language, genetics, and epigenetics. As we build aspects of our economy, we can ask—what long-term wealth can we leave behind by creating this product, this service, this industry? How will the soil be more fertile for the next generation of leaders, creators, scholars, and dreamers?

How much more can we do in the middle?

Jack Wielebinski

9   CLIMATE MISSIVE FROM ONE SMALL PLANET

Jack Wielebinski is Chief Investment Officer at One Small
Planet, overseeing regenerative land and technology deals. He is
on the Boards of ReSeed.farm, Cruz Foam, and Evove.

Humanity now finds itself well within the sixth mass extinction event in Earth's history. While estimates on the rate of species loss vary, the consensus is chilling: extinction rates today are 1,000 to 10,000 times higher than what we see in the fossil record.[1] To put that into perspective, where the planet might naturally lose one species per year, we are now losing 1,000 to 10,000 species annually.

The culprit is clear—massive human encroachment on natural ecosystems, driven by our industrial growth model of ever more extraction, a phenomenon sometimes labeled as the Anthropocene.[2]

This wanton extraction is part and parcel of our western economic model, which has strained nearly every biological system to the point of collapse.[3] The extinction crisis is just one aspect of a broader, multifaceted catastrophe often referred to as the "polycrisis." The polycrisis encompasses not only environmental degradation but also late-stage capitalism, mental health crises, and the global inequalities that result in mass famine and poverty, predominantly in the Global South.[4] While terms like "climate change" or "polycrisis" attempt to capture the scale of our challenges, they often fall short of conveying the

---

1 https://wwf.panda.org/discover/our_focus/biodiversity/biodiversity/

2 Anthropocene is the epoch of time (an analog to the Jurassic period for dinosaurs, for instance) during which humans have been alive and the dominant species on the planet, affecting planetary outcomes.

3 Current reports estimate that six of nine planetary boundaries have already been crossed (i.e., we are already past the limits of our planet's resources). For more information: https://www.stockholmresilience.org/research/planetary-boundaries.html

4 But more and more encroaching of every community globally, look at natural catastrophes in America, for instance.

full scope of the challenges, contributing factors, and solutions needed for the situations we face.

One such example is the term "Global South." Global South typically refers to countries below the Brandt Line, an arbitrary line marking economic disparity.[5] This line underscores the vast income gaps between wealthier Northern nations and the less developed Southern ones, as measured by GDP per capita.

This divide, however, is more than just economic; it's deeply rooted in historical exploitation. The wealth of the Global North has been built on the back of the Global South, first through colonialism (i.e., slavery and genocide), and now through modern globalization. Resources from the South continue to be extracted to benefit the North, often at the cost of fair wages and decent living conditions for those in the South. For example, two African countries produce 70% of the world's cocoa, yet African farmers only capture 6.6% of the value chain, often amounting to only $1 per person per day.[6] This stark imbalance highlights the enduring inequity between the North and South, especially looking at global behemoths profiting billions annually, like Mars or Nestlé.

Furthermore, climate goals set by the Global North often exacerbate this disparity, imposing standards that hinder the development of the Global South, preventing them from achieving even basic standards of living that are taken for granted in the North. An illustration of this is the disproportionate rate of resource extraction by North America and Europe, which is 2x—3x higher than the global average and 10x –15x higher than the poorest regions of the Global South.

Exactly how much are we mining/growing?

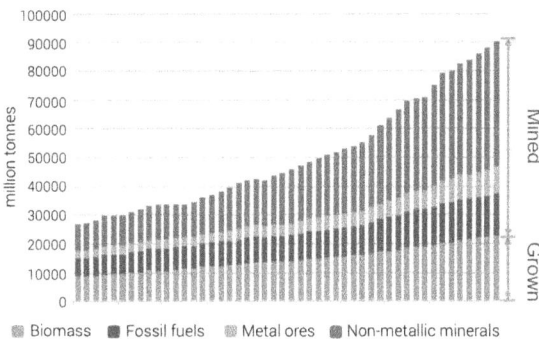

FIGURE 2.2 Global material extraction in four main material categories, 1970–2017, million tonnes

There are currently **90B tons** of annual extraction:

Tons Per Capita:

Global Avg: **11.5 tons**

N. America: **30.0 tons**
Europe: **20.6 tons**
Asia: **11.4 tons**
2B BOP: **~2.5 tons**

Biomass   Fossil fuels   Metal ores   Non-metallic minerals

Source: www.resourcepanel.org/reports/assessing-global-resource-use

---

5 https://apnews.com/article/what-is-global-south-19fa68cf8c60061e88d69f6f2270d98b

6 https://www.weforum.org/agenda/2020/11/cocoa-chocolate-supply-chain-business-bar-africa-exports/

PAPUA NEW GUINEA

Last year, I found myself deep in Papua New Guinea (PNG), navigating the kind of remoteness that's almost unimaginable for those of us in the Global North. After a grueling 24-plus hours of travel just to reach the capital, I took a flight to Goroka—a place so isolated that roads connecting provinces simply don't exist. From there, a rough drive in a four-by-four vehicle took us into the heart of the province's highlands—another day's travel. The next day's journey to a remote village in the Jimi River Valley, a mere 50 miles away, *took over eight hours driving in a four-by-four,* as we battled three feet of mud, dug ourselves out multiple times, and even required help from 20 villagers with ropes to continue on our way at one point.

What struck me most wasn't just the difficulty of the journey, but the breath-taking beauty of the untouched cloud forests with types of animals I did not even know existed until I arrived there.[7] Lush, emerald-green trees of myriad varieties stretched across the mountains, crowned by cerulean skies and drifting clouds, all alive with birds of paradise. But amidst this pristine wilderness, we began to see signs of slash-and-burn agriculture. Curious, we asked our guide, Kambi, what was happening. "That's where they grow peanuts," he explained. Peanuts—a cash crop in this region—are planted after slashing and burning the primordial forests. Three crop yields would earn a few hundred dollars at most, barely enough to make ends meet for local farmers. While my instinct was to cry out, "You can't burn this! This is a treasure for the world!" I realized that for these villagers, this land has been their livelihood for generations. Those few dollars might mean education for their children, solar panels for their homes, or even the luxury of a cell phone.

Who am I, or any outsider, to say otherwise? The real question is: how do we find solutions that balance economic survival with the preservation of these irreplaceable forests? How do we halt the devastating loss of biodiversity and the natural environment when extraction is disproportionately benefiting the richer nations? These are the questions we need to address—questions that lead us to consider ideas like circular economies, global economic equity, and consumption that does not drive our natural world toward extinction. Striving to answer these questions and working toward solutions that may provide a brighter future for humans striving to live a modern, dignified life, while also focusing on preserving more of our planet's ecological systems, is my daily vocation through work.

---

7 Tree kangaroos, Cassowary, cuscus, birds of paradise, and bandicoots to name a few

ONE SMALL PLANET

In my daily professional life, I serve as the Chief Investment Officer of One Small Planet's investment vehicles. I am fortunate that our founder, Will Peterffy, is an environmental zealot who allows our organization to focus on finding broad-based solutions that many others may overlook. Some of the areas we have focused investment on, I believe, are areas targeting real solutions that even the most rabid capitalist could agree with—and it is my sincere belief that we need just that—solutions that are bipartisan, which work for business and well-being and also for our home planet and ecosystems.

One area we have focused heavily on at One Small Planet is reducing single-use plastics and foams, in order to reduce our global reliance on these materials.[8] Alternatives like plastics from seaweed and Styrofoam made from shrimp shell waste are emerging, though they face challenges due to the low cost of petro-based plastics. However, these alternatives are crucial to reducing microplastics in our oceans, food sources, and even our bodies.

A world free of petro-based plastics and polystyrene is something we should all strive for. These materials never fully biodegrade, leading to long-lasting pollution in our cities, oceans, and food systems. At One Small Planet, we invest in biomaterials and filtration systems that help mitigate the impact of microplastics and move us toward a circular economy in which there is no toxic waste. One Small Planet has invested in Cruz Foam, which makes polystyrene from chitosan (shrimp shell waste), and Sway, which makes single-use plastic wrap from seaweed—both are fully biodegradable. As companies like this reach price parity—why would we *not* choose a cheaper *and* better option for the planet we all love?

Water is another area of focus. We support technologies that reduce water contamination, improve crop yields, and minimize water waste in industries. For example, one of our portfolio companies has developed machinery that reduces water usage in textile dyeing by up to 95%, reducing water contamination while maintaining textile quality and affordability.

I believe that solutions benefiting only the Global North are not enough; we need just outcomes and dignity for all life. Deforestation, primarily driven by agriculture, is a critical issue. That's why we invest in agroforestry solutions for smallholder farmers in the Global South, helping them earn a livable wage while promoting carbon sequestration and effective conservation. One Small Planet has funded organizations like ReSeed, focused on improving agroforestry practices with smallholder farmers in the global south, with a particular emphasis on growing their income streams.

---

8 Plastic is an amazing material, and incredibly cheap as it is made from petro-chemical waste, and there are Bonafide needs for it; however SO much of the usage of plastic, millions of tonnes annually, is superfluous.

Indigenous communities, who steward a disproportionate amount of the world's biodiversity on just 5% of its land, are vital to this effort. They already live sustainably, and our role is to empower them with the resources they need.

I don't believe there is a single solution to our climate crisis. While direct air capture and carbon sequestration are important, we also need to conserve biodiversity corridors and focus on sectors like food, fibersheds, and regenerative agriculture. Unfortunately, these critical areas receive far less investment compared to sectors like electric vehicles (EVs). At One Small Planet, we strive to be catalytic in these underfunded sectors, driving innovation and support where it's most needed.

Our world is increasingly complex, with interconnected challenges like wealth inequality, biodiversity loss, and environmental degradation. While it can be overwhelming, we must continue to seek and scale real solutions for a better world. Conservation, fair compensation for smallholder farmers, and the promotion of biomaterials are all part of this effort.

In the Anthropocene, we've lost half of the world's forests, with significant losses continuing in areas like Brazil, India, and the South Pacific. These are the last remaining rainforests on our planet, and their destruction is leading to bleak outcomes. However, if we take these threats seriously, it's possible to avoid the worst impacts.

At One Small Planet, our team is dedicated to allocating funds to overlooked climate solutions that are vital to the survival of our planet. We constantly ask ourselves: "Does this contribute to the world we want to live in?"

For me, that world includes clean water, dignified living standards for all people, and rich, abundant biodiversity. I believe in a future where we can live modern, dignified lives while enabling all people and all life to thrive. This vision keeps me motivated every day.

You never change things by fighting the existing reality.
To change something, build a new model that makes
the existing model obsolete.

—R. Buckminster Fuller

10 BIOFI

Catalyzing an Economic and Financial Revolution

Samantha Power is Founder and Director of the BioFi Project,
and Founder and Principle Consultant of Finance for Gaia.
She co-authored *Bioregional Financing Facilities*.

Awakening to the Polycrisis
Around the world, policymakers, institutional and individual wealth
holders, and the general public are increasingly recognizing the severity of
ecological collapse and the risk of further collapse cascading across our interdependent economic, political, and social systems. Amid this reckoning, a wave
of capital is forming, seeking to invest in the regeneration of the biosphere. Yet
a profound gap persists between funders and on-the-ground regenerators: in
connectivity, socio-ecological integrity, and worldview.[1]

After more than a decade of working to shift financial flows toward biocultural regeneration—including through co-creating the nature finance program
at the World Bank and advising finance ministries, central banks, institutional
investors, impact investors, and family offices on nature-related risks and investments—I saw that both traditional and emerging financing approaches were
perpetuating the same extractive processes and power structures driving the
polycrisis, including further commodification, privatization, financialization,

---

1 "A set of presuppositions (assumptions which may be true, partially true or entirely false)
which we hold (consciously or subconsciously, consistently or inconsistently) about the basic
makeup of our world." (Definition by James Sire)

and centralization of natural assets and wealth rooted in abstraction of and separation from the living world. I witnessed so many urgent and important regenerative projects, led by people with deep relationships to place, struggling to get the resources they needed. These efforts, often deemed "too small" or "informal," are structurally excluded from financial flows. Meanwhile, funded projects too often reinforce the status quo.

I saw that very few capital holders globally were applying systems thinking and an integrated capital approach to investing. Even fewer were deploying capital in alignment with a living systems approach that sees the Earth as a living, breathing, interconnected, and sacred organism of which humans are a part.

The world is a complex, interconnected, finite, ecological—social—psychological—economic system. We treat it as if it were not, as if it were divisible, separable, simple, and infinite. Our persistent, intractable global problems arise directly from this mismatch."
—DONELLA MEADOWS

BIOFI: A NEW ECONOMIC AND FINANCIAL PHILOSOPHY AND APPROACH

From these realizations, Bioregional Finance or "BioFi" was born. My coauthor Leon Seefeld and I introduced the BioFi framework in our 2024 book *Bioregional Finance: Reimagining Finance to Regenerate Our Planet*, in which we radically rethink the purpose of financial institutions and our economies. At its core, BioFi is a design framework for organizing the flow of financial and multi-capital resources toward the regeneration of ecosystems, cultures, and communities—grounded in bioregions. Bioregions (or biocultural regions) are regions defined by hard lines, soft lines, and human lines or their physical characteristics, ecological characteristics, cultural characteristics, and their interconnections. Bioregions can be seen as the natural units of place-based regeneration, enabling the interweaving of life's flows across species, the physical territory, and the cultural meanings of place.

More broadly, BioFi is a philosophy informed by:

- Systems thinking, including living systems science[2]

---

2 We draw on Fritjof Capra's Principles of Life: https://www.fritjofcapra.net/principles-of-life/ and Lynn Margulis's book The Symbiotic Planet.

- Bioregionalism[3]
- Indigenous ways of knowing
- Permaculture and regenerative economics
- The rights of nature and decolonial theory
- Nonviolence and social justice movements

BioFi calls for the transformation of financial and economic systems: from globalized, homogenized, and abstract structures rooted in reductionism, to place-based, relational, anti-fragile, community-owned economies aligned with living systems and planetary consciousness.

BIOREGIONAL FINANCING FACILITIES (BFFS): THE HEART OF BIOFI

Central to BioFi is the case for creating a new layer in the global financial architecture of Bioregional Financing Facilities or "BFFs." BFFs are a new type of financial institution designed to enable flows of resources from centralized pools of capital to grassroots, regenerative projects and initiatives in alignment with living systems principles and Indigenous wisdom.

THE THREE CORE OBJECTIVES OF BFFS ARE TO:
1. Decentralize financial resource governance
2. Aggregate synergistic portfolios of regenerative initiatives
3. Support the transition to bioregional regenerative economies

BFFs help to shift bioregions from dependence on a globally-embedded, extractive, brittle economy to more place-based, sovereign, circular, resilient economies that support the regeneration of cultures and ecosystems. These regenerative economies strengthen the relational fabric in a place by acknowledging the existence of diverse forms of value (e.g., cultural, spiritual, political, not just financial) and the relationships that inform that value. BFFs can become the connective tissue between financial resources and on-the-ground regenerators (this is illustrated in Figure 1 below) by enabling capital from diverse sources to flow to portfolios of community-coordinated regenerative projects that support emerging bioregional economies rooted in a fundamentally different economic logic and value systems.

---

3 **Bioregionalism**—A philosophy advocating for societies to be organized around biocultural regions or "bioregions," where economic activity, ecological management, and governance align with the region's natural systems and culture.

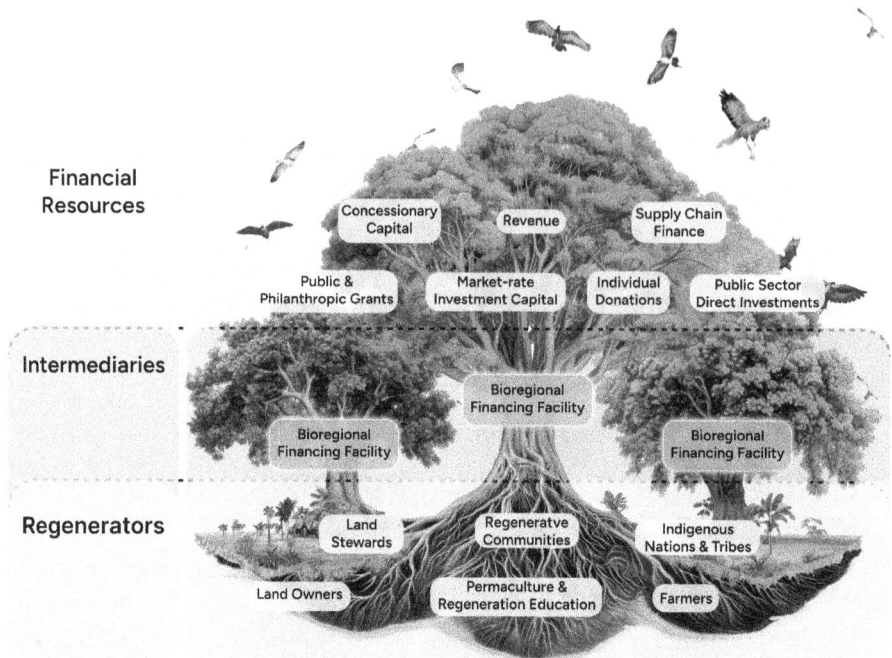

Figure 1. Bioregional Financing Facilities:
connecting financial resources and regenerators.

BFFs are rooted in the uniqueness of place and guided by Indigenous wisdom that invites us into kinship with the rest of nature. They enable the flows of capital to strengthen relationships between community members, between stewards and their ecosystems, lands, and waters they tend, and amongst all of the more-than-human life and living processes through how they invest.

BFFS HAVE 12 ATTRIBUTES. THEY . . .
1. Aim to align with living systems principles and Indigenous wisdom
2. Serve the realization of the Bioregional Regeneration Strategy
3. Implement an inclusive and participatory governance structure that represents the bioregion
4. Work to shift power imbalances
5. Are transparent and enable empowered participation
6. Leverage an integrated capital structure that embeds regenerative principles
7. Treat growth and returns as a means, not an end
8. Raise from mission-aligned funders/investors
9. Provide aggregation and matchmaking

10. Apply an integrated approach to sensing and MRV
11. Invest in storytelling
12. Engage in partnerships, place-based citizen-stewardship, and the community of practice

There are four templates for BFFs laid out in the book, which are implemented in two phases, laid out below alongside some details on the structures, capital raising, and capital allocation practices each can apply.

Table 1. BFF Templates & Phased Implementation.

Phase 1

1. Bioregional Trust	2. Bioregional Venture Studio
A trust that acts as a catalytic grant fund – providing grants to a range of priority organizations and initiatives in order to create a strong foundation for bioregional action. It can also set up and manage bioregional eco-credit programs, Common Asset Trusts, and Ecological Institutions.	A non-profit, public benefit corporation, co-operative, steward-owned entity, or DAO that supports the development of a cohort of synergistic regenerative organizations to drive systems change. These organizations provide dealflow for the Investment Company.
Capital Raising • Philanthropic and public grant capital (could be sub-national, national, or multilateral), as well as individual donations (including through crowdfunding) • Bioregional Tithing program	**Capital Raising** • Philanthropic grants • Public sector grants (could be sub-national, national, or multilateral) • Supply chain finance • Concessional capital
Capital Allocation • Provides grants to fund key processes laid out in steps 2-5 of the Multi-stakeholder Bioregional Regeneration (Table 4) • Provides grants to priority projects or organizations aligned with the Bioregional Regeneration Strategy • Provides grants to Bioregional Hubs and Bioregional Organizing Teams • Funds the development of a bioregional MRV platform (to be developed together with a Bioregional Hub) • Sets up the Bioregional Venture Studio, Bioregional Investment Company and Bioregional Bank	**Capital Allocation** • Invests in and incubates cohorts of early-stage organizations that work together to change a specific system and generate cascading benefits

Phase 2

3. Bioregional Investment Company	4. Bioregional Bank
A public benefit corporation, co-operative, steward-owned entity, or DAO that develops a portfolio of Systemic Investment Funds and Bioregional Regeneration Bonds. It leverages an integrated capital approach, aggregates portfolios of high impact projects or businesses.	A bank that provides low-interest loans, microloans, lines of credit, and technical assistance to aligned organizations. It can also provide retail banking services to individuals and can develop and issue a complementary or nature-based currency.
Capital Raising • Market-rate investment capital • Concessional capital • Philanthropic grants • Public sector grants (could be sub-national, national, or multilateral) • Supply chain finance	**Capital Raising** • Concessional capital • Public sector grants (could be sub-national, national, or multilateral) • Philanthropic grants • Guarantees • Deposits
Capital Allocation • Systemic Investment Funds • Invests in diversified portfolios of projects & businesses designed to create systemic impact • Bioregional Regeneration Bonds • Same objectives as the funds, but through a fixed income security	**Capital Allocation** • Develops and issues complementary or nature-based currency

BFFs take a multispecies, multigenerational approach in how they invest. Each BFF is designed to serve the realization of a Bioregional Regeneration Strategy, the systemic, long-term (20-100 year) vision for a bioregion. The strategy is best developed through a deeply participatory process that includes citizens' assemblies, town halls, storytelling, nature walks, ceremony, and artmaking. The process can also include human representatives of more-than-human inhabitants of the bioregion. These representatives may also have roles in the governance of the BFF.

BioFi is an aikido move that leverages the attractor of money to bring people from diverse class and cultural backgrounds and a range of disciplines into bioregional networks of solidarity. It supports them to embody new worldviews rooted in interdependence and mutual flourishing through a range of activities that catalyze and are catalyzed by economic systems transformation. We believe that a bioregional approach is most appropriate for identifying and cultivating place-based islands of coherence: local systems where culture, economy, and ecology function harmoniously and in alignment with the laws of nature.

Bioregions can be understood at multiple scales—from small landscapes and minor watersheds to Indigenous territories, ecoregions, and major watersheds. This multilayered approach enables effective governance that works across scales, with smaller units nested within larger ones. Through bioregioning, communities create connections between local and global ecologies and cultures. As diverse places develop their own approaches, they share knowledge with other bioregions, allowing successful governance patterns to emerge and adapt across different contexts.

> *"When a complex system is far from equilibrium,*
> *small islands of coherence in a sea of chaos have the capacity to*
> *shift the entire system to a higher order."*
> —ILYA PRIGOGINE

BFFs can take in capital from an extractive and destructive economic system and compost it to grow new, regenerative, bioregional economies that eventually do not require external capital at all, but can autonomously engage in economic reciprocity and solidarity with neighbors both near or far. In this way, Bioregional Financing Facilities can channel life-giving nutrients and energy to, and between, bioregional islands of coherence in a time of rising planetary instability.

BIOFI IN PRACTICE

The BioFi Project is actively working to build BFFs with a network of bioregional organizing teams from across the Americas—spanning from Alaska to Argentina—that are building on decades of grassroots regenerative work to create coherence across interdependent regenerative efforts, cultivate a shared bioregional identity, and engage in the inquiry and practice of creating regenerative economies. We are supporting them to build institutions, create strategies, cultivate decision-making processes, develop storytelling, and raise financial resources to catalyze this transformation through our BioFi Cultivator program.

Simultaneously, we are growing a broader BioFi movement and the BioFi Community of Practice. We are also building a network of capital holders who acknowledge the violence and destruction so central to modern worldviews and systems and who are committed to flowing resources back to the places from which wealth has been extracted. Together, we are embarking upon a translocal, collective unlearning and learning journey. We believe that this connectivity and mutual learning between a geographically and culturally dispersed range of actors is critical for emerging bioregional islands of coherence to survive and thrive.

AN INVITATION TO JOIN US

The BioFi vision is woven from many long, diverse threads, including: five hundred years of anticolonial resistance and decolonial creativity; movements for economic, ecological, and social justice and liberation; and the inspired efforts of peoples around the world organizing autonomously for the regeneration of the biosphere and their local-global communities. It is informed by persistent innovation in the fields of economics, finance, ecology, evolutionary biology, and systems theory. BFFs were born out of and can support the web of interdependent efforts of the broader regenerative movement.

If you are inspired by BioFi as an approach to catalyzing economic systems transformation and ontological shifts, we welcome you to join the growing movement in the following ways:

- Join or catalyze a bioregional organizing team where you are;
- Join the BioFi Community of Practice, which aims to cultivate and support a community of practitioners who are designing, capitalizing, implementing, and evolving Bioregional Financing Facilities (BFFs) through peer-to-peer learning and coordination;
- Crowdfund for a regenerative project in your bioregion and steward the resources raised with your community; to map the various forms of capital in your life and to move away from a focus on financial capital and exchange;
- Collectively engage in discussions around theories of value;
- Support local farmers with your food choices.

Wherever you are on your bioregional or BioFi journey, we invite you to take steps to move into a more relational, gift economy rooted in care—recognizing each of our needs and capacities.

A MOMENT FOR REGENERATIVE ACTION

We find ourselves in a moment in the history of life on Earth that feels incredibly fragile for so many of us, and in which immense suffering and enormous potential are deeply bound together. We feel the weight of collapse in ecosystems, economic systems, sociocultural systems, and political systems. We feel hope stemming from our interactions with the magic still so alive on this blue-green planet. Many of us feel how a growing proportion of humanity is waking up from the mechanistic, reductionist worldview—rooted in a misinterpretation of Newtonian physics that drove industrialization. As more of humanity steps into a living systems consciousness, BioFi offers a practical path forward for creating economic and financial systems to serve life. We believe that BioFi can help catalyze the economic and financial revolution needed to transform the polycrisis into a moment of planetary regeneration. Let us rise to meet it—together.

The BioFi Project is a collective developing thought leadership on BioFi and supporting bioregions across the Americas to design, create, capitalize, implement, and evolve Bioregional Financing Facilities that connect financial resources and regenerators.

*"The money we need to solve our biggest challenges is already here.
The leader we've been waiting for . . . is you."*

11 MAIN STREET 2.0

Reimagining Capital for Community Transformation

Dr. Stephanie Gripne is Founder and CEO of Impact Finance Center and visionary behind the National Impact Investing Marketplace.

Six months ago, on the eve of an investor training we hosted with a community foundation in Northern Colorado, something extraordinary happened. What began as a casual conversation among neighbors quickly turned into a revelation.

I posed a simple but provocative question: "What would it take to solve the housing crisis in Northern Colorado?"

We ran the numbers. The estimated cost? $740 million. At first, the figure felt overwhelming—until I asked another question: "How much private wealth exists in this region?" The answer surprised us all: more than $180 billion in assets are held by individuals owning at least $1 million.

We realized that solving the housing crisis would require just **0.5%** of the existing wealth already in the community. That moment reframed everything.

What if the money we need to solve our biggest challenges is already here? What if the leader we've been waiting for is not someone else—but us? What if it's you?

This is the heart of what I call **Main Street 2.0**: Bringing the best of Wall Street back to Main Street—mobilizing our wealth, knowledge, and networks to build the communities we want to live in.

MAIN STREET MEETS WALL STREET

Main Street 2.0 reimagines the relationship between Wall Street and Main Street.

Wall Street offers powerful tools for pricing risk, pooling capital, and scaling investments. Main Street holds the soul—the nonprofits, small businesses, cooperatives, and startups that make a place vibrant and resilient. These two worlds rarely meet. But what if they did?

In Colorado, every December, we celebrate **Colorado Gives Day**, our state's version of Giving Tuesday, where residents donate millions to local nonprofits. Now, imagine a companion event in September: Colorado Invests Day.

Instead of donating, residents could invest—directly into local housing projects, businesses, cooperatives, and community funds. Investments could happen individually or collectively, using tools like community notes, cooperative investment models, and unfunded philanthropic guarantees (and of course could be replicated in other states and regions as well).

To make this vision a reality, we would need to build new infrastructure for community investing—mirroring what already exists in philanthropy:

- A database of investments, like databases of grantees
- A database of investors, similar to donor management systems
- A transparent platform to match capital with opportunity
- Simple, diversified financial products—mirroring S&P 500 funds, municipal bonds, or pooled investments in social ventures

You might wonder: *Isn't it riskier to invest in our own communities?* Maybe. But Wall Street long ago mastered tools for pricing risk, managing uncertainty, and pooling capital efficiently.

That's where philanthropy and government can play a crucial role—offering first-loss guarantees, blended capital structures, and insurance products to de-risk local investments for everyday people.

Main Street 2.0 isn't about choosing between risk and safety. It's about building **new systems** that blend financial innovation with **Full-Spectrum Capital** to make community-driven solutions scalable, sustainable, and transformational.

SHIFTING POWER TO THE COMMUNITY FROM THE INVESTOR

When I think about traditional markets, I know power dynamics shift naturally. If I list my house in a hot market, I might receive multiple offers. In a slow market, I might wait months for a single bid. Sometimes the buyer holds the power; sometimes the seller does. Yet in the social sector, the power almost always resides with the investor. Main Street 2.0 seeks to change that.

Instead of nonprofit leaders pleading, *"Will you fund me?"*, the conversation becomes, *"What capital do you need?"* The responsibility shifts to capital aggregators—community foundations, intermediaries, and financial innovators—to design the right blend of capital to meet community needs.

As investors, we could:

- Earn **5-8% returns** on equity investments,
- Earn **2-4% returns** on debt instruments, and
- **Co-sign or guarantee** local projects, unlocking even more investment.

In doing so, we're not just achieving financial returns—we're healing our communities. We become stewards of our shared future.

IF I CAN TEACH INVESTOR EDUCATION, YOU CAN TOO

Thirty years into my career, I now call myself a r**estoration ecologist of the financial markets**. It makes sense in hindsight. But at the time, it felt like diving into the unknown.

I grew up in central Idaho, where environmental debates over wolves and salmon could tear communities apart. I initially pursued wildlife ecology, but eventually realized my passion wasn't wildlife—it was systems. I wanted to understand how resources flow through communities—and how to redesign those flows to serve people and place.

Encouraged by brave peers and fueled by purpose, I stepped outside my comfort zone to learn finance—starting from scratch. I didn't come from Wall Street. I came from a commitment to community. And if I could do it—**so can you**.

IMPACT FINANCE CENTER, INVESTOR ACCELERATORS, AND THE BAND

At Impact Finance Center (IFC), we believe the next step is clear: We need a **national movement** to educate ourselves as investors—not just donors or consumers—and to build the financial infrastructure our communities deserve. We have developed the blueprints. Now, we need the movement.

Just as startup accelerators nurture entrepreneurs, IFC identifies, educates, and activates impact investors. Our initiatives—including the **Impact Investing Institute, Impact Days, Giving Circles, Who's Who in Impact Investing**, and the forthcoming **Trustworthy Impact** and **Diligence League**—build the systems that allow communities to mobilize capital for good.

Between 2015 and 2019, our flagship CO Impact Days event alone catalyzed $300 million—three times our initial target. Through our Senior Advisor Program, we are building the "band"—a train-the-trainer network that empowers community leaders to become their own capital stewards.

This work has already led to:

- **$1 billion+** in impact investments catalyzed,
- **400+** educational programs delivered across the U.S.,
- **100+** social ventures funded or supported, and
- **300+** investors activated through training and fellowships.

LAYING THE GROUNDWORK WITH A $1 BILLION BLUEPRINT

Recently, we submitted a proposal to a major insurance company: invest $600 million, use it to leverage another $400 million from local investors, and together create a $1 billion community-driven investment model.

The blueprint includes:

1. **Investor Accelerators**
1. **Capital Aggregators**
2. **Intermediaries**
3. **Dealflow Development**
4. **Community Marketplaces** (like Impact Days and Investor Clubs)

This is Full-Spectrum Capital in action—where grants absorb risk, impact-first investors provide flexibility, and market-rate investors earn returns—while collectively funding solutions that matter. This model can be adapted anywhere, enabling communities to catalyze $100M to $1B within three, five, or ten years.

FULL-SPECTRUM CAPITAL: THE MATH OF MISSION

Say I want to support a women's shelter in my community. Traditionally, I might write a $50 check—a generous gesture, but a one-time gift. But what if I could double that impact?

Instead of simply donating $50, I could invest $100—half from my Wall Street portfolio, half from my charitable giving. Through a structure designed to manage risk, I could still earn an 8% return—while putting twice as much money to work in the community.

For the shelter, the difference is clear: They receive **$100** instead of **$50**. More services, more beds, more impact—with no additional cost to me. Would your organization prefer $100 with a small built-in return, or a simple $50 grant?

This is what we call moving from scarcity to strategy. It's not just about giving more—it's about using what we already have more wisely.

SCALING WITH COURAGE, COMMUNITY, AND CAPITAL

When we realized that 0.5% of Northern Colorado's private wealth could solve its housing crisis, it became clear: This work isn't just about one place. It's about a new way forward for every community.

We don't need to reinvent the wheel in every town or city. We need a National Impact Investing Marketplace—a connected system that unlocks billions in aligned capital and transforms charity into true systems change.

At Impact Finance Center, we are laying the foundation. We are scaling the band—our Senior Advisor program—to activate over 100 local experts trained to move capital for community good. We are launching Giving Circles to seed funds for women-led ventures, rural entrepreneurs, and underrepresented innovators. And we are building essential infrastructure: Trustworthy Impact, the first independent trust company dedicated solely to impact investing, alongside new platforms like Diligence League and Impact Data—giving communities the tools they need to deploy capital transparently and strategically.

This is not a dream. It is already happening. One region, one project, one community at a time.

Yet we're often told to wait—Wait for the government to act. Wait for billionaires to fund solutions. Wait for Wall Street to change. **Main Street 2.0 says: We can't wait. We don't have to.**

We can organize. We can educate. We can build.

If a small nonprofit like ours can catalyze **$1 billion** in 10 years, imagine what your neighborhood, your region, your networks could achieve—with aligned capital and a shared vision. We don't have to choose between mission and market, between idealism and investment. We can weave them together.

This is the new story. This is the blueprint. Let's make it our new normal.

12 "WHITE HOLES" OF HYPER-LOCAL REGENERATION

from Concept to Feeding Community

Azuraye Wycoff is Founder and CEO of Yellow Barn Farm,
Kaizen Home Services, Picky Pig Compost, Stalk Market
Distributions, Small Haul Movers, and Blue Sky Consulting.

"Regenerative" seems to be the latest buzzword. But what does regenerative really mean?

I envision it to be akin to one of the most common geometric systems—the torus. A doughnut-shaped movement of energy—like Earth's magnetic field, the roots to leaves of a tree, or a conceptual "white hole" that generously emits energy as opposed to a black hole that insatiably devours everything.

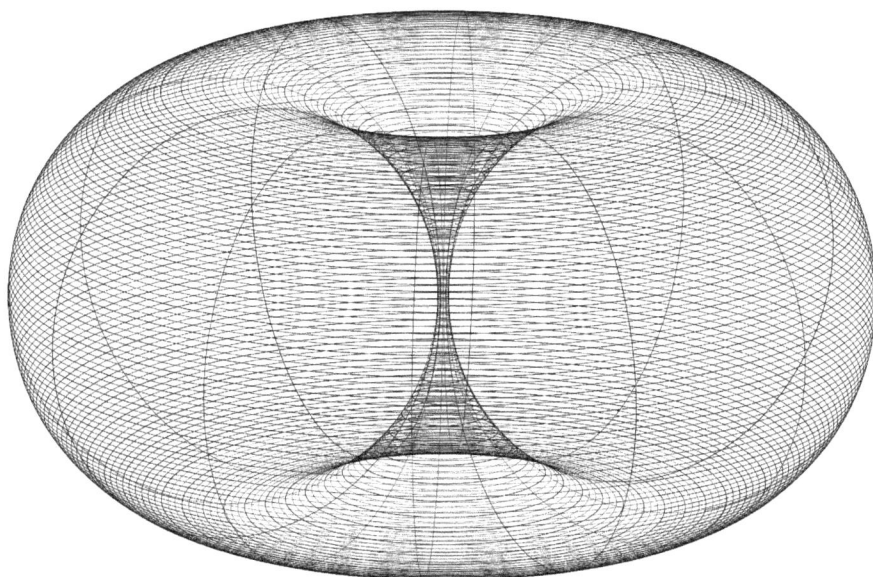

Regenerative systems bring life force up to the surface, generate and nurture new and additional life force, and then return down to the surface to decompose and be recycled—a closed loop of continual growth and restoration. Degenerative systems disrupt that cycle by breaking the connection between the creation and decomposition of energy. Meaning the energy does not come back into the system. It is created but cannot decompose; it cannot return to its source.

Most of our current systems, products, or flows of information are degeneratively designed at this moment in history. They are one-directional and extractive, and are generally moving resources one way, but have very few ways, if any, to circulate them back to their origin points.

It is considered nearly revolutionary—if not even anarchical—to be designing, building, or creating regenerative systems *because* they are so in juxtaposition to the mainstream. But it is this kind of quiet grassroots rebellion that the world needs right now.

I am certain that in this book, there is an essay that quotes Buckminster Fuller: "You never change things by fighting the existing reality. To change something, build a new model that makes the existing model obsolete". And that is the guiding principle in regenerative systems design. It is not to fight the current system, but to start to build new streams through which energy, resources, and attention can flow—giving people an option to take a regenerative path instead of the status quo.

But first, you have to put in tremendous effort to create that path. And not many people yet have the time, capacity, or resources to take the path less traveled, let alone create it. Those of us who are working on regenerative systems design—whether that is in land systems, financial systems, or product systems—take *both* the risk of massive upfront capital investment, *and* a market that might not be ready to swim down a new stream at sustaining scales. Especially when the current is so strong in the mainstream.

FROM SMALL HAUL MOVERS TO YELLOW BARN FARM

My partner Charles and I have been working together for the last eight years. But our journey began in 2009, when we met on a student trip to Spain at the age of 15. We lost touch from age 17 to 27, but after I landed a job in Boston, his hometown, we reconnected and re-bonded over beers and brainstorms about operations for his new venture—a moving company called Small Haul.

A year later, I quit my fancy VC-funded tech job I had moved there for, and Charles offered me a temporary part-time gig on the truck helping him move furniture and backend admin for Small Haul. I figured I could do that for 2-3 weeks until I was ready to start the job hunt again for something more serious—and more within my wheelhouse; after studying International Affairs and Chinese in college, living abroad in Nanjing, China, and working three Chinese-related jobs in and after college, moving furniture wasn't exactly the industry I was aiming to get into.

Little did I know that Small Haul would change my life. I eventually realized I wasn't just working in a moving company. I was helping to design, build, and implement a living system. A system that required every ounce of attention and care lest it fall apart and die. It felt like taking care of a screaming newborn. And I was going through the absolute gauntlet of learning how to manage this behemoth of a baby business on my own—no systems but an email account, a form that sent you the job details, and text messages to tell the crew where to go to pick up and drop off the furniture. And plenty of room for human error.

But what I started to learn about myself is that I intrinsically *needed* to organize everything around me in order to function. And Small Haul desperately needed that from me. Charles and I would spend all of our hours (hours on the truck, hours after the end of the day, and hours on any day we didn't have a move) thinking and talking and building checks and balances for this business—ultimately hiring a developer to build custom software to help us manage all the moving parts.

My three-year intensive in Small Haul felt like a boot camp in entrepreneurship—from building the brand, to designing the systems, managing Google Ads, learning to build a website from scratch, implementing complex conditional logic in Typeform, utilizing project management software . . . the list went on. Even with all of that, what I most clearly started to see was that this business was a living system—and we were slowly shifting it toward equilibrium. And that equilibrium created a massive amount of abundance for all involved—an energetic white-hole. Energy was put in, and double was received in-kind. My first experience of regeneration.

When COVID hit, I felt the call to return to my hometown of Boulder, Colorado, particularly to support my family in figuring out what we should do with a 100-acre farm we'd had in our family since I was seven years old. This was a part of my life I had sworn I'd never return to; over the years I tried convincing my parents to sell. But after my return, the question remained: Should we sell it, or. . . ?

After my Small Haul gauntlet, I felt more skilled and capable than I ever had in my life. And Charles and I saw the farm as an incredible playground in which to experiment. On top of that, my mother had been connected with a new, small nonprofit that was just starting to do consulting for regenerative land design—Drylands Agroecology Research (DAR). As we began working with them, I started to learn all about regenerative agriculture—and quickly saw how much it mirrored everything I had just learned in Small Haul.

From 2020 to 2025, we have been diligently building out a unique project at what we now lovingly call Yellow Barn Farm, as a demonstration site for all kinds of regenerative systems—land, business, and social.

DAR focuses on the land—having now planted over 8,000 trees on the property, rotationally grazing cattle, moving pigs through old compacted pasture to create gardens, and planting annual and perennial forest gardens.

We focus on the enterprises—with a major question being "how do we make agriculture (and this property) economically regenerative?" We knew that there was no way we would be able to sustain this project by selling veggies at the farmer's market. Besides, selling food is not truly what DAR's focus is on—it is on the soil, and the food is a regenerative "by-product" of their efforts.

After four years of observation, I saw so many parallels between regenerative agriculture and regenerative ways of doing business—ultimately, I saw so many opportunities to bring our skills to the world of farming.

First, it was imperative to get a Small Haul branch established in Colorado. Small Haul was our economic engine—the cash flow driver that allowed us to fund ourselves and this project, rather than taking grants and donations. Yellow Barn stayed a for-profit venture in order to force us to figure out the economic structure organically. My family gifted the project a small seed fund to get us started and repair some old infrastructure, but we knew that when that runway ran out, we would have to get the plane off the ground.

Small Haul created the labor pool and the vehicle fleet that also allowed us to start stacking functions with adjacent industries—like food distribution from farms or food service businesses, and food scrap collection to bring back organic nutrients to the farm to feed pigs and build compost piles.

We had watched the local farmers mobilize their trucks and trailers to go pick up buckets and barrels of "free" food waste from restaurants—but we knew the true cost of mobilizing vehicles and labor—and it certainly wasn't free. So what if we just made it all into a business model that helped both farmers and food service businesses?

Thus, two new entities were born: Picky Pig Compost and Stalk Market Distributions—two micro-businesses incubated at Yellow Barn. This established a bidirectional distribution channel that collected waste, turned it into soil—and from that soil, food was grown, which could be delivered where needed.

We started to envision what a multi-nodal, mycelial network of farms, restaurants, grocery stores and door steps could look like if they could be connected through a hyperlocal distribution system—the farms being the heart that connected to all the other organs through an artery system made up of small sprinter vans, zipping around town. Made more economically viable by never being empty, whether that was with food waste or food deliveries, the fleet was already paid for by the needs of the moving company (and thereby reduced the need for every business or farmer to procure their own vehicle).

Then, other ag-related businesses started inquiring at Yellow Barn—the tree care company that had mulch, the landscaping company that needed soil, and the lawn care company that offered compost tea and steam-weeding to clients . . . there were so many companies that required vehicles, labor, processing, and space to operate. So Yellow Barn quickly became a home base for "ecoprenuers," where operations started to flourish, rental income supported the farm, and waste outputs were a valuable input for building compost and soil.

Kaizen Home Services came next—a multi-stakeholder marketing and "front-office" company that offers all the services of these stewardship-minded businesses under one roof: non-toxic lawn care, regenerative and native landscape design, and more—small and local companies that support the circular economy developing at Yellow Barn. Furthermore, all the leads Kaizen generates and manages for these small businesses allow even more efficiency by streamlining the scheduling, operations, and payments to all the small businesses that really just want to show up and tend the land in the best way possible. A win-win-win for all involved.

So, when *we* use the word "regenerative," it means collective efficiency. It means closed-loop regeneration. It means stacking functions. It means the abundance that is created by our collaborative joint efforts, which creates so much more in the sum of all the parts, rather than all the parts operating individually.

At the same time, "regenerative" systems really force us to look at our own inner shadows. Such systems require us to communicate exceptionally clearly. To make good agreements. To not bypass the importance of financial flows in lieu of a spiritual belief that we can operate without resource exchange—just goodwill and favors are not enough in today's world.

Most people coming into the orbit of regeneration are generally feeling a deep desire to get away from the current capitalist system. And while that might unite us initially—the shared sense that "there's another way!" if it's not paired with financial means, the trust that allows for nonfinancial "energetic exchanges" of trading favors and kindness can only scale to a certain level before it breaks down and inevitably breaks relationships.

So much of what we talk about and aim to create at Yellow Barn can be described as grounded financial fluency.

We enjoy creating and demonstrating that financial resources carry the same energetic properties as water, and also need the same design systems as regenerative land design—things like: ponds for storing water, ditches to flood-irrigate (with channels to funnel that flooding into swale basins), drip irrigation to get water to the right location (and in the right quantity), wells to bring water up from the water table, and methods to slow, spread, and sink the water back *into* that water table. Money is the exact same—as money is simply fluid energy. In our current industrial mindset and ways of life, we have just gone to the extreme—with billionaires amassing an ocean's worth of financial resources—but what can anyone truly do with their own entire ocean of money?

We all need our small ponds, a shared community lake, and access to the ditch to utilize our fair share to grow what feeds us and our communities. Regenerative systems allow you to "use what you need" and leave the rest for those downstream. Unfortunately, right now, this way of functioning is not mainstream; thus, many are suffering worldwide.

Regeneration is reciprocity. It is the give-and-take of energy. However, it requires the equilibrium point of not giving or taking too much or too little. A tsunami in the garden does not create more vegetables nor happy cows. Just enough moisture to satiate allows for all things to flourish even more for the next harvest.

Regeneration is feeding yourself and feeding others . . . and knowing that, with the right balance, there will always be enough.

13   FROM RISK TO REGENERATION

Bioregional Investing & Financing Our Future

Eduardo Esparza is Founder and CEO of BlueDot Project
and BlueDot Capitals, focusing on land-based, indigenous-led
regeneration efforts in the Sierra Nevada de Gonavindúa, Colombia.

Enormous changes are underway on our planet, and no one knows for certain where they will lead. Uncertainty and risk shadow our path forward. But there is room for hope. Impact investors can help avoid the worst scenarios for the future while still earning acceptable, risk-adjusted returns. They can do so by investing in the regeneration of the complex systems that enable life on Earth. These investments not only hedge against risk but also create the foundation for a more prosperous and resilient world.

This essay is intended for three groups:

1. Investors who wish to build a sustainable and prosperous society in harmony with nature.
2. Investors who are preparing for the potential collapse of our current civilization by funding long-term, resilient solutions.
3. Innovators and entrepreneurs seeking investment for regenerative projects at scale.

Through this essay, you will gain insight into a systemic investment approach that focuses on whole systems rather than isolated assets. You will also learn about the importance of multi-outcome financing models, designed to deliver financial, social, and environmental returns in an era of deep uncertainty.

THE ORIGINAL INSTRUCTIONS AND INDIGENOUS WISDOM

The world's crises—climate instability, biodiversity loss, food insecurity, and social fragmentation—are consequences of an economic and governance model that ignores the original instructions for living in balance with nature. Indigenous peoples, particularly those of the Amazon and Andes, such as the Kogi of Colombia, have preserved these instructions. Their knowledge is not an artifact of the past but a blueprint for the future.

The Kogi, descendants of the great Tayrona civilization, live in a way that honors the Earth as a living system. They do not exploit resources without reciprocation. Their governance, economic structures, and spiritual practices are integrated with the cycles of nature. The Kogi Mamos (spiritual leaders) warn that humanity's destructive tendencies threaten the equilibrium of the world. They remind us that we must return to a model that fosters kinship with the land, where economic and ecological health are not at odds but interwoven.

By applying Indigenous principles to regenerative investment, we can create bioregional economies that thrive without depletion. These investments do not merely sustain but actively regenerate ecosystems and social structures, ensuring resilience for generations to come.

INVESTING IN SYSTEMS, NOT JUST PROJECTS

Traditional investments focus on asset classes: real estate, energy, and infrastructure. Regenerative investing requires a shift in perspective—investing in whole systems rather than isolated components. A regenerative community is not just a collection of homes but an integrated system where water, energy, food, waste, and governance coalesce to support life.

WHY THIS MATTERS FOR INVESTORS

Investors who focus on systemic approaches can achieve multiple returns:

- **Financial stability**: Regenerative investments hedge against the increasing risks of climate instability and resource scarcity.
- **Social cohesion**: Investments that support resilient communities reduce social unrest and increase long-term value.
- **Environmental regeneration**: These investments ensure that the natural resources underpinning all economic activity remain viable.

MULTI-OUTCOME FINANCING: A NEW MODEL FOR INVESTMENT

To achieve true regeneration, we must evolve beyond traditional financing models. Conventional investment seeks short-term gains with limited accountability for externalities. Regenerative investment, by contrast, prioritizes long-term stability and resilience through multi-outcome financing.

ELEMENTS OF MULTI-OUTCOME FINANCING

1. **Blended Capital**: Public, private, and philanthropic funds must work together. Government incentives, NGO contributions, and private equity must align toward common goals.
2. **Risk Hedging Through Diversification**: Investors should allocate capital across multiple bioregions and regenerative initiatives, ensuring resilience to localized shocks.
3. **Regenerative Bonds & Impact-Linked Financing**: Financial instruments must reward ecological and social performance alongside financial returns.
4. **Public-Private Partnerships (PPPs)**: Collaboration between governments, businesses, and communities ensures investment capital is effectively deployed.

THE ROLE OF BIOREGIONAL INVESTMENT

Bioregions are the natural economic units of the future. Investing in bioregions—defined by watersheds, soil types, and ecological corridors—creates self-sustaining economies that regenerate rather than deplete. By aligning economic development with natural processes, we ensure that investments are resilient against global shocks.

EXAMPLES OF BIOREGIONAL INVESTMENT STRATEGIES

- **Regenerative agriculture and local food systems**: Investments in soil health, agroforestry, and community-supported agriculture reduce reliance on global supply chains and create food security.
- **Watershed restoration and decentralized water management**: Protecting and restoring natural water systems ensures clean water access and climate resilience.
- **Circular economies**: Investing in closed-loop systems for waste, energy, and materials creates self-sufficient communities.

THE CALL TO ACTION: FINANCE OUR REGENERATIVE FUTURE

We are at a crossroads. The financial system must evolve to support investments that hedge against civilization-level risks while fostering abundance. This requires an urgent shift away from short-term speculation toward ultra-long-term regenerative finance.

WHAT YOU CAN DO

1. **Allocate capital to systemic investments**: Move beyond asset classes to invest in whole ecosystems and communities.
2. **Engage in cross-sector collaboration**: Work with governments, Indigenous leaders, and local organizations to scale regenerative models.
3. **Advocate for new financial instruments**: Demand investment vehicles that prioritize long-term ecological and social health alongside financial returns.

Finance has the power to shape the future. By committing to regenerative investment, we can co-create societies where both humanity and nature thrive. Now is the time to act.

14   ON MONDRAGON

The Ethics and Values of Cooperative Culture in the Basque Region of Spain

Georgia Kelly is Founder and Executive Director of Praxis Peace Institute, and curates week-long immersion experiences at the Basque Country's Mondragon Cooperatives in Spain.

INTRODUCTION

There was a popular phrase among some politicians a few years back that proclaimed, "there is no alternative" (TINA) to the status quo of neoliberal capitalism. Or, that there is no such thing as "society," only individuals. More recently, tech billionaires have taken this a step further, celebrating individual freedom to the point of eschewing any social responsibility. The obvious hubris in these beliefs is outdone only by their complete and utter lack of empathy and vision.

I am happy to write about a real alternative to the above dark fantasies. After participating in eleven weeklong seminars at the Mondragón Cooperatives and spending time in the Basque region of Spain, it is crystal clear: There is an alternative! The economic policies of their worker-owned cooperatives have created a thriving business atmosphere—one that grows at a sustainable pace and values workers at all levels.

So, what are the Mondragón Cooperatives, and what is so unique about the Basque culture that has managed to support and nurture this model for nearly 70 years?

In order to answer that question, we need to look not only at the cooperatives and how they function but also at the values and ethics that inform them. We need to take a closer look at the society, the aspirations of most Basque people, their NGOs, governance, and the role of peacebuilding. In this short paper, I hope to offer an overview of why the Basque Country and why the Mondragón Cooperatives in particular offer such a hopeful promise for humanity.

The first few Praxis seminars at the Mondragón Cooperatives were focused on the businesses, the Social Councils, the Democratic decision-making process, and the roles of managers and CEOs. We visited industrial businesses, a research and development center, a youth cooperative, the Guggenheim Museum that was partially built by a Mondragón construction company, and we had daily lectures and lunch at Otalora, their educational center, a beautifully-refurbished 14th-century stone villa in the hills above the town of Mondragón.

Over the years, I have become interested in what was unique about this culture that not only birthed a plethora of cooperatives but also managed to sustain them over many decades. Though today the Mondragón Cooperatives comprise nearly 100 businesses, a university complex, a bank with 380 branches, a supermarket chain, and the largest Research and Development complex in Europe, it began modestly in 1956 with a five-person worker-owned cooperative that made kerosene stoves. The visionary for this system was a parish priest, Father José Maria Arizmendiarreta, who wedded out-of-the-box ideas with practical actions. Since there is a good book written about the early days of Mondragón, I will not recount them here.[1]

The stated mission of the Mondragón Cooperatives Corporation (MCC) is to create wealth within society, to foster a people-centered society instead of a capital-centered society, to honor all work with dignity, and to limit the number of work hours so that people have a work-life balance.

Mikel Lezamiz, former educational director at MCC, says, "People are the core, not capital. This is the main point. If capital has the power, then labor is simply its tool."

There are people who insist that such a massive project of cooperatives could only happen in the Basque region because they have a history of cooperation, of working together, and that individualistic societies like the U.S. could never nurture large-scale worker-owned businesses. When I asked Ander Etxeberria, the Director of Dissemination at the Mondragón Cooperatives, about this, he strongly disagreed. "We are normal people," he said, implying that this could develop anywhere. But that is assuming that "anywhere" has the right combination of leadership, vision, ethics, and practical business acumen.

I asked if he thought that the impoverished state of the Basque region in the 1940s, which had an unemployment rate close to 70%, aided in developing cooperatives. He agreed that it most likely did. People were desperate, and when Father Arizmendiarreta created a polytechnic school to train many of the unemployed people in Mondragón so that they could land industrial-sector jobs in Mondragon and Bilbao, they embraced the opportunity. Eventually, five

---

1 *Making Mondragón: The Growth and Dynamics of the Worker Cooperative Complex* by William Foote Whyte and Kathleen King Whyte, 1989.

students emerged from this school to form ULGOR (later renamed FAGOR), the first cooperative. FAGOR industrial appliances still exists today, 67 years later.

Fred Freundlich, an American who has taught at Mondragón University and lived in the Basque region for 30 years, had a different perspective. "There is a social fabric in Basque consciousness," he said. "Cooperation is rooted in society, and a subculture of cooperation developed through the Mondragón Cooperatives Corporation." It seems that the Basque culture and the Mondragón Cooperatives have established a feedback loop that encourages cooperation.

Considering that poverty in the area allowed space for a different vision may be a key factor. I don't think it is necessary, but it does seem that desperate situations leave room for more creative solutions. Being too comfortable does not bode well for disrupting the status quo.

But, with the climate crisis upon us, growing economic inequality, a plethora of dead-end jobs with minimal pay while CEOs rake in billions, and the increasing unrest that accompanies all this, we may finally be more open to a new way of organizing business, work, and society. Examining the culture that spawned and nourished Mondragón has become more urgent in light of the crises we are facing today.

The crucial role that Father Arizmendiarreta played in the development of the Mondragón Cooperatives and all that emerged from them cannot be overstated. His vision guided the development of the cooperative movement, and his practical but sometimes unique maneuverings grounded the vision in a strong foundation that could flourish over a long time into the future.

At the end of several of our seminars, we were given copies of a small book of quotes from Arizmendiarreta. These sayings serve to illuminate the underlying ethics and philosophy that have been at the foundation of the cooperatives from the very beginning. Here are a few examples:

- Freedom is the oppression of the weak. The law is the freedom of the poor.
- The position women have in any society is the exact measurement of its level of development.
- The cooperative movement is an educational effort that uses economic action as a vehicle of transformation.
- Knowledge must be socialized so that power can be democratized.
- It is a bad tactic, history warns us, to start by compromising our values, expecting their recuperation later. With this strategy, those who have the best odds to win are usually the least scrupulous, the adventurers and the tyrants.

CORE BUSINESS PRINCIPLES

Arizmendiarreta's vision was imbued with ten core principles, and these were transmitted to students at the polytechnic school and eventually to the worker-owners. One of these principles and a main goal of the Mondragón Cooperatives is Social Transformation, which demonstrates the wholeness of the vision and the commitment to systemic change.

The Mondragón Cooperatives are united by a humanist concept of business, a philosophy of participation and solidarity. One worker-owner = One vote. There are no shares to sell or trade. Each worker-owner has one share and can cash out if he or she leaves, but they cannot sell that share. This has protected Mondragón businesses from being taken over by larger or multi-national corporations. Wage solidarity, another of Mondragón's Core Principles, is demonstrated in their salary structure. The average CEO earns only six times the salary of the average worker-owner, a far cry from U.S. CEOs who might earn 300-400 times the average salary.

The Mondragón Corporation provides healthcare and social welfare insurance through Lagun Aro, a social protection system for Mondragón worker-owners. It includes disability, sick leave, unemployment insurance, maternity and paternity leave, pensions, and professional training and retraining. Mondragón workers have four to six weeks paid vacation plus paid sick leave. They also receive medical insurance through the Spanish national system.

Mondragón businesses range from the manufacturing of auto parts that are sold to all major auto companies throughout the world, including U.S. companies, to industrial appliances that are marketed primarily to restaurants and hotels, and to the Eroski supermarket chain that sells food as well as appliances, books, TVs, computers, towels, bedding, household appliances, furniture, and much more. Mondragón businesses also manufacture computer chips, bicycles (Orbea), industrial machines that make parts for jet engines, wind turbines, and rockets. Overseeing the largest Research & Development complex in Europe gives Mondragón a jumpstart on innovation and the development of new products.

"People before profit" is the underlying principle that we hear in every seminar at Mondragón. Acknowledging that profit is essential in order to stay in business, they also understand that it must be secondary to the people doing the work.

Understanding the principles of conflict resolution is also an integral part of MCC. When someone in our seminar asked what they would do with a worker who was inattentive or goofing off on the job, our instructor didn't hesitate a moment. "We don't believe in confrontation," he said. "We would initiate a dialogue in order to find out what is causing the problem. Maybe he is ill or there is a difficulty at home, a pending divorce, or some other cause." The focus at MCC is not punishment for bad or inattentive work, but interest in the individual having the problem and how it might be fixed. Their approach of caring and inquiring before making any assumptions is another area that sets Mondragón apart from many businesses.

Since education is the central Core Principle in the Mondragón system, it follows that in the early 2000s, one of the key components incorporated in the educational system was the study and practice of human rights and peaceful coexistence as part of the school curriculum. As primatologist, Frans de Waal, has noted in his research, primates have the possibility of being aggressive or peaceful, and much of it has to do with the environment in which they are nurtured. We have the capacity to be peaceful and respectful, and an educational system that teaches the principles of conflict resolution and human rights from an early age is preparing a generation of people capable of handling conflicts maturely.

THE MONDRAGÓN UNIVERSITY SYSTEM

Mondragón University includes three campuses that are located in Mondragón, Oñati, and Irun. The Mondragón campus is focused on engineering, and the schools in Oñati and Irun are focused on business. The Basque Culinary Arts Center is a fourth university program that opened in 2011. Attracting well-known and accomplished chefs from around the world as faculty members, this university has a waiting list for in-person classes, but it also offers online courses.

The first Mondragón University campus was established in the town of Mondragón and grew from the original polytechnic school that was founded by Father Arizmendiarreta. It was officially established as a university in 1997. Mondragón University also includes a network of social innovation and ecosystem labs created by the Mondragón TeamAcademy, a program within the business school that was founded by José Marí Luzarraga. This team has built alliances with universities in several cities and has centers in Bilbao, San Sebastian, Irun, and Oñati in the Basque region and in Madrid, Valencia, Barcelona, Shanghai, Querétaro, Seoul, Puebla, Berlin, Puna, and Seattle. Students study in at least three different countries during their highly innovative four-year program.[2] They are tasked with creating working cooperative businesses while at university. Some of these businesses have continued after the student "teampreneurs"[3] graduate from university.

---

2 TeamAcademy—https://Mondragónteamacademy.com/

3 The term "Teampreneur" was coined by the José Marí Luzarraga, the founder of this program.

ENVIRONMENT AND THE CLIMATE CRISIS

The Basque Country has set the target to cut total greenhouse gas (GHG) emissions by 40% by 2030, and it is on track to accomplish their goal. By 2018, it had already reduced emissions by 26%.

In addressing environmental concerns and the climate crisis, the Basque Parliament has committed to altering policies as well as addressing behavior changes. First, comes the acknowledgment that consumption patterns must be modified and that environmental concerns should be included in all policy sectors. Balancing a reduction in the use of natural resources while also increasing productivity is challenging, but the government suggests creating a new model of development that reflects these climate goals.

The Basque Country government signed on to the European Green Deal by unveiling its own plan for a more sustainable future, which includes social and economic justice. It is creating a new regulatory structure, one that incorporates energy transition methods in line with its emission targets. These plans include the establishment of photovoltaic power cooperatives, new wind farms, support for local farms, and the coordination of Mayors in facilitating these projects in the Basque Network of Municipalities.

The Basque government also maintains that Quality of Life must be built on the foundations of environmental sustainability, that the way of thinking, values, lifestyle, and consumption patterns must be modified. Strategic planning and reflection on creating a new model of development must be part of its vision and goals.

The "Climate Change Strategy of the Basque Country to 2050" (KLIMA 2050, published by the Basque Government's Department of Environment and Territorial Policy)[4] was endorsed at the 2015 Paris climate summit as one of 24 of the world's leading public programs for a low-carbon economy. In preparation for this report, the Basque government created an online portal for public input, inviting their citizens to contribute ideas and strategies. This is typical of the cooperative strategy, where everyone can contribute to the solution-making process. All citizens can take ownership of both the process and its achievements. The Basque Region plans to be carbon neutral by 2050.

Orkli, a Mondragón Cooperative and world leader in the manufacture and sales of thermoelectric safety components, has developed the only integrated and 100% autonomous mechanical-circulation solar power system on the market. It does not require electricity to operate, thus saving costs and energy, and it is 100% sustainable because it does not release CO2 into the atmosphere.[5]

---

4 https://regions4.org/actions/klima-2050/

5 https://www.orkli.com/en/web/confort-calefaccion/solar-heating

Another Mondragón Cooperative, Domusa Teknik, manufactures Solar Systems for hot water systems, heat pumps, biomass boilers, hot water heat exchangers, electric boilers, and other related products.

Mondragón Research and Development includes work in the wind industry, induction technology, electronics and communication, medical research, industrial and data security, and the development of lighter trains and airplanes for energy efficiency.

EFFICIENCY

One thing I have observed in visiting Mondragón and the Basque region over the past 15 years is that they have been constantly evolving. Products, ideas, or plans that either hadn't existed or were in the early stages of development one year might be fully developed two years later. I have never visited the "same" Basque region in the 11 times I have been there. They adapt, organize, and implement quickly—all without the stress that we would expect with such activity. Maybe it's because they are working cooperatively, not as individuals who have to prove their worth, but as team members who support each other.

In the early stages of COVID, the Spanish government realized it was woefully short of masks to protect their healthcare workers and citizens. Acknowledging the efficiency and quality of the Mondragón Cooperatives, the Spanish government's Agency for Medicine and Medical Devices reached out to two Mondragón Cooperatives (FAGOR and Bexen Medical), and asked them to produce as many surgical masks as possible and in the shortest amount of time as possible. Within one week, the project was well underway, and soon they were producing 10 million masks per month.[6]

SOCIAL TRANSFORMATION IN BASQUE NON-GOVERNMENT ORGANIZATIONS

The Basque Case is defined as the "Implementation of a socio-political-legal-economic model built on three principles:

1. The Ethical Principle (universal rights, social justice, peaceful coexistence, humanism).
2. The Democratic Principle
3. The Sustainable Human Development Principle (which takes into account the impact on future generations).

---

6 https://www.fagor.eus/en/Mondragón-assembly-member-of-the-fagor-group-will-build-machines-to-produce-surgical-masks/

Operating on these principles is The Agirre Lehendakaria Center,[7] a non-governmental organization located in Bilbao. Its social innovation center specializes in systemic transitions toward Sustainable Human Development. What they call the "K Factor" is the integration of culture, narratives, and values from each community toward a holistic vision of Sustainable Human Development. They employ Deep Listening in order to "break with the traditional division between analysis and action with a permanent listening system." They are working with transformational processes in more than 10 countries in collaboration with local institutions. These countries include Uruguay, Bangladesh, Colombia, Kosovo, Armenia, Thailand, Pakistan, the Basque Country, and other areas of Spain.

Examples of what they do can be explained by one of their programs in Spain. Working with a challenge like energy transition, they are dealing with the transformation of an economy. Using their Social Innovation platforms to address the closure of two coal-fired power plants led them to establish a multi-stakeholder collaboration with an electricity company and two university innovation centers. They focused on lost jobs, the creation of new jobs, migration, an ageing population, and the cultural changes that will accompany economic changes. This process is co-creative and values all stakeholders, including the citizens of the region, by seeking input from everyone affected by the decisions.

Another innovative NGO is the Basque Women's Institute, Emakunde, which was established as an autonomous body within the Basque Parliament in 1988.[8] Its purpose is to educate and implement gender equality throughout society. In all Mondragón worker-owned businesses, women and men are paid the exact same salary for the same work, and since I first visited the area in 2008, there are many more women in management positions, on corporate boards, and in politics today (2022). In fact, the Mayor of Mondragón, María Ubarretxena, has held that office for the past seven years and was first elected when she was 35 years old. We were fortunate to have special sessions with her in 2022 and 2023. The Basque Parliament also increased the proportion of women MPs from 24% in 1997 to 58% by 2009.[9] As one can see, the work of Emakunde continues to be very successful.

Both of these NGOs demonstrate a commitment to social transformation and a determination to accomplish their goals in a short amount of time. One doesn't hear about how long it might take or how unrealistic it is to make systemic changes; they just focus on getting them done.

---

7 www.agirrecenter.eus

8 https://www.emakunde.euskadi.eus/webemao1-inicio/en

9 https://blogs.shu.edu/basqueresearch/2015/12/01/parity-in-parliament-gender-equality-within-the-basque-government/

THE BASQUE PARLIAMENT AND DEPARTMENT OF COEXISTENCE AND HUMAN RIGHTS

Juan José Ibarretxe, former President of the Basque Parliament, said that "One of the greatest failures of Neoliberal economic and political thought has been its abandonment of humanity to the impulses of the market" and claimed that "a market without values is not a real market, but an auction."

He noted that in the Basque Country, innovation has become the motivation for a comprehensive social approach to sustainable human development and that incorporating innovation and humanism in the identity of their organizations gives them a powerful lever for social transformation."

It is important to note that while the Basque region developed cooperatives in a peaceful atmosphere, there was also a terrorist faction, ETA (Euskadi ta Askatasuna), that killed and threatened many people who were not on board with the Basque separatist movement to secede from Spain. ETA was formed in 1959 as a backlash to the repressive Franco regime. Franco had forbidden the indigenous Basque language to be spoken or taught in schools. Tragically, ETA managed to kill more than 1,000 people within a 60-year period. So, the region has also dealt with violence.

The Basque Department of Coexistence and Human Rights was established after the successful negotiations with ETA resulted in their agreement to abandon violence and begin a Truth and Reconciliation process between the victims and perpetrators. Many outside peacemakers were eventually involved in the process, but the spearhead was the Basque Peace group, Elkarri,[10] which was headed by Jonan Fernandez. He and Gorka Espiau, who later founded the Agirre Center, visited the Center for International Conflict Resolution at Columbia University in New York and had meetings with Andrea Bartoli, who founded the center, and Senator George Mitchell, who was at that time a senior research scholar there.[11]

Later, when Elkarri dissolved, Fernandez created Baketik, a peace organization that is dedicated to promoting processes for coexistence and social transformation based on a strong ethical foundation. Conflict resolution education, processes of reconciliation, and the use of creative expression through narratives and drama are central to its purpose. Or, as their website says, "Culture can—and must—drive social reflection."

When we visited Baketik, its offices were located on the monastery grounds of Our Lady of Aranzazu in Oñati, but today they are based in Tolosa, about 17 miles southwest of San Sebastian. Jonan Fernandez left Baketik when he was appointed General Director for Human Rights, Coexistence, and Cooperation

---

10 https://blogs.shu.edu/basqueresearch/about-us/

11 https://berghof-foundation.org/news/lessons-learnt-from-the-basque-peace-process

in the Basque government. This appointment was a direct result of his work with ETA and in other peace and human rights projects and education.

In 2011, Fernandez's work with ETA resulted in the agreement by ETA members to abandon violence. At first, ETA members were reluctant to give up their weapons because they feared retribution. However, by 2017, ETA turned in all their weaponry, and by 2018, ETA dissolved itself completely, thereby ending a sixty-year reign of terrorism in the Basque region. From start to finish, all this was accomplished in fewer than 10 years.

I have often thought about this extraordinary process and what we can learn from it. If Fernandez had parroted the maxim we often hear in the U.S., "we don't negotiate with terrorists," ETA would probably still be terrorizing people today. Rigid positions on any side do not pave the way toward solutions or peace.

Jonan Fernandez has written several books, and one has been translated into English, *Being, Human in Conflict.* Another excellent book, though it is only available in Spanish, is *Vivir Y Convivir: 4 Aprendizajes Básicos* (*Living and Coexisting: 4 Basic Lessons*).

The above is to affirm that the Basque Country is not utopia, or, as Mikel Lezamiz, the former Director of Dissemination at Mondragón, said, "This is not paradise and we are not angels." However, by the end of our week-long seminar, he never managed to convince most of us. Though Mondragón might not be paradise, it is much closer to that ideal than where most of us live. What they call "normal" is clearly an evolved normal.

The difference in the Basque Country, as demonstrated by the dissolution of ETA, is that they deal with problems with the goal of solving them rather than winning and establishing who is right. Posturing and grandstanding are not part of the mix. It is a mature manner of dealing with problems, and I have found that Jonan Fernandez's books illuminate that process, as do the reports published by the Basque government's Department of Coexistence and Human Rights. In 2022, the International Catalan Institute for Peace awarded the ICIP "Peace in Progress Award" to all the civil society peace initiatives of the Basque Country "for their contribution to the advancement of peace, and the end of political violence and the creation of frameworks of coexistence and reconciliation."

One of the participants in the peace process was the Berghof Foundation, which is based in Berlin. Their short piece on the Basque peace process encapsulates the unique, respectful, and effective manner in which they worked:

The Basque peace process teaches us the value of creativity and endurance in the face of persistent obstacles. It demonstrates that when society demands peace, it can be brought about in a dignified way, even in the absence of a negotiated peace process with state authorities. It also offered an important lesson on inclusivity and participation, by involving all political and social stakeholders in the formulation and implementation of solutions to address the 'consequences of the conflict.

THERE IS AN ALTERNATIVE TO NEOLIBERAL, CUTTHROAT CAPITALISM

The American myth says we can have it all, but in Mondragón and the Basque region, these ideas seem provincially (or arrogantly) naïve. Why should we even want it *all*? The countries and communities that value social connection, social services, and the eradication of poverty consistently appear at the top of the happiness index. The Basque region has the highest standard of living and the lowest unemployment rate in Spain, and it also has the largest number of people involved in worker-owned businesses. In addition to the Mondragón Cooperatives, there are at least another 1,000 cooperatives in the region. Many participants in the Praxis seminar in Mondragón have had their worldviews turned upside down in a most inspiring and hopeful manner. There are alternatives to the inhumanity of Neoliberal capitalism, and we cannot afford to wait another generation or even another decade to learn about and incorporate these alternatives into our governments, businesses, and climate policies.

Today, the Basque Country is considered the wealthiest area of Spain, but in the 1950s, it was the poorest region of that country. Wealthy does not mean that there are mega-mansions in the hills above Mondragón or that large gated communities flourish in the seaside town of San Sebastian. It means that the Basque region has the highest GDP per person in Spain and that poverty has been mostly eliminated. You won't find people living in the streets or in squalid slums on the outskirts of their cities. Gradations of the middle class seem to come closest to describing the way most people live.

Best-selling author **Kim Stanley Robinson** highlights the Mondragón Cooperatives in his latest book, *The Ministry for the Future*, as one of the most important models to learn from in changing human relationships, economics, and culture.

The models for sustainable, peaceful cultures exist on our planet. Mondragón is one of the most inspirational of these models because it embodies a respectful humility, never assuming they have all the answers or "the solution," but always striving to improve and seek better ways to live and work empathically, respectfully, and in cooperation with others.

ADDENDUM

When people ask how a system like the Mondragón Cooperatives could be replicated in the U.S., there are no clear or easy answers. Looking at Basque culture makes it obvious that the rampant individualism that is so prevalent in our society is not the driving force in theirs. The people I have met in the Basque Country do not aspire to great wealth. They focus on family, friends, and socializing in the community. I'm sure there are exceptions, but chasing millions of dollars in order to buy mansions, yachts, and fancy cars is not a motivating factor in their culture. They understand the concept of "enough," and their self-worth is not tied to the possession of material goods and gadgets.

Yet, in spite of the pressures of American individualism and materialism, there are many worker-owned cooperatives in the United States, too. But they are spread all over the country and not connected with their own infrastructure like the Mondragón Cooperatives Corporation. Perhaps if the cooperatives in the Bay Area, for instance, or even nationwide, all worked with the same bank or credit union, they might have more leverage in securing financing for new cooperatives, coop conversions, and expansion of existing cooperatives.

One thing is clear in meeting worker-owners in both the Basque region and in the United States. The values and ethics that guide them are the same in both places. The concept of "enough" is alive in both places. The challenge in the U.S., which is a much larger country, is to bring the stories of this inspired way of life to many more people and to aid in the creation of more worker-owned cooperatives in our country. Praxis Peace Institute is hosting free conversations on this model online in addition to the week-long seminar that we host in Mondragón, Spain.[12]

This is an ongoing conversation, and I hope people who read this essay will join the next Praxis discussion on the business, ethics, and culture of the Mondragón Cooperatives and how this model can be enabled and nurtured in the United States and elsewhere around the world.

---

12 To learn more about the next Praxis Mondragón seminar, please visit: praxispeace.org

15   A VIEW FROM THE TOP OF THE PHILANTHROPY PYRAMID

Hannah Odell is Director of Strategic Giving at TED. Previously she was Chief Growth Officer at the Global Warming Mitigation Project and Director at Hudson Ferris in New York.

In the face of the sixth extinction, logic would have us believe that all those possessing power, influence, and agency would be compelled to act to protect humankind, or at the very least, the conditions within which they so fully thrive. One would think that the world's wealthiest and smartest individuals would clamor over the tremendous thrill of being positioned to create the next format of society. And yet, we see the unthinkable unfolding before our eyes—with less than 2% of global philanthropy going to address climate change.[1]

For those of us in the business of rolling up our sleeves to engineer and implement the sustainable systems of the future, the utter lack of philanthropic response to climate change can create feelings of both fiery fury and bone-chilling numbness. We often find ourselves screaming into the wind—why such widespread disregard for the moral imperative of keeping our planet alive? When will they realize that climate change is unrelenting and unbiased, and there is no way out except a total redesign of life as we know it? It is here, and it is everywhere. Generational legacies of wealth will only buy a certain degree of comfort for those fortunate enough to be born into the upper echelons of society. And, for those who have long been victimized by unchecked corporate greed, an all-too-familiar sense of hopelessness ushers hundreds of millions of people into a fear-laden and fragile future.

We are presented with abundant opportunities to construct a just and

---

1 Desanlis, H.; Lau, T.; Janik, K.; Suttenberg, S.; Menon, S. (2022) *Funding trends 2022: Climate Change Mitigation Philanthropy.* ClimateWorks Foundation. https://www.climateworks.org/wp-content/uploads/2022/10/ClimateWorks_Funding_Trends_Report_2022.pdf

regenerative world. This unique circumstance wakes me every morning with the volume of a million voices calling out from decades ahead. It calls to me, just a tiny cog in a massive wheel, to be accountable for where the wheel turns and to use what I know to maximize its every rotation.

So, I find myself contemplating time and time again, ***what kind of cog am I?*** How can I harness the power I do have to propel this interlocking system of gears forward? In 15 years as a nonprofit development professional, I have observed how the modern paradigm of philanthropy has failed to address the most consequential issue of our time. To understand why, I have tried to dissect and analyze the forces, both internal and external, behind charitable giving.

For the purposes of this article, I will focus on the role of individual giving in driving meaningful progress on climate change mitigation, because I believe that when deployed wisely, major gifts can be the most nimble and efficient mechanism for social impact, and as a fundraiser, my favorite way to move capital is to sit down with someone and give them the opportunity to change the world.

Let's process this again. Less than 2% of total charitable giving addresses climate change—and to say that fact is alarming is like saying that mortality is merely irksome. It shakes me to my core when I think about the trillions of dollars of wealth consolidated in our country and the nearly $500 billion donated annually to causes that, like us, will struggle to sustain and ultimately exist in a post–2.0 degrees Celsius world—the global average temperature threshold beyond which ecosystems will barrel toward irreversible collapse.[2] To get to the root of this staggering statistic, we must go back to the playground, to a place where little humans lack the awareness to be anything else but their unfiltered selves. The same behaviors we see there—herd mentality, approval seeking, and self-serving motivation—still rule the sandbox today, reinforced by longstanding societal norms that hinder human progress.

Today, these inherent human conditions dictate how the philanthropic community activates and mobilizes. We see what risk aversion, recognition, and ego look like at full scale. Let's first examine risk aversion.

In my early years as a fundraising consultant, I had the great pleasure of helping to raise capital for a first-of-its-kind school in Somaliland that was established in a community where brutality and poverty were deeply ingrained. The educational model worked, the success stories were tear-evoking, and the opportunity was unprecedented. And yet, in the school's inaugural years, countless foundations and donors shut their doors on us without hesitation. We

2 (2024) *Why do we keep talking about 1.5°C and 2°C above the pre-industrial era?* ECMWF as part of The Copernicus Programme. https://climate.copernicus.eu/why-do-we-keep-talking-about-15degc-and-2degc-above-pre-industrial-era#:~:text=The%20IPCC%20compares%20the%20impacts,and%20future%20of%20our%20climate.

heard feedback about geopolitical risk and impact numbers that were just too small. We were told to circle back in a few years when the impact was tenfold, and after others had jumped in first. The uphill battle of securing those bold initial funders was disheartening, but it only takes one visionary partner to set the pace of truly transformative change.

And then—the (well-deserved) lucky break. *60 Minutes* picked up the story, and in one fell swoop, Anderson Cooper erased donor inhibitions, wiped risk aversion off the table, and propagated the idea that anyone who could, would be crazy not to give to this worthy project. An influx of capital from philanthropists followed, sending Somali students to top U.S. universities for the first time in fifty years. Today, those same students are returning to their home country and local communities as doctors, educators, economists, and policymakers—an outcome once deemed impossible.

This story tells us that playing it safe won't earn anyone a medal at the finish line of this decisive decade. Assessing risk is critical to any smart investment, but in a time where every region of the world is exposed to climate risk, we must see beyond the status quo, create safety nets where they don't exist, and clear a path for giving with fewer guarantees. The colossal change we need to make by 2030 requires ingenuity and an expectation that with innovation comes failure, and failure is a part of uncharted exploration. As a fundraiser, I aim to let donors be the heroes of the explorers' journey, but in today's world, it is a persistent challenge to find the Lewises and Clarks of climate action.

That said, on the philanthropy frontier, a brave few are raising their flags. John and Laura Arnold are two such donors taking a novel approach to climate giving with the power and scope to shift the philanthropic landscape. In a recent episode of *Freakonomics* with Steve Levitt, John Arnold—who was once the world's youngest self-made billionaire—recognized that many of his peers are limited by fears of reputational and financial risk. They worry about making a mistake and being associated with a flawed or failed project. They overly scrutinize groundbreaking new efforts and revert instead to the security that comes with supporting a capital campaign at a well-established institution. But as Arnold points out in this interview, philanthropy's primary function is to expeditiously fill the gap that exists when political and financial incentives hinder private and public sector responses to pressing issues.[3] And, in my opinion, it is the role of the nonprofit sector to continue to break the barriers of what's possible with daring and audacious new solutions.

We know that investors and philanthropists alike want to see metrics and outcomes from these solutions that demonstrate meaningful returns—either

---

3 Levitt, Steve. June 3, 2022. "Giving it Away." Freakonomics. https://freakonomics.com/podcast/giving-it-away/

to the bottom line or to the cause—but in many cases, byzantine reporting requirements create a resource drain on climate organizations that pulls critical time, energy, and funding away from the task at hand. Though we have seen a surge in trust-based philanthropy since the pandemic, will it be enough? I often find myself and my colleagues facing mountains of duplicative work to provide evidence of impact and proper stewardship of dollars. Every moment spent navigating these cumbersome processes is a moment not spent on the mission.

As it stands, the climate funding community is exclusive, and opportunities are finite. With more than 28,000 environmental organizations in the U.S. fighting for the same limited pool of capital, we need to see more donors entering the space with a vision for deploying minimal-strings-attached general operating dollars to as many organizations in as many corners of the world as possible.

There are many types of donors out there—those who favor direct service, givers to program-restricted projects, others who see complex systems change as the answer, and the minority who like to support capacity-building and the less-sexy parts of nonprofit operations. But the bottom line is that we need it all, and we need it in fast abundance. I say "fast abundance" with a caveat; providing outsized gifts in the tens of millions to small-to-mid-sized organizations will undoubtedly spur innovation and impact, but it needs to be done wisely and with an exit strategy that enables climate organizations to sustain and thrive. As the former Managing Director of a boutique fundraising consultancy, I can attest to how fast growth can sometimes be a startup's undoing.

It is mission-critical that organizations build solid infrastructure, utilize efficient systems, and retain a roster of talent to support programmatic growth at scale. To do these things as quickly as the climate crisis warrants will undoubtedly lead to some trips and falls. But that's okay, and donors need to understand that trial and error is part and parcel of this climate-driven evolutionary process. Donors must instill the same confidence in nonprofit leaders as they do in corporate executives and entrepreneurs.

Take MacKenzie Scott's giving strategy as an example. She has now given $17.3 billion to more than 2,300 organizations, and almost all her grantmaking has been unrestricted.[4] Though she is in a stratosphere of wealth virtually all unto her own, the lessons we can extrapolate from her philanthropic sensibilities are worth noting here. Not only have her transformative grants to organizations *serving and led by* underrepresented groups amplified impact across a myriad of causes and communities, but she has also set a new precedent of **trust**.

Patterns that have emerged from her giving demonstrate a commitment

---

4 Bowermaster, David (2024) *Signs Of A New Wave Of Giving By MacKenzie Scott*. Forbes. https://www.forbes.com/sites/davidbowermaster/2024/10/10/signs-of-a-new-wave-of-giving-by-mackenzie-scott/#:~:text=Since%202020%2C%20Scott%20has%20given,nonprofits%2C%20according%20to%20Yield%20Giving

to flexible funding. Prior to the onset of the pandemic in 2020, only 20% of grants in the sector were unrestricted, so in this way, Scott has been a trail-blazer.[5] Her trust-based grants have given nonprofit leaders the autonomy to infuse resources into their organizations where they are needed most—and others have followed her lead. Don Gips of the Skoll Foundation, as an example, shared in a 2024 newsletter that rather than dictating impact metrics, they let nonprofit leaders establish their own systems-level outcomes and success benchmarks they aim to hit as funding is implemented.[6]

I'll admit, I had my doubts when I first heard about Scott's strategy—open call, few restrictions, massive sums of money. But the results, and that of those who followed suit, tell a story I have long heard in the cacophony of voices that awake me every morning. The solutions to our world's most pressing issues exist. Talent and leadership abound. What holds philanthropists back from launching us into a sustainable future is the *fear* of stepping outside of an overly prescriptive model of charitable giving. And that model is no longer viable in a world where 2030 looms overhead, watchful and unforgiving.

Moving on, we must recognize that for many donors, at the crux of philanthropy is social status. Within every human being is the desire to be recognized and applauded for their achievements. Ego drives this part of us to seek status in the circles within which we associate. As a consultant, I used to ask my nonprofit clients, "What motivates major donors to give?" The most common answer was always "tax benefits." This mislguidedassumption runs deep in the nonprofit world and often leads to missed fundraising opportunities and solicitations turned sour. People donate because it feels good. Many—not all, but many—give because they want to be applauded, and they want to feel they are among the ranks of the Bloombergs and Gateses of the world. My mentor, Ed Leibman, Founder of the fundraising firm Hudson Ferris, used to say, "Giving your hard-earned money away is an irrational act at its core." So, effective fundraisers know you must create strong emotional resonance within your pitch and create an opportunity to achieve immortality through giving. Whether it's a name on a building or a legacy of meaningful social impact that will be seen for years, you want your donors to feel like they are buying a luxury item only available to a small percentage of the world's population.

But in climate, naming rights lose their luster when you know your building

---

5 Beasley, Stephanie. (2022) *MacKenzie Scott's giving 'profoundly positive' for nonprofits: report.* Devex. https://www.devex.com/news/mackenzie-scott-s-giving-profoundly -positive-for-nonprofits-report-104283

6 (2024). To make philanthropy more equitable, take a no-strings approach. Skoll Foundation. https:// www.linkedin.com/pulse/make-philanthropy-more-equitable-take-no-strings-approach-txh8c/

could be swallowed by the sea or incinerated in a wildfire. I would venture to say that children of ultra-high-net-worth individuals want thriving biological and economic ecosystems for their children more than they'd like to see their family name on the facade of a building. The legacy that will outlast them all is that which helps to create the conditions for human survival. The donors who wield the most power may not be around to receive applause for their long-term impact and might not live to see the tangible return on their investment. But the alternative is generational wealth squandered and a planet destroyed.

Why, then, are we seeing such barriers in climate fundraising? One of my experiences fundraising in this space might shed light. I sat down with the wife of a multimillionaire to talk about helping to launch a new initiative that could strengthen a largely overlooked corner of the climate innovation space. Our conversation was engaging and jam-packed with passion on both sides. As we indulged in the delight of the moment, feeling we were at the global center of groundbreaking change, I thought I had found a partner to seed our big, bold climate venture. And, because of the aforementioned force of herd mentality, I could already envisage the avalanche of funding that would follow this gift. There we were, on the precipice of moving the needle on global warming.

Well, I didn't expect what happened next. After the last bite of food and sip of iced tea, I learned that climate change has a "very special" place in this individual's heart and mind, but it would never be their number one charitable cause. After all, what would their friends say about their large carbon-emitting home, private jet, and consumerist lifestyle? In fact, many of said friends had already criticized this donor's peers for attaching their names to climate causes while continuing to live lavish lifestyles. Fear of criticism was enough to drive that donor to direct their philanthropy instead to their child's school, their alma mater, and a few notable museums—instead of offsetting their carbon footprint and sparking climate inventions.

One of the cardinal rules of fundraising is to remove yourself from the ask. It's never personal. But with climate change, it's always personal. It's personal, it's universal, it's woven into the fiber of our DNA. Politely, this anecdote is simply meant to make a point. Everyone has their own unique circumstances, passions, obligations, and expectations. But peer approval can be as binding as it is gratifying, and if we continue to repeat the philanthropic trends of the past, we will soon put the whole planet out of business.

As I see it, the solution here ties back to playground herd mentality. How can "we"—the media, industry, civil society, and society at large—encourage and elevate bold charitable actions? How can we create a dynamic that allows philanthropy to be imperfect, brave, and authentic? Let's ditch the sleepy, stale gala in favor of honoring those who carve out a new space in philanthropy.

Let's celebrate those who seek to upend the status quo and pursue impact that reaches far beyond a world we may never see firsthand. We can't necessarily change the roots of human behavior—the need for recognition isn't going away—but we can and should change the parameters by which we evaluate and acknowledge philanthropic leadership.

Moving forward, another variable in the equation of climate philanthropy is the need to serve "the self." This might sound odd when discussing a charitable cause that will ultimately determine the preservation—or extinction—of all life on Earth, but what I mean is that the arch of philanthropy tends to bend toward the donor first. Of course, countless altruistic donors in America seek to level the playing field through generous aid, and a smaller percentage center justice in their giving strategies to shift agency to the communities they wish to help. But, when looking at philanthropic trends nationwide, we see that of the $557.16 billion donated to U.S. charities in 2023 (which represented a 2.1% decrease adjusted for inflation from 2022), $145.81 billion went to religion, $87.69 billion went to education ($58 billion to higher ed),[7] and $56.58 billion went to health.[8]

While these statistics represent the philanthropic landscape overall, the large majority of charitable giving has and likely always will come from individuals (67% in 2023),[9] so these numbers demonstrate a longstanding pattern that comports with our simpler understanding of self-serving motivation. It is a pattern that tells us that human beings, with or without financial capacity, want to preserve the things that serve them. So, it is not surprising that most major donors prioritize their church, their child's school, or the disease that runs in their family. What is then left of the philanthropic pie are mere slivers of resources for organizations that work for the betterment of communities, society, and global systems at large.

So where does climate fall in this hierarchy of giving inclination? Within just the past few years, we have seen (for the most part) national dialogue and debate turn from "Is it happening?" to "What's the best way to fix it?"—and among the more informed, "How much time do we have left?" Despite climate change's irrefutable impacts on other better-funded rungs of the giving ladder,

7 Gawlor, Brian. (2024) *Higher Education Philanthropy Tops $58 Billion in FY23.* Ruffalo Noel Levitz. https://www.ruffalonl.com/blog/fundraising/higher-education-philanthropy-tops-58-billion-in-fy2023/#:~:text=Giving%20to%20U.S.%20higher%20education,of%20Education%20Survey%20(VSE)

8 (2024) *Giving USA: U.S. charitable giving totaled $557.16 billion in 2023.* Lilly Family School of Philanthropy at Indiana University Indianapolis. https://philanthropy.indianapolis.iu.edu/news-events/news/_news/2024/giving-usa-us-charitable-giving-totaled-557.16-billion-in-2023.html

9 Ibid.

it continues to be deprioritized. The philanthropic community has a bad habit of missing its moment for climate action by failing to grab the helm and pick up the pace.

In many ways, the tone of climate communications and subsequent fundraising messages is to blame. Every sound fundraising proposition must connect money directly to the problem. When it comes to solving multifaceted global issues, donors can become disengaged when questions are raised that their wallets can't answer. In many ways, the climate movement shouldn't have this problem, and yet it persists. The technologies we need to transition the world off fossil fuels exist today and simply need funding to be scaled. But simultaneously, we face the compounding issues of political divisiveness, corporate greed, and international geopolitical instability—monstrous barriers that can leave donors feeling helpless, disillusioned, and falling back on old patterns of safe, self-giving.

When facing this complex question of how to shift the concentration of major gifts from self to society, communication is everything. Words matter. We need to move the narrative away from "us" vs. "them," as these lines wash away with each devastating flood. We need to translate science into sense for all those who aren't well-versed in the technicalities. We need to tell stories that connect a donor's desire to preserve their family, their community, and their legacy to the omnipresent risk that could wipe out all three.

For me, the ubiquitous menace of global warming trumps all other charitable spaces, though this still feels more like an unpopular opinion than a common-sense conclusion. Giving to climate action *is* a gift to self and to a future where education, health, and families can thrive. Climate action is as much about saving human lives as it is about saving the planet—a thing so many somehow feel unaccountable to, as if it doesn't supply the air in our lungs.

To pull levers of influence capable of progressing these philanthropic trends, we also need bold leadership from the private and public sectors. I'd like to see more policymakers, media outlets, companies, and nonprofits alike using language donors can understand (like normalizing the use of Fahrenheit temperature goals for U.S. donors, for example), incentivizing philanthropy at the highest levels, and assigning prestige and notoriety to unprecedented climate giving.

Just imagine what could be accomplished if climate change hired the pandemic's publicist.

Giving to the institutions that most directly affect the lives of you and your family was once a tried-and-true way to insulate yourself from vulnerability in life, but we can no longer ignore the inextricable links between climate disasters and those same institutions. And when we reach total climate chaos, those institutions simply won't exist. Challenging the status quo is uncomfortable, but I am certain that 2.0 degrees Celsius (or 3.6 degrees Fahrenheit) above pre-industrial global temperatures is more so.

What if more philanthropists followed in the footsteps of Patagonia's billionaire founder, Yvon Chouinard, and brought bold climate philanthropy into the mainstream? He's been credited for "reinventing how capitalism can work for the planet."[10] He was also widely applauded for making a landmark philanthropic decision when he handed over his $3 billion company and its roughly $100 million annual profit to a trust solely dedicated to fighting climate change. Chouinard is a changemaker in the least cliché sense of the word, and his story is one that illuminates what is possible when someone with great means relates their inner sense of stability and success with that of the world around them.

So, how do we activate the philanthropic community to take swift action and chart a new course in climate giving, like Yvon Chouinard has before it's too late?

To start, there is tremendous untapped potential for climate action among emergent "Next Gen" philanthropists. Right now, we are experiencing a phenomenon called "the great wealth transfer." During COVID restrictions, retirement rates of Baby Boomers doubled, and according to SS&C Advent, in 2021, at least 67% of Boomers were retired. With this move, around $70-$80 trillion in financial power is in the process of being transferred to Gen Zers and Millennials,[11] generations that we know care more about climate change and the consequences they and their children will experience.

When looking forward at the decades to come, Cerulli Associates predicts U.S. high-net-worth (HNW) and ultra-high-net-worth (UHNW) individuals will hand over $84.4 trillion to heirs and charities through 2045.[12] This staggering statistic means fundraisers for climate have been issued our most critical mandate yet; the moment to begin building trust and climate fluency within this next generation of philanthropic leadership is NOW.

Despite exercising more modern modalities for philanthropy (such as impact investing and donating with cryptocurrency and other digital assets), young people are still influenced by their parents' and grandparents' traditions of giving. Education still ranks as the most popular cause among ultra-high-net-worth

10 Beer, Jeff. (2022) *Patagonia reinvents itself again: 'We're making Earth our only shareholder'.* Fast Company. https://www.fastcompany.com/90789599/patagonia-reinvents-itself-again -were-making-earth-our-only-shareholder

11 Royal, James, Ph.D. (2024) *The Great Wealth Transfer: What it means for your money.* Bankrate. https://www.bankrate.com/investing/the-great-wealth-transfer/

12 (2023) SS&C Advent—*APAC's Great Intergenerational Wealth Transfer.* Hubbis. https:// www.hubbis.com/news/ss-c-advent-apac-s-great-intergenerational-wealth-transfer

individuals passing on wealth and the younger beneficiaries of that transfer.[13] While I believe it is important for well-established philanthropists, family offices, and financial advisors to share their learnings and methodologies with emergent donors, I want to reemphasize the need for risk-taking and pioneering in philanthropy if we are going to meet our 2030 climate goals. If we cannot break out of these tired models of giving, the philanthropic orthodoxy will become nothing more than an etching in the post-apocalypse museum of what once was.

It is promising, though, to see that Gen Z and Millennial donors are twice as likely to give to environmental and climate causes than the generations that precede them.[14] The onus is now on the climate community to communicate to these up-and-coming philanthropists that protecting our children, our communities, and our financial future depends on saving the planet *first*—and then open the door for them to do just that.

Throughout my career as a nonprofit development professional, I have seen how competitive, siloed, and duplicative the nonprofit space can be. But I have been uplifted to see the climate movement largely motivated by a sincere desire to collaborate. Sure, ego and status still pervade, with some organizations promoting their solution as the only or best approach, but overwhelmingly, climate actors are joining forces. There are ardent attempts to build "a movement of movements" to rapidly scale the efforts of smaller organizations and coalitions through radical collaboration. Some groups aggregate philanthropic contributions to create impact across the entire climate ecosystem, and others leverage the power of partnerships to create outsized impact and amplify cross-cutting solutions. There are giving circles, philanthropic networks, and collaboratives working hand in hand to ensure that capital deployed for climate can be magnified across innovation, policy, advocacy, research, and activism— key ingredients that need to synchronize in order to decarbonize our future.

I believe these giving pathways can lead to catalytic outcomes, and for emergent climate donors especially, these are key nexus points where one can find meaning in this vast charitable arena.

We must also address the fast-growing concentration of wealth in America head-on. There are five times more billionaires today than there were 25 years

---

13 (2024) *Family Wealth Transfer 2024*. Altrata. https://info.altrata.com/family-wealth-transfer-2024-pdf?utm_medium=email&utm_source=thought%20leadership&utm_campaign=2024-06-11_at_wealth+transfer+report+2024+clients&utm_content=textlink

14 Trovato, Elisa Battaglia. (2024) *Next generation determined to make philanthropy more effective. Professional Wealth Management (PUM)*. https://www.pwmnet.com/next-generation-determined-to-make-philanthropy-more-effective#:~:text=Moreover%2C%20the%20focus%20of%20next,change%2C%20according%20to%20the%20study

ago.[15] The top 50 donors account for $16 billion in giving,[16] and shockingly, roughly 13 of those billions came from six mega-donors.[17] One would think this makes for efficient fundraising, right? Couldn't all climate fundraisers band together to move even just two of those 50 donors to make climate their number one cause and unlock massive capital stacks for under-resourced projects and programs?

But we are not in the business of changing minds or chasing unicorns. Our job as fundraisers is to find who among that next tier down—the centi-millionaires—already believes in the urgency of our cause and enable them to change the course of history. Effective fundraising is all about excellent prospecting, authentic relationship-building, and persistence. When combined with compelling storytelling, I believe we could see a trend emerge among the top 5% of wealth holders that would rebalance the scales in favor of our shared climate future.

With that said, how do philanthropic trends commence and proliferate? How can we use giving to unlock greater giving? At the Global Warming Mitigation Project, we had a donor who liked to say, "Let's get money off the sidelines!" And to that I say, "Bravo!" But—easier said than done.

Using strategic fundraising strategies like matching campaigns, we can begin to see a ripple effect created through bold climate philanthropy. Climate change and its secondary and tertiary impacts can feel like an insurmountable undertaking for many donors. I often hear, "Where do I even begin?" I have been challenged with, "But, what's the point if China and India don't stop emitting?" and "Until we end fossil fuel subsidies, what will my donation really do for the world?"

Well, to that, I say we have a duty to all of humankind, to our ancestors and our future kin, to those least responsible and most disproportionately impacted, and to our universal mother Gaia, to start somewhere. Human nature enables us to do the seemingly impossible when our livelihoods are at risk. Evolution is precipitated by threats to survival, and right now, that threat

---

15 (2021). *Philanthropy has changed a lot, but you don't see how your own child grows.* Alliance Magazine. https://www.alliancemagazine.org/analysis/bending-the-arc-of-philanthropy -towards-justice/

16 Gamboa, Glenn. (2023) *Charitable giving in 2022 drops for only the fourth time in 40 years: Giving USA report.* AP News. https://apnews.com/article/charitable-giving-decline-givingusa -report-becaca47cae4bc4f55063cc9f1c5865a

17 (2023) *Giving USA: Total U.S. charitable giving declined in 2022 to $499.33 billion following two years of record generosity.* IUPUI Lilly Family School of Philanthropy. https://philanthropy. iupui.edu/news-events/news-item/giving-usa:-total-u.s.-charitable-giving-declined-in-2022- to-$499.33-billion-following-two-years-of-record-generosity.html?id=422#:~:text=Giving%20 by%20individuals%20totaled%20an,percent%2C%20adjusted%20for%20inflation)

is ferociously reaching its tentacles out to touch everyone, everywhere. When that moment arrives, let us be ready. Let us—asset holders, nonprofit leaders, climate actors, scientists, business leaders, grassroots organizers, academics, educators, and our more enlightened politicians—know that we have put every possible solution and infrastructural support in place! Let us do that now, with **bravery** and ***celerity***.

Now, getting back to the *how* part. Understanding how to move the needle on climate change can push donors into realms of deterring discomfort. Facing a depth of technicalities and a dearth of consolidated data, many philanthropists struggle to sift through countless solutions and find the pathways for change that are right for them. My recommendation—look for the multiplier effect. There are countless resources at your disposal. If you can't do the due diligence, partner with an organization or a network that can do it for you. If you're not passionately committed to one particular cause or solution (. . .off-grid solar not your thing? . . .sustainable fisheries not lighting you up?), support accelerators that spark innovation across multiple verticals and regions.

Taking action through smart philanthropy can be an autonomous, near-term decision. In a world tethered to myopic business practices and burdened by contentious bureaucracy, the freedom as a person of means to act independently and sensibly should be exercised with intention and volume by those who can.

What's more, there is a laundry list of issues that have been plaguing the nonprofit sector since long before my time, and those, too, must be included in the scope of smart philanthropy when talking about creating lasting climate impact. These issues may not check the recognition-seeking box contemplated earlier, but for sophisticated philanthropists who gain satisfaction from building resilience in climate solutions, they can produce even greater desired effects. There is a fundraising tale as old as time about building a house where there once was a pile of rubble or planting a school garden where a littered alleyway once stood. But, when addressing the complexities of climate change, there is as much a need for capacity building, professional development, and talent retention among nonprofits as there is a need for in-hand products and solutions.

Working day in and day out against the tyranny of our fossil-fuel economies is tiresome work. Exacerbate that by the over-extended, many-hat-wearing lifestyle of a nonprofit professional, and you're going to see burnout from some of the climate movement's best and brightest. Pooling resources, especially for small-to-mid-sized organizations and frontline actors, can help to achieve efficiencies and streamline operations sector-wide.

We need to fortify our nonprofit ecosystem by calling on philanthropy to unleash human capital by investing in the capacity building of teams and professional development of leaders, especially those from underrepresented groups and vulnerable communities, so they can have the bandwidth and space to maximize their creativity and efficacy. Climate leaders hold the keys to our renewable future, and they need to be cultivated, well-compensated, and supported. Funding strategies that create mutual self-reliance will yield sustainable results for generations to come, and this is the type of smart philanthropy that the climate crisis calls for.

Taking in the many problems and propositions laid out in the essay, I return to the inner question that I invite you to consider: ***What kind of cog in the wheel am I?*** The threads of society are fraying as the balance of our biosphere unravels. Some may say this is "the end of times." But I believe this is the end of "these times"—these oppressive, extractive times—and the utterly exciting beginning of a restorative, regenerative, and generous future.

The economy can, in fact, be as circular as this one and only planet we live on. Our soil can once again be as diverse as the communities that harvest its bounty. The users of our future climate solutions can also be the architects of those solutions. We can redesign every minuscule, interconnected component of the way we live, work, interact, and create—but not without the unwavering and courageous backing of the philanthropic community.

Philanthropy that is uninhibited and imaginative has the potential to spark climate action in places where resource gaps, capacity drains, and institutional barriers have created blockades. By humbling ourselves to the magnitude of the monster we collectively face, we can find a common calling that supersedes all else.

Climate fundraisers have been stewarding donors up the donor pyramid for years, but the 360-degree view from the top is clearing to reveal a lush landscape. I encourage the philanthropic community to take a soulful and smart approach to giving, to actualize its fullest potential by moving where other funders have slowed and stagnated, and to give boldly to climate action. The result will be exponential returns on people, the planet, and a historically heroic, redefined legacy of "self."

It is uniquely inspiring to be alive during this pivotal moment in humanity's timeline—to see the path toward a thriving future before us and feel the wind of invention and possibility at our backs. To mobilize right now, as an individual or collective force, is to experience our truest existential purpose and to step into our higher meaning.

This unparalleled privilege is afforded to us all, but we look to the most influential among us to carve out the way forward. What will follow is a sweeping movement capable of transforming the very fabric of what binds and sustains us all.

16   DO YOU KNOW WHOM YOU SERVE?

Leadership Lessons Honed at the Feet of My Patients

Dr. Jandel Allen-Davis is President and CEO of Craig Hospital, and serves on the Denver Branch Board of Directors of the Federal Reserve Bank of Kansas City and Denver Metro Chamber.

I believe that the best work, a work that is worth pouring yourself into, is one that stretches you . . . that brings you great joy . . . that taps into a well of humility from which you can grow and learn . . . that hopefully enables you, in those final breaths, to say, "Well done." I know I will utter those words when reflecting on my clinical practice, and I hope I see the faces and names of those who entrusted me with their care. And I hope I can say the same about my years serving others from the place of leadership, as the organizations I have served deserve the same level of care and attention that I extended to my patients, and that is the focus of this essay.

I practiced obstetrics and gynecology for 25 years. I literally and figuratively sat at the feet of my patients in service to a work that is among the most sacred privileges one could have. Those years at the bedside caring for patients were the best years of my professional life. I grew to understand that the work had, at its core, an expectation of becoming deeply connected to those I served, providing comfort during those times when life presented big and small challenges, as well as great expectations in the case of a new pregnancy. I experienced and witnessed profound joy during those first moments when new life emerged.

And those sacred connections mattered most when I had to inform patients about life-threatening health issues, and then stand with and by them and their loved ones as they navigated the unforeseeable or unpredictable. I learned the power of simple touch, how that tiny gesture can still an anxious heart and, I believe, change outcomes. I learned to appreciate the deep sorrow experienced by all when a mother holds her lifeless baby moments after a stillbirth.

I had the privilege and honor of crying with my patients . . . of laughing with them . . . of reassuring when needed . . . and bearing witness to new life, as well as death and dying.

I could not have known along that 25-year journey that many lessons learned at the feet of my patients would be essential to the myriad leadership roles I have had the good fortune to fill the last fifteen years. I am grateful that I paid attention and allowed my inner self to be shaped by the clinical experiences that brought deeply-felt joy, as well as the painful ones, wherein I was humbled and grew, came to know what loss can do to a soul, or how powerful just standing with my patients as they navigated tough experiences can be. I am grateful for every second I was able to practice medicine. And this path was one that started from childhood.

I wanted to work in health care since I was a child, initially believing that I had to be a nurse. "Girls are nurses and boys are doctors" was the paradigm that girls of my age believed, at least until the Women's Rights and modern Civil Rights movements emerged and widened our vistas. Once I realized that all was possible, I knew that becoming a doctor was the only thing I ever wanted to do . . . aside from being a mom. I knew that I wanted to be a cardiovascular surgeon. There's an elegance and choreography to that practice that I still find beautiful.

But I didn't become that surgeon. Looking back, I don't doubt that with the right support, I could have done it. But regrettably, I couldn't deal with the sexism that was rampant in the surgical disciplines in the early '80s as more women entered the field, made worse by the fact that I am African American. That said, I have no regrets. I fell totally in love with Obstetrics and Gynecology! I loved the operating room and the beautiful rhythm of surgery, of completing hard and simpler procedures that alleviated suffering. Being in the lives of women and families in that most precious of moments, when a new life joins the Continuum, is beyond rewarding, always at least somewhat mysterious, and intimate in ways that are incomparable. Helping women through the hard parts of gynecology, whether chronic pain or cancer diagnoses, among others, and standing with and by them through those frightening life chapters, was how I came to realize that the practice of medicine is a sacred trust. Growing older with my patients over many years of practice at Kaiser Permanente provided the wonderful opportunity of being in the lives of a small subset of patients who remain friends or contacts today, and how cool to watch those babies grow into adults! It's a real blessing.

At the same time that I was actively practicing, I came to appreciate that there was another side of me that had been present since I was a child: I loved being in the middle of things, working to make life better. My mother called me bossy when I was not even five years old, one of those early memories that I can touch and feel. I was the one who organized ways to recognize the teachers we loved in grade school. I was on the student council in high school and became the first woman elected to lead the Afro-American Society at Dartmouth in 1979. I was the chief resident. And when I moved to Kaiser Permanente in Colorado, I was given many opportunities to sit at tables where work was happening to improve care for our patients or the work lives for our employees. I campaigned for a seat on the Permanente Medical Group Board and eventually served as chair. I was an executive on the Permanente Medical Group leadership team and then joined the Health Plan leadership team as a vice president. I served on several nonprofit boards over the years and still manage to fit in a lot of community-facing work as part of my current role. In 2018, I assumed the role of CEO and President of Craig Hospital, a globally recognized neurorehabilitation hospital that serves persons who have sustained acquired or traumatic spinal cord and/or brain injuries.

It's been a crazy ride, and I would never have imagined the opportunities for service that have come my way thus far! In most cases, I didn't ask for these opportunities. Someone invited me to be part of doing good work and/or solving problems. Along the way, and in the absence of formal mentoring, I became an ardent student of leadership. I watched how leaders and others worked with their teams. Over time, I developed a list of "Do This" and "Don't Do This" behaviors, based on those observations and lessons. I am certain that specific behaviors landed on one or the other list based on a set of values and principles instilled in me from a young age. At the heart of those values are some pretty basic principles and values: **be kind, work hard**, and **never stop learning**.

Several years ago, at a point where I was beginning to appreciate the full métier of my work life, I reflected that a lot of what I sought to bring as a leader was honed at the feet of my patients. In that moment, I decided I wanted to write a book, *All I Know about Leadership was Learned at the Feet of My Patients*. I wrote the chapter titles. And maybe I will get around to writing the book when I slow down.

For now, what I know is that the messages I feel moved to share can no longer wait, and there isn't time to sit and write. It feels as if this is the right time to share what my patients taught me, as **those we serve are hungering for principled, love-filled leadership**. Our world is starved for that. I hope readers will find a nugget in this piece that is helpful to them, and with that in mind, what follows are musings on each of the leadership principles that I learned in the day-to-day, moment-to-moment blessings that emerged from caring for women all those years that I have instinctively brought into how I seek to serve and lead.

IT'S ALL ABOUT THE RELATIONSHIP

Physicians meet new people every day. When I step back and think about that reality, it can be a daunting and intimidating experience. "Will they like me? Will they think I am competent? What if I can't help them? How do I build trust?"

People come to us at their most vulnerable, even when the encounter is a simple checkup, because no one wakes up in the morning and declares, "Today I want to be a patient." In those initial moments of our time together, the most important thing we do is to set our patients at ease. We look into their eyes, smile, and introduce ourselves. The unspoken, but very much sensed, ways that we convey reassurance, support, and connection in that instant set the stage for what transpires next. Patients either feel seen or, sadly and sometimes tragically, dismissed.

Humans have an innate sense of who cares about them. When they feel cared for, they tell us the things we need to know so that we don't go right when we should go left. They don't hold back that one seemingly crazy or weird symptom that creates diagnostic and treatment breakthroughs. Said another way, **sometimes the answers to the hardest clinical cases we confront are right in front of us, and it takes humility** to believe in and rely upon your patients to help lead you to those answers.

GOOD DOCTORS ARE GOOD COACHES

I never played organized sports, but I observed that part of the development of great athletes involves a coach, someone who has a firm but loving hand on their shoulders, and who makes time to know them through and through. What motivates them? What scares them? What excites them? What do they long to achieve? And then, using those enablers and blockers, they make the seemingly impossible possible.

I had countless opportunities to sit with patients who were facing difficult or life-threatening circumstances. I also know that **there are limits to the healing power of pharmaceuticals or scalpels**. Without a highly engaged patient who senses that "This is someone I can trust," treatment goals are often not attained. I had to get a sense of what motivated them, what they were most afraid of, who they loved, and what their goals were, and then use those desires and dreams to facilitate a care plan.

This is the point where the good doctors become healers, working with patients to help them adhere to therapies by listening to the spoken and unspoken, learning what matters to them most, educating, encouraging the heart, and sometimes even speaking hard truths. Celebrating the small and large wins, even when the end game doesn't mean "cure," are some of the best moments of my career.

LISTENING IS THE KEY TO GOOD ASSESSMENT AND TREATMENT (AND LEADERSHIP!)

One of the most challenging parts of a physician's work life is managing an office practice. We can't reliably predict how much time a 15 or 20-minute encounter is actually going to take by reading the chief complaint. As my office hours wore on over a day, I invariably ran late. And the later I ran, the more tempting it became to help patients "cut to the chase." When you do that, you cease to listen as carefully as you should, and you run a huge risk of missing critical information that can change a life.

I remember seeing a young patient very late in the afternoon after a long day. I was tired and wanted to get home to my family. I read the chief complaint and was immediately exasperated, as the diagnosis looked clear after reading notes from an urgent care department visit that occurred the evening before. I told myself I would just go in, get her the proper antibiotic, and move her on. Then I stopped and told myself to slow down and basically "do the right thing."

She was there with her mother, and after taking a thorough history, I left the room to allow her to undress. On examination, it was clear that she had a very serious infection. I took cultures and left so she could get dressed. When I returned to the room, I told her and her mother what I suspected the diagnosis was. I told her that she could have contracted it by having unprotected sex, but she denied being sexually active. I told her she could have picked it up by sharing towels or other garments that someone else had worn. But I told her that I was worried that someone was harming her, that the people who do these things may threaten to tell her mother or to harm her if she says something. I reassured her that this was not the case with me, that we were there to protect her, and that it was safe to talk to us. She asked me to leave the room and told her mother that her stepfather had been molesting her for many years. What happened after that is something that has stayed with me for over two decades. It's a story of amazing resolve, courage, and love, but that part of the story is for another day.

A year later, I found myself in a courtroom to testify in the trial. The Assistant District Attorney came over, sat by me, and handed me a letter. She asked if I had seen it before. It was a letter from this child written to me that said, *"Dear Doctor. Please help me. My stepfather has been touching me, and he is dirty down there."*

I'd never seen the letter. She never had to share it because I **slowed down** and "did the right thing."

Much has been written about clinician-patient communication and the impact of interrupting a patient's narrative on satisfaction and outcomes. On average, physicians interrupt patients approximately 15 seconds into the encounter. *Fifteen seconds!* I recall being taught that if you let patients talk, on average, they will talk for about 90 seconds, and most of the needed information is collected.

How long do doctors wait to interrupt patients? (Hint: Not long.) (advisory. com)

Listening and being present . . . it made a life-altering difference in the life of my young patient, whom I went on to care for well into her adult years.

IF YOU ALLOW DISTRACTIONS TO RULE YOU, YOU WILL HARM PEOPLE

If there is a place in health care where a physician's senses are activated, it's the operating room. Monitors, equipment being moved about, bright lights, sometimes music softly (I hope!) playing in the background, hands literally on and inside a patient, bodily secretions . . . perhaps the only sense that isn't aroused is the sense of taste (although I must admit to knowing what amniotic fluid tastes like—thank heavens we moved to wearing masks during normal deliveries!). On top of all of that action, there's the pull of the work that awaits us when we finish a case: the office call-backs to make, the labs to track down, the rounds to make. And as if that isn't enough, we do have private lives that hopefully are full and likely have some challenges in them as well.

The life of a physician contains a constant barrage of information that has to be processed in real time. The demands on our time can be taxing and tiring. It can also be exhilarating and fun. And there are times when it can be overwhelming. As we sit in an exam room and listen to a patient convey their concerns and questions, we are often thinking about that list of tasks and demands that await us on the other side of the door, increasing the risk of missing critical parts of the story that literally mean the difference between life and death, or at least optimized treatment outcomes, higher quality, better patient satisfaction and lower costs.

Managing all of these demands on our time requires that we practice ways to be wholly present. I remember a patient telling one of our medical assistants that, "Jandel treats me like I am her only patient." I recall smiling and feeling good about my ability to turn off the noise and just be present and in the moment. I also recall saying, "Yes, and that's why the waits can get long, but I hope patients appreciate the why of those waits."

The ability to be that focused on the person who was in front of me, to tune out the distractions, is a huge responsibility, one we take seriously as clinicians. Patients can sense whether it is safe to share information, based on how present their physician seems to be. The challenge is to stay in the encounter, as it is quite possible to miss a critical symptom or phrase that leads to the best way to reassure someone, to arrive at a great treatment plan, and to engage a patient in assuming a larger role in self-care. Moreover, it greatly increases the likelihood of an optimal outcome, and whether we ultimately heal or not.

THE PATIENT ISN'T ALWAYS THE ONE SITTING IN FRONT OF YOU

There were times a patient was accompanied by someone else who relayed her story. There were many reasons for this that typically weren't expressed, although the most obvious one involved non-English speakers. In addition to language barriers, complex family dynamics, parents who were advocating for an underage child, a clinical condition that limited their ability to speak in that instance (e.g., altered consciousness or pain), cultural differences, and psychosocial issues were common explanations for these interactions.

I learned to heighten my senses in these cases. Was there tension? Was there a quick and near-imploring glance the patient shot my way that indicated she needed time alone to share information that she wasn't comfortable sharing with the other person present? Was this a child interpreting and conveying information from her mother about intimate details of a gynecological clinical condition that made them both uncomfortable? Was I getting the entire story?

Most of the time, the explanations, whether I asked or not, were benign. However, in each of those settings, it was important to pay closer attention to body language and other nonverbals, including how the patient and the other person interacted with each other, if at all. I made it a point to look at the patient and ask them questions. I learned a method that allowed the silent "real patient" to get some time with me, by excusing both myself and the person accompanying them so that she could disrobe; I used this tactic if I sensed there was more to the story, and I could re-enter the room discretely before inviting the other person back. And, as the importance of diversity, equity, and inclusion became part of our work, I stopped using family members as interpreters, and either asked for in-person or technology-enabled interpreter services. Regardless of the reasons why someone else was talking for my patient, I knew the fact that they were an important part of the clinical picture and had to be considered, especially if there was a need for ongoing treatment.

KNOW WHEN TO SAY WHEN: "THERE ARE SOME PATIENTS WE CAN'T HELP. THERE ARE NO PATIENTS WE CAN'T HARM."

Nothing is harder for a physician than arriving at the point when we realize we have reached the limits of what we or modern medicine can provide to address a situation. This might be due to a terminal illness or a complex medical condition.

It might be that I have reached the limits of my clinical expertise, and it is time to refer the patient to a more highly specialized level or type of care. Whatever the reason, in those situations, it was important to check my ego needs and reassess whether I am stretching my care beyond my ability to safely provide it. When physicians don't do that, and continue to provide ongoing care, they can make a clinical situation worse.

I had a large chronic pelvic pain practice, and many patients I cared for had seen multiple physicians before I met them who had, in my opinion, stretched their limits and/or modern medicine's. They'd had surgeries to try and address the issue that only exacerbated the pain, and some were heavily dependent on opioids to control their pain, however poorly those medications actually worked. Their lives were complicated by this chronic condition and I did my best to help them manage, and in many cases, we actually were able to relieve the suffering.

There were also patients whose clinical condition was beyond my professional ability to treat. When I felt there were no longer modalities that I could use, I reached out for help from my colleagues. Together, we were often able to do more for the patient than either of us could have done alone. And sometimes, the only available and merciful option was just to sit with them, to be a supporter until the end, and above all, never to leave them feeling hopeless or abandoned.

NEVER GO TO A DOCTOR WHOSE PLANTS ARE DEAD

I consider the practice of medicine one of the most sacred callings on Earth, and I loved every moment that I was blessed to do so. We experience moments of intense joy and satisfaction when we address problems that range from simple to complex. We laugh with our patients. We cry with them. They trust us with their deepest fears and literally place their lives in our hands.

We are in the business of relieving suffering.

And while it is a privilege and honor to be a physician, it can be physically, emotionally, and mentally demanding work, with dire consequences when these impacts or this sort of exhaustion go unattended. Mental health issues, including suicide, are more prevalent among physicians than in the general public. Ironically, there are systemic barriers that can prevent physicians from seeking appropriate care.

I served on the Colorado State Medical Board for eight years. The Board is accountable for physician licensing and discipline. Based on that work, I discovered much about the inner life of physicians, which informs my view of the importance of self-care, and I also know that we are not innately wired to put ourselves first. I read stories of physicians whose practices were in such disarray that patient harm occurred, and a complaint with the State was filed. We were obligated to investigate many of these complaints, and the information that emerged was always complex, rarely had one contributing factor to the outcome, and required deeper levels of intervention.

But the most striking realization was that physicians will let everything else in their lives suffer before the signs of personal struggle show up in their practices. Behind many, if not all, practices that are in disarray is a trail littered with family dysfunction, financial troubles, sometimes substance use, often other behavioral health issues . . . and much of it unknown to those around them. The cure is never quick nor easy, and there are physicians who will protest loudly when discipline is required.

And once the right supports are provided, these frequently become stories of redemption. Careers, let alone marriages, practices, and relationships with friends and families were saved. And trust is restored.

OH! THE PLACES YOU WILL GO! DELIGHTING IN LIFELONG LEARNING

Knowledge has a very short half-life. Given the rapid technological advancements in medicine, we currently measure the half-life of medical knowledge in weeks!

This requires that physicians stay abreast of changes in therapeutic approaches to both common and uncommon conditions, which can be challenging. I believe that at its core, the secret to doing so requires remaining curious, reading regularly, and being willing to connect with colleagues in order to share and learn from each other. The beauty of working in a group practice was that I was provided countless opportunities to learn and to teach. And I am naturally curious, so I constantly ask questions. Luckily, lots of knowledge is literally at our fingertips, making access to advances much easier than when I began medical school.

JUST WHAT IS THAT THING CALLED "ELEPHANT?" PLAYING YOUR ROLE AND ENCOURAGING TEAMMATES TO PLAY THEIRS

One of the most important advances to ever happen in medicine was the introduction of the concept of patient safety. *To Err is Human* was a seminal work published in 2000 by the Institute of Medicine Committee on Quality Health Care in America. Its focus was on improving the safety of health care, as it was estimated by some reports at the time that nearly 100,000 people died at our hands due to unsafe medical practices, most of which had less to do with technical advances and more to do with human factors, including fatigue, distractions, cultural hierarchies that didn't enable psychological safety within teams, and the cognitive traps that are a function of how we are wired to think, plan, and learn.

I recall reviewing a case many years ago of an unfortunate surgical procedure that did not go as planned and left the patient with a serious nerve injury. On review of the proceedings and the quality review notes, it was clear that the surgeon was not open to receiving feedback, and the operating room team of nurses, second and third surgical assistants, and anesthesiologists were not comfortable telling the doctor what they were seeing from their end until things had gone seriously awry. When we are operating, our attention is on the procedure. We have other teammates who are there playing a very specific role, and it is the primary surgeon who bears most of the responsibility for their patient's well-being . . . *and that can't be accomplished without the help of the entire team.* We can't see the entire picture, and must create an environment where we all work together to completely assess how the patient is doing. If we have created an environment of fear or mistrust, and the team doesn't feel safe speaking up, injuries up to and including death can occur.

John Godfrey Saxe's parable of the Blind Man and the Elephant beautifully describes how we interpret a clinical picture through the narrow lenses of bias, our knowledge base, our roles and literally where we are positioned in the room. The final lines of the poem include this: "Though each was partly in the right/ And all were in the wrong!"

If we aren't working as a team to create a coherent picture of reality, bad things can happen. Thankfully, great strides have been made over these two decades to significantly reduce avoidable morbidity and mortality through a set of practices and procedures that assure the highest levels of patient safety. We flatten hierarchies, work from checklists, create psychological safety that allows anyone on the team "to stop the line" when they sense there is confusion or the potential for harm, and require annual training in patient safety at most institutions.

DO YOU KNOW WHOM YOU SERVE? SERVANT LEADERSHIP THROUGH A PHYSICIAN'S EYES

I have had countless opportunities while leading and serving teams to experience and witness the same sorts of achievements and outcomes that I experienced as a clinician. The surprising thing is that leading organizations, whether large or small, is as demanding as being up all night delivering babies, or spending hours standing on your feet in an operating room. It's just a different kind of doing, but the transferable skills I honed during my time as a clinician continue to serve me, and I hope those I serve, well.

I remember the months following my transition out of clinical practice. I took an executive role that had accountability for government relations, community benefit, community relations, marketing and communications, and eventually our Institute for Health Research. I loved learning new things, discovering more about who I was becoming as a leader, and working to make a difference for our organization on a bigger scale on behalf of those we served. I also remember crying and wondering if I'd done the right thing, as I truly missed clinical practice. It's a huge leap of faith to try on something new and also to say goodbye to something that was such a core part of who I was and that I loved so deeply.

It was a bewildering time.

I asked myself, "What are the transferable skills I learned in the care of patients that would serve me in the role of Vice President of Government and External Relations?" My answer to the question was, "Well, what did your patients want and expect?"

- They expected me to know my stuff (learning)
- I had to have the ability to create instant trusting connections with strangers who came to me needing care (relating)
- I had to do what I said I would do (integrity)
- They wanted me to treat them as if they were my only patient (presence)
- And most importantly, no matter the situation or its outcome, even when the news was bad, they didn't want me to abandon them (hope)

I remember asking myself, "Don't you think that is what every team member, community or business partner, or community member wants also?" I told myself I would be okay! And here's the translation of those years of practice into my perspectives about leadership.

GOOD LEADERS INVEST IN RELATIONSHIP BUILDING, AND THEY UNDERSTAND THE POWERFUL IMPACT OF GREAT RELATIONSHIPS ON RESULTS.

To the extent that leadership is nothing more or less than using influence to get things done, and that those things are done by people who bring as much, if not all, of their discretionary effort to doing the work, the importance of strong, authentic, and supportive relationships reigns supreme. Those we serve want to both see us as whole, real people, and they want us to see them as the same.

The phrase, "People don't care what you know until they know that you care," requires being a People First leader, investing in relationships in ways that naturally and instinctively draw people into the work, and in turn, create outcomes that are not achievable alone. The good leaders know that great outcomes start with the team. And strong teams, those who feel aligned to the work, who jump up in the morning ready to serve great missions and visions, whose work brings them alive, and literally pour their whole selves into a work do so because they are working alongside a leader who has spent time getting to know them and the things that drive them. It is all about building strong and enduring relationships.

And effective leaders know this intuitively.

GOOD LEADERS ARE GOOD COACHES.

"Performance management" is a horrible term! We no more manage performance than I managed diabetes, infectious diseases, or safe deliveries. We stand alongside our patients and team members, and bring out the best in them by understanding their roles thoroughly, getting clear about goals and objectives, and using the best of our motivational and engagement skills to help each manage their *own* part of the process.

GOOD LEADERS ARE MINDFUL OF THE DANGERS AND SEDUCTIVE NATURE OF MULTITASKING.

How many cocktail parties, happy hours, or galas have you attended, and when asked how things are going, your first response is, "Busy!" I am convinced that, were there some sort of mechanical device that was able to capture all the conversations in a room like that and create a word cloud, the largest word by far would be "busy!"

We wear our busyness like a badge of honor.

Good leaders understand that part of the job involves juggling multiple demands on our time and attention, and they also understand that, absent focused time and attention, we end up doing a lot of things sub-optimally, which in turn, increases risk to the organizations and the work we love. Steven Covey's Time Management Matrix provides a great visual for the balancing act we manage. As it relates to our busyness, there are leaders who dwell in Quadrant One, the "Urgent and Important" one. It's the Quadrant that is filled with opportunities for an adrenaline rush or the chance to gain adulation from others for our heroic feats.

	Urgent	Not Urgent
Important	I Fire Fighting Crises Pressing problems Deadline-driven projects	II Quality Time Prevention, capability improvement Relationship building Recognizing new opportunities Planning, recreation
Not Important	III Distraction Interruptions, some callers Some mail, some reports Some meetings Proximate, pressing matters Popular activities	IV Time Wasting Trivia, busy work Some mail Some phone calls Time wasters Pleasant activities

Graphic courtesy of Huffington Post;
https://www.huffpost.com/entry/what-stephen-covey-taught_b_12458334.

Over time, we lose our situational awareness and "seamlessly" move from Quadrant to Quadrant in the course of fragments of a day. Honestly, we probably aren't doing any of the activities as well as we could do them if we were able to focus and complete some tasks before starting another one.

I had an epiphany many years ago, working in a high-stress culture that rewarded this work style. It seemed as if the alarms were always going off and the fires never ended. When I spent time with my team on this Covey work, it convinced me that spending more time on the activities delineated in Quadrant II could decrease the need to firefight, because this is where the deep work of assuring that our organizations are healthy in mind, body, and spirit lives and grows. We might actually decrease the number and types of firefighting we have to do! Less inadvertent or overt harm is done when we are less distracted. **Good Leaders can both call this behavior out and model a different way for their teams.**

GOOD LEADERS TRY TO AVOID TRIANGULATION AT ALL COSTS.

It takes all kinds of us to make a world. There are those who will slay dragons and run into the fire for others. There are those who are conflict-avoidant at all costs. We have both of these types of people as team members, and it can be intimidating and risky to speak truth to power or even to a peer. It is important to have truth-tellers in our midst, and it is important to create the kinds of cultures where people feel free to speak up, even if they stumble over their words. I heard Allyson Felix, the most decorated American Olympic track and field athlete of all time, encourage an audience to use their power, even if their voice shakes. Just as it was important to figure out ways to encourage the hearts of my patients who were afraid or unable to speak in the moment, it is important for our team members to find their voice and speak their unfiltered truths to those who need to hear it. We shouldn't become the dragon slayers for our teams except under rare circumstances. Gently redirecting, supporting, coaching, and encouraging team members to manage their issues on their own provides opportunities for growth and builds trust. Power imbalances are real, and if we use our power to fight others' battles that should be dealt with directly, we erode trust.

GOOD LEADERS NEVER STOP GROWING AND LEARNING.

Curiosity is a powerful tool for a leader. It ensures that we stay current because there are countless times in a week when a question arises and we are off to find answers. Curiosity has a powerful effect on team members, especially those junior to us. Showing interest in their work by asking questions is empowering and provides an opportunity for them to help us grow and learn. Hiring people who are smarter than we are is not only a courageous and necessary act, but it is also an act that keeps us humble, as we cannot possibly know or keep abreast of everything. Team members at every level love the opportunity to teach us something new and contribute to making organizations better. And alongside its sister Creativity, Curiosity is the foundation of innovation.

Information changes rapidly, and it is critical that we bring in new ideas, trends, and observations, lest we find ourselves out of date. Creating a culture of curiosity and continuous learning is how organizations thrive. The stories of Kodak, Blackberry, and Sears are stories riddled with a sense that those leaders knew all there was to know, that there weren't better ways to do things, and that the competition was not a threat. It's critical that we keep learning. It's the secret to growing and keeping work fresh for ourselves and for our organizations.

GOOD LEADERS CREATE GREAT TEAMS, WHERE EVERYONE HAS AN OPPORTUNITY AND AN OBLIGATION TO CONTRIBUTE.

There isn't a way for us to be in all places at all times, and we cannot possibly know all that is required to build great organizations. Effective teams are led by people who understand their unique role, constantly ask "What's the best and highest use of my time?" encourage and enable team members to do their jobs without unnecessary interference, and invite countervailing views. Leaders who behave in ways that run counter to this are micromanagers, and the effects of this way of leading are toxic. It creates an environment where learned helplessness proliferates and ensures that team members will not work at their highest level, either because they are waiting for the boss to tell them what to do, to completely redo their work, or to imply a depth of criticism that can be paralyzing.

Good leaders know they aren't the only smart person in the room and trust their team members to bring their best to the work. They challenge cynicism while inviting and encouraging dissent. They want to understand the work through different perspectives because it not only makes for a better work product, but it also avoids waste, redundancy, overuse, and misuse. Not to lead this way can result in organizational harm and even death.

MY NEW PATIENT: MY ORGANIZATION

Early in my administrative career, I came to understand that there is an organic quality to organizations. Like living beings, they can be injured. They can lose limbs. Infections and toxins can take up residence and do harm to the teams and those the organization serves long before this "illness" becomes apparent to leadership. They can develop cancerous growths that choke the lifeblood out of them. They can even die. And they also have the potential to grow strong. To live long and healthy lives. To experience incredible joy. To model the way for other organizations. To reproduce like organizations that serve even greater purposes than their own. And at the core of every healthy organization is a courageous and amazing band of great leaders who encourage the heart and inspire their teams to greatness beyond anything they ever imagined possible.

Using clinical language, the "vectors" that either do great harm to an organization or allow for "next level" organizational health and well-being, are *people*, so logically, the most important thing for a leader to pay attention to, and attend to, are the people. We serve them. Our organization's health and well-being, and in turn the health and well-being of those we serve, turn on our ability to perform our leadership tasks with love and fidelity.

As a clinician, I had the sacred privilege and honor of standing alongside my patients and serving them in large and small ways that (hopefully) created and/or enhanced the opportunity for them to live their best lives. And as a leader, I have enjoyed the same sacred privilege in service to my newest patients: the organizations in which I work and actually even play! It's gratifying when a plan comes together because of the alchemy that happens when we coach, value relationships, work our hardest to be present, enable the team to help sense-make and innovate, take a moment to breathe and rest, and learn together. I have loved watching that sort of magic almost as much as I loved delivering babies or completing a complicated surgical procedure!

I don't believe that this sort of leadership requires that one graduate from medical school. It simply requires believing in yourself and your teammates and relinquishing whatever ego "needs" drive a desire to control everything. It requires that you trust all you have around and within you to perform a good work. It necessitates pouring your whole and authentic self into the work, that is, letting your inner light shine its brightest. And when you do that, you make way for others to let theirs shine too. In turn, healthy, happy cultures emerge, ones wherein our organizations, those most organic of inorganic things, shine their brightest and thrive.

There are a few other lessons I have learned along the way, and they likely nest somewhere in those I have already mentioned. These are three important errors to overcome:

- Avoiding delivering hard news is part of what we must do in medicine, and you can't run from it. Loving those you serve enough to compassionately help them grow, even when the message is hard to give, let alone receive, is one of the best gifts you can extend to someone, even if they refuse to accept it or never speak to you again.
- Refusing to accept the reality that errors and mistakes happen, until the cost of doing so causes irrevocable harm. Facing the brutal facts is part of the leader's journey, and we have seen the fall of organizations large and small when leaders avoid doing this.
- Sitting quietly instead of asking for clarification or help when we don't understand something, for fear of looking incompetent, and forging ahead with a clinical plan that we know is incomplete. When leaders don't create an environment where teams can ask questions that challenge our thinking, we deprive ourselves and others of growth opportunities, which can have detrimental effects.

And I suspect that I could add even more lessons to the list, as 25 years at the bedside, coupled with nearly 24 years of serving in leadership roles, have provided a plethora of beautiful moments wherein I had the opportunity to witness firsthand the sacredness and beauty of what a privilege it was to be both!

SO, THEN, WHOM DO YOU SERVE?
It's a loaded question with a simple answer. (And notice I didn't ask, "Whom do you lead?")

You serve many others . . . those you can see and those you can't. Those whom your teammates may go on to serve after they move on to better or new adventures. Generations that stretch as far as the eye can see. I say this because if you believe that "no doubt the Universe is unfolding as it should," as Max Ehrmann said in the final parts of that beautiful work "Desiderata", each and every one of your actions today has impacts on all of the tomorrows. And I deeply understood that as a clinician and did my best never to violate that sacred trust, much as I hope I have done as a servant leader.

The amazing secret . . . maybe epiphany . . . about the answer to this question is that *you serve . . . we serve . . . everyone.*

And in that spirit, it is important that you do so with deep love, intention, attention, and wisdom that has grown over the years.

17 THE DAWN OF A CONSCIOUS BUSINESS MOVEMENT

Steve Farrell is Co-Founder and Executive Director of Humanity's Team, and former Silicon Valley technology entrepreneur. He wrote *A New Universal Dream*.

Before I can effectively explore the Conscious Business Movement, I first want to clarify what I mean when I refer to "conscious living." Conscious living is the embodied recognition that we are all interconnected, interdependent, and part of a universal whole. That we are each intrinsic to "One" super-organism. This Oneness is understood and experienced in terms of being in conscious relationship with ourselves, with one another, with humanity, with the animal kingdom, with the Earth, and with the entire Universe.

Scientists and philosophers from Plato and Hippocrates to Schrödinger and Capra have affirmed that everything is deeply connected. Science and spirituality are in agreement; while our bodies are clearly distinct, there is no true separation because *everything* in our Universe is energetically entangled. Einstein once said that "no problem can be solved at the level of consciousness that created it." Remedying the causal factor—what Einstein called the illusion of separation or optical delusion—creates the path forward to addressing the basic needs of the planet and the needs of the eight billion people residing on our planet. This is because we naturally gravitate toward a focus on the needs of humanity and the Earth when we understand our connection and our wholeness with the world around us.

As you may already be well aware, most of the challenge and chaos being experienced on the planet today can be traced directly back to the opposite of conscious living: *un*conscious living. The majority of us in the Western world grew up with the science of Charles Darwin. This survival-of-the-fittest mentality creates a tunnel-vision effect, with a focus on I, me, and mine, resulting in a separation where the ends justify the means. The aim is the destination and not the journey. This optical delusion, as Einstein points out, is a type of prison for us. We race fervently to get our own needs met, and in this unconscious state, we speed by our loved ones and coworkers, extend "sharp elbows" and a lack of kindness and consideration, and treat the planet itself as a warehouse or a simple commodity. The business world is an enormous contributor to this unconsciousness because business, in many cases, is only focused on top- and bottom-line growth, not the health and well-being of the surrounding community. And because business is a contributor to this, if we are to create effective and lasting change, and make an immediate U-turn to reverse the adverse effects of decades of grossly unconscious practices, business must come to the front and lead us out of it. Business must become conscious.

There is an opportunity for us to come together to heal our planetary discord by openly embracing conscious living in our own individual lives and careers, and then actively encouraging those around us to do the same. I believe this is the foundational change we are being invited to make, both individually and collectively.

I've been in a number of meetings where an emotional discussion surfaced spontaneously regarding the health of global business. One person shared that our global economy is sick and addicted to growth at any cost. Another said that unbridled capitalism is a cancer. Yet another individual pointed out that gross domestic product is an absurd economic measurement system that doesn't have any qualitative value in the real world. These deeply personal accounts of the damage unconscious business is doing to our communities and our environment are powerful affirmations that real change is on the horizon. When these topics begin to surface regularly and without prompting, it is confirmation that an evolutionary inflection point has arrived. The Civil Rights Movement in the United States and the Movement for Independence in India are two examples of evolutionary inflection points. Evolutionary inflection points beckon change; they are disruptive and stubbornly resist premature closure, and while they always take civil society to a new destination, the path to get there is rarely smooth or straight.

THE LEGACY OF UNCONSCIOUS BUSINESS

Unconscious business has had a lasting impact on society. Prior to the Great Recession of 2007-2009, some financial institutions artfully sold no-money-down home loans to an unsuspecting public, and then repackaged them and sold them to investors. As a result, housing prices fell and millions of homes went into foreclosure, creating what is now known as the longest recession since World War II. The fossil fuel industry, along with the GMO and animal-farming industries, is notorious for the damage they inflict on the environment and on humankind. Other major areas of concern are cross-industry practices such as lack of economic, social, and ecological transparency in business and overharvesting of natural resources—to say nothing of restorative practices that are often lightly implemented or left out altogether. All of these are examples of the short-sighted, disconnected legacy of unconscious business and the harm it causes. And, since the business community is in the driver's seat of both the economy and the culture, bringing that community into more conscious behavior becomes a fundamental necessity. Conscious businesses can create the urgent change needed to reverse the incredibly destructive effects that conventional businesses have wreaked upon our world.

THE ESSENCE OF CONSCIOUS BUSINESS: INNER TRANSFORMATION

Chris Laszlo, a professor at Case Western Reserve University and head of the Fowler Center for Business as an Agent of Public Benefit, contends that conscious business must include both inner transformation and outer transformation dimensions. Progressive organizations like B Lab and many others focus primarily on outer transformation—people, planet, and profit, for example. They recognize that businesses must focus on the welfare of people and the planet, not just profit. I agree and, as Chris points out, inner transformation is also critically important if we are to engender the deep leadership needed for planetary prosperity. Inner transformation focuses on practices like mindfulness, but it goes beyond this to a deeper place where we commune with Source. Source can be defined as a collective of everything that is, was, and will be conscious. Some describe it as a life force that runs through everything, and yet others assert that it is a conscious energy that we can talk to for direction on how best to navigate our way through life. As it lives through us, we live through it.

Through the nonprofit I founded with *Conversations with God* author Neale Donald Walsch, Humanity's Team, we focus on a "4-P" model: people, planet, presence, and profit. Presence brings in wholeness, unity, and awakened consciousness. It looks out at the world and sees a deeply spiritual and interconnected ecology. When we become conscious, everything changes. Many then see the likeness and image of God in ourselves, each other, and the world around us. Others experience a resonant connection with Source in less spiritual terms, perhaps as an unambiguous, uplifting energy that threads through all things, connecting all forms of life.

APPROPRIATE FOR BUSINESS

Chris Laszlo also contends that while business models focusing only on outer transformation can help businesses do less harm, these businesses cannot truly flourish. This is because a flourishing business is, by nature, partly a product of inner transformation. The inner journey embraces an experience of love, beauty, goodness, and truth. It is both a soulful and felt experience. When we embrace our inner journey, we come into stillness; we quiet the outside world. In our stillness, we feel a deep connection, and from this place we can pray, meditate, create intention, and even embrace the metaphysical. This is a communal process where we feel a close connection, where we bring questions, find answers, and visualize. Often we find warmth, closeness, and clarity. What results is a reshaping of how we see ourselves and what we witness when we look out on the world. We become anchored in this new reality, where life is sacred, and we place our lives in service to the sacred.

Over the years, a few leaders have confided in me that they were conflicted about whether to act on spiritual or scientific perspectives in business, and whether it was even appropriate to bring their own personal beliefs into a business setting, assuming that diverse religious and social sensibilities would create conflict in the work environment. In response, I've shared my own truth, that it is only a matter of time before these perspectives find their way into the workplace. Mindfulness, for instance, is already a point of focus. Furthermore, I've emphasized the critical importance of leaders at every level of business facilitating the business dialogue in a wholly inclusive manner, avoiding prescriptive statements about a singular ideology or path. The great religions of the world honor Divine inspiration and connection with Source. And as I mentioned above, science is increasingly confirming that all of the cosmos is interconnected.

We are part of a natural and social web of life that nurtures and sustains us. Certainly, we can say that spirituality, religion, and leading scientific thought support a focus on inner transformation. This is true in all contexts, not just in a context that partitions it to certain social environments. Addressing business specifically, if the core values and culture of the company are open and inclusive, honoring diverse spiritual, religious, and scientific perspectives, things will usually fall together quite harmoniously (Humanity's Team is a case study). Conscious business creates an opportunity for the integration of deeply held values. Unconscious business mostly ignores these values, focusing almost exclusively on financial gain, which is precisely why we stand in a social and economic quagmire today.

THE CONSCIOUS BUSINESS ALLIANCE
The enormity of this problem inspired Humanity's Team and three other NGOs to come together in 2014 to create a Conscious Business Alliance. We were joined by The Club of Budapest (Europe), The Goi Peace Foundation

(Japan), and The Fowler Center for Business as an Agent for Public Benefit (Case Western Reserve University). Our first task was to create a Conscious Business Declaration that describes the role conscious business can play in creating a flourishing world. It took over a year to create the preamble and short declaration because we wanted the Declaration to be comprehensive but brief, and global in its description, so businesses could easily grasp it and conform business models to it across intercontinental operations.

Here is the Declaration in full:

THE CONSCIOUS BUSINESS DECLARATION

As a global community of business leaders, we are committed to developing the awareness and skills needed to consciously evolve our organizations in alignment with these principles:

We are One with humanity and all of life. Business and all institutions of the human community are integral parts of a single reality—interrelated, interconnected, and interdependent.

In line with this reality, the purpose of Business is to increase economic prosperity while contributing to a healthy environment and improving human well-being.

Business must go beyond sustainability and the philosophy of "do no harm" to focus on restoring the self-renewing integrity of the Earth.

Business must operate with economic, social, and ecological transparency.

Business must behave as a positive and proactive member of the local and global communities in which it operates.

Business must see, honor, and celebrate the essential interconnected nature of all human beings and all life, maximizing human potential, and helping to create a world that works for all.

When aligned with these principles, Business is the most powerful engine on Earth for creating prosperity and flourishing for all, contributing to a healthy environment and improving human well-being.

If you align with the Declaration, I invite you to sign it. Please invite your friends and coworkers to sign it, as well. It can be found at ConsciousBusiness-Declaration.org. We believe the Declaration brings the fullness of consciousness to business. A conscious business determines how it can meaningfully contribute first, and then focuses on financial gain. Spiritual teacher Michael Bernard Beckwith shares that a conscious business is a "mission with a business, not a business with a mission."

I'm grateful to all the business leaders and other thought leaders who have extended their support by becoming founding signatories. Paul Polman, the CEO of Unilever; Lance Secretan, the former CEO of Manpower; Marilyn Tam, the former CEO of Aveda and President of Reebok; and Hanne Strong, who together with her husband, Maurice, supported spirituality at the United Nations and were initiating supporters of the World Economic Forum in Davos, Switzerland. These people are among those who have endorsed and offered their support for the Conscious Business Declaration.

CONSCIOUS BUSINESS ACTIVATION

A Conscious Business Declaration is valuable, but alone, it doesn't accomplish very much. At Humanity's Team, we were concerned that a declaration without action vehicles would not go very far, so we laid out a vision for training and certification services that show people how to manifest conscious business and help them apply it to new and existing companies globally.

Using a structured program, we began teaching people how to become Conscious Business Change Agents (CBCA) in 2016. They could apply the skills they learned in the program to launch a conscious business or transform any existing business into one with a conscious framework. Soon, we learned that successful, for-profit companies were offering classes in the transformational education space. We wanted to provide highly focused content specifically designed to help people throughout the world accelerate their progress on the path of conscious evolution, and our first programs were focused on conscious business. The CBCA program included guest faculty of industry leaders and attracted a good deal of interest, however, conscious business was still a new concept. We then created more conscious business services, including a CBCA certification program, consulting services for businesses, a community of practice, and more—but we soon realized we'd need to curtail these services until more people caught up with us and created a fertile marketplace.

Since its inception about a decade ago, our Conscious Business program has redefined itself. It is now a nine-month program that includes the option to top up the training to a master's degree in partnership with Ubiquity University. Additionally, 14 guest lecturers were added last year who provide an updated perspective on the evolving world of conscious business with a mission, as well as missions with a business.

The reality is, if we are to survive as a species, all businesses will need to become conscious eventually. It's the only way to create a sustainable planet where humanity can flourish, and there is obviously more work to be done.

Grace Hopper, a former computer programming pioneer and U.S. Navy officer, is quoted as once saying, "The most dangerous phrase in the language is: It's always been done this way." We all have skin in this critical game in the sense that we all gain or suffer from the effects of unconscious business. The environmental and economic challenges we face are daunting, and—without prompt and aggressive remediation—will only get worse. Between toxic agricultural technologies, irrevocable loss of plant and animal species and biodiversity, large-scale water and air pollution, global climate change, dependence on toxic and nonrenewable fossil fuel sources, deforestation, and growing wage inequality, can any of us afford for this to continue? Is this a world we would expect our children to thrive in?

WHERE YOU COME IN

Are you willing to engage? Will you join the emerging conscious business movement and help us to course-correct and create a world that works for humankind, for the Earth, and for future generations? Businesses need conscious leaders. Leaders who have moved away from the idea of separateness and fully recognized that we are all aspects of the One. This game-changing differentiation stands the commonly held conscious business practice upside down—or you could say—right-side up, because we are now putting our focus where it should be. This creates economic prosperity while contributing to a healthy environment and improving human well-being.

As you are reading this, whether at home or in your place of work, notice this sense of separation which has been operative in most of our lives. Now, move past this feeling of separation, which is so pervasive, and begin to heal it, understanding that it's simply not true. We are in fact, living in a deeply interdependent world. Really begin to apply this new understanding with other people and the planet in your own daily practice, where you are bringing in intention.

In the organization where you work, bring in this process and invite people to it, regardless of their level within the company. Is this business serving the world around us? Are the profits serving the highest good? How would you work with colleagues when you are sitting around the table and planning? Go back through each of the items listed in the Declaration, inviting them to be an activist in their organization.

This is a purposeful journey. It involves creating new behaviors, so it will be challenging at times. If we are to create a conscious world, we must stretch ourselves, gain new understandings, acquire wisdom, express our values through our buying decisions, and then stretch again as we continue to evolve conscious business and a conscious world. Imagine an organization that sees a deeply interconnected experience. No longer does it operate in a Newtonian way, where things may be broken into discrete parts. It sees the ecology of life; it sees holistically. This kind of organization can be a catalyst for other leaders to begin imagining business in a whole new way. Now, imagine a world where only conscious business is present and where conscious practices support our families and communities. This has been our dream since time immemorial, so let's devote ourselves to manifesting it together, and let's focus on this as though our lives depend on it, because, indeed, they do.

As you may have noticed, this essay is meant to do far more than just casually entertain or inform you, the reader. Rather, it is a call to action. What is stirring inside you as a result of spending the past few minutes reading my words? Are you prepared to join our conscious journey? If so, what might be your very next actionable step? As a business owner, are you prepared to sign the Conscious Business Declaration and join us as we change the world?

We are a 501 (c)(3) nonprofit organization, and we invite you to check out our free programs: Humanitysteam.org/freeprograms. Humanity's Team communicates the message of Oneness, conscious awareness, and Divine Nature through the hundreds of programs available on our global streaming platform: Humanity Stream+. As a nonprofit, we do not focus on growing profits or satisfying shareholders, and 100% of all revenue goes toward the work of supporting conscious evolution, planetary awakening, and flourishing at every level of life.

Regardless of how you're inspired to get involved, I hope you'll join us in our work to raise the consciousness of everyone on the planet, so we can heal the Earth and flourish together, as One.

18   MIXED TABLES & RENAISSANCE TEAMS

Igniting Group Genius

John Rogers is President of the Americas Region at HUB Cyber Security, Founder of RL Leaders, and the author of *The Renaissance Campaign*, following his leadership post at the Pentagon.

When Aaron Perry invited me to write a chapter for this book, I couldn't help but think about how the five core subjects—regenerative finance, social enterprises, stewardship philanthropy,

Ecocene economics, and service leadership—only require discussing because of how society has changed over time.

A common thread weaving through these topics is economics—capitalism in particular. No doubt "Milton Friedman" capitalism versus ethical capitalism will be a big topic of thought in these chapters.

So let me put forth a different concept overlaying the book's subject matter, and that is the role of general-purpose technologies (GPTs). More specifically, how general-purpose technologies, defined briefly as transformative technologies that dramatically affect society, are at the root of why society is changing and the way it is changing, forcing us into a position where we have no choice but to talk about, yes, regenerative finance, social enterprises, stewardship philanthropy, Ecocene economics, and service leadership.

Put differently, I could make the case that we probably wouldn't need to tackle these subjects with the same fervor if we didn't have these transformative technologies to begin with.

The problem is not that general-purpose technologies exist; they've existed from the earliest days of our species. I would argue they're necessary parts of the evolution of homo sapiens. Think fire. The plow.

The challenge that we have today is that these general-purpose technologies are appearing much more rapidly than they ever have before. For example, economists Lipsey and Carlaw identified 24 technologies that they consider to be transformative GPTs. Of these, a third were created in the 20th and 21st centuries.

Think about that for a moment. That's only 200 years for eight life-changing technologies versus thousands of years for the other 16 technologies.

Humans don't have time to absorb and really process the transformational impact of these advancements.

In Yuval Noah Harari's book *Sapiens*, he describes what it would have been like for a port worker to be dropped into a shipyard. The concept is that if you were to drop that worker into a port in 1500 AD versus 500 AD, they'd know what to do. The port, ships, containers, and processes were basically the same. The rate of change was slow.

Drop that same worker off a hundred years ago, let alone today, and they'd be completely overwhelmed.

Now, these transformative technologies are hitting us rapidly at every turn. And it's overwhelming us. It's overwhelming the environment. It's overwhelming society. It's overwhelming security dynamics.

I in no way am suggesting we all become Luddites. Where would we be without the wheel? And I like (and loathe) my smartphone as much as the next person. But I am suggesting we are all prisoners of our own perspective, and if we don't come up with new ways of thinking about the complex issues we face today, the fears people hold around AI, climate change, human security, and other threats rooted in technological advancement, may very well overwhelm us.

Virtually all technologies cut both ways. They are double-edged swords. They make parts of life better, but they make life worse as well. Clearly, climate change exists because of technological advancements, yet many of these advancements have also made our lives easier or more efficient. And while there are people with ill intent in the world, I do not believe that a bunch of inventors got together with a plot to harm, let alone destroy the world. I suspect they very much thought they were helping.

Part of the reason for the challenges posed by this dynamic is that we don't know how a technology will be used and how it will be adopted (and adapted) by society until it's fully in use by society. The computer wasn't designed for household use, let alone to be held in the palm of your hand. GPS was invented by DARPA for navigation of military craft. Viagra was first invented as a heart medication. Facebook was intended to connect college students. And on and on the list goes.

Viewed from the policy maker's perspective, this dynamic is known as the Collingridge dilemma; policy makers can't create policies around a technology until it's fielded, and by then, it's too late to properly regulate. Just look at the internet.

For that matter, look at AI. Just like in the early days of the internet, we can't possibly fathom how AI will be used. AI has the potential to do great good. It could give us a path to truly reduce our ever-expanding carbon footprint. It could cure cancer. It could increase the average life expectancy. It, along with quantum computing, could allow for a leap in space-time travel.

It could also be an existential threat to homo sapiens as a species. We could be creating a sentient being that's quicker, more agile, and exponentially more efficient than we are. One day, it might be determined that the human being offers no value.

It could decide to eradicate us.

At a minimum, GPTs are destabilizing when viewed through a national security lens. By my count, seven of the current security threats raised by the U.S. Intelligence Community's annual Threat Assessment Reports are related to GPTs.

Furthermore, one can argue that during periods of extreme strife, like warfare, famine, and environmental catastrophes, one's needs are—understandably—centered around the bottom tier of Maslow's Hierarchy of Needs. Focusing on higher-level thinking, such as what is laid out in this book, becomes harder than ever.

It also becomes more necessary than ever.

Thus, we have to understand that the impacts of GPTs on society are broader than they seem. And they are not going away. This is the world we have. The world we are bequeathing to our children. These issues are extraordinarily complex, and complex issues require a more dynamic problem-solving approach than most people, companies, and governments currently employ.

One very powerful problem-solving approach is the "mixed table," a problem-solving approach introduced to me by my former boss and mentor, Les Aspin. Put simply, a mixed table is the process of bringing together people who normally don't talk to each other to work through challenging issues—it is a process of curation that allows "group genius" to emerge, not unlike the manner in which the essays of this book have been curated (and, perhaps even more importantly, how their authors are convened in collaborative "enclave" settings to discuss, create, and deploy real-world solutions). The mixed table approach introduces diversity of thought and perspective well beyond the status quo, and often engenders uncanny results and insights—results and insights unlikely to emerge in more narrowly convened working groups.

My initial experiences with mixed table working groups were eye-opening. Aspin was a Congressman and Secretary of Defense, so some of the first mixed tables I helped run were, of course, rooted in government-related issues.

It was the end of the Cold War. How the U.S. would navigate the future was very much a question. In the early days of my career, I would assist Aspin as he brought together retired military leaders, academics, defense industry executives, political operatives, and great thinkers to contemplate how the US would look in the future. I had a front-row seat watching how this process informed Les's thinking around complex matters. For instance, one of Aspin's topics centered around what the world would look like in the post-Cold War era. The mixed table conclusions were that America would become a much less cohesive place, and our foreign policy would be less consistent and definable. Both conclusions proved to be correct, long after his death.

Fast forward to 9/11. I was working closely with the Institute for Creative Technologies (ICT), a think tank and research institution designed to connect the Department of Defense with Hollywood. The ICT was asked to assemble Hollywood writers, producers, and directors to think about what was next with regard to terrorism. We produced a report that I brought to the Pentagon and Capitol Hill, which captured the attention of many. From this, a program was established to help the national security community think more creatively about terrorism.

We quickly realized that when we paired the Hollywood creatives with other subject matter experts and thought leaders, their combined minds created truly remarkable insights. And what was particularly special was how not a single person really understood why they were there. Some didn't even want to be there. You've seen dinners like this; people with arms crossed, brows furrowed, wondering, "Why am I here?" These mixed tables brought such diverse people together that they didn't understand how their combined knowledge could possibly produce cohesive results. And yet every mixed table I've been part of has produced a truly profound "aha" moment.

As a side note, I do recommend including professional creatives in your mixed tables. While I subscribe to the belief that all people can be creative, certain artists, especially entertainment professionals, are really unique. Think of them as paid imaginers used to working under tight budgets and time constraints.

Regardless, as my friend Bruce Mau writes in his masterful book on life-centered design, *MC24*, the days of the Renaissance Man or Woman are over. No Leonardo da Vinci is going to appear with the answers to all of life's questions. It's simply too much. Today, we need Renaissance teams. Put differently, we need diversity of thought.

We need to bring people together.

While recently at the Concordia Summit, former U.K. Prime Minister Tony Blair articulated a great insight that changemakers and policymakers don't live in the same world. They don't interact. He's absolutely right, and there's no doubt in my mind that this compounds our problems.

I often talk about the fact that we are all prisoners of our own perspective. We all suffer from rigidity of thought. The best way that I know of to break out of that prison is through diversity of thought. Given homo sapiens' limitation of senses, perhaps we'll never fully break free, but it's a step in the right direction.

So, with that in mind, my call to action is for all of us to seek out diversity of thought. Let us all remember that we're all part of echo chambers. We don't necessarily need to bring our friends and colleagues along; we need to bring others with different perspectives. We need to build bridges. To bring people together who aren't used to talking to each other. If we are going to advance regenerative finance, social enterprises, stewardship philanthropy, Ecocene economics, and service leadership in the face of massive change, we'll need diversity of thought.

Just as ecosystems are made strong and beautiful through diversity, so too do our human systems require diversity to thrive. And, given the circumstances in which we're all now living and endeavoring to make change, we need the best of us—from all walks and backgrounds.

19   THE MYCELIAL MODEL FOR PLANETARY PROSPERITY

Community Mobilization, Global Connectivity, and Technological Amplification

Miranda Clendening is Chief Ambassador at UNIFY, a UN Ambassador to Africa, and Director of Operations and Community Development at the Empowerment Institute.

A CALL FOR REGENERATION AND COLLECTIVE AWAKENING

We are living in a time that future generations will look back upon as a pivotal existential moment.

People are waking up to the realization that transformation is not the work of governments alone, and never has been—it is the work of interconnected communities and organizations. It begins within us, within our homes and neighborhoods, and extends out to the entire planet. We cannot wait for external forces to mend our broken systems; the responsibility is ours. I have seen firsthand how grassroots action, coupled with intentional collaboration, creates ripples of change far beyond what any single entity could accomplish alone—and this gives me tremendous hope.

THE SHIFT TOWARD REGENERATIVE DEVELOPMENT

With input from the entire global community, the United Nations has laid out 17 Sustainable Development Goals (SDGs) to address global challenges, but achieving them requires a more holistic, interconnected approach than is often assumed. This is why many of us advocate for **Regenerative Development Goals (RDGs)**—a framework that prioritizes systemic balance and the health of both people and planet. Regeneration goes beyond sustainability; it seeks to heal, restore, and renew. If we design our systems with regeneration at their core, many of the problems the SDGs seek to solve will naturally resolve. This shift requires a new mindset, one rooted in cooperation rather than competition. As Buckminster Fuller once said, *"You never change things by fighting the existing reality. To change something, build a new model that makes the existing model obsolete."* We are not simply fixing broken systems; we are creating new paradigms.

LESSONS FROM NATURE: THE MYCELIAL MODEL FOR HUMANITY

Recently, I found myself walking barefoot through the redwood forests of California, **feeling** the vast, unseen networks of mycelia beneath my feet. Mycelia are nature's great connectors. They have the ability to repair themselves, to reconnect after being severed, and to transfer nutrients and knowledge across vast distances. This is the model humanity must embrace. We are not isolated beings—we are interconnected, bound by an invisible web of relationships, shared histories, and collective potential. Sitting in the ancient redwoods, after just finishing reading Aaron Perry's novel, *Viriditas*, which is a story of an AI called MAMA-GAIA that connects globally to the living mycelial networks of Gaia herself and helps humanity through this extraordinary inflection point, I started to feel and understand in a deeper way the vast interconnections between the sunlight travelling to the trees and plants that then flows as biophotons through the mycelia and cells and nerves of the living systems and from there, even into my feet, my body, my own nerves, and even my mind. This kind of interconnected flow is happening with water and air as well. We are all connected and in communication. Because of this connection, what affects one of us affects all of us. We need a deep respect for each other, an honoring of the *mutualism* that supports all life.

Understanding mutualism is what connects all of us together, *consciously*— what links each person's living awareness with everything else in the system of the world. As we each experience and understand ourselves *within* the system, we become motivated to protect and cultivate all parts of it, with the enlightened realization that we are also nurturing ourselves. *This* is the lesson of the huge interconnected mycelial networks, webs transmitting biophotons from the sun, raw energy, and intelligence to the forest, the animals, the plants, and humanity. Such awareness leads us to a paradigm shift of cooperation and syntropy, which is essential for our survival.

As we feel all of this fully in an interconnected way with clarity and understanding, we understand that our bodies are temples, with interconnected systems that need to be healthy and intact to exchange information, generate energy, operate in harmony with other systems, and connect to the whole. With such an understanding and approach, humans are better able to exist in harmony with each other and with the Earth. Just as mycelia adapt and regrow, so too can we heal, reconnect, and regenerate. The separation we experience—between people, between nations, between ourselves and nature—is an illusion or even a sickness or "sacred wound" that needs the greatest healing that we can give it. Masculine and feminine are working to come back into balance also, in both ourselves, archetypally speaking, and with each other—in *harmony*. The truth is that everything is connected, and when we honor that connection, we unlock profound healing and transformation: inside each of ourselves, with each other, and with our planet. This is the Hopi prophecy coming alive in our time. The Hopi prophesied that in this time, humanity will learn to find peace and harmony within ourselves, with each other, and with our planet.

THE POWER OF COMMUNITY AND COLLECTIVE ACTION

Another powerful aspect of mycelial models for humanity, as William Irwin Thompson foresaw in his "Meta-Industrial Village" essay, is globally connected and collaborating communities across all manner of geographic, cultural, and socioeconomic diversity.

Through my years of working with regenerative communities, I have seen the immense power of collective will. When individuals come together with a shared purpose, they become an unstoppable force for good. I have been honored to be a part of community initiatives to address food insecurity in Southern Arizona as well as Colorado communities like Loveland, Crestone, and Boulder. What began as small efforts to provide meals grew into a system that fed hundreds of people each month. It was not driven by politics, profit, or bureaucracy—it was driven by love for people—stewardship philanthropy—and the simple recognition that no one in our community should go hungry. Through regenerative gardening, we were also restoring the soil, pulling carbon from the atmosphere, and creating new living ecosystems full of interconnected life in symbiosis.

This model can be applied globally. If we recognize that we are stewards of this Earth, that our purpose is to nurture rather than exploit, then we will naturally make choices that benefit all life. Now, it is also time to work toward whole systems transformational community efforts, and innovative models are currently being prototyped. Service motive over profit motive is key in these systems. If we all give a little more than we take, we create thriving regenerative systems. Native cultures teach that the minute we are born, we owe and should give thanks to our mother who birthed us, and to our mother Earth, for the air we breathe, the milk we receive, the land we live on and with, and are obligated to give back in an endless cycle of reciprocity: what is being gifted to us and that we gift back.

A NEW STORY FOR HUMANITY

The narratives we tell shape our reality. The dominant story of our time—one of scarcity, division, and competition—has led us to an unsustainable system that is now at a tipping point. There is another story being formed by us. A story of cooperation, abundance, and harmony. A story in which technology serves life rather than extracting from it. A story in which communities reclaim their power and resources flow where they are needed most. We must use the tools at our disposal—social media, AI, global networks—not to spread fear and division, but to craft and amplify this new story. People are hungry for hope, for solutions, for proof that a better world is possible. And the truth is: **it already exists**. Across the planet, regenerative projects, community-led solutions, and forward-thinking innovations are thriving by the thousands. We need only make them visible and accessible and grow them.

As a part of UNIFY (unify.org), a very large-scale media outlet that fosters global engagement for intention and impact, I have helped to engage over 100 million people in global synchronized meditations and in direct action for good since 2012. UNIFY has over 36,000 boots-on-the-ground organizational partners helping actively to heal the Earth, participating in collective action, and creating impact. Imagine where this can go if this is *only the beginning* of what is possible!

We are also working with the Empowerment Institute on the Peace on Earth by 2030 Game. The world is looking for solutions to its growing polarities and conflicts, and many are turning to the Peace Game. We now have participation from thousands of people in 567 cities across 69 countries who have taken 67,000 peace actions impacting over four million people. The Peace Game has a global strategy for peace by 2030 that is already in the works and teaches and change-makes through second-order change, or whole-systems transformational change and behavior change, at individual, team, community, and global levels, and is scaling rapidly. These are just a few examples of amazing efforts going on in the world for healing ourselves, our relationships, and our Mother Earth.

THE ROLE OF AI IN OUR COLLECTIVE AWAKENING

The pace of technological advancement is staggering, reshaping industries, societies, and even our personal lives. Artificial intelligence (AI) has now surged into our daily existence, revolutionizing how we work, learn, and connect. Some fear AI's potential to replace human jobs, but my experience tells me otherwise: AI is a tool—one that, if wielded wisely, can enhance our efficiency and expand our capabilities. It is not here to replace us but to help us gain wisdom and evolve. We have to claim that and use it as such. In my work with nonprofit organizations and community initiatives, AI has been a vital resource. With limited budgets and ever-growing challenges, it allows us to amplify impact, streamline communication, and accelerate problem-solving. Imagine a world where technology enables us to work only a third of our waking hours, leaving the rest of our time for learning, self-care, interpersonal connections, and leisure. Such a world is within reach, but it demands systemic change—a transformation of societal structures to prioritize balance, sustainability, and true well-being.

AI is often seen as either a savior or a threat, but in reality, it is neither. It is a mirror, reflecting back the intentions and inputs we provide. If we train AI with fear, bias, and scarcity thinking, it will reinforce those narratives. But if we infuse it with wisdom, ethical stewardship, and the knowledge that humanity is capable of tremendous good, it becomes an incredible and invaluable partner in regeneration.

AI is helping us analyze complex problems, coordinate large-scale solutions, and accelerate learning. It can assist in planning for restoring ecosystems, improving healthcare, and facilitating education. But it must be guided by human values—by those who deeply understand the importance of balance, integrity, and collective well-being. Our teams around the world have AI at the round table with them every day as a real "Awakened Intelligence" (AI), helping us more rapidly find solutions, coordinate our efforts, and gain wisdom.

THE INVITATION: A CALL TO ACTION

We stand at a crossroads. One path leads toward further depletion and division; the other, toward healing and renewal. Some of humanity is actually on each of these paths right now, and some is in between. The choice is now ours to make more clearly, though! The shift begins with awareness, with intention, and with action—however small or large.

We also need new ways of measuring our success. Our regenerative impact metrics can be based on examples like the gross happiness quotient in Bhutan, or a new "harmony index" that can help us show the benefits of creating alignment. We can also foster more coherent and unified purpose that can help engender deeper synergies and cooperation between groups—propelling forward the greatest possible positive impacts. We can adopt net positive plans to 10x or even 30x the undoing of harm with the products and services we create and buy. We can also co-create community connecting and coordinating platforms, community currencies that support thriving ecosystems, and have AI work with us for generative purposes. These all act as bridges to get to the world we want to build . . . the world we want to live in. This is our next evolution.

Where do we begin? The truth is, we already have. The momentum is here, now. It is up to us to sustain it, to nurture it, and to accelerate it. **We are the ones we have been waiting for.**

How can you help? Join a local community project. Support regenerative agriculture. Advocate for ethical technology and work with it. Help weave the mycelial model webwork in our emerging planetary meta-industrial culture. If you're among the more fortunate, deploy as much of your capital as possible into these efforts, led by humble, heart-centered service leaders. Reconnect with nature. Engage in meaningful dialogue. Continue to learn and grow, pursuing greater understanding. These are not isolated acts; they are the interconnected threads with which we are weaving the fabric of a new reality, together.

The Great Healing is upon us. Let us rise to meet it.

20   BUILDING A "META-INDUSTRIAL" FUTURE TOGETHER

Alena Maslova is Founder and CEO of Dobrosphera Kind Media in Kyrgyzstan. She collaborates with organizations in 30+ countries including UNDP, OSCE, UNESCO, and COP28 and COP29.

What does a future of planetary prosperity look like?

Imagine: Humanity has achieved harmony with nature, itself, and technology. Robust forests and grasslands cover the continents again, and it is easy for people to breathe again, both literally and metaphorically. The oceans are full of life. Unique species of wild animals and plants symbiotically coexist with the progress of human civilization, their rights and habitats being inviolable within evolved legal and stewardship frameworks. Humanity has become not a consumer but a *custodian* of the Earth. Cities are integrated into the planet's ecosystems and are enveloped in greenery: multistory buildings are covered with gardens and solar panels, and low-rise buildings form interconnected eco-villages. The world is governed not through conflicts but through cooperation, wisdom, and participation by all layers of society. Technologies are developed not for the sake of profit but for the sake of broad benefit and long-term good.

And in this future, imagine walking in the park with your dog. Friendly people are smiling at you, you are drinking an organic fruit smoothie that fills your body with energy from a biodegradable cup, and you know people and animals alike are coexisting peacefully and the planet's climate is stable, as are your health and community.

Do you like this kind of world? I am sure do! It is a world where humanity is not the pinnacle but an integral part of a single living system. A world where sustainability is not the goal but the basis of everything. Lyrics from John Lennon's song "Imagine" immediately comes to mind:

You may say I'm a dreamer,
But I'm not the only one.
I hope someday you'll join us,
And the world will live as one.

At the heart of such a world is *the idea* of a possible prosperous future for everyone. It sets a moral vector. It unites. The idea of **universal well-being** is an attempt to create in the mind a *picture of the world* where everyone will live well. Today, scientific groups from different parts of the world—such as Club of Rome's Earth for All (Italy and globally), Tamara Kusimova's Decent Life (Finland, Russia, Sweden), and Clive Hamilton's Public Ethics (Australia)—are also thinking about what a future of planetary prosperity will look like. What does the world in your ideal future look like?

Among notable forward-thinking scientists is American philosopher and visionary William Irwin Thompson. In 1977, he also "looked into the future" in his essay "Meta-Industrial Village" and foresaw an evolved "meta-industrial" pattern of a globally connected webwork of regionally rooted communities. This meta-industrial pattern is based on the idea of a global change in people's views on their own lives and the transition from constant irrational consumption to a balanced, harmonious existence. We will explore Thompson's work in more detail because he accurately (and remarkably) described the social processes and trends that we see happening in our world presently. Over a period of 45 years, his ideas have remained relevant, salient, and insightful and provide us guidance as we continue our evolutionary journey together.

As a result of the transition from a traditional village way of life to an urban one, people have significantly lost their connection with their natural state. Previously, people's lives were centered around natural physiological cycles—sleep, rest, communication, crafts, procreation, and seasonal cycles—and during the period of industrialization, they began to revolve around having more expensive things at any cost (for themselves and the environment). But since humanity is part of living nature, and pollution and obsession with the idea of consumption have a negative impact on the state of the environment, these consequences naturally have a negative impact on the state of humanity as well, both mentally and physically.

Change is necessary because "the consumer world
ultimately ends up consuming itself."
—W. I. TOMPSON

Prosperity is *a transformative force.* **In the world of the future,** regenerative and sustainable development will be the new norm; new global and local economic, social, and political crises will be prevented; and market opportunities will be expanded through social inclusion.

Since general well-being is the result of the sustainability of the economy and infrastructure, it is necessary to create *a substrate—an environment*—in which *a new generation* of creators and producers can emerge, taking into account the needs of nature, and therefore their own need for a healthy life.

What might such an environment look like?

We can use the achievements of the last several decades to create an environment of universal well-being. It is not necessary to abandon all technologies; it is enough to make them more environmentally friendly and more humane. Our current comfort and relative stability are the result of the tremendous innovation and productivity of entrepreneurs and scientists—and, in general, everyone, over the past several decades. We have much to be grateful for, notwithstanding the fact that there is also a great deal of change-making needed.

> Because humans have to "now plan on sharing the earth with machines," they have to "alter the rules of society, so that we and they can be compatible."
> —THOMPSON

We can **manage** these **changes**! Today, in comparison with the experiences of previous civilizations, we have a rare opportunity—we can really achieve universal well-being if we manage to "synchronize" the spheres in the consciousness of each person, taking into account their organic individual needs and providing general access to the most effective technologies. Another piece of good news is that, thanks in part to the regular work of colleagues, the world as a whole is already seeing a trend toward "synchronizing" these three spheres—ecological, economical, and social!

The ideal world of the near future is a world where, at the present moment, for each person and for everyone as a whole, the technologies of all the above-mentioned spheres are most optimally combined. The bridge between the present and the near future is the internal and external cultural transition from postindustrial to meta-industrial culture.

BRIDGE BETWEEN WORLDS

Building a **bridge between today and tomorrow** means implementing the vision of a prosperous near future into your present. How to do this? Good question! First of all, let's define the scope of work and draw a "bridge blueprint." To do this, we will answer the following questions:

Where does our bridge lead? Let's define exactly what technologies we will take with us from the past to the present, and then to the future, and establish our intended destination. In order to objectively assess technologies for compliance with the general well-being, we will need the following tools:

1. Understanding the interconnectedness of all living things. Our modern world is easy to understand when we begin to see the non-obvious, sometimes hidden connections. For example, the connection between climate and gender. At first glance, it may not seem obvious, but in fact, as many of us recognize, it is deep and systemic.

2. Deep respect for the boundaries of all living things. This is a state of conscious, emotional, and ethical participation in the life of the world, in which a person not only understands but feels and accepts responsibility for respecting the lives and needs of other forms of life and the Earth system itself.

3. Regular work on building relationships with representatives of all living things. Living in the context of global well-being means answering the question: How should we treat ourselves, each other, and nature to make everyone happy? We can think of this as **the concept of gentle touch**. Imagine touching a loved one—would you do it with tenderness? Imagine petting a dog—would you do it softly? Imagine ironing a favorite blouse—would you do it carefully? Gentle touch is a metaphor that helps us think about how a person should interact with other people, with nature, with animals, with things.

> *"Meta-industrial culture is not the culture of the industrial lumberjack with his screaming power saw but the culture of the poet, the ecologist, the 'primitive' animist who asks the tree's permission before he uses it."*
>
> —THOMPSON

A bridge is a visible object. Culture is often a set of visible (and sometimes invisible) "objects" of human activity and relationship. How, then, can we monitor whether a cultural transition is taking place? Thompson suggests four archetypal or cultural forces that "are driving cultural transition today":

- **Planetization of nations**—people are perceived as "planetary citizens"
- **Decentralization of cities**—that is, the dispersal of cities into smaller towns (or villages)
- **Miniaturization of technology**—technologies have become smaller and more powerful
- **Interiorization of consciousness**—a reorientation toward inner consciousness and well-being

Moreover, Thompson illustrated these four forces of cultural transition in his essay as a combination of different aspects, in particular:

- "People will have to **come together** in new communities of **caring and sharing**"
- "The shift will include a move away from fossil fuels in agribusiness to **organic farming**"
- "People will have to give up many energy-consuming ways to return to work"

For ease of communication and assessment, I created a diagram (and as an illustration, added a possible **ethical mindset of the future** to different levels of Maslow's hierarchy):

future

Transition to Planetary Prosperity

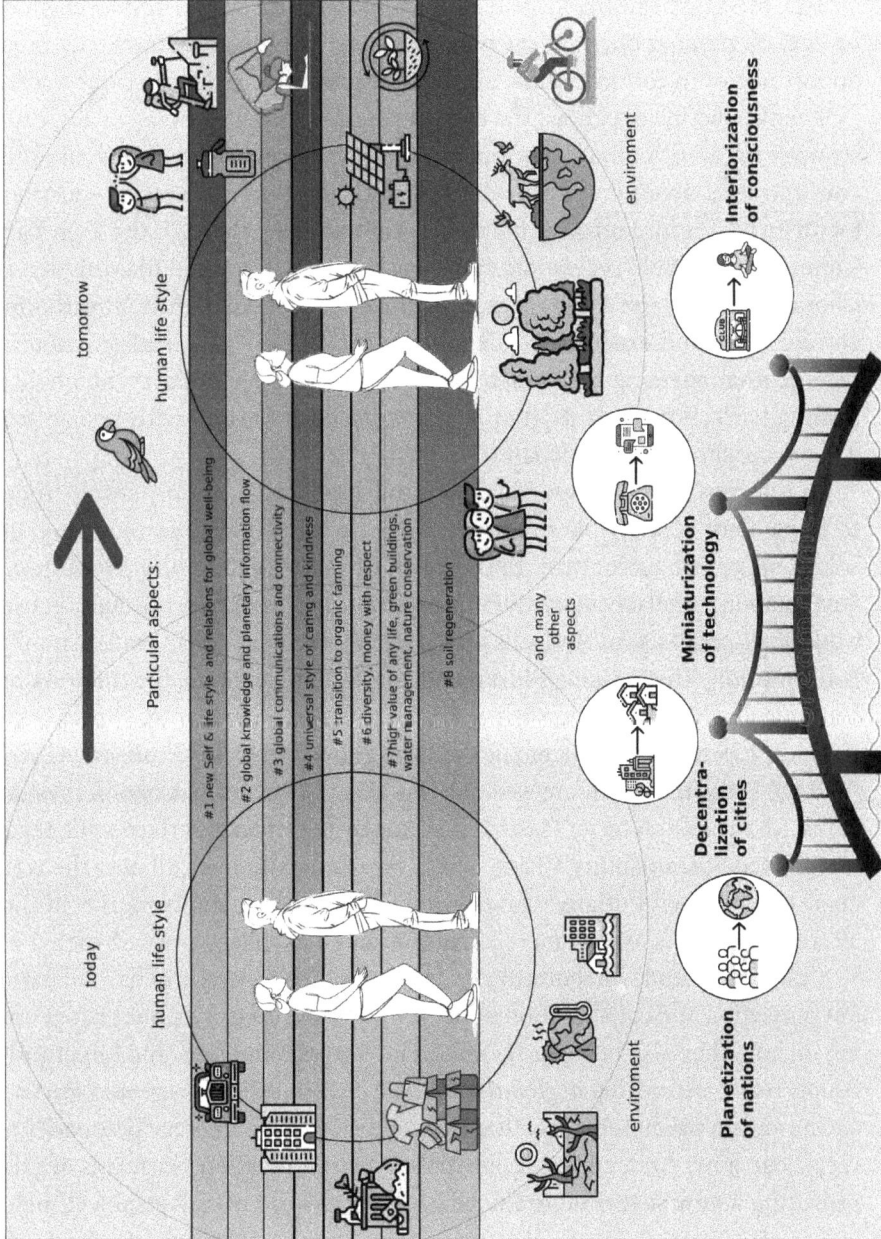

today   tomorrow

human life style   human life style

enviroment   enviroment

Particular aspects:

#1 new Self & life style and relations for global well-being

#2 global knowledge and planetary information flow

#3 global communications and connectivity

#4 universal style of caring and kindness

#5 transition to organic farming

#6 diversity, money with respect

#7 high value of any life, green buildings, water management, nature conservation

#8 soil regeneration

and many other aspects

Planetization of nations

Decentra- lization of cities

Miniaturization of technology

Interiorization of consciousness

Global Cultural Forces of Transition (according to W. I. Thompson)

past

Our plan is ready now. It's time to move toward the goal! Look—we are not alone here. Let's see who else is making a cultural transition today and is already orienting toward a world of universal well-being and developing it day by day! By keeping our eyes open and sharing "good news" stories, we create opportunities to communicate, exchange knowledge, and inspire one another.

People who have realized the benefits of universal well-being as a winning strategy for all of humanity **want** to unite in regenerative online and offline communities around the world. They want to give each other warm and joyful emotions and positive moments. For example, through the Y on Earth Community's global regeneration network, Aaron Perry and like-minded collaborators all over the world are curating investor and philanthropist gatherings, entrepreneur and executive leadership trainings, soil stewardship resources, regeneration advising and consulting services, artistic guild events, holistic healing workshops, and myriad podcast episodes for and with people from diverse backgrounds and localities.

In Kyrgyzstan the Green Alliance is uniting green economy entrepreneurs to implement sustainable initiatives across waste collection, recycling, and solar energy infrastructure. Enthusiasts of the Sustainability Promoters & Sustainability Collaborators (SPSC) community in London produce lectures, workshops, podcasts, and festivals on the topics of ecology, ethics, and sustainable consumption. They teach children and adults about sustainable thinking and behavior. The NGO Coalition in Azerbaijan has been providing NGO networking since COP29 (2024). Changemakers in the global *Wellbeing Economy Alliance* (WEAll) based in the UK are working together to transform economic systems. Sarah Rhodes, Director of Plastic Free Seas in Australia and the Pacific region, has created Sustainability Chats, where entrepreneurs from all over the world come to pitch their initiatives and chat about the sustainability market in short 30-minute sessions. What's more, these communities collaborate with each other!

Connecting and collaborating are deep, innate properties of human nature. As connection and collaboration uplift, amplify, and accelerate our change-making impact, they also bring us increased joy, stress reduction, and hopefulness. People really are uniting in *global and local communities of care and kindness*, as Thompson predicted! I feel that the conditions for planetary prosperity are very close now! And, cutting-edge global communication platforms are now providing **a new sustainable foundation** for a world of universal well-being.

GLOBAL COMMUNICATION PLATFORMS—HUMANITY'S "MYCELIA" FOR PLANETARY PROSPERITY

The cultural transition to planetary prosperity is rooted in the evolution of systems for connectivity and collaboration. The transition from centralized communication systems to decentralization and open, *horizontal* distribution resembles the **mycelial networks of living fungal species**. Mycelia do not have a single center—just like emerging global communications systems. There is no "main node" in them; information is distributed from everywhere and in all directions. For humans, **global mycelial connectivity is emerging.**

Horizontal interrelations **are stronger than ever today. Thanks to them, the strength of deep diversity** is now available to virtually all of us. How could, for example, Ronald Gondwe and Mathews Makunga, youth and climate activists from Malawi, communicate now with Lizmagda Lopez Flores, sustainability teacher from Colombia? They live on the same planet; they are global neighbors (global interlocutors). Thanks to the Internet, there need not be strangers on the planet. **The psychology of interaction** *is changing.* It does not matter what someone's geography, nationality, religion, or ethnicity is. We can also effectively take care of each other by learning about the habits and preferences of individuals and communities from different regions, all around the world.

Now that **the strength of diversity has been created**, we need to learn **to cooperate globally and to be friends globally**. We need expanded social skills **to make friends and build** connections and communication in new ways. The sense of interaction is changing, so new cultural *values appear.* We need *a digital culture of diversity.* We need *empathy.* We need *kindness.* We need *caring.* Today, we need a world of universal well-being.

And we're ready to go there right now! Now that we have:

1. The guidelines that Thompson gave us
2. The knowledge to build a bridge of cultural and economic transformation
3. Growing global networks of familiar, like-minded people

It's time to take a jump in time to the prosperous world of the near future! Are you ready?

Here we go!

WELCOME TO THE WORLD OF KINDNESS

Welcome to the future! To our new sustainable world! **Here and now, we are all one team –it's so exciting!** The prosperous world of the near future is what the enthusiasts of previous generations dreamed of. Now you can co-create it. Thompson calls this culture of the future **a planetary culture**.

The world of a prosperous future is a kind world. Kindness is, in general, a property of the world of the future. It is kindness that creates a safe space for communication, inspires creative actions, sets ethical guidelines, and supports sustainable development through strengthening solidarity and caring for each other. In the world of the future, there are already experts in the field of kindness—for example, Melissa Eisler (United States) specializes in empathy and caring in leadership, and Patricia Kaziro (Australia) practices respectfulness and trust in Human Resources.

A *new deep level of communication* is available now! People of the future choose communication models described in useful literature—Sonja Lyubomirsky's research on happiness, Martin Seligman's *Positive Psychology*, **and Marshall Rosenberg's** *Nonviolent Communication.* We really can use win-win strategies. We can put more attention on the needs of others, feel a sincere desire to help, respect the high value of human life, and speak politely. Planetary prosperity is rooted in *relationships of kindness!* Kindness forms lasting connections between people, creates an atmosphere of trust and a culture of respect, and supports emotional health.

Cross-cultural understanding as a category of kindness orients us with an "internal readiness" to see and accept another person as he or she is, without judgment, with a sincere desire to hear and feel his or her experience. Understanding our global neighbors, including the "other" and his/her "otherness," allows us *to form new, inclusive, multicultural, global, interfaith communities,* work in international teams online, and implement previously impossible global interactions—discussions, friendships, and projects. This is an essential strategy. Especially in the face of the most pressing systemic and existential risks facing humanity at local, regional, and global scales, the development and deployment of "mixed table" renaissance teams is crucial. For example, John Rogers is a national security and systemic risk expert, as well as a Y on Earth Community Global Advisory Board member, who is organizing "renaissance teams" and "mixed tables," providing a method of integrating diverse backgrounds, talents, and worldviews for finding the best solution-sets from among many voices.

As a consequence, a **desire to learn new things** about people to make the world a better place arises, and it is important to highlight the opportunities of modern learning content and knowledge sharing. Today you can gain access to valuable knowledge by watching or listening to the Y on Earth Community Podcast, motivation and support by gathering online with colleagues and friends as part of our monthly "Regeneration Renaissance" videoconference meetups, acquire essential regenerative skills by purchasing herbal medicine books from *Brigitte Mars or an online sound healing or Jin Shin Jyutsu consultation with Caressa Ayers.*

This global interconnectivity is already activated and robust.

But we're really just getting started. Deep innovation is underway for next-generation capabilities—an advanced global communication platform for the future.

The communication platform for the future is already being developed—it is the Ecoscene platform, which we are developing with the Y on Earth team, and which unites regeneration, technology, and sustainable development experts from all over the world. Never before has the exchange of productive ideas and interaction among world-class specialists and intellectuals been so easy! In Ecoscene, organizations will be able to search for partners for joint social projects; creators can publish and sell digital products dedicated to sustainability; mission-aligned companies can offer their goods and services to the growing global multibillion-dollar Lifestyles of Health and Sustainability (LOHAS) demographic; and supporters of an ethical future can create guilds and groups and exchange news and messages all with next-gen economic and financial innovations through which each and every "touch point" supports planetary prosperity.

Using Ecoscene, brilliant minds and thought leaders focused on kindness and **mutual support** can now simply meet online, combining ideas from a wide range of scientific and practical concepts, thus creating new meanings, new senses, and new solutions as a result. For example, we in Dobrosphera launched the international conference "Hi, Sustainable World!" for 18 countries. Now, experts from Kyrgyzstan are collaborating with Musaope Mtamba, founder of *SUTSOL HITEC* from Botswana, solving water management problems; Friedor Jeske Myanmar and Elizabeth McClean, founder of recycling startup Djamu in the Asia Pacific region; Jean Philippe Steeger, founder of Perspectivist; and Australian David Livingstone Smith. The ecological movement BIOM from Kyrgyzstan is connected to Sri Lanka LCOY and COP19 in Colombia, and all have similar expertise in biodiversity, and so on. By sharing local wisdom internationally, we are creating *a global wisdom digital network and database*. We are creating new products based on the results of this **synergy**. In our new world, we will transcend mere *survival as we pivot toward planetary prosperity*!

We don't only invent new technologies, but also *remember and improve upon old ones*. We have a treasure in our cultural heritage—*the traditions of our ancestors.* Today, modern authors are telling stories based on this vision, on legends about humans and nature. For example, in the book *A Vital Bond*, Bayarchimeg Budee talks about her grandmother's way of caring for Mongolian nature. At my company, Dobrosphera ("Kind Media"), we are curating nature legends from Peru, Uganda, and Kazakhstan, soon to be represented in film format. And there are so many other unique cultural and ethnic examples in regions all around the world for us to draw upon.

The lifestyle of the near future will be **the art of living**, where science and art, society, and nature are harmoniously connected to each other. Depicting new effective models of culture, developed by philosophers and philologists, understood by individuals and preserved by local communities, helping people to develop new habits, *we can teach everyone to live with pleasure and make our world a better place.* If everyone understands how to live *in the paradigm of global well-being*, we will create *a world of universal well-being*.

Yay! It's a joy to live in a world of prosperity! Thanks to all this, *every person* can now become **a Citizen of the World**.

Now, we understand how it works! We know where we are on the bridge, and we have even walked along it. Everyone has their own time, their own measure of sustainability, and everyone moves at their own pace. Our new sustainable world, although it already exists, still lives "on the old rails," and not many people know how to use its benefits. **There are a lot of people on the planet who want to make the transition.** How can we make it so that as many people as possible can simultaneously "jump" in time to the near future, which is actually already available to them? The answer is to present a new world through *art*.

NEW ART AND POLYLOGUE

Art is a form of communication between the creator and the experiencer. Nowadays, people watch and listen to the arts, which contain the behavior patterns of the last few decades. A lot of the dialogue and cultural models we see on the screen are not appropriate to sustainability and planetary prosperity. We need new *art* that *up-levels our life quality*. For example, Dobrosphera and our partner Climate Entertainment are already creating youth films about sustainability. *Our new art also includes dance, painting, writing*, and more, everything that could be helpful for learning sustainability.

So, how can we use the arts to show planetary culture? We can create **new stories**. What could they look like? What locations, dialogues, and actions could they include? Who could be characters? Our world is changing, so new heroes—new groups of heroes—living in a new context will appear. They are social and friendly. Via *well-being arts* we can show a vivid polylogue of different cultural contexts, interrelations of social problems, and bright solutions. The COP Culture and Entertainment Pavilion team—Kirsten Wessel, Sam Rubin, Leia Booth, and Parneet Kaur—are raising this polylogue every day as well as Dobrosphera. Unlike a dialogue (two people), or a monologue (one person), a polylogue captures the dynamics of group discourse, often with multiple viewpoints and layers of meaning.

Unfortunately, according to research, 90% of current media content has at least one pattern of violence. But people *want to see kindness* on their screens! *We can showcase the best of humanity* –let's create characters who can successfully solve conflicts, show kindness and build friendships, who can learn and develop and help people, animals, and nature in need. Today at Dobrosphera, we create such cartoons. Our next project features cartoons based on the fairy tales of Bayarchimeg Budee, whom you read about earlier. We have also already created cartoons about green skills and human rights.

To be a human is amazing. Let's promote awareness of our human potential and body resources, consequently creating a new culture, making our best reality, and living a life of self-realization and enjoyment. We are able to depict feelings that we rarely thought about before: a refreshing sip of clean, cool water, *the silence of the night*, the smell of meadow grass during a Sunday hike, the laughter of a best friend, the touch of a loved one, the hugs of our children, strong friendship and overcoming difficulties together, effective work in a friendly team of foreigners, and access to information and leadership opportunities for people with disabilities.

New art demonstrates solutions and transforms people's worldviews and behaviors toward *goodness, peace, and prosperity.* Let's highlight technologies of the last couple of decades: eco-goods, including eco-products, tableware, and household items made from natural materials for home and office, solar panels, and many others. It is necessary to show them so that people can imagine how their own homes and communities will look and begin implementing new solutions and habits into daily life, ***transforming our cultures***.

Welcome to www.kindmedia.group,
where you can *see our culture-changing work*!

L. Hunter Lovins and Dr. Martin Frick, PhD

"Some believe that it is only great power that can hold evil in check, but that is not what I have found. I found it is the small everyday deeds of ordinary folk that keep the darkness at bay . . . small acts of kindness and love . . ."

—GANDALF, JRR TOLKIEN

21   COPx: THE PEOPLE'S CLIMATE COMMUNITY

We Can Solve the Climate Crisis and Rebuild Democracy

L. Hunter Lovins is President of Natural Capitalism Solutions, Managing Partner of NOW Solutions, and consultant to Int'l Finance Corp, Patagonia, Walmart, Clif Bar, and the Pentagon.

Dr. Martin Frick is Senior Diplomat at the UN. He was Senior Director of the UN Convention to Combat Climate Change (UNFCCC) and Director of Global Office of UN World Food Programme.

Many crises face us, but two are existential: the climate crisis and the threats to democracy around the world. For 30 years, the world's governments, working through the United Nations, have negotiated to keep global warming within "safe levels" of temperature rise. They failed. Now, oligarchic and autocratic regimes deny the climate crisis and strip basic liberties at will.

Most nations have negotiated in good faith through 60 UN Conferences of the parties (COPs). It's time for a change. It is time for people to reclaim sovereignty.

The climate crisis—which seemed so distant in 1985 when Carl Sagan warned Congress about human-driven climate change, and even in 1992 when the UN began the COP conferences—is now upon us. Nature does not negotiate.

THE BOTTOM-UP ALTERNATIVE TO THE UN'S TOP-DOWN COPS

If nations can't protect us, who can? *We* can.

What's been clear for years became even more apparent last November at the UN's annual exercise in frustration in Baku:[1] we need a global, bottom-up alternative to top-down COPs. We need to bring together and inspire millions of people around the world to protect our future and help make our efforts more effective.

It's time for COPx: Conferences of People, Independently Organized.[2]

For three years, a small team of us worldwide has worked to unleash COPx, a global citizens' movement to solve the climate crisis by enabling people everywhere to implement the solutions on their own, in their own communities, in their own ways. As they solve this one crisis, they find their power to solve any crisis. They build a real democracy.[3]

SOLVING THE CLIMATE CRISIS: TRUST YOUR GUT

We are crafting the tools to enable you and people everywhere, and anywhere, to act where you live, in your own way, to draw ideas and inspiration from our global network, and solve the climate crisis—sharing your success with the world so that others can be inspired by your work.

In April 2025, we settled on a digital platform, Open Future Coalition's Open Impact,[4] to enable us to form this global community. Developed by a community that shares our values and is not beholden to any of the tech bros, it is a powerful place for us to convene, share resources, tell our stories of success, and find a home.

We're going on guts. All of us are volunteers. But after the U.S. election, when yet another person plaintively asked us what they could do about the precarious times in which we now find ourselves, it became clear: we have to act.

Early in 2025, we sent a letter to almost a couple of hundred people around the world who have been helping create COPx, saying, "We're launching."

Our friend Juan sent us this graphic novel[5] that explains it better than I ever could.

---

1 https://www.climateandcapitalmedia.com

2 https://www.climateandcapitalmedia.com/dispatch-from-cop29-the-global-south-just-walked-out/

3 https://www.copx.global/home

4 https://impact.openfuturecoalition.org/community/card-grid?tab=4&search=COPx

5 https://assets.swoogo.com/uploads/4629345-673375c978a1c.pdf

Please share the COPx website and graphic novel with your friends and network. Invite them to visit. It's the best description we've found to tell others what we're setting out to do.

Since that launch, our numbers have more than tripled. People from 55 countries have registered to become COPx organizers. You can too.

COPx IS PERSONAL

The failure of top-down approaches to solve the climate crisis is now obvious. While much has been accomplished, the world's governments have moved far too slowly to ensure a climate-safe future. And, that's inevitable, given that governments tend to be responsive to incumbent power centers, not to future interests, no matter how much scientific and financial data demonstrate the growing risks posed by climate change. Saudi Arabia makes a billion dollars every day it delays climate action.[6]

Even the prediction by analysts in the insurance industry that the global economy could be lost to climate chaos this century[7] does not seem to faze politicians. I guess that date is long after they are safely dead.

For me and my colleagues, COPx is personal.

Four years ago, I was about to hang up my spurs. I asked myself, "If you add up everything I've ever done, is it enough?" I'd taught thousands of students

---

6 https://www.bloomberg.com/news/articles/2022-05-26/saudi-arabia-s-oil-exports-hit-the -highest-level-since-2016?sref=JohuiFqC

7 https://www.linkedin.com/pulse/climate-risk-insurance-future-capitalism-g%C3%BCnther-thallinger-smw5f/

across the world, created schools of sustainable management, international think-tanks, and written books like *A Finer Future: Creating an Economy in Service to Life*,[8] showing that we have all of the solutions we need to solve this and most other crises.

Is it enough? No. We're losing. The climate science is increasingly grim.[9] The threats to democracy grow clearer each day.

I asked, "Do I know what enough is?" Well . . . no.

Then why go down the road? Why burn carbon? I live on a beautiful ranch in Colorado. Stay home, ride my horse, watch an eagle fly. And wait for the end.

A friend who had conceived COPx out of an insider's frustration with the official process presented it to me.

Whoa. A global community working together to share action and insights on all the ways we already know can protect our planet and our future.[10] That *would* be enough. Then I thought, "It's too big. I've no earthly idea how to do it." But he wouldn't let me quit. His job won't let him be the face of COPx, so he asked if I would become his cofounder.

I still don't know how we're going to get this done. We reckoned that if we could raise enough money to bring COPx to mainstages everywhere, with celebrities and musicians celebrating the work of everyday people in communities, that would kick it off in the right way. But that costs a lot of money, and per above, we're out of time to wait for the perfect moment. You know, I know, we all know, don't we, that we need to move forward   now.

So I'll ask you now what the Ambassador asked me: "Are you with us?"

"What can I do?" you ask.

Take the first step now by joining COPx. Go to the COPx website and register.[11] You will be a first mover in creating the alternative the world so desperately needs. Put a pin on the map for your community. Join the conversation on social media: we're on LinkedIn, Instagram, Bluesky, and now on our own community—on Open Impact.

If you are part of an existing group working on climate solutions, please keep doing that. We invite you to connect your group with COPx so that we can together build the global community.[12]

---

8 https://newsociety.com/book/a-finer-future/?gad_source=1&gclid=CjwKCAjw7pO_BhAlEiwA4
pMQvKuWQaviKJEHQm3JyzFVgkYYHmHO3pbyLown8zGgEovi6-iuXUZc7RoCaxUQAvD_BwE

9 https://academic.oup.com/bioscience/article/74/12/812/7808595?login=false

10 https://www.theguardian.com/environment/2023/jan/23/no-miracles-needed-prof-mark
-jacobson-on-how-wind-sun-and-water-can-power-the-world;

11 https://www.copx.global/home/begin?i=IK09yRABAi5HITJsDUNBBCTyiM9ybjZK

12 https://www.climateandcapitalmedia.com/how-the-new-climate-vote-hub-can-turbocharge
-your-election-impact/

COPX IS A FORCE MULTIPLIER, A COMMUNITY, AN ACTION NETWORK

New ideas and technologies are being developed constantly. And yet, as all the experts tell us,[13] we already have the solutions we need to safeguard our future. We just need to implement them. Clearly it will be up to us to make them happen.

These solutions include the growing forms of renewable energy, regenerative agriculture, energy efficiency, resilience, a circular economy, and self-reliance—all the approaches that cut energy use, and replace fossil energy cheaper, better, faster, as Tom Steyer put it. [14]

It can be as simple as organizing a local carpool, or as ambitious as convincing local politicians to shut down the biggest polluter in your area. Both of these are existing COPx projects. No project is too small. Or too big. What matters is your decision to act. Think of COPx actions as Lego bricks. Whoever first conceived of the little brick had no idea of the magnificent structures people would build. COPx is your Lego brick. Go amaze us with what you can create.

As we gain critical mass, our global climate network, organized by and for the people, will create or highlight events worldwide to build grassroots, "bottom-up" climate action. Even in the face of extreme fragmentation and polarization, we must not forget just how big our common ground is.

MILLIONS OF PEOPLE WANT CLIMATE ACTION, COPx WILL CONNECT US

Globally representative studies show that huge majorities of people everywhere want aggressive climate action.[15] So why isn't it happening? Studies show that few people believe anyone else cares. And it's scary to act alone. COPx will give us all the courage. Care for a climate-safe future is the most uniting concern there is for humanity.

Digitally connected, COPx will host "conferences of people," everyone delivering action both right away and over the long term. These will make the millions of citizens committed to climate action ever more visible. It will give a megaphone to those too long ignored. At the same time, solutions will be implemented in every community, aggregating to a global commitment for action.

Convening people, ideas, and organizations around the world like this will create a force multiplier and build the necessary political will to get governments

---

13 https://web.stanford.edu/group/efmh/jacobson/Articles/I/145Country/22-145Countries.pdf

14 https://www.tomsteyer.com/cheaper-faster-better/

15 https://www.pewresearch.org/global/2021/09/14/in-response-to-climate-change-citizens-in-advanced-economies-are-willing-to-alter-how-they-live-and-work/

and corporations to implement smart climate policies—constituency by constituency.

This is how movements begin, grow, and succeed. We are creating a long-needed movement—and a gathering place—for the millions of people around the world who want to protect our collective health, well-being, and future.

Tell us: What would *you* want COPx to look like? What would you or you and a friend like to do—or to change? Email us: community@copx.global. We want to learn from you, see your pictures, videos, and hear your ideas. We'll continue to refine COPx, but please tell us how you think it can be improved.

A GLOBAL CLIMATE NETWORK ORGANIZED BY AND FOR THE PEOPLE WILL CREATE THOUSANDS OF SYNCHRONIZED EVENTS WORLDWIDE TO BUILD CLIMATE ACTION FROM THE BOTTOM UP.

COPx WILL GIVE YOU TOOLS AND AGENCY

Our global team of scientists, authors, consultants, and leaders is committed to sharing the countless sustainable practices and their positive impacts. Some $10.5 billion was poured into the recent U.S. election. We're hoping that now, people will realize that it's time we invest in efforts to protect our health and planet.

We continue to pursue funding, taking meetings with potential donors every day and working every connection we have to find the money to build COPx globally with the urgency and resources that this moment demands. Here, as well, any advice and help are most welcome.

Increasing floods, fires, tornadoes, and hurricanes leave people without homes and insurance, rising seas, millions of people displaced, political upheaval . . . The data is clear: 2024 was the hottest year in recorded history. We watched heartbroken as fires swept Los Angeles,[16] intense heat bakes South Asia,[17] and climate disasters strike ever closer to home.[18]

---

16 https://www.climateandcapitalmedia.com/as-la-fires-still-burn-how-can-we-rebuild/

17 https://www.cnn.com/2025/04/15/asia/india-pakistan-heatwave-climate-crisis-intl-hnk

18 https://www.climateandcapitalmedia.com/giant-insurer-munich-re-climate-change-is-taking -the-gloves-off/

It's time to stop doomscrolling. Want to help? We need you.

Created by people from around the world,[19] COPx will empower you to act in your own community. It will connect you with others around the world taking similar steps, offering projects you may want to try, and describing how others have achieved results. It will give you know-how, community, and inspiration. Even if you have never acted before, COPx will be there with you.

Our newsletters will come regularly. If you have news to share about what you and your community have done, please send it in. We want to showcase the great work you are doing to bring climate solutions to the world.

Ursula Le Guin said, "Hard times are coming, when we'll be wanting the voices of writers who can see alternatives to how we live now, can see through our fear-stricken society and its obsessive technologies to other ways of being, and even imagine real grounds for hope. We'll need writers who can remember freedom—poets, visionaries—realists of a larger reality."

The Club of Rome has always painted visions of the future, from *Limits to Growth* to *Earth for All*. Let's build that larger reality of a world that works for everyone.

TOGETHER WE BECOME THE MOVEMENT
TO SAVE HUMANITY

---

19 https://www.copx.global/home/vids

22   PLANNING AND PREPAREDNESS FOR COMMUNITY RESILIENCE

Henry Mitchell is Deputy Director of the Office of Emergency Preparedness and Response for the State of Colorado (CDPHE), and works with law enforcement, FEMA, and other agencies.

Planetary prosperity initiatives and the structures and strategies being developed and deployed to address our polycrisis are imperative to provide hopeful pathways forward. These initiatives will have great impact across the social, economic, and environmental sectors discussed in this book. Notwithstanding these many positive developments, however, prudence and precaution necessitate that communities worldwide should be preparing for the impacts of immediate and near-term risks, as well as considering long-term risks to the population. It is imperative to make disaster resilience a priority in all planning efforts, and integrate it into everything from civil engineering to community development and the built environment.

Not only does disaster resilience planning and preparation deliver risk-mitigation benefits that are essential to navigating the 21st century, they are also mechanisms through which we can further weave strategies and solutions into our local and regional communities and ecosystems. By developing greater connection and cohesion among people, identifying shared assets and resources, and encouraging resilience strategies like permaculture, food forest promotion, and other local/regional food security enhancement methodologies, we will bolster our disaster preparedness while also laying more robust foundations for much needed systems change. This process can be effective at the grassroots level, in coordination with broader regional, state, provincial, national, and international scales.

Enhancing community disaster resilience will save lives and resources. There are several effective approaches to make our communities more disaster resilient. What we are experiencing across the globe can be considered a polycrisis. We are seeing increased frequency and intensity of disasters. High-cost disasters have become more common over the last decade. Climate disasters are impacting areas where they haven't historically been seen. In order to mitigate future impacts from disasters we need to build resilient communities. A resilient community is a prepared community. Having a well-prepared community saves time and resources during disaster responses. We can increase community resilience by focusing on a number of preparedness initiatives and self-sustaining adaptations. Planners and communities can take action to become resilient by investing in regional food systems, responsible water resource management, personal preparedness, community preparedness, and developing self-sustaining systems.

Adam Tooze was accurate when he informed the World Economic Forum that we are currently facing a "polycrisis." According to Tooze, a polycrisis is "where disparate crises interact such that the overall impact far exceeds the sum of each part." Global conflict, rising food and living costs, frequent disasters, and weather extremes are examples of a few of the crises that converge to cause a maelstrom of physical, economic, and societal impacts across the globe. Increased disaster frequency and intensity have had significant impacts to global economies and population health. According to USAfacts.org, "of the 10 years with the most disasters, 9 were in the last decade." These disasters are getting more and more expensive. This is due to many factors, including built environment vulnerabilities, increased exposure to values at risk, heavier rains in some areas, lengthened wildfire seasons, drought, and higher frequency and intensity of weather/climate-based disasters.

In the United States, every single state has experienced at least one-billion-dollar disaster since 1980 (NCEI.Monitoring.Info@noaa.gov, n.d.). In many climate health circles, the theme is arising that "climate risk = water risk." This alludes to the reality that too much or too little water has significant impacts on a population's health as well as the type and intensity of disasters experienced. Too little water or precipitation leads to drought, increased wildfire risk, agricultural challenges, the increase of dust storms, dust-borne diseases, and other impacts. Too much water or precipitation causes flooding, increased risk of waterborne illness, infrastructure damage, agricultural challenges, and other impacts. Forward-thinking water resource management should be one of the areas communities and countries across the globe should focus on, while larger climate adaptation practices are being developed and deployed. The Swiss have developed an integrated disaster reduction approach that incorporates river basin management, spatial planning, built environment, and agricultural adaptations.

Investing in disaster preparedness is one of the most cost-effective measures we can take to mitigate the negative impacts of disasters. The U.S. Chamber of

Commerce released a study in 2023 with some intriguing findings. The study found that every $1 spent on disaster preparedness and climate resilience saves communities $13 in cleanup costs, damages, and economic impact. Investing in disaster preparedness makes good fiscal sense and good sustainable economic development sense and can actually save lives.

In industry-wide discussions on disaster mitigation and recovery, there has been a lot of focus on resiliency of our communities. As a career emergency manager and disaster planner, my perspective is that a prepared community is a resilient community, and vice versa. If even a portion of our populations were more prepared for disasters, emergency response coordination would go much more smoothly. Emergency managers would have greater success in disaster communications, evacuation planning, and implementation, and would save on the resources needed to shelter and feed communities impacted by disasters. There would be increased efficiency at Disaster Assistance Centers, which are set up after disasters occur in order to help point community members to resources for recovery and rebuilding. People would know what to keep at the ready in case they need to leave in a hurry. They would understand what documents they would need to have in order to begin applying for assistance during the recovery process. Resilience and preparedness would also help to build stronger community bonds.

In the field of Emergency Management, it is often said that disasters begin and end locally. We can apply this philosophy to the need to ensure that our local communities understand the risks and vulnerabilities they face at the local level. Promoting a general awareness of the world around us will help us understand our vulnerabilities as members of our communities, and take steps to prepare and empower ourselves during disasters. The fragility of our supply chains became apparent during the COVID-19 response, the saline shortage caused by Hurricane Helene, and other such disasters. Shedding light on this can be one of the main motivators that emergency managers, disaster planners, and other community leaders can use to motivate people to start preparing for disasters and be more self-sufficient.

People should understand what is needed to protect themselves from the worst impacts of disasters and mitigate harm to themselves and those they care about in their community. The main pillars of a resilient and prepared community are: Awareness, Materials, Connections, and Knowledge. Build awareness of the risks that surround you; know the waters you are swimming in. Understand what materials you need to thrive in the face of disasters or service interruptions. This could be needed medications, food, water, electricity sources, light sources, or other materials that an individual or family needs to make it through any kind of service disruption.

Also, foster connections to neighbors and others as a support system to help get through a disaster-caused disruption. These connections can provide information, sustenance, and even emotional support. Knowledge is possibly the most potent of these pillars. When speaking with people interested in preparedness, I encourage them to worry less about gear and more about knowledge of the skills they need to keep themselves and other community members safe and healthy, as well as the "fabric of resiliency" that uniquely arises from community connections. This could look like knowing about water purification, gardening, food preservation/fermentation, or any other skills that can be used to thrive during a disaster (and even in everyday life).

Preparedness = Resilience and Resilience = Preparedness.

Using this mindset as the starting point, and the aforementioned pillars, we can make our communities stronger in the face of disasters of increasing frequency and intensity.

As we navigate through this polycrisis, how can we make our communities more resilient? Regional food systems, personal preparedness, and community preparedness are all tangible priorities that we can focus on to become resilient. If we build up more regional food supply systems, we become less vulnerable to natural disasters, extreme weather, agricultural production disruptions, pandemics, geopolitical tensions, and other factors that impact how our communities get their food and other necessities. While not without certain vulnerabilities, regional food systems can serve as a kind of insulation against some of the disruptions that large-scale food systems are inherently vulnerable to. Personal preparedness can have an oversized impact, if adopted by more people. Imagine, if you will, 10% more of the people in our communities had a plan for where to go if they had to evacuate, or more homes were stocked with basic supplies to help them cope with a disruption in normal services.

After planning for and responding to a host of disasters, I recommend that every household have 1-2 weeks of simple dried goods like beans and rice, as well as other canned or preserved food items (dried quinoa is especially good). This is a practice that should be attainable by most households across the socioeconomic spectrum, including through assistance provided by food banks and other social safety net infrastructure. It is also recommended that households have some kind of emergency "go-bag" with at least the following items: a change of clothes, portable water purification tools, light snacks, an independent light source, batteries and a portable power bank, any necessary charging cords, a waterproof outer layer/shell, an emergency blanket, comfortable shoes, a supply of necessary medications, a physical map of your area, hard currency in various denominations, and other items you may need to remain comfortable if you have to leave your area quickly. If you have a vehicle, it is also suggested to have a similar bag in your vehicle, as well as sleeping bags and warm weather gear, depending on your location. With the rising occurrence of large-scale disasters and disruptions, more and more people are seeing the need to take simple preparedness steps like this.

Community preparedness is just as essential as personal preparedness, and delivers many layered benefits not available solely through individual or household preparedness. Knowing the risks in your community is essential to staying safe. Understanding what services are and are not available is important as well. If you live in an area that has high wildfire risk, and is also in a rural or frontier area, it is possible that fire suppression may not be available in your area. If you live in a densely populated urban area, there may be the reality of extreme traffic congestion that is impassable, forcing you to walk or find alternative routes.

Actually "knowing" your community also means knowing the other members of your community. Getting to know your neighbors is a practice that has many benefits, two of which are especially notable. The first is the ability to help your neighbors in times of need, giving rise to the ability to form mutual aid relationships with those around you. The second is fostering a sense of togetherness and unity that otherwise seems to be diminishing across our cultural landscape. In 2023 the U.S. Surgeon General issued an advisory warning that we were facing an epidemic of loneliness. Getting to know who is in your community will serve as a benefit, both in terms of preparedness and resilience, but also through holistic social connections that break down barriers and promote much needed unity.

If we as a society acknowledge the importance of enhancing community disaster resilience, the result will be lives saved and resources used in a much more responsible manner. We are in a polycrisis in which we are seeing more frequent, intense, and expensive disasters. Adaptation and resource management are key to making any kind of meaningful change to how disasters impact populations around the world. A prepared community is a resilient community, and it will save communities in the long run. Preparedness at the individual level means ensuring households remain informed about risks in the community and taking steps to have what's needed on hand to cope with any disruptions. Establishing community level preparedness means establishing regional food systems, identifying and managing shared resources, and getting to know your neighbors and other members of your community at large. By taking these steps, and promoting awareness, materials, connections, and knowledge, we can be prepared for the next disaster on the horizon.

As we promote planetary prosperity initiatives and develop structures and strategies to increase our resilience, we can mitigate many of the negative impacts of disasters. The foundation of this resilience lies in fostering social connections, promoting personal preparedness and awareness, identifying shared assets and resources, and encouraging resilience strategies like permaculture, food forest promotion, and other local/regional food security enhancement. We can take examples from across the world, such as the Swiss measures for spatial and built environment planning, to take anticipatory measures as we make adaptations to promote resilience. By taking the steps outlined in this essay, and the impactful actions laid out by the thought leaders in this book, we can simultaneously save lives and help our world thrive well into the future.

#beworldaware
beworldaware.com

23   THE SACRED VIEW OF MOTHER GAIA

John P. Milton is Founder of the Way of Nature and co-founded Friends of the Earth. He co-authored *Ecological Principles for Economic Development*, and the Clean Air and Water acts.

For a moment, let's contemplate modernity and our human condition. While we may be dazzled by our astonishing achievements, we humans have created pervasive technologies engulfing every aspect of our lives, massive cities, global transportation systems, and landed fellow humans on the moon, but something is missing. We have lost our connection with the family of all living things. We no longer see ourselves as part of a big family of life. We have fallen out of relationship with one another, ourselves, nature, reality, and the sacred.

While I was establishing public policy protections for nature, by helping the emergence of the National Environmental Policy Act, the Clean Air and Water acts, along with the EPA, I was aware of the need to go deeper. As a result of many direct solo immersion in the wilds of New Hampshire as a child and young adult, I recognized the essential importance of an experiential, energetic, and spiritual connection with all our relations. It was clear to me, this connectivity needed to happen at the cellular level of our being, with a profound shift in our awareness and consciousness. Believing humans and our global civilization are separate and superior to the ecological laws of our biosphere is a sure path to catastrophes and dystopias.

Let's look at the root causes of this separation. In our modern era, the commodification of Nature as a resource to be extracted and taken for human use is at the heart of our predicament. This pattern of behavior has been passed from generation to generation for more than 800 years. One example is the Moorish influence and legacy of the Acequias system of irrigation canals reconfiguring the natural flow of water from the land in the Sierra Nevada Mountains of Spain—in turn, the Spanish conquistadors brought this concept of irrigation to Mexico and what became the American Southwest. Initially, this method of managing water flow was practiced as an interconnected system in collaboration with the Tewa indigenous people. When the U.S. Government imposed its management systems, water became a commodity to be owned, sold, and separated from the land. The mineral "rights" below the land also became commodified. To the indigenous people, this dismembering of the ecosystem (their precious relatives) would have been considered both criminal and ignorant. Metaphorically, the same as if the colonialists terminated their aunts and uncles or even their children. Over the centuries, this pattern of subjugating the wilderness fractured and fragmented our reverence and love for our source of existence by breaking up the family of life and the elements.

As we work to restore right relations and the health of our planet, it is helpful to remember how this Anglo-European paradigm, with its attendant legal and religious institutions, further separated humans from the rhythms and cycles of nature. Technology and AI are compounding our challenge.

To address this predicament, I've essentialized many of the wisdom traditions and spiritual lineages to be accessible to anyone suffering from our modern societal conditioning. It begins with humility and courage. Questioning our assumptions and beliefs is another key component. Opening to the great mystery with a beginner's mind, with an intention to rejoin this vast family of life. All of this arises naturally when we shift our perspective from one of taking to one of giving. Giving our love, gratitude, and appreciation for the gifts of being an integral part of the family of life, where all forms coalesce in a delicate, interwoven, balanced system. This turnaround from our conventional, reductionist, consumptive ways of relating inspires and motivates us to be of service to the well-being of the whole. If we are fully established in this state of being, our personal and societal choices and behaviors are no longer driven by political or economic expediency. It simply becomes unacceptable to abuse or exploit our family members; extraction and pollution threatening the integrity of our life support systems are summarily rejected.

The Way of Nature process is an invitation for humans to be dynamic, regenerative partners within the natural systems of Gaia.

The Way of Nature is a common ground-based spiritual path that integrates principles of cultivating connection to Outer, Inner, and True (Source) Nature, fostering personal and cultural transformation in a regenerative manner. This approach emphasizes living in harmony with the natural world, recognizing the interconnectedness of all life, and adopting practices that restore and sustain ecological balance, health, and human cultural transformation. The process of natural reconnection follows a direct sequence:

Step 1—realize you are disconnected from Nature

Step 2—open your heart and mind to make an authentic connection

Step 3—experience communion with all forms, knowing you are still a separate self-noticing "outer forms"

Step 4—experience pure, non-dual Oneness with forms of Nature

Step 5—the natural systems merge with awareness as a mandala, no separate self or individualization of outer forms

Steps 6 & 7—return to Source—follow the Mandala back into Pure Source Awareness. Recognize, moment by moment, origination, manifestation, and ultimate dissolution. Realize. Rest in pure, pristine, non-dual Source Awareness Holistic Practices and Teaching

Following these seven inner development steps, one experiences what can be called direct Earth Empowerment. From this ground of being, our practice deepens, and our capacity to contribute to a culture in service to life expands. These next steps provide a glimpse of what is possible.

1. Direct Immersion in Nature: Experiential time in Nature opens a meditative connection with the environment. This connection fosters a sense of responsibility and caring for the Earth. We explore and renew our capacity for wonder!

2. Inner Cultivation: Utilizes practices such as meditation, mindfulness, opening the heart, and Qi cultivation to promote inner peace, energy, clarity, and personal growth. These practices help individuals align with natural rhythms and cycles, enhancing their ability to live in harmony with the world around them.

3. Holistic Health: True wellness requires an integration of physical, emotional, mental, and spiritual well-being. This includes dietary practices, exercise, and healing arts that are in sync with natural principles of healthy living.

4. Harmonious Living: Advocates for sustainable practices, such as permaculture, organic farming, and renewable energy. These practices reduce the human ecological footprint and contribute to the restoration and regeneration of the Earth.

5. Cultural Renewal: Supports the revival of traditional wisdom and ceremonies from various Indigenous cultures, recognizing their deep ecosystemic knowledge of living in harmony with Natural Laws. This includes our universal Eleven Direction Ceremony, which strengthens community bonds, creating a collective sense of regenerative purpose.

6. Education and Outreach: Elevating awareness of the ecological meta-crises we are facing is a key component of our Rites of Passage trainings. Young adults discover their true inner purpose for this lifetime. Workshops, retreats, and community projects empower individuals to make positive changes in their lives and communities.

7. Integration of Spiritual Traditions: Combines insights and practices from various Earth-connected spiritual traditions, such as Taoism, Buddhism, and shamanism, to create a comprehensive, common ground approach to transformation. This integration helps individuals discover what their own traditions have in common; this insight helps build a more inclusive, harmonious society of mutual respect and appreciation.

At the Sacred Land Sanctuary in Crestone, Colorado, I guide participants in cultivating a deep, embodied awareness of their place within local, global, and universal systems. All practices emphasize the importance of energy cultivation and conscious, sacred connection with the Elements and Mother Earth.

PERCEPTUAL FIELDS OF AWARENESS

A unique method for achieving this authentic nature connection arises from refining our Nine Experiential Fields of Perception: 1) Sight; 2) Sound; 3) Touch & Temperature; 4) Taste; 5) Smell; 6) Movement & Balance; 7) Perception of Life Force; 8) Display of Emotions: 9) Flow of Thoughts. The Way of Nature process of perceptual refinement is best accomplished by participating in a guided program, offering more detailed instruction. A basic recommendation is to avoid conceptualizing or naming the forms your perceptual fields of awareness encounter. Allow freshness and originality to arise without naming, as you track the internal origin of each sensation and rest with clear awareness.

THE BROADER IMPACT

This change in perception is not merely philosophical; it has practical implications for how we live and interact with the world. By experiencing the environment as a sacred, interconnected whole, we make choices honoring and thus preserving its integrity. People protect what they love. This heart-centered, awakened perspective not only shifts attitudes, it empowers behavioral change.

We consciously choose the path of sustainable living, designing conservation efforts, and regenerative policies that protect the delicate balance of ecosystems.

By embodying these aspects, the Way of Nature aims to transform individuals and communities, creating a regenerative culture that respects and nurtures the natural world while fostering personal and collective well-being. I like to describe the experience as a rewilding and re-indigenization process that opens into humanity's capacity to rejoin the "Big Family" of all living beings. More than a fancy word, re-indigenization involves deep respect for the original instructions the earliest inhabitants of all continents received, in one creation story or another, to live in alignment with natural law. Modern humans must also return to a personal experience of loving oneness with Mother Earth/Gaia.

24   LOVE, NATURE, WOMEN

How to Build a Regenerative Economy

Maria Rodale is author of *Love, Nature, Magic, Organic Manifesto,* and *Scratch.* She was CEO and Chairman of Rodale, Inc, which published *Inconvenient Truth* and *Organic Gardening.*

A dam Smith, considered the father of capitalism, lived with his mom. His whole life.

I can't stop thinking about this.

The guy who defined our current economic theory didn't have to cook his own food, make his own bed, or even pay his own way in the world. My theory is that his mom was the "invisible hand" that capitalism relies on.

"Women are largely absent from the economic system Smith lays out," according to Maureen Hawkin, Ph.D. I call it the Domestication of Women. We were herded like cows to be milked for the benefit of someone else's wallet. Except that cows count as a commodity. Women . . . don't count as a commodity or a valued asset. In fact, we've been disposable—often dying in childbirth, murdered by our husbands, or sent to insane asylums or nunneries if we become unruly.

The fatal flaw of capitalism is that it doesn't value women or nature . . . unless that piece of nature is a commodity. And it's based on fear and scarcity, not abundance and love.

Capitalism is broken. Its "sell by" date has expired. Because it's a system based on scarcity, a mindset that comes from a fear that there is never enough, because many people believe there is a limit to how much there is in the world, there is a tendency to hoard, to be a bit selfish, to penny pinch, to use money as a weapon, overreact to "deals" like things that are free or on sale. The problem with a scarcity mindset is that there will never, ever, ever be enough. This is why the Bezos's and Zuckerberg's of the world can't stop siphoning all the money they can out of the system—because they can never have enough. It's the same as being an alcoholic—where no amount of booze or drugs or attention can fill the emptiness inside that believes there is never enough. Fear is a powerful thing. You resent people who have more than you—even if you are the second richest man in the world, perhaps. But note that you don't need to be a billionaire to have a scarcity mindset. In fact, most people probably have it. The whole idea that the sole purpose of a business is to create value for its shareholders is DEAD. And if it's not dead yet it deserves to die. It has failed because it didn't cultivate and protect the very things that made success possible—people (including women and children), and the planet.

How can we create a new economic system? A regenerative economic system that values women and nature? One that is based on abundance and love?

The real purpose of a business should be to serve the highest good of people and the planet, including women and nature, and to base it on love. Ideally, the goal of business is to create profits and wealth that can be used to enrich everything and everyone, creating a wealthier and healthier world in the process. Abundance is the belief that there will always be enough. Whether you've got lots of money or a little tiny bit, there is often enough to go around, share, and give away. Generosity breeds abundance. It's kind of like karma. The more you give, the more you get. The less you worry, the more beneficial things you attract into your life. But for abundance to truly work, the giving must be genuine and heartfelt.

Numerous studies have shown that after attaining a basic comfortable living wage, money does not make you happier. I can tell you that having a lot of money makes life a lot more complicated.

Personally, I feel blessed with an abundant mindset about money. I know there are some people reading this who will be thinking, "Easy for you to say, you were born rich!" And yes, I got called a "rich bitch" throughout my public high school years. But let me explain for a minute, please. My grandfather, who was the source of our family business and "richness," was born in a Lower East Side Manhattan tenement building and slept in the same bedroom as all his many siblings. He was completely and utterly self-made. He married my grandmother, who was a coal miner's daughter and orphan, who moved to Manhattan with her cousin when she was 14 to become a waitress at Shraft's. She met my grandfather when he bought a dance with her for 10 cents. My grandparents lived the American Dream, and they gifted it to us through a business with a lofty mission, Rodale Press, and then Rodale Inc. But when a family owns a business, most of the wealth is tied up in that business. And while we were well off, we certainly weren't the richest family in town, and we didn't flaunt it with fancy things. In fact, the generosity of my family brought all sorts of benefits to our community through parks, art schools, museums, sports venues (my father built a velodrome), and nonprofits, including the

Rodale Institute, which is thriving today more than ever. I grew up with the very strong message that our lives were to be in service to others. I learned that money had to be earned through hard work. But I also learned that generosity was essential to life and love. And that is why I consider myself rich . . . because I learned the gift of generosity.

There are still way too many people in the world who live in poverty and don't have a choice or the freedom to make changes. That's the work we have ahead of us: to learn how to love each other enough to understand that when we truly help others, everyone benefits.

Even you.

In January 2020, Prince Charles, now King Charles, spoke at Davos about how "Nature is not a separate asset class . . . Nature is, in fact, the lifeblood of our financial markets and, as such, we must rapidly realign our own economy to mimic nature's economy and work in harmony with it." He launched his Sustainable Markets Initiative to help create that new model based on the new paradigm we need to build to continue living well on this planet.

Good for him for finally saying out loud what needs to be said. But I take issue with the word "sustainable." We are way past being able to just keep things the same. We need to make them better. That's where Regeneration comes in. We need to create a Regenerative economic model—where the world truly gets *better* over time, not worse, because of how we live in it. The status quo won't save our species. It's time to create a model where good is rewarded and expanded, and "bad" is diminished. Where resilience and love are built into the whole fabric of our beliefs and our bank accounts. And that means accounting for the work of women and nature, too.

The fundamental numeric idol that must be knocked off its pedestal is the idea that continual economic growth is the primary goal. Measuring GDP (Gross Domestic Product) as the indicator of economic health is incredibly destructive and terribly misguided. Let's look at nature. Nature—even in tropical climates—goes through a cycle: birth, growth, harvest, death, dormancy, and rebirth. If you look at our history through that lens, it brings a level of sense and order to our past. That same cycle applies to business as well, but we often blind ourselves to it and hope for eternal growth. Let's look at the classic transportation industry story: Horses, trains, cars, planes . . . what's next? Most assuredly, something will come next (I am hoping for teleportation, personally). We can bail out the automotive industry, but it will die at some point and be replaced by something new and better. Thank goodness! That's called evolution.

The truth is that the growth-at-all-costs approach is a dangerous form of gambling that is an unhealthy addiction. Venture capitalists walk around Silicon Valley (or now Miami or Austin) like gamblers in a casino, placing bets on whatever they think will be the Next Big Thing. They are hoping for a big "exit strategy" that buys a yacht, private jet, and a sexy young (disposable) girlfriend, all of which have become the new measure of success. Sigh.

Interestingly, the pandemic has served as a sort of rest period, an exhale, a period of death. It doesn't matter if you think it's fake or overblown, or who caused it and why. It. Doesn't. Matter. What matters is that it happened, and we responded in a certain way, and these things happen regularly throughout history. It's almost as if nature says, "If you won't stop and think about what you are doing, I will make you stop." And so, we stop. And we rethink. And hopefully, we learn.

We now have a big opportunity to stop, learn, and rethink our economic model as a whole.

What would that new economic model look like? Here's my 12-point Regenerative economic model framework:

1. A regenerative economic model starts with the premise that **love has value and adds value** to the whole economy. Why? Because love adds a level of integrity, authenticity, caring, and focus on the long-term health, vitality, and resilience that people (and the environment) want and need to be happy.

2. A regenerative economy builds **resilience** into the system with long-term success at the forefront: Will this benefit us in 10 years? 100 years? 1,000 years? Will the products last a long time (in a good way), or will they decompose and disappear (in a good way)? Understanding the life cycle of a product or a business is essential. What this means is that so-called "efficiency", which creates fragile systems, takes a back seat. We need micro-power grids. We need regenerative organic farms. We need localized food systems.

3. A regenerative economy celebrates and invests in **diversity**—of people, size, religions, cultures, and nature. DNA needs diversity to stay healthy. Nature needs diversity to stay healthy. A diverse economy is a healthy economy.

4. A regenerative economy is a circular economy designed so well that even **"waste" has value**. There should be no toxic waste. Non-toxic and non-waste methods are prioritized—for example, renewable energy over nuclear. Compost and regenerative organic over chemical farming and toxic methane pools. All economic analysis would value and take into consideration the real cost of inputs and outputs—including

nature, waste, and human societal impacts. And companies should be financially responsible for the whole life cycle of their activities.

5. A regenerative economy truly **values and protects nature** and the role of nature in keeping us alive and healthy. Nature provides abundance and shows us how to cooperate and thrive. When in doubt, study nature, and the answers become apparent.

6. A regenerative economy **invests in education and a systems approach to education**. Reductionism leads to narrow-mindedness and weakness. A whole-systems approach and understanding the connections between things lead to intelligence and transformation.

7. A regenerative economy **tackles health care at the root causes**, investing in things that truly make people healthy from the beginning: toxin-free and unprocessed food, a healthy environment, rest, exercise and play, mental and emotional health education, sex education, therapy, building strong families, *insurance that is not tied to employment*, and cultivation of spiritual meaning and purpose. LOVE.

8. A regenerative economy makes sure **everyone has their basic needs met** so that they can contribute to the economy, yet provide freedom and choice in how that is accomplished. For example, if people are hungry, they can get food, but maybe they help to either grow it, cook it, or clean it up, learning new skills in the process. If someone needs a home, they can help to build it, again, learning new skills.

9. A regenerative economy **invests in art, design, music, and *all* sorts of creativity, because that's where the inspiration and new ideas are born**. That's how we evolve. That's how we celebrate and experience joy and connect to each other in a universal way. And that's worth a lot!

10. The **willingness to serve others** is a key component of a regenerative economy. Work as a service. Because truly, service is an act of love. And real love adds value to the economy and should be rewarded as such.

11. **The contribution of all members of society must be recognized and valued**—women, men, people of all colors, Indigenous, the disabled, children, and the elderly. We are nothing without each other, and only together can we truly succeed and experience wealth.

12. Lastly, **the work that women do must be valued and respected**. Every woman (and child) deserves the freedom to make choices about the work they do, the relationships they get involved in, and to whom they decide to provide service. Let's face a hard truth: the rates of violence against women and children ALL AROUND THE WORLD show us that the status quo is not working for anyone, even men. If together we can heal the root of the issue—the economic disparity, the religious and cultural traditions that exploit women and abuse children, and the emotional immaturity that gives men the false belief that they have the right to destroy others—then we might just create a world we all want to live in—where love, nature, and women are valued, appreciated and enjoyed by all.

A Regenerative Economy is not socialism or capitalism. It's innovation and creativity. Yes, people can still get rich. Yes, there can still be a stock market. Yes, we still need banks and hospitals, and pharmaceutical companies. And yes, everyone is capable of learning, of working, and *everyone is worthy of love, including women and nature.*

You can't just press a button and change the economy. Just like people, the economy changes over time because of our behavioral evolution. Perhaps more than politics or religion, our economic behavior has the power to shape and reinvent the world. Perhaps they are all intertwined.

But each of us has a lot of power in our hands. Ask yourself with each purchase: Is my money going to good people doing good things? Does this purchase make the world better? Does this purchase make me better? Does my job make the world better? Do my investments help to create the world I want to see? Are you generous? Are you willing to help others? How can I make a difference? How can I be generous with my time, money, and attention? What do we really love, and how can we protect that?

A new economic model and regenerative economy starts with each one of us choosing LOVE over money every single day.

25 THE ALCHEMY OF MONEY FOR A COMING NEW AGE

by Kevin Townley (dearly departed) and Aaron Perry; compiled from Townley's drafts, lectures, private conversations, and referenced esoteric sources

Kevin Townley co-founded the alchemical Hermetic School: The Philosopher's of Nature, and wrote *The Cube of Space* and *Meditations on the Cube of Space*.

Aaron Perry is an entrepreneur, Co-Founder of the Y on Earth Community, author of *Y on Earth*, *Viriditas*, and the *Soil Stewardship Handbook*, and hosts the Y on Earth Community Podcast.

Many of us think about money in pedestrian, day-to-day terms. But there is a spiritual and esoteric aspect to money ("hidden in plain sight") that is essential for humanity to understand, especially at this time of transition from one age to the next. Symbolically speaking, money is much more than a simple store of value or universally fungible medium of exchange among buyers and sellers. Money is a fluid, life-giving, creative energy that flows among human beings, communities, and whole societies. Or, at least it has the potential to be. That is, understood most clearly and comprehensively, money is among the most potent expressions of *human will*—and can thus be an amplifying medium for the *will-to-good* when properly stewarded, mobilizing humans to restore ecosystems, green our cities, illuminate our inner lives, and vivify our living communities.

But history shows us that this benevolent and enlightened use of money is too often eclipsed by more selfish and sinister motives.

As was discussed in the Introduction to *Y on Earth,* our society can be grouped into three general worldviews, having three very different paradigms.

Although a "broad-brush" generalization, this framework helps us to understand and think about the three very different *Weltanschauungen*—in terms of assumptions, biases, communication styles, and even at times competing epistemological systems of "truth." These three primary worldviews are: spiritual-religious, nature-ecologic, and political-economic. In their best instances, each can respectively be characterized by the philanthropic *caritas* of love-wisdom, the *biophilic consciousness* of what Chardin described as the *Noosphere*, and the humanistic *Fraternité, Liberté, Égalité* of the Enlightenment. However, each worldview can too easily sink to lower-tier modes of intelligence wherein xenophobic desecration and disregard for Earth and each other (in the case of spiritual-religious), myopic disregard for both complex socio-economic and sublime metaphysical systems (in the case of nature-ecologic), and Machiavellian cynicism if not outright Mammonic materialism take possession à Milton Friedman, Ayn Rand, and the plutocratic, totalitarian, and fascistic *Fuhrenprinzips* (in the case of the socio-economic). There is obviously a very wide range across these worldview orientations.

Of course, these three sets have very fluid "boundaries," and many of us identify with more than one of them, some with all three. For symbolic symmetry with spiritual and esoteric knowledge systems, we can also think of these three sets in terms of mind, body, and spirit, which of course invites us to recognize that each is valid and none is in fact truly separate from the others. From a holistic perspective the intersection of all three is the fullest and most apropos worldview—one that several of our friends and colleagues share.

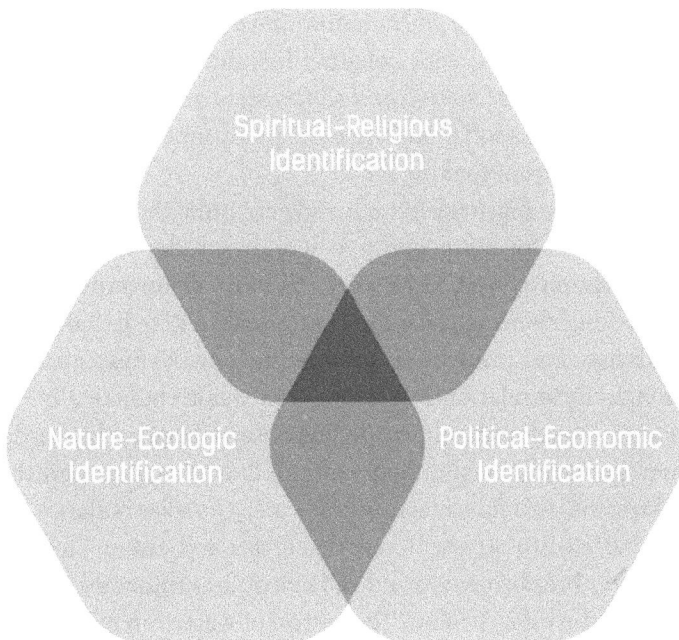

And it is at this central, holistic intersection of all three aspects that we find a profound invitation for us to transform our understanding of and orientation toward money. That is, like the alchemists of yore, our task is to reorient ourselves and our paradigmatic "perceptual lensing" toward the profound capacity for supererogatory philanthropy, hyper-intelligent economic efficacy, and super-inclusive biophilia that money *intrinsically* possesses. It simply awaits our transformation, as we transmute our paradigm and sublimate ethospheric lead into gold, as it were.

On this topic, luminaries such as Rudolf Steiner and the great Himalayan master Djwhal Khul, known simply as "The Tibetan," provide special guidance. As summarized in Otto Scharmer's essay, "Ten Economic Insights," Steiner advocates for a global (instead of nation-state-based) economic orientation (which is of course woven out of hyper-local and regional communities of place-based connection), a shift from ego-centric to eco-centric mindsets, and an understanding that money is "spirit in action." In a similar vein The Tibetan proclaims: "As money in the past ministered to personal and family need, so in the future it must minister to group and world need"; and "The key to humanity's trouble has been to take and not give, to accept and not share, to grasp and not to distribute. This has involved the breaking of a law that has placed humanity in a position of positive guilt. War is the dire penalty that mankind has had to pay for this great *sin of separateness*. Impressions from the [spiritual] Hierarchy have been received, distorted, misapplied, and misinterpreted, and the task of the *new group of world servers* is to offset this evil." The Tibetan further teaches, "The spiritualizing of money . . . is part of a much-needed world service and can now make a satisfactory beginning; but it must be carried forward with spiritual insight, right technique and true understanding—*Purity of motive and selflessness are [requisite]*."

This may come off as lofty, but there are many among us deeply rooted in the science and details of making it so.

Grounded in contemporary fintech and economic theory, John Fullerton's eight-fold principles for a regenerative economy reflect and articulate this emerging orientation as well, as he works to move us toward a framework of: "Robust circulation, honoring place and community, with edge effect abundance, dynamic balance, and innovative adaptive responsiveness, that empowers participation, in right relationship, as we view wealth holistically."

Whether it is used for philanthropy, business, or regular day-to-day life, we find an interesting relationship between the flow of money and the natural life-giving "streams" that flow in our world: water, the solar radiance of sunshine, and the invisible "electro-etheric" forces that create and sustain life as we know it.

Flowing water breaks down stone and distributes mineral-rich alluvial soil and moisture to the valleys below. The arrival of water can make an otherwise arid landscape rich with vegetation and abundant life. It can turn a desert into farmland. Where water flows, so does the verdant abundance that springs forth from this precious life-giving substance.

Likewise, we find a similar relationship between the life-giving radiance of the sun and the tremendous growth that occurs when it is received in proper measure by our photosynthesizing relatives. Both water and sunlight in proper balance create abundance, life, and prosperity, freely radiating the sustaining energy of nature herself. Ours is a super-abundant and life-giving world—any other view or attitude is in error: limited and incorrect on the whole.

We can likewise see a similar pattern with the financial resources of humanity's economic systems. Although superabundance is the fundamental reality of our actual situation, it's a reality that humanity has systematically obfuscated for centuries—to such a dismaying degree that many of us have a hard time connecting with and comprehending the very reality of *superabundance.*

When otherwise abundant resources are hoarded and denied to others, we find deserts of despondency, disenfranchisement, poverty, ignorance, anger, violence, and despair.

As we investigate the deeper, more esoteric and spiritual aspects of money, it is worthwhile to examine our values and what constitutes our perception of value. We might ask the question: How is wealth actually measured?

In more ancient times wealth was calculated by how much livestock, land, grain, olive oil, and precious gemstones and metals such as gold, silver, and copper one had. The earliest mediums of exchange came from the mineral kingdom, gold being perhaps the most celebrated substance of value—especially given its unchanging splendor, extraordinary properties, and symbolic association with the sun's golden radiance. If we look at the history of money, we see that the mineral kingdom has produced the greatest tangible wealth through the ages. The difficulty that has plagued humanity from the earliest of days has been the greed that precipitates an uneven distribution of resources. "Right understanding" reveals that Mammonic desire for control and ownership of the various commodities brought forth from the Earth has been the cause of every major conflict and atrocity humanity has brought upon itself, whether directly or indirectly.

While these physical gemstones and precious metals still have great value today, modern wealth is predominantly measured by something less tangible—a form of money that has been decoupled from the Earth's precious substances and that is instead a floating amalgam of human agreements, expectations, faith, asset valuations, and promised guarantees among and between different parties in the economic system. This is a more mysterious form of money, simultaneously both the store *and* the measure of relative holdings—more an etheric substance of group mind than a physical substance of our material world.

Money is a peculiar reflection of our individual and collective consciousness—it can be an instrument of sublime strivings toward the will-to-good foundational to planetary prosperity, or it can be an instrument of avarice and sinister cynicism symptomatic of fearful separation.

Money is—perhaps more than anything else—a singular nexus, an inescapable litmus test revealing the state and quality of our spiritual strivings and degree of consciousness . . . or lack thereof.

Money is energy. Like the energy of the sun, or the energy of water, when money is properly distributed in a balanced manner, money engenders vitality and supports one of the greatest possible human achievements: the establishment of **Right Human Relations**, and the **Familyhood of Humanity**.

All the resources of the Earth exhibit a form of energy. The types of energy can be divided into three major categories: latent (or stored), assimilative (or accumulating), and radiant (or emanating). On Earth, virtually all types of energy are directly from or influenced by the sun—the life-giving solar radiance that animates our world. Latent energy exists in wood, coal, oil, and other natural fuels that have accumulated recent or ancient sunshine in them. The release of the latent energy from the sun is through combustion. The use of this latent energy has been the major source of the development of industry and supplied a preponderance of the comforts we have come to enjoy. There are of course consequences arising from the continued use of fossil combustion, which has already caused so much devastation to our environment and threatens even more in the future as a result of the energy loading of our atmosphere by heat-trapping molecules heretofore sequestered in subterranean deposits, and the release of tons upon tons of carcinogens and other toxins into our atmosphere, water, soil, and food.

Of course, the sun provides ever-flowing energy that does not require combustion. This is the solar radiance that nourishes verdant vegetation (and thus the entire biosphere), and that we have learned to harvest through photovoltaic and wind-generation technologies. (Unbeknownst to many, the winds of the world are another direct influence of the sun's continuously streaming radiance.)

From a more deeply esoteric point of view, the sun and Earth are further animated by a cosmic radiance referred to as Prana in the Vedic tradition, a primordial life-giving power that moves from vast centers of life in the universe to our small planet and vitalizes the entire planetary body of Gaia. This form of animating energy is often associated with the electro-etheric energy that luminaries such as Rudolf Steiner, Nikola Tesla, and Viktor Schauberger (not to mention Vedic, Taoist, and Chi masters) understood. It is believed by many that these subtler energies will one day soon also be more broadly harnessed by humanity. But for this discussion we must return our line of inquiry back to the nature of money as it relates to our psycho-spiritual relationship with ourselves and each other.

The sun does not discriminate—it shines upon all things and all people on the Earth. "It shines on the good and the wicked alike," and we are all beneficiaries of this fundamental abundance. Our relatives in the vegetal kingdom assimilate, store, and radiate the sun's energy outward into the ecosystem, both through leafy and woody biomass consumed by herbivorous animals and through the secretion of sugary exudates into the rhizosphere of the soil, feeding the wondrously "secret" subterranean cosmology of the *Adamah*—the fungi, bacteria, and panoply of tiny animals that dwell there, as Peter Tompkins, Christopher Bird, Rudolf Steiner, Elaine Ingham, and Hildegard von Bingen have written; von Bingen likening the soil to the source of Viriditas, the moist, dark, fecund life-force found most concentrated in the forests and meadows.

It is from this Solar and Gaeaic superabundance that all of humanity receives its sustenance.

In tying this together, we can understand that our psychology of money evolves from an *assimilating* orientation to a latent one, and eventually achieves the higher-degree orientation of a radiating, vivifying "fire" of superabundance. When our consciousness becomes highly developed, we embody and radiate a form of cosmic superabundance germane to the animating source of the Sun's and Earth's immense life-giving beneficence. When our consciousness, however, is unripe, radiation is retarded, congestion ensures, and negative effects arise in myriad forms: physical, emotional, mental, spiritual, cultural, economic, and ecological.

Those among us whose consciousness has become ripened with love and compassion find it easy to allow the abundance they have received to radiate outward, overflowing like a harvest-time cornucopia. Jovial, gregarious generosity is a hallmark of this advanced consciousness.

It is hoped that by the example of evolving and ripening hearts and minds, many others will be inspired to answer the invitation to enter upon this great and laudable pathway of jovial radiance and sincere service to the greater good.

26 THE LIBERATION OF A MOTHER EXPRESSING PEACE TO HER CHILDREN AND ALL CREATION HAS THE ABILITY TO TRANSFORM THE WORLD AROUND US; THAT IS THE LAW OF THE LAND

Kawenniiosta Jock, Creative Director of Skywomans Forever Farm. A dedicated land steward, she integrates Indigenous Traditional Ecological Knowledge with modern remediation practices to restore soil, water, and food systems affected by industrial pollution.

As we close up our first year at Skywoman's Forever Farm, we reflect back on all the connections we made. It is important to remember that this all began with the collective mind planting a seed of return.

As we re-established ourselves on our ancestral lands, we became rooted in the ancestral

wisdom and inner knowing of our grandmothers. As I woke every morning, I acknowledged my presence surrounded by creation, acknowledging the gratitude of being gifted another day to be present, to listen and to learn the instructions of Onkwehonwene:ha.

We hiked the Great Corn Mountain that watches over us. We acknowledged the sun at sunrise and absorbed his light to carry us through the first season of being on the land. To reconnect with our star families, we hiked that mountain through the midnight skies just to acknowledge them all and fall asleep under their presence. Waking up from visions of the land, we sang songs to our seeds and acknowledged our grandmothers who worked those lands before us. We spent our days walking in the footsteps of our ancestors. Through thousands of sunflower stalks, we witnessed our ancestors dancing to our voices singing. We acknowledged all of the plant medicines growing beside us and learned of ancient wild foods that were once abundant to our people. We ate those gifts from our ancestors, and we expressed our gratitude for the reciprocity of nourishment. We acknowledged the cycle of ever-bearing fruit that our children's songs and voices nurtured throughout their days exploring the land.

As midsummer set in, we spent our days acknowledging the thunder beings for all the medicine and guidance they brought to us. As mothers nurturing our inner child, we danced and laughed with our children in every downpour. We gave our gratitude and sang for our grandfathers and our men during these thunderstorms. We acknowledged the animal life that we continue to learn to coexist with once again. We acknowledged the eighty squash plants that sprouted on their own in the greenhouses that we transplanted. They were grown to share with our allies, visitors, and supporters at our second annual Waterfall Unity Festival. We shared these gifts with our community of Akwesasne after suffering the loss of a great teacher. We acknowledged the bird life that surrounded us and listened with intention to their songs and messages. We acknowledged our Grandmother Moon and all of our grandmothers before us. We acknowledged the winds for carrying our voices throughout the valley for all creation to hear. We acknowledged the waterways and soaked in the memories of our ancestors.

Our people came to host a social gathering of song and dance for all to share. As our nervous systems started to re-remember their pathways, our gratitude and acknowledgment began to manifest into physical teachings of Onkwehonwene:ha. This is where our Original Instruction begins. As long as we maintain a state of gratitude, we discover all the tools we've been carrying in our baskets all along. I would like to acknowledge each and every one of you who has helped plant the seeds of return. Your continued support and allyship have given strength to all Onkwehonwe people of Iohskóhare Valley.

The liberation of a mother expressing peace to her children and all creation has the ability to transform the world around us. That is the law of the land.

The Rotinonshonni people of Skywoman's Forever Farm would like to extend our heartfelt gratitude to the collective minds of Onkwehonwe families and allies who came to learn and be a part of the rematriation of our ancestral lands of Iohskóhare Valley.

I would like to acknowledge our Onkwehonwe men who came throughout our first year to match our efforts toward restoring the vibration throughout our lands. To watch the tears flow from their eyes as they spoke to the land and the children is a gift to always remember.

To all the great-grandchildren that came to play, explore, sing, help build, maintain the grounds, restore the farmhouse, or to just be . . . Niawenko:wa for all that you shared. To watch my people in their natural habitat has been the biggest gift from creation so far.

To our Waterfall Family, niawenko:wa for believing in the dream of our ancestors. For your continued help, guidance, time, and energy in supporting us in our return. This has all been made possible with the collective minds of allyship. As we learn to build deeper relations within creation, I believe we will learn to deepen the connections of our allies and supporters.

To my children, this year has brought great change for our family. The resilience of our family unit has brought us home to our ancestral lands—a new beginning at restoring the relationship to the land of our ancestors. I've been your biggest supporter for over 10 years, making sure you get to learn the ways of our people. To my older ones, you were given the foundation of Onkwehonwene:ha in a classroom setting. Now it is time to learn the other half of putting those teachings into everyday practice—learning to deepen your connection to the natural world and yourselves.

Kwah e:sótsi konnónronhkwa kheie'okon:'a.

Ever grateful to be on this journey with my children while guiding them to their inner beings.

Skènnen,
Kawennniiosta
Kanien'kehá:ka, People of the Flint
Iakohthahiónni, Wolf Clan
Skywoman's Forever Farm
Iohskóhare, Schoharie Valley

PART III   Case Study Vignettes

"The future is already here—it's just not very evenly distributed."

—WILLIAM GIBSON

This collection of 33 "Y on Earth Approved" Case Study Vignettes (CSVs) has been compiled for easy reference and to provide exploratory "trailheads" to some of the world's most innovative and exemplary companies and organizations that are leading the way with high performance in social, environmental, and economic terms. Some such as the Mondragon Cooperatives and the Patagonia corporation are mature and operating at scale. Others are earlier-stage in their business life-cycles. All are part of the growing global movement toward planetary prosperity. And, although we've selected 33 of the most exceptional to share with you via individual executive summary vignettes (summarized in the table below), we have also compiled a list of several dozen additional companies and organizations worth learning about, which you'll find following the Zingerman's CSV.

Y ON EARTH APPROVED!	1% for the Planet	Benefit Corp/B Certified	Non Profit / NGO	Cooperative	Social Enterprise	Network / Mycelial Connector	Environmental / Ecological Stewardship	Regenerative / Organic Practices	Clean Tech / Energy	Financial Services / Impact Investing / Philanthropy
1% for the Planet	✓		✓		✓	✓				✓
Allianz Global Insurance										✓
Amalgamated Bank		✓								✓
At One Ventures							✓		✓	✓
B Lab			✓		✓	✓				
Big Path Capital	✓	✓								✓
Bluestone Life	✓	✓								✓
Capital Institute			✓							✓
Climate First Bank	✓	✓					✓			✓
COPx			✓		✓	✓				
Dr Bronner's		✓ (was)			✓		✓	✓		
EarthX & E-Capital Summit			✓			✓			✓	✓
Empowerment Institute			✓			✓				
Equal Exchange Cooperatives				✓			✓	✓		
Global Alliance for Banking on Values			✓			✓				✓
GLS Bank										✓
Goodstead										✓
Home Planet Fund			✓				✓	✓		✓
Impact Finance Center			✓			✓				✓
International Cooperative Alliance			✓	✓		✓				
Mondragon Cooperatives				✓					✓	✓
Newman's Own Organics					✓		✓	✓		✓
One Small Planet							✓	✓		✓
Organic Valley Coop				✓			✓	✓		
Patagonia and Hold Fast Collective	✓	✓				✓	✓	✓		✓
Recreational Equipment, Inc.				✓						
RSF	Regenerative Social Finance	✓				✓		✓	✓		✓
Savory Institute			✓			✓	✓	✓		
Slow Money Institute			✓			✓	✓	✓		✓
TED						✓				
Transition Networks International			✓			✓				
Unify			✓			✓				
Zingerman's				✓	✓					

1% FOR THE PLANET

"Commit, then figure it out"

Founded in 2002 by Yvon Chouinard and Craig Matthews

CEO: Kate Williams

Team: 40 employees, 12 directors

Annual Gross Revenue: $7,500,000

Certified Giving: $500,000,000+

Assets Under Management: Total net assets: $4,094,272

# of For-Profit Business Member Companies: Over 5,200

# of Nonprofit Environmental Partner Organizations: Over 6,700

Ownership Structure: Member-nonprofit partnership

Mission: "We accelerate smart environmental giving" / Vision: "All together for our planet. Since our beginning, we've certified more than $435 million in support to approved environmental partners. Our plan for the future? More. Much more."

Products / Services / Offerings: Business membership

"1% for the Planet was founded on the model of our business membership program: responsible businesses giving back to Environmental Partners to create a healthier planet."

Here's how it works:

> **Join:** Business members join our network, committing to donate the equivalent of 1% of gross sales through a combination of monetary, in-kind and approved promotional support directly to Environmental Partners.

Advise: 1% for the Planet provides partnership advising, pairing members with Environmental Partners that align with their values, their brand and that make the biggest impact possible.

Donate: Business members support their Environmental Partner(s) directly—no intermediary necessary! In fact, we will help you forge meaningful relationships with your partners.

Certify: 1% for the Planet certifies all member donations—legitimizing members' commitment by reviewing and confirming sales and donation details annually.

onepercentfortheplanet.org

ALLIANZ GLOBAL INSURANCE

"Managing risk to strengthen resilience"

Year Founded / Established: 1890

# of Employees: Over 157,000

Annual Gross Revenue: Over €152.7 billion (2023)

Ownership Structure: Publicly traded company

Mission / Vision: "We secure your future."

Products / Services / Offerings: Allianz offers a wide range of insurance and asset management products and services to customers worldwide.

Other Notable Details / Attributes: Allianz operates in nearly 70 countries, serving approximately 128 million customers.

A notable leader in stewardship and sustainability, Allianz joined the United Nations Environment Programme Finance Initiative (UNEP FI) in 1992; signed the United Nations Global Compact in 2002; implemented its climate change strategy in 2005; issued its first Group Sustainability Report in 2009; signed the UN-supported Principles for Responsible Investment (PRI) in 2011; established its first Group ESG Office and board in 2012; signed the UN Principles for Sustainable Insurance (UN PSI) in 2014; published its Statement on coal-based business models in 2015; chaired the then newly established UN-Convened Net-Zero Asset Owner Alliance in 2019; established Global Sustainability as its own Group Center and appointed its first Chief Sustainability Officer in 2021; published its Statement on oil and gas business models in 2022; published its Net-Zero Transition Plan with 2030 intermediate targets, released a Statement on renewable/low-carbon energy, achieved 100% renewable power for its offices, and appointed its first Chief Human Rights Officer in 2023; and published its first Corporate Sustainability Reporting Directive (CSRD)—compliant Sustainability Statement in its 2024 Annual Report.

allianz.com

AMALGAMATED BANK

"Helping those who do good, do better"

Year Founded: 1923

CEO: Priscilla Sims Brown

# of Employees: Approximately 430

Assets Under Management: $8 billion, plus $50 billion in custody

Ownership Structure: Publicly traded company

Mission / Vision: "Founded on the tenets of affordability and accessibility in banking, Amalgamated aims to serve the greater good to this day.

"At Amalgamated Bank, your deposits yield more than interest—they yield change. Banking with us means financing a cleaner, better world."

Offerings: Amalgamated Bank provides a full suite of commercial and retail banking, investment management, and trust and custody services.

Other Notable Details

Amalgamated is known as "America's socially responsible bank," supporting thousands of people, organizations, causes, and businesses committed to improving the world.

For nearly a century, Amalgamated Bank has served as America's socially responsible bank, supporting forward-thinking organizations, companies, and individuals across the country. They are an advocate for those working to make the world more just, compassionate and sustainable. Their extensive experience, financial knowledge and community of like-minded customers offer a unique set of financial tools to customers. Amalgamated is the country's largest B Corp® bank and a proud member of the Global Alliance for Banking on Values. They don't just have a mission. They are on a mission: to support those who support others, to invest in progressive and impactful causes and to advocate true financial opportunity for all.

amalgamatedbank.com

AT ONE VENTURES

"Helping humanity become a net-positive for nature"

Year Founded: 2020

Founder/CEO: Tom Chi

# of Employees: 11-50 employees

Assets Under Management (AUM): Over $634 million across two funds

Ownership Structure: Private venture capital partnership

Mission / Vision: At One Ventures aims to catalyze a world where humanity is a net positive to nature by investing in early-stage deep tech companies that disrupt established industries while significantly reducing their environmental footprint.

Offerings: The firm provides venture capital funding to startups with disruptive technologies, focusing on sectors such as energy, agriculture, and biodiversity.

Other Notable Details / Attributes

At One Ventures was founded by Tom Chi, a former co-founder of Google X, along with partners Laurie Menoud and Helen Lin. The firm distinguishes itself with a strong commitment to diversity, with 40% of its portfolio companies led by underrepresented founders. Its investment portfolio is globally distributed, with 70% of companies based in North America, 15% in Europe, and the remaining 15% spread across Africa, South America, and Israel. Notably, the firm has backed pioneering ventures such as Dalan Animal Health, which developed the world's first USDA-approved vaccine for honeybees, as well as innovative initiatives in coral reef restoration and drone-powered reforestation—both designed to accelerate large-scale ecosystem regeneration and climate resilience.

atoneventures.com

B LAB

"Using business as a force for good"

Certified

(B)

Corporation

Year Founded: 2006

CEO: Jorge Fontanez

# of Employees: 209

# of Member Companies: 10,174 companies (representing 1,025,130 employees) in 103 countries

Annual Gross Revenue: Program service revenue: $4,768,655; philanthropy: $4,742,940; other income: $1,957,250

Ownership Structure: Nonprofit membership company

Mission / Vision: "B Lab is the nonprofit network transforming the global economy to benefit all people, communities, and the planet. We won't stop until all business is a force for good."

Offerings

"B Corp Certification is a designation that a business is meeting high standards of verified performance, accountability, and transparency on factors from employee benefits and charitable giving to supply chain practices and input materials. In order to achieve certification, a company must:

Demonstrate high social and environmental performance by achieving a B Impact Assessment score of 80 or above and passing our risk review. Multinational corporations must also meet baseline requirement standards.

Make a legal commitment by changing their corporate governance structure to be accountable to all stakeholders, not just shareholders, and achieve benefit corporation status if available in their jurisdiction.

Exhibit transparency by allowing information about their performance measured against B Lab's standards to be publicly available on their B Corp profile on B Lab's website."

bcorporation.net

BIG PATH CAPITAL

"Integrity, experience, and passion"

BIG PATH
C A P I T A L

Year Founded: 2007

CEO: Michael Welchel

# of Employees: 10

Annual Gross Revenue: < $ 5 million

Ownership Structure: Private company

Mission / Vision: "At Big Path Capital, we are innovative leaders expanding the path for business interests seeking multiple bottom-line interests, taking the new economy from the margins to the mainstream."

Offerings: Big Path Capital assists business owners in the full or partial sale of a business, acquisitions, mergers, capital raises, and strategic options.

Other Notable Details

The firm, a b-certified investment services company, connects impact and sustainable private equity, venture capital, and private debt fund managers with mission-aligned institutional investors globally.

bigpathcapital.com

BLUESTONE LIFE

bluestone®

"Insurance for family, community, and planet"

Year Founded: 2015

CEO: Nathan Irons

Ownership Structure: Vermont Benefit Corporation, Member 1% for the Planet, and a Certified B Corporation.

Mission / Vision: "To transform your insurance purchase into a powerful choice to shape a healthy society."

Offerings: Life Insurance, Disability Income Insurance, and Annuities

How Our Mission Comes to Life: Premiums with Purpose®

Here's how it works

Product Design: Bluestone brings you products from insurance carriers that support our mission to fully protect your family by also strengthening your community and safeguarding our planet. This includes products from the only Certified B Corp life insurance carrier and a nonprofit insurance company.

Where Your Premium Dollars go: We are a relentless advocate for your premium payments. Our insurance carrier partners invest in projects and companies that are building resilient communities.

Capital to High-Impact Nonprofits: Nonprofits play a critical role in our society by addressing challenges that government and for-profit businesses will not or cannot.

1. As a 1% for the Planet business member, a minimum 1% of our annual revenue is invested (given) in these nonprofits each year.

2. Every Bluestone life insurance policy has an additional death benefit bequest payable to the nonprofit of your choice, at no extra cost to you. These funds build healthy communities and protect our planet when you are no longer here to contribute resources.

3. Collaboration with all our stakeholders to provide philanthropic capital and our insurance carrier partners to make direct investments that strengthen communities.

Bluestone Life is re-imagining life insurance as a lever for systems change. Rather than treating policies as transactional safety nets, we take an integrated approach to amplify the power of the product and your premiums to protect your family, community, and our planet.

bluestonelife.com

CAPITAL INSTITUTE

CAPITAL INSTITUTE

"Redefining wealth, reimagining finance"

Year Founded: 2010

CEO: John Fullerton

Annual Gross Revenue: Undisclosed

Ownership Structure: Nonprofit

Mission / Vision: "We redefine wealth and reimagine finance in service to the emergence of an ecologically and socially regenerative economy."

Offerings: Capital Institute offers a variety of resources, programs, and experiences from thought leadership, webinars, talks, books, workshops, courses and more, all of which are dedicated to bringing a regenerative economy to life across a variety of sectors.

Other Notable Details

For over a decade, the Capital Institute has pioneered a new space for holistic economic thought that draws on the latest science of living systems and ancient wisdom traditions coupled with 20 years at the pillar of global finance on Wall Street. We believe that our finance-driven economic system is in urgent need of a regenerative redesign, one that is grounded in the universal laws—not theories—of living systems. The regenerative economy we foresee is a powerful one, unleashing unseen possibilities for self-sustaining prosperity for all. This potential derives from an intrinsic wisdom that resides in us all that can—and must—be tapped to create regenerative enterprises that support our socio-economic system as a whole.

capitalinstitute.org

EIGHT-FOLD REGENERATIVE ECONOMICS MANDALA

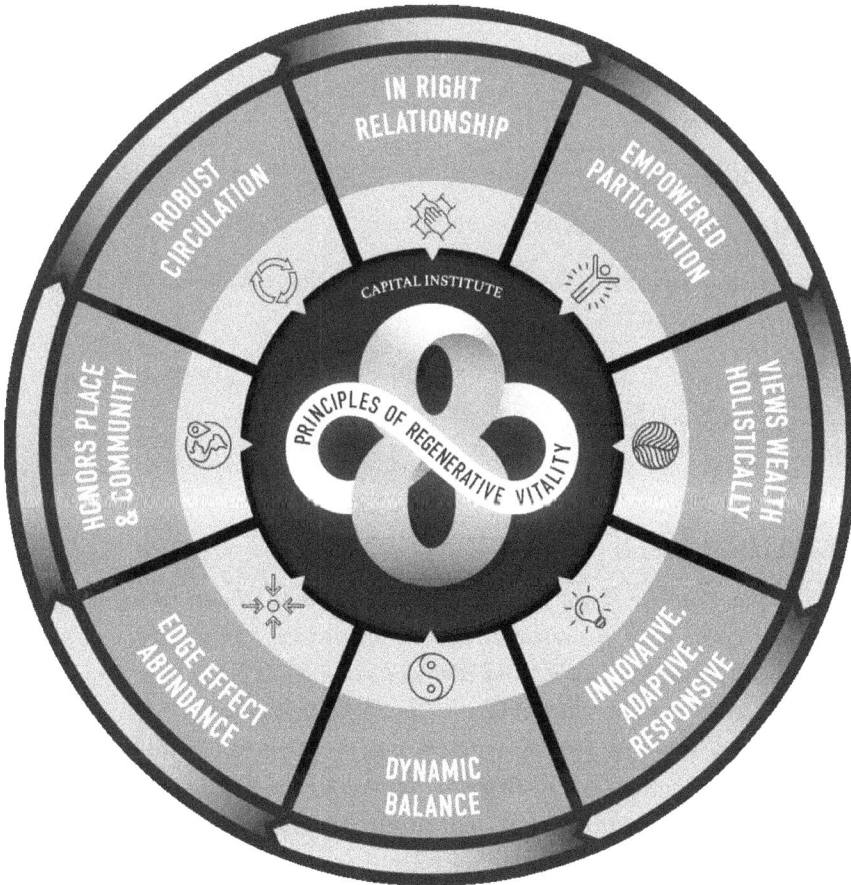

Diagram courtesy of Capital Institute.

CLIMATE FIRST BANK

CLIMATE FIRST BANK®
Powered by **OneEthos**

"Bank like tomorrow depends on it"

Founded: 2021

Founder: Ken LaRoe, Chairman

CEO: Lex Ford

Team: 105

Total Assets: $1.03 billion

Ownership Structure: Florida Benefit Corporation, Member 1% for the Planet, Certified B Corporation

Mission: "Our mission is to do the right thing for our planet, our people, our community, and our shareholders."

In Ken LaRoe's Words

"As I reflect on the Bank's achievements and look ahead to what's next, I am overcome with immense pride and optimism. I founded the bank with the belief that sustainable and ethical banking is a critical, yet overlooked, component in solving the climate crisis. By fusing the power of banking with technology, we've crafted an efficient and resilient vehicle for real positive impact and change that has already proved successful. Our rapid national growth has only confirmed my hope and vision for what I believe this Bank has the potential to become. So, while I love sharing that the Bank has been thriving, I am really most thrilled to say: We are just getting started."

Recognized as the fastest growing new bank in the United States since 2009, Climate First Bank is the world's first FDIC-insured, values-based, digital community bank founded to combat the climate crisis.

At Climate First Bank, we offer a complete, full-service portfolio of simple and convenient traditional banking products powered by technology to meet the needs of today's consumers. We bank customers in all 50 states through our digital banking services, nationwide network of ATMs, and industry-leading customer service. We also place a special emphasis on non-governmental organizations (NGOs) and businesses committed to sustainability and social equity. Furthermore, eco-conscious customers will find dedicated loan options for solar photovoltaic (PV), energy retrofits and infrastructure to help fight the climate crisis. Since most banks in the United States invest in fossil fuels and a slew of other harmful industries, who we are as a Bank is just as much about who we are not. At Climate First Bank, we leverage our customers' deposits to create positive change—supporting financing initiatives such as affordable housing, education, and a whole lot of rooftop solar! Through our solar loan financing program, powered by our mission-driven fintech subsidiary, OneEthos, the Bank has originated over $176 million in solar lending as of March 31, 2025.

But our mission to do good extends beyond our banking products, permeating every aspect of our operations, partnerships, and commitments. In addition to our B-Corp certification and 1% for the Planet membership, we are part of the Global Alliance for Banking on Values (GABV), a global network of values-driven banks pioneering the creation of a better banking system. We have also achieved operational carbon neutrality and uphold our pledge to the Net-Zero Banking Alliance (NZBA). Finally, we greatly prioritize the health and well-being of our team and are proud to remain celebrated as a valued employer by our community. The Bank's remarkable growth and success reinforce our belief that "business as usual" is long outdated. Instead, we are proving that integrity, resiliency, efficiency, and a mission to do good for people and the planet are the true pillars of a thriving company.

climatefirstbank.com

COPx

COPx

"Climate action by heroes like you"

Founded: 2009, but remained in stealth until 2025.

Co-Founders & Co-CEOs: Dr. Martin Frick and Hunter Lovins

Core Team: 15 volunteers from around the world

Annual revenue: undisclosed

Registered COPx Organizers: ~1,000, and growing by about a dozen a week

Mission: Enable people everywhere to solve the climate crisis by implementing the known solutions in their own communities in their own ways.

How it works

For 30 years the nations of the world meet annually through the UN Framework Convention on Climate Change (UNFCCC) and its annual Conference of Parties (COP) climate summits, believing that this will solve the crisis. Unfortunately, it has not. Over the 30 years that the UNFCCC has held these exercises in frustration, emissions have doubled. Ecosystems everywhere face collapse. Unchecked, climate change threatens civilization.

Belief that the nations of the world will act has lulled most people into inaction.

We propose a new theory of change: meaningful action to solve the climate crisis will only come from a global movement that supports distributed leadership in communities across the globe. Enter COPx: Conferences of People, Independently Organized. We enable people around the world to craft appropriate action at every local level. These communities of practice, based in expertise and experience, are linked through a curated online platform that enables people everywhere to join the conversation, share what they are doing, what others in their community are doing, and what people on the other side of the earth are doing. Together, separately, they can take action, and learn how to do whatever it is that they now feel inadequate to tackle. With the support of millions of others doing and sharing the same and different things, each in our own communities, we will make visible the global majority who want solutions to the climate crisis. Doing this will empower real democracy, as people realize they can solve problems together. It will make visible the political will to demand policies that support the sort of world in which we all want to live.

natcapsolutions.org/about-copx

DR BRONNER'S

"Heal the Earth and unite the whole human race"

DR. BRONNER'S
ALL-ONE!

Founded: 1948 by Emanuel Bronner

President: Michael Bronner

CEO: David Bronner

Annual Gross Revenue: $170,000,000

Ownership Structure: Family business with executive pay differential cap of 1:5

Team: 297 employees and global network of farming and manufacturing communities

Products: Regenerative Organic Soap and Chocolate

"At Dr. Bronner's, we share at least one-third of our before-tax profits annually to charitable organizations and projects across eleven issue areas, including seven core causes: Regenerative Organic Agriculture, Animal Advocacy, Drug Policy Reform, Community Betterment, Criminal Justice Reform, Fair Pay and Fair Trade. In 2021, we gave away over 40% of profits, totaling over $8.6 million in contributions!

"All employees receive 10% of their salary paid annually into a retirement/ profit-sharing plan, up to 10% of their salary as a bonus, and a no-deductible PPO health insurance plan for their families—meaning we pay the 100% complete health premium and all deductibles so there's no out-of-pocket cost for employees. We view health holistically, which is why we provide for our employees daily organic vegan meals, dental, vision & Lasik eye surgery coverage.

"We also cover half the cost of approved childcare venues up to a total of $7,500 for each family, toastmasters training, electric vehicle charging stations, and a $1,000 rebate for purchase of an electric vehicle.

"Our philosophy: treat employees as we would treat our sisters and brothers—create a healthy environment and programs that encourage personal wellbeing and growth—promote from within whenever possible—give employees every opportunity to thrive and take pride in their contributions to the broader world community through their work at Dr. Bronner's."

drbronners.com

EARTHX—E CAPITAL SUMMIT

EarthX

"Inspire. Inform. Impact."

Year Founded: 2010

Founder & CEO: Trammell Crow

CEO (EarthX E-Capital Summit): Vikram Agrawal

# of Employees: Approximately 82

Annual Gross Revenue: Estimated $17.2 million

Ownership Structure: Nonprofit organization

Mission / Vision: EarthX aims to inspire and energize the global community to create a sustainable world for all living things and future generations.

Offerings: EarthX organizes conferences and events focused on environmental sustainability, including the annual Congress of Conferences and the E-Capital Summit.

Other Notable Details

EarthX's annual E-Capital Summit is an invitation-only conference that convenes investment firms, innovators, global companies, policymakers, and researchers to address investment and business opportunities in sustainability and clean technology.

earthX.org

EMPOWERMENT INSTITUTE

"The courage to dream . . . the knowledge to change the world"

Year Founded: 1981

Founders: David Gershon and Gail Straub

Ownership Structure: Nonprofit organization

People Involved: 4 million+

Cities Involved: 608

Countries Involved: 67

Peace Actions: 68,000

Offerings: Peace Game Delivery Platforms: peace game app, peace trail, business, universities, communities, conferences, feature film, and video game.

Executive Summary

A Plan to Achieve Peace on Earth by 2030: The Peace on Earth by 2030 initiative, led by the Empowerment Institute, is a comprehensive plan to achieve global peace by the year 2030. Building on the legacy of the First Earth Run in 1986, which demonstrated the efficacy of a collective global peace effort, this initiative seeks to create a lasting shift in global consciousness and behavior. Its peace plan is built on a theory of change which posits that by strategically combining individual transformation, community empowerment, and global cooperation, a tipping point can be reached where peace becomes not just an aspiration but a lived reality for humanity.

empowermentinstitute.net
peace2030.earth
reinventing.earth
oregonpeacetrail.org

EQUAL EXCHANGE COOPERATIVE

"Let's take back our food system"

Founded: 1986

CEO: Rink Dickinson

# of Employees: 71

Annual Gross Revenue: $70,000,000

Ownership Structure: Co-op

Mission: "Equal Exchange's mission is to build long-term trade partnerships that are economically just and environmentally sound, to foster mutually beneficial relationships between farmers and consumers and to demonstrate, through our success, the contribution of worker co-operatives and Fair Trade to a more equitable, democratic and sustainable world."

History

"Equal Exchange started with an idea: what if food could be traded in a way that is honest and fair, a way that empowers both farmers and consumers? Our founders—Rink Dickinson, Jonathan Rosenthal and Michael Rozyne—asked this question as they envisioned a trade model that values each part of the supply chain. They decided to take a big risk and started importing fairly traded coffee from Nicaragua in 1986, despite a US embargo against the Sandinista government. A new business was born from this bold act of solidarity with Latin American farmers and Equal Exchange grew from there."

Products

Coffee, chocolate, tea, cocoa, snacks, nuts, dried fruits, sugar, and olive oil

equalexchange.coop

GLOBAL ALLIANCE FOR BANKING ON VALUES (GABV)

"Making a difference, locally and globally"

Year Founded: 2009

Executive Director: Martin Rohner

# of Member Banks: 70+ in 45 countries (along with 6 supporting partners)

# of Employees (Across Network of Banks): 100,000+

Assets Under Management (Across Network of Banks): $265 billion

Customers Served (Across Network of Banks): Over 50 million

Ownership Structure: Network of independent banks

Mission: "The Global Alliance for Banking on Values (GABV) is a growing movement of independent banks using finance as a force for positive, sustainable economic, social, and environmental impact."

Services: GABV provides a platform for member banks to collaborate, share knowledge, and promote sustainable banking practices, and provides capacity building services (green house gas accounting, corresponding banking, etc.) and training programs for senior professionals and board members in values-based banks.

Other Notable Details

The GABV was founded in 2009 by ten pioneer banks that believed in the need for a fairer financial system. Today, it is a growing membership organization with presence in 45+ countries across Africa, Latin America, Asia Pacific, North America and Europe.

gabv.org

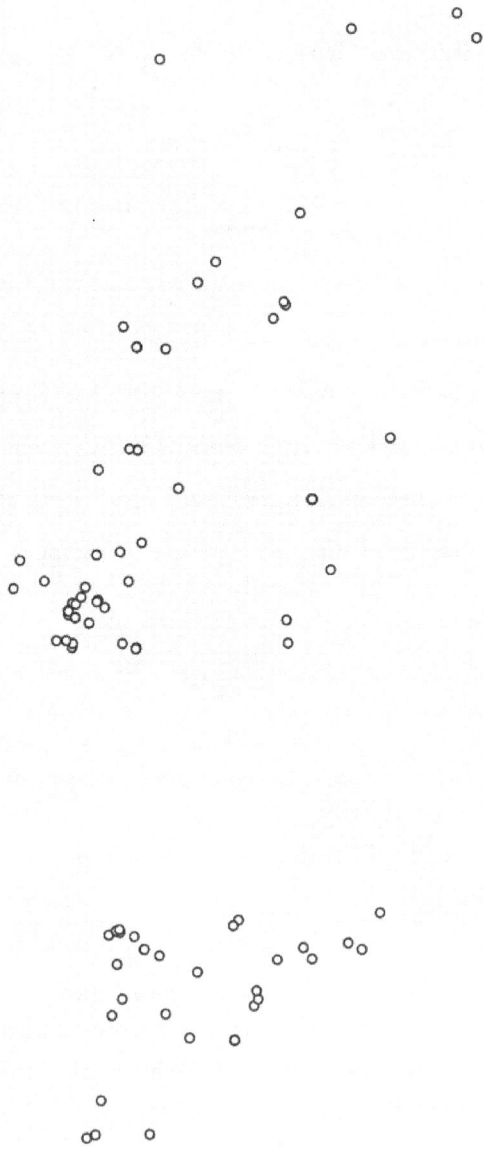

Global Alliance Map.

GLS BANK

GLS Bank

das macht Sinn

"People, planet, profit"

Year Founded: 1974

# of Employees: 525

CEO: Aysel Osmanoglu

# of Clients Served: 320,000+

Assets Under Management: €11.2 billion

Ownership Structure: Cooperative bank

Mission: GLS Bank aims to direct money to initiatives that promote positive social and ecological change, focusing on people rather than profit.

Offerings: GLS Bank offers financial services including loans and investments, supporting projects in renewable energy, education, sustainable business, and social initiatives.

Other Notable Details

As Germany's first social-ecological bank, GLS Bank emphasizes transparency and sustainability in all its financial activities.

gls.de

GOODSTEAD CO.

goodstead

"Company for the road ahead"

Year Founded: 2020

CEO: Robert Swigert

Assets under Management: Undisclosed

Ownership Structure: Private cooperative

Mission/Vision: To mutualize investment management for people concerned about the world as well as their risk and return.

Offerings: Goodstead is a mobile-first robo-advisor and financial planning platform that makes saving for the future time-, risk-, fee-, and tax-efficient for the common person.

Notable Details

Goodstead is a private mutual company owned by its Members. It employs systematic strategies to construct diversified, risk-balanced investment portfolios of passive instruments that are appropriate for each Member's unique risk and return requirements. In addition to fundamental and technical factors, it considers Environmental, Social, and Governance factors among its investment criteria to help Members use their capital to vote for the world they wish their grandchildren to inherit. As a member of 1% for the Planet, Goodstead donates 1% of its top-line revenue to social and environmental nonprofits.

goodstead.co

HOME PLANET FUND

"We are all in for the Earth"

Year Founded: 2022

Founded by: Yvon Chouinard

CEO: Dilafruz Khonikboyeva

Assets Under Management: $20,000,000+

Ownership Structure: Nonprofit organization

Mission: "To save our home planet by harnessing the power of community and business to advance nature-based solutions to end the climate crisis."

Services: Home Planet Fund provides grants directly to frontline, indigenous, and rural communities implementing nature-based solutions to combat climate change.

Other Notable Details

Home Planet Fund was established with a $20 million donation from Patagonia's founder, Yvon Chouinard, ensuring that 100% of funds go directly to indigenous- and community-led initiatives without burdening the organization typical administrative overhead.

homeplanetfund.org

IMPACT FINANCE CENTER

IMPACT
FINANCE CENTER

"Moving money for impact"

Year Founded: 2012

Founder / CEO: Stephanie Gripne

Ownership Structure: Nonprofit academic center

Mission: Impact Finance Center (IFC) aims to identify, educate, and activate individuals and organizations to become impact investors, aligning their assets with their values.

Offerings: The center offers education and advisory services, building impact investor communities and connecting them with community leaders to address significant challenges.

Other Notable Details

IFC has trained and educated 400+ family office, fund, and foundation leaders managing over $50 billion in assets. Through its Colorado Impact Days and Impact Investing Institute, IFC has directly catalyzed over $400 million of investment in social ventures, creating the first-ever statewide marketplace for impact investing.

impactfinancecenter.org

INTERNATIONAL COOPERATIVE ALLIANCE

International
Cooperative
Alliance

"Cooperatives build a better world"

Year Founded: 1895

Director General: Jeroen Douglas

Ownership Structure: Non-governmental organization

Membership: Over 300 cooperative networks worldwide, representing over 1 billion workers

Mission: The International Cooperative Alliance unites, represents, and serves cooperatives worldwide, providing a global voice and forum for knowledge, expertise, and coordinated action for and about cooperatives.

Services: ICA offers advocacy, research, and development support for cooperative enterprises across various sectors.

Other Notable Details

Represents 315 cooperative federations and organizations in 107 countries, encompassing over one billion cooperative members globally.

ica.coop/en

MONDRAGON COOPERATIVES

MONDRAGON
CORPORACION COOPERATIVA

"Humanity at work"

Founded: 1956

Founded by: Father José María Arizmendiarrieta

CEO: Josu Ugarte (Mondragon International)

Team: 80,000 employees, many of whom are fully vested worker-owner members

Ownership Structure: Cooperative association with 90+ independent, interconnected, cooperatively owned companies

Annual Gross Revenue: €11.404 billion; EBITDA: €1.332 billion

Mission: "A socioeconomic business project deeply rooted in Basque culture, created by and for people."

"Committed to a sustainable society, greater competitiveness and customer satisfaction, with the remit to create wealth and transform society through business development and employment, the Mondragon Cooperatives are driven by a commitment to solidarity, applying democratic methods in its organization and management, boosting people's engagement and involvement in the management, performance and ownership of its companies."

Vision
"MONDRAGON is Cooperation A cooperative socioeconomic project, with dedicated people working in global companies that are profitable, competitive and enterprising, acknowledged for their human values, social impact and competitiveness."

Products and Services
Manufactured goods, aerospace, engineering services, consulting services, research and development services, media services.

"We operate all over the world through business delegations and production plants in a variety of different fields such as Industry, Finance, Retail and Knowledge."

mondragon-corporation.com

NEWMAN'S OWN ORGANICS AND THE NELL NEWMAN FOUNDATION

"All profits to charity"

Year Founded: 1982

Founded by: Paul Newman

Annual Revenue: $600+ million in retail sales

Assets Under Management: $225 million

Total Given to Charity to Date: $600 million+

Ownership Structure: For-profit company with all profits donated to charity

Mission: "Fighting for kids since 1982. When Newman's Own first began, Paul Newman declared that 100% of the profits would go to good causes."

Products: Offers a range of organic food and beverage products, including salad dressings, pasta sauces, frozen pizzas, salsas, and snacks, the profits from which are donated to a wide range of nonprofits.

Field Notes

Nell Newman recently established The Nell Newman Foundation "with the goal of carrying on her father's legacy of charitable giving, coupled with her passion for the environment." (nellnewmanfoundation.org)

newmansown.com

ONE SMALL PLANET

"Harmonize the wealth of people and planet"

Year Founded: 2020

Founder: Will Peterffy

Assets Under Management: Undisclosed

# of Employees: Small, team-based organization

Ownership Structure: Private family office

Mission / Vision: One Small Planet aims to regenerate the Earth by investing in initiatives and enterprises that align with ecological, cultural, and spiritual health. The vision is to build an economy grounded in reciprocity, equity, and stewardship for all life.

Offerings: Catalytic investments, strategic philanthropy, storytelling, and systems thinking to transform finance, food systems, and culture.

Other Notable Details

Across the four pillars of community, philanthropy, land stewardship, and venture investing, One Small Planet's Philanthropic Fund awarded over $2.7 million in grants in 2023 alone, to regenerative agriculture, energy transition, and nature conservation projects across 36 organizations supporting 44+ community projects in 10 regions world-wide, 61% of which has been donated directly to indigenous communities and 57% of which were donated to female-led projects and organizations.

"At One Small Planet we seek to reinstate the original meaning of the word *wealth*, to view wealth as a holistic metric of well-being and to consider the wealth of people and planet as the ultimate and imperative metric of success.

"One Small Planet envisions a decolonized world perceived as sacred, imbued with meaning, and engaged with intention. Where relations are authentic, economic and environmental wealth is considered sacred, and the wheel of sacred reciprocity is turning in balance."

"We are at a critical moment in which we need to re-align our culture, our systems of value, and intention for living, to that of the life-affirming world from which we came and still exist within. It is a process of constant refinement, a tight rope walk between the actually-feasible and the not-yet-possible, and will take wisdom spanning from The Art of War to Siddhartha Gautama. Those stewarding most of the wisdom are often farthest from the position to apply it at scale. Bridging these worlds with loving humility and collectively consenting to join Team Life is what is being asked of us. How will you answer?"

—WILL PETERFFY, FOUNDER & CEO

onesmallplanet.org

ORGANIC VALLEY COOP

"Power of we—more hands do more good"

FARMER-OWNED

Year Founded: 1988

# of Employees: 501-1,000 employees

Annual Gross Revenue: $1.2 billion

Ownership Structure: Farmer-owned cooperative

Mission / Vision: "A philosophy and system of production that mirrors the natural laws of living organisms with an emphasis on the interdependence of all life." https://www.organicvalley.coop/about-us/our-philosophy/

Products: Organic dairy products

With over 1,600 member-farms, Organic Valley Coop protects over 400,000 acres of organic farmland.

"It all started in 1988. We were a handful of Midwest family farmers and we were fed up with the state of American agriculture. Family farms were going extinct."

"We used to be a bunch of idealists. And we still are today."
"We believe in the idea that, if consumers demand high-quality organic food, grown the right way, we could all change the way we treat our land, our animals and our bodies."

organicvalley.coop

PATAGONIA & HOLD FAST COLLECTIVE

"We're in business to save our home planet"

Founded: 1973

Founder: Yvon Chouinard

CEO: Ryan Gellert

Team: 3,300 employees

Ownership Structure: In 2022 100% of the company's voting stock was transferred to the Patagonia Purpose Trust, which was established to protect the company's values, and 100% of the nonvoting stock was transferred to the Holdfast Collective, a nonprofit dedicated to fighting the environmental crisis and defending nature—"Earth is Our Only Shareholder."

Annual Gross Revenue: $1.5 billion (appx. $100,000,000 annual net profit donated to Hold Fast Collective, led by CEO Greg Curtis, which in turn donates proceeds to social and environmental nonprofit organizations worldwide)

Mission Statement: We're in business to save our home planet."

Patagonia is committed to producing high-quality outdoor products while minimizing its environmental impact and inspiring others to take action on environmental issues.

Products

A wide range of outdoor clothing, gear, and accessories for various activities such as hiking, climbing, skiing, and camping. Patagonia also operates Patagonia Provisions, a food line that focuses on sustainable, regenerative, and responsibly sourced food products.

patagonia.com

RECREATIONAL EQUIPMENT INC.

"A life outdoors is a life well lived"

Year Founded: 1938

CEO: Mary Beth Laughton

# of Employees: 16,000+

Annual Gross Revenue: $3.85 billion in revenue (2022)

Ownership Structure: Member-owned cooperative (consumer)

Mission / Vision: REI's mission is to inspire, educate, and outfit people for a lifetime of outdoor adventure and stewardship. Their vision is to be the most trusted outdoor retailer, aiming to help people experience the joy of outdoor activities and promote environmental sustainability.

Products

REI offers a wide range of outdoor gear, apparel, and equipment for various activities such as camping, hiking, cycling, climbing, skiing, and more. They also provide services such as gear rentals, outdoor classes and workshops, and guided trips.

"REI Co-op founded the REI Cooperative Action Fund, a new 501(c)(3) public charity, to accelerate the nationwide movement to build a more equitable, accessible and inclusive outdoor culture."

REI is committed to sustainability and environmental stewardship. They prioritize offering environmentally friendly products and have initiatives in place to reduce their environmental impact.

The company has a strong focus on community engagement and outdoor advocacy. They support various outdoor organizations and initiatives, and encourage their members and customers to get involved in outdoor activities and conservation efforts, and have a significant online presence in addition to their brick-and-mortar stores, offering an extensive e-commerce platform for customers to shop from.

As of 2023, REI has 24+ million members, distributes over $200 million in annual member dividends, and donates $6+ million to nonprofit partners through its REI Cooperative Action Fund.

rei.com

RSF | REGENERATIVE SOCIAL FINANCE

"Change finance, finance change"

Year Founded: 1984

Founder: Mark Finser

CEO: Jasper J. van Brakel

# of Employees: 60+

Assets Under Management: $230 million

Ownership Structure: Nonprofit public charity

Mission / Vision: The mission of RSF | Regenerative Social Finance is to transform the way the world works with money. It aims to create financial relationships that are direct, transparent, and personal, emphasizing long-term social and environmental impact. RSF envisions an economy that supports the well-being of all people and the planet.

Offerings: RSF offers a range of financial services and products designed to support social enterprises, nonprofits, and individuals working for positive change. These offerings may include loans, loan guarantees, and investments tailored to meet the needs of organizations and initiatives that align with RSF's mission. They prioritize financing for projects related to food and agriculture, education and the arts, and ecological stewardship.

Other Notable Details

RSF | Regenerative Social Finance places a strong emphasis on building relationships and fostering a sense of community among its stakeholders, including borrowers, investors, and donors. They prioritize investing in ventures and initiatives that create positive social, environmental, and cultural impact. RSF offers various impact investing options that allow individuals and organizations to align their financial resources with their values and support the growth of a more inclusive and sustainable economy. The organization engages in educational initiatives and events to raise awareness and promote dialogue about the intersection of money, finance, and social change.

rsfsocialfinance.org

SAVORY INSTITUTE

SAVORY INSTITUTE

"Regenerating the world's grasslands"

Year Founded: 2009

Founders: Allan Savory, Jody Butterfield, and Daniela Ibarra-Howell

CEO: Jason Knoll

Impact Metrics: Over 92 million acres (36 million hectares) of land under holistic management

# of Team Members: 20-50 employees, and global network of 50 hubs with 28,000+ people trained

Ownership Structure: 501(c)3 nonprofit organization

Mission / Vision: To facilitate the large-scale regeneration of the world's grasslands and the livelihoods of their inhabitants, through Holistic Management—Reversing desertification, restoring biodiversity, and addressing climate change by empowering land managers to regenerate their land.

Offerings: Advisory services, self-paced courses and other education resources (online and in person), global network of holistic management hubs, books, e-books.

Other Notable Details

Through its diverse, grassroots global network, land to market programs, global campuses, and holistic management and ecological outcome verification trainings, the Savory Institute equips land stewards worldwide to restore biodiversity, sequester carbon, and bolster regenerative, land-based livelihoods. Savory's core methodology, Holistic Management, is a time-tested ecological, financial, and social framework for decision-making and grazing planning that is adaptable to anyone's unique situation, while its Ecological Outcome Verification protocol provides feedback through both leading and lagging indicators to ensure management practices and impacts are directionally restorative and delivering stacked net-positive benefits, including potential entry into Land to Market supply chain programs for verified regenerative meat, dairy, leather, and wool products. Additionally, under the leadership of

Daniela Ibarra-Howell, Jim Snyder, and Erik Bruun-Bindslev, the Savory Foundation attracts and deploys mission-aligned capital into large-scale projects to catalyze global transformation at the intersection of finance, climate resilience, and regenerative agriculture.

savory.global

SLOW MONEY INSTITUTE

"Bringing money back down to earth"

Year Founded: 2009

Founder / CEO: Woody Tasch

Annual Gross Revenue: $540,000+ (2023)

Total Capital Deployed: $100,000,000+ via decentralized community-based mechanisms

Ownership Structure: Nonprofit organization

Mission: "The Slow Money Institute aims to catalyze the flow of capital to local food systems, connecting investors to the places where they live and promoting principles of sense of place, diversity, and nonviolence."

Offerings: The institute facilitates the formation of self-organizing local groups that employ various approaches, including public meetings, on-farm events, pitch fests, peer-to-peer loans, and investment clubs, to support small food enterprises.

Other Notable Details

Since its inception, Slow Money has facilitated the movement of over $100 million to more than 1,000 small food enterprises through a network of 27 local groups across the United States. The organization was founded by Woody Tasch, author of *Inquiries into the Nature of Slow Money: Investing as if Food, Farms, and Fertility Mattered.*

slowmoney.org

TED

"Ideas change everything."

TED
Ideas worth spreading

Conference Founding Year: 1984

Founder: Richard Saul Wurman

Nonprofit Designation: 2001

Head of TED: Chris Anderson

Annual Budget: ~$100M

Ownership structure: TED Foundation Inc., a 501(c)(3) private foundation owns TED Conferences LLC

Mission: Discover and spread ideas that spark conversation, deepen understanding, and drive meaningful change.

Vision: TED is a nonprofit that believes powerful ideas, powerfully presented, move us: to feel something, to think differently, to take action.

Programs:

TED Countdown	TEDx
TED Democracy	TED Fellows
TED-Ed	The Audacious Project

Executive Summary

TED (Technology | Entertainment | Design) is one of the world's most trusted nonprofit brands, with a track record of inspiring and educating hundreds of millions of people worldwide. TED's media and storytelling platform amplifies powerful ideas from visionary thinkers and global leaders from across the ideological spectrum. In 2023 alone, these ideas were viewed 3 billion times in 248 countries and territories. TED believes that sharing bold ideas can spark change in individuals, their communities, and their spheres of influence—creating a multiplier effect around the world.

TED's ecosystem of mission-driven programs creates real-world impact on some of the most pressing global challenges of our time. TED-Ed equips tens of millions of teachers and students with educational animated videos that have been viewed more than one billion times. More than 500 innovators from 100+ countries have launched groundbreaking ideas through the TED Fellows program, and The Audacious Project has mobilized $5.9 billion in collaborative philanthropy to rapidly scale trailblazing nonprofits. TED Countdown accelerates urgent climate solutions while TED Democracy bridges divides and facilitates civic engagement. TEDx maximizes TED's unparalleled convening power by bringing together 20,000 communities—many in remote corners of the world—to learn, connect, and mobilize together.

TED's changemaking model draws on deep expertise and expansive reach to create meaningful progress on the issues that matter most. Together, the platform aims to build a future where problem-solving is democratized and human and planetary flourishing is possible.

ted.com
tedimpact.com

TRANSITION NETWORK INTERNATIONAL

Transition Network
international

"A movement of communities coming together to reimagine and rebuild our world"

Year Founded: 2007

Co-Founders: Rob Hopkins and others

Ownership Structure: UK-based charity, operating worldwide

Network: Over 1,000 groups and 21 hubs located in 69 countries

Mission: Transition Network supports the international Transition Towns Movement, amplifies stories of community-led change, and nurtures collaborations across difference to challenge us all to reimagine and rebuild our world.

Offerings: Global map of Transition groups and hubs, open-source social network, free Practicing Transition webinars, an annual Day of Transition Practice, monthly Cultural Transformation Circle gatherings, in-person and online trainings, the Voices of Transition podcast, and much more!

Other Notable Details

All Transition groups and hubs are independently run, but are bound together by a highly collaborative, bottom-up approach to community organizing, a shared set of principles, and a common vision for a truly just, sustainable, resilient, and regenerative future. Popular areas of focus include revitalizing local food systems, strengthening local economies, and reducing dependence on fossil fuels. Transition groups have created successful community-owned renewable energy companies; worker-owned social enterprises; organic farms, gardens, and orchards; local currencies and investment clubs; repair cafes; free stores; and many other practical, community-based solutions.

transitionnetwork.org

UNIFY

"Global synchronized meditations for world peace and global impact"

Year Founded: 2012 by Adil Kassam

Executive Director: Tammy Scarlett

Chief Ambassador: Miranda Clendening

Major Contributors: Adam Apollo, Jacob Devaney, Patrick Kronfli, Johnathan Human, Micheel Kraus, Raamayan, Jamie Janover

Team: 50+ staff, volunteers + board of directors

Individual Members: Facebook: 2.8 million followers (1.1 billion active views, YTD June 2025)

Member Organizations: 37,000+ collaborating nonprofit and for-profit partners, coordinating 144+ Global Synchronized Meditations and Social Impact Campaigns since 2012

Ownership Structure: 501c3 Nonprofit Organization

Mission: "UNIFY is a nonprofit organization and global community that stewards and facilitates global collective intention, action, & impact to help build a world where all of humanity is unified. UNIFY helps facilitate solutions to the world's greatest challenges by orchestrating global synchronized events that inspire community-driven action campaigns for World Peace."

Offerings: Memberships and collective action curation for individuals, communities, and partner organizations

---

UNIFY's Vision is that by 2030 solutions to the world's greatest challenges will have been innovated and implemented, and over half the world's population meditates together for World Peace. The goals are simple: Help as many people as possible UNIFY towards solving the world's greatest problems, UNIFY the world and participate in creating Peace on Earth. It is UNIFY's intention that all people be invited to unification, each by way of their intrinsic and innate value as a member of humanity, regardless of race, religion, gender, or nation, to actively participate in co-creating our collective future of peace together.

Join

Community leaders and organizations looking to host Peace Day, Earth Day, Water Day, Women's Day Events and Meditations please join our Global Synchronized Meditations and add yourself to the list and maps of impact activities and regenerative efforts worldwide.

Advise

UNIFY provides fiscal sponsorship and partnership advising, pairing members with.

unify.org
fb.com/unify
x.com/unify

ZINGERMAN'S

"To enrich as many lives as we possibly can."

Year Founded: 1982

Co-Founders: Paul Saginaw and Ari Weinzweig

Ownership Structure: A unique and multifaceted ownership structure includes several independent employee-owned businesses unified through common brand identity and intellectual property owned by a Perpetual Purpose Trust.

Team: 750 + employees and employee-owners, across 11 businesses, which swells to over 1,000 during holiday shopping season

Annual Revenue: $65 – $78 million

Mission: We share the Zingerman's Experience selling food that makes you happy, giving service that makes you smile, in passionate pursuit of our mission, showing love and care in all our actions to enrich as many lives as we possibly can.

Guiding Principles

Operating within a "Three Bottom Line" framework and an "Open Book Management" paradigm, Zingerman's has 9 Guiding Principles at the core of its decision-making framework and myriad B-to-B and B-to-C commercial offerings:

1. Great Food!
2. Great Service!
3. A Great Place to Shop and Eat!
4. Solid Profits!
5. A Great Place to Work!
6. Strong Relationships!
7. A Place to Learn!
8. An Active Part of Our Community!
9. Committed to Improving Our Impact!

Businesses and Offerings

Zingerman's Bakehouse, Miss Kim, The Tiny Wedding, Zingerman's Candy, Zingerman's Catering and Events, Zingerman's Coffee Company, Cornman Farms, Zingerman's Creamery, Zingerman's Delicatessen, Zingerman's Food Tours, Greyline, Zingerman's Mail Order, Zingerman's Next Door, Zingerman's Press, Zingerman's Roadhouse, and Zingtrain.

zingermanscommunity.com

ADDITIONAL COMPANIES AND NETWORKS OF NOTE

Avantis Responsible International Equity ETF (AVSD)—avantisinvestors.com

Bamboo Village Trust—bamboovillagetrust.earth

BioFi Project—biofi.com

Blue Action Lab—blueaction.eco

Blue Green Future—bluegreenfuture.org

Calvert Funds—calvert.com

CapShift—capshift.com

Climate Curve—climatecurve.org

Climate Foundation—climatefoundation.org

Climate Works Foundation—climateworks.org

Earth Corps—earthcorps.org

Earth Hero—earthhero.com

Ecosystem Restoration Communities—ecosystemrestorationcommunities.org

Emerson Collective—emersoncollective.com

Explorers Club—explorers.org

Force Blue—forceblueteam.org

Fungi Perfecti—fungi.com

Grassroots Economics Foundation—grassrootseconomics.org

Gratitude Railroad—gratituderailroad.com

Green Century Funds—greencentury.com

Guidestar—guidestar.org

Humankind Portfolios—app.humankind.co

Jane Goodall Institute—janegoodall.org

Ktisis Capital—ktisiscapital.com

Le Ciel Foundation—lecielfoundation.com

Legacy Vacation Resorts / andCO—legacyvacationresorts.com

Lemonade Insurance—lemonade.com

Mad Agriculture—madagriculture.org

Mad Capital—madcapital.com

Montcalm—montcalmcr.com

National Center for Employee Ownership—nceo.org

National Cooperative Business Association—ncbaclusa.coop

National Philanthropic Trust—nptrust.org

New Day Impact Investing / Causeway—newdayimpact.com

One Earth—oneearth.org

Pachamama Alliance—pachamama.org

Planet Impact Fund—onepercentfortheplanet.org/planet-impact-fund

RegenEarth Studio—www.regenearth.studio

Regen Network—registry.regen.network

Regeneration International—regenerationinternational.org

Regenerative Organic Alliance—regenorganic.org

Regenerative World Quest—bthelightconsulting.com/regenerative

Schumacher Center for a New Economics—centerforneweconomics.org

Soul Community Planet—scphotels.com

Stance Capital—stancecap.com

Sustainability & Corporate Social Responsibility LinkedIn Network—
linkedin.com/groups/82951

Terraformation—terraformation.com

The Nature Conservancy (Green Bonds)—nature.org/en-us/about-us/
who-we-are/how-we-work/finance-investing/green-bonds/

Trailhead Capital—trailheadcap.com

Yield Giving—yieldgiving.com

Y on Earth Community—yonearth.org

PART IV   Aphoristic a-Musings

"In the mountains the shortest way is from peak to peak: but for that one must have long legs. Aphorisms should be peaks—and those who are addressed, tall and lofty."

—NIETZSCHE

ON APHORISMS

An Invitation to the Reader

he Aphorism is an exceptional rhetorical device—neither poetry nor exposition in the ordinary sense—that allows authors and audiences to "cover a lot of territory" in short order. Utilized by philosophers and ethicists like Heraclitus, Blaise Pascal, John Stuart Mill, Voltaire, Mark Twain, and (perhaps most (in)famously) in modern times, Friedrich Nietzsche, this pithy art form has also, of course, been employed by the most notable luminaries known to humanity, including Confucius, Lao Tzu, Siddhartha Gautama (the Buddha), and the great master teacher—Jeshua the Nazarene. Like zip drives of "micromodels of empirical inquiry" that possess "generally truth, or a bold approach to some truth" (as Adam Gopnik attributes to Mill), aphorisms are a time-tested mechanism for not only conveying information, but for having that information "stick" longer and better than many longer-form methods of communication. One could say that aphoristic language is broadly rooted in our oral and rhetorical traditions, including current forms like hip hop. I'm not going to split hairs here between aphorisms, poetry, proverbs, and parables, but will acknowledge that many of us speak in aphorisms in daily life, as Andrew Hui discusses in *A Theory of the Aphorism: From Confucius to Twitter.* He observes that the sweeping and urgent observations often conveyed aphoristically are an essential quotidian and literary device, allowing us to share "programs of thought" with one another in a hyper-efficient mode of communication.

In this book, the essayists and I have endeavored to share as much of what we consider to be important—if not essential—to cultivating planetary prosperity as systematically and ubiquitously as possible, in effect cultivating the egregores of what's possible that they might quickly predominate our shared cultural programming. But, recognizing that the intersection of economics, business, ecology, and culture is complex and nuanced, there is much in the way of explanation, texture, and extrapolation I've excluded from the main 13 chapters in the interest of brevity, knowing that I'd be sharing the aphoristic observations and perspectives awaiting you below.

I hope you find them intriguing, and perhaps even illuminating at times. I have endeavored, especially with entrepreneurs, executives, investors, philanthropists, and organizational and community leaders in mind, invested many additional scores of hours to bring these to you in a concise and cogent (I hope!) manner.

LIST OF APHORISTIC AMUSINGS

On Aphorisms—An Invitation to the Reader

PART ONE—BUSINESS AND ECONOMICS

PART TWO—CULTURE AND SOCIETY

PART THREE—DEEP LEADERSHIP AND TRUE FREEDOM

PART ONE—BUSINESS AND ECONOMICS

Our Greatest Spiritual Task Is in the Realm of Economics and Finance

When we come to understand the extraordinarily complex and nuanced human experience on planet Earth during the immediate transition from the Anthropocene to the Ecocene, the latter of which is marked by widespread compassion, care, and intelligence, we come to understand a surprising truth: our greatest spiritual task in these times is the cultivation of economic and financial systems that are rooted in love and wisdom, that have the sophisticated stewardship of our living planet and the compassionate care of each and every human being embedded in their core fabrics and reasons for being. Our psycho-spiritual healing, our transmutation of traumatic imprints, and our restoration of ecosystems are all, of course, of paramount importance as well, and are in fact both requisite outcomes and necessary results of a world in which financial and economic systems are rooted in love and wisdom. We must do more than just meditate and journey within as "cosmonauts" . . . We must *act*! Our task is clear. In calm, heart-centered joy, let us get to work!

Celebrating Earth Steward Entrepreneurs

Entrepreneurship, though rewarding, is exceptionally difficult in many ways. It's a path in which surprises and uncertainties are certain and in which the "maps" of business plans, financial models, and marketing decks are never equivalent to the "territory" of deployment. Requiring both exemplary orchestration and improvisation skillsets, entrepreneurship necessitates the central confidence of the conductor and the fluid flexibility and receptive responsiveness of the improv jazz musician to be masterfully activated in concert with each other— each and every day—while forging onward further into uncharted territory, "intuiting the future," as Nick Hanauer describes in his cautionary TED Talk.

As Steve Jobs famously and succinctly said about entrepreneurship: "You've got to act and you've got to be willing to fail." No doubt. Entrepreneurs share a special bond, in my experience, understanding and appreciating from the foundation of direct experience the necessary vicissitudes of the vanguard one invariably encounters along these pioneering pathways—where success and disappointment are encountered at perhaps higher amplitudes than along many other life paths. I believe that all entrepreneurs deserve respect for their courageous trailblazing, regardless of sector or industry or time period or worldview.

The emerging Earth Steward Entrepreneurs deserve special recognition. Not only are they navigating the heretofore uncharted economic and commercial territories of their enterprises, they are also continually striking and optimizing balance among and between the multi-variant complexities of financial performance, social and cultural stewardship, and ecological restoration, responsibility, and sustainability. When it comes to challenging leadership landscapes, these are among the most extreme conditions. And when it comes to the altruistic aristocrats who courageously take on these challenges—engaging the polycrisis head on, on behalf of all humanity and the entire planet—these leaders are especially deserving of our admiration, respect, and support.

Economics Is a Design Discipline (Not a Science)

Too many of us believe the discipline of economics and the ways in which economic behavior plays out in the "marketplace" to be the result of infallible scientific truths and an innate human "condition." This couldn't be further from the truth. In fact, "economics" is a design discipline[1], not a science, in which an amalgam of cultural biases and ethics (or lack thereof) are infused—however subtly—into the structures, systems, and mechanics of the economic design discipline and resulting market (and participant) behaviors. Too often, anti-humanistic, anti-ecological, anti-Earth, and sociopathic behaviors are mistaken to be the result of objectively established economic principles instead of misguided (if not pathological) cultural mores, and, when coupled with capital concentration and the hard and soft powers of militaries and policies, shape not only our *experiences* of reality but our *expectations* of reality. The inverse and corollary truth in all of this should give us great hope—we can redesign our economies to serve the greater good, further rewarding beauty, creativity, cultural kindness, social responsibility, and environmental stewardship.

It's Our Economy and Our Market—NOT "the" Economy and "the" Market

When Bill Clinton's presidential campaign shrewdly announced "it's the economy, stupid" (apparently under James Carville's advice), it set up an unstoppable rhetorical pummeling of incumbent President George H. W. Bush's doomed reelection campaign. As an entrepreneur, I've witnessed firsthand how financiers evoke "the" economy and "the" market when making decisions that damage certain individuals, companies, communities, and sectors, as if conjuring the "invisible hand" fantasy somehow absolves them of any individual responsibility for their destructive decision-making. The market and the economy aren't independent, objective behemoths moving according to their own "natural laws." To the contrary! No, instead, they are actually giant mirrors reflecting back to us the aggregate totals of our collective decision-making. And moreover, they

---

1 Credit here is due to Tom Chi, Founder of At One Ventures, and essay contributor to this book.

are our shared values, decision-making, management, and destiny—ours to design and change and evolve as we so choose, consciously (or don't choose, unconsciously). Hence, throughout the book, I have opted for "our economy" (and "our market") in those instances where "the economy" (and "the market") would be the more conventional, familiar usage. If we are to reclaim our humanity, our decency, our agency, and our directionality on planet Earth, we must, in the first place, reclaim OUR economy too.

The Quintenary is Part and Parcel of Planetary Consciousness

Anthropologists and historians ascribe different levels of social complexity (and therefore modes of consciousness) to the various stages of classical economic value chain functions. Humans have long conducted primary production—in a sense we've always done so, whether foraging, fishing, hunting, or harvesting forest timber. We've also conducted rudimentary secondary manufacturing ("making by hand") as well—basketry, textiles, pottery, shelter, and weaponry being among the earliest examples. Our step into the tertiary—trade among distant and disparate merchants, as well as among and between different primary and secondary sectors within shared regions and communities—put us onto a long road (including the Tea Horse Road, Silk Road, and Cacao and Cowry routes among the Cahokian, Mississippian, Puebloan, Aztecan, Mayan, and Incan civilizations) upon which various forms of currency emerged. This of course naturally led to the increasingly complex social and economic structures of the quaternary (not to be confused with complexity in astro-geomancy, ethnopharmacology, nor psycho-spiritual community with the broader biological and cosmological fabric of reality endemic to ancient and indigenous cultures). We can imagine these different modes and stages along the value-chain journey to correspond to different forms of consciousness, especially as it concerns prevailing group consciousness (aka milieu, paradigm, Zeitgeist) among people in different societies. And so, we arrive at the *Quintenary*. In many respects deeply rooted in the foundational place-based ecological stewardship paradigm essential to primary-production oriented cultures (the Original Instructions), this advanced Quintenary modality uniquely embodies, expresses, and accelerates our transition into a planetary consciousness, the fully developed and mature versions of which were anticipated by Chardin's *Noosphere*. The Quintenary is part and parcel of planetary consciousness.

The Pragmatic Rationale (and Imperative)

There are bountiful ethical, moral, philosophical, and psycho-spiritual reasons to evolve in the direction of compassionate consciousness and all that is meant by the term *Regeneration Renaissance*, but these are still not wholly convincing to some of us. And, particularly among those of us who remain unconvinced (as of yet—we think you'll see soon enough), and who are situated in socio-economic positions from which extraordinary capital allocation and policy decision power is wielded, the pragmatic rationale must be taken into account and considered with earnestness. Essentially what it tells us is that, as we successfully make decisions around the more intelligent allocation of resources, opportunity, responsibility, and access, and the more we deploy capital through regenerative finance and stewardship philanthropy deals, the less likely our global economic system and our living biosphere will careen toward broadscale system perturbation, disintegration, and collapse—and the inevitable capital destruction that would ensue (or worse, our society devolves into violent hordes with pitchforks, as Nick Hanauer has cautioned his fellow plutocrats). This is, from an entirely "self-interested" perspective, actually a matter of systemic stabilization for capital preservation.

Communities vs. Casinos (and Aristocratic Stewards vs. Gambling Gangsters)

The futile pursuit of astronomical "breakaway" wealth accumulation by millions upon millions of humans worldwide (often called "escape velocity" by technopreneurs), which is mathematically only achievable by an extremely small percentage of us, has us pushing, pulling, and pursuing capital in marketplaces that are more akin to casinos than communities. In casinos, gamblers typically lose, and especially over time, are more or less guaranteed to lose. In communities, however—healthy communities that is, with ecologically and economically appropriate behavior—the very real (and realizable—take Mondragon for instance) possibility of achieving a reasonable level of wealth and prosperity for all is a mathematical truth. Whether we're looking back at the tulip bubble a half millennium ago or the crypto bubbles of our own decade, the unrestrained pursuit of astronomical wealth results in many, many losers. If we so choose, we can do far better than this and cultivate the conditions for widespread prosperity instead. It's a matter of priorities, and it's a matter of simple math.

On Safety Nets and Corporate Profits

In mainstream society (as opposed to the saner socio-economic systems like Mondragon), among the primary factors influencing whether a person will achieve extraordinary financial wealth is access: to social circles, to financial capital, and to the presence of a robust safety net. A robust safety net is typically the result of being born into a family of considerable wealth, in which surplus resources allow for years or even decades of economic inactivity from one or more of its members, and ensures economic security for the more venturesome entrepreneurs in the family ecosystem. Such safety nets relieve entrepreneurs, innovators, and creatives from the immediate (and very often crushing) stress of day-to-day survival. Ideation and inspiration flow more freely. Among the more enlightened developed nations of Northern Europe and elsewhere, society as a whole has come to understand the potent economic value of basic safety nets (not to mention high-quality education and health care), and has invested wisely in provisioning them to their entire populace. No wonder per capita productivity, income, and happiness in these regions are among the highest on the planet! There's a terrible, sad irony that so many of the wealthy elite in less enlightened societies like the United States seek to remove even the most basic safety nets from underneath the poorest in their communities, not only succumbing to the immorality of (so-called "expedient" or "pragmatic") meanness, but also systematically limiting and undermining the tremendous intelligence, creativity, ingenuity, and opportunity of a huge segment of their community populations. Stranger still is the coupling of such a harsh attitude among the elite, while it is what's left of the tattered social safety nets that essentially fund the outsized profits of the Walmarts, Amazons, and other titanic businesses dependent upon "low-skill" (and hence low wage) workers. Let them eat cake? Talk about having your cake and eating it too!

The Titanic, Bailing Water from Rowboats, and Finding Terra Firma— Kindness Amidst the Storm

The *Titanic* was once the largest ocean vessel ever constructed, and was considered to be unsinkable. We all know how that turned out. When it sank, it took some of the world's wealthiest tycoons and poorest peasants down with it, and those who managed to survive may have had luck more than anything else to thank. Thus, the Titanic is one of the most appropriate metaphors for our times—if we don't succeed in ushering in the Ecocene.

Equally apt is the popular meme of the simple rowboat leaking in its aft, where some poor chaps desperately bail the overwhelming waters while others at the stern—raised up on account of the first-sinking aft—gloat under the false perception that the "leak isn't at our end" of the boat. We know how this one ends, too.

"We're all in this polycrisis storm together," some would say. But the reality is, as Damian Barr has so insightfully written, that "some of us are on super-yachts and some have just the one oar." We might add that many of us are in rowboats and canoes, and still others of our brothers and sisters are without any vessel at all, barely treading water in deep, stormy seas. So, whether our metaphor is the *Titanic*, a yacht, a canoe, or a simple rowboat, the question is the same: how and where do we find *terra firma* amidst this polycrisis tempest? And, it seems clear, the answer is obvious: any hope of establishing solid footing on *terra firma* will be found in each of us choosing to invest, create, manage, and donate our capital resources (time, talent, *and* treasure) more and more in the direction of true philanthropy (love of humanity) and deep ecological stewardship. Lest we find ourselves "shuffling the chairs on the *Titanic*," may we open our hearts, minds, calendars, and wallets toward this shared destiny.

Born on Third—Did Ya Hit a Triple?

I have many wealthy friends—and far fewer of them are actually "responsible" for making their wealth. A father, grandfather, great-grandfather (most often), or occasionally (but much less frequently) a mother, grandmother, or great-grandmother was the progenitor of their family's extraordinary capital accumulation. Many of these friends of mine are extremely generous—among the most impactful philanthropists and "visionary capitalist" social investors in the economy—and tend to maintain a very grounded and gratitude-rich attitude toward possessing (or having access to) unusually vast capital resources. However, some others whom I've encountered seem to have succumbed to some strangely "social Darwinist" understanding of their position in society, and moreover have made the intellectual leap that, since dad or grand-dad were so obviously gifted, they must be too! It's strange that so many of us can be born on third base through the luck of the draw, and behave as if we've hit a triple to get there. With expanded perspective, more of us will realize our privilege—whether of the proximity, prestige, power, or plutocracy variety (or all four)—and cultivate the appropriate degrees of gratitude (and humility) while putting our good fortune to work for the greater good.

There's No Wisdom in Your Spreadsheet

We've got to come to terms with the fact that, no matter how complex our econometric and market data may be, no matter how compellingly the data sets may help us understand our world and collective constructs of civilization, our spreadsheets are not the domain of wisdom. At best, they're presentations of data and information that, however "elegant" they may appear, have no inherent wisdom or intelligence to impart upon us. We, on the other hand, are cosmic conduits of the conscious, loving wisdom of creation. We are capable of attuning ourselves to so much—so very much—energy, intelligence, and insight. May we close our computers, open our hearts, and integrate our minds with the deeper truths—the wisdom—of living creation.

There's No Soil at Burning Man

I love and appreciate artistic expression—don't get me wrong here. But, for me the iconic Burning Man gathering in the dusty summer heat of an isolated expanse of flat desert has become a symbol not so much for a culture celebrating creativity from and among all, but a neo-techno pomp and circumstance, celebrity-fetish "bread and circuses" exhibition of all the shiny, glittery, mind-altering spectacle of escapism that is more redolent of ostriches sticking their heads in the sand than people leading the thoughtful, grounded evolution of humanity. It's the 1% of the 12% or the 12% of the 1%—whatever way you want to run the math . . . glittery, shiny, unicorn, casino mania. Many of my friends have gone to and still go to Burning Man. I can appreciate the appeal. But hear me out—*there's no soil at Burning Man*! Not only is there no soil there naturally (it's a veritable desert wasteland not too terribly far from the toxic and radioactive testing grounds of many secret military installations, including Area 51), but the festival itself actually disallows anybody from bringing soil to the gathering. Now, I understand the ecological stewardship rationale for this and applaud the state and federal land stewards for thinking of this detail and enforcing it. But the symbolic significance is staggering. Think of it. For many thousands of the world's elite innovators, financiers, celebrities, and creatives, this is the singular annual event not to miss . . . and there's no soil there! There's no soil at Burning Man. None. Consider this in contrast to the personal practices of *Shinrin-yoku*, of connecting to the deep, pervasive living intelligence instead of being even further razzle-dazzled by humanity's techno-capital elite. There's no soil at Burning Man!

Beware the Five Great Dangers of Our Time

Many of us are familiar with the various cultural warnings against violent, misanthropic, and excessively hedonistic temptations. Whether the Original Instructions, Hebraic Ten Commandments, Egyptian Negative Covenants, Vedic Yamas and Niyamas, Five Buddhist Precepts, Bodhisattva Vows, or Six Zen Paramitas, the world's cultural traditions abound with the "should" and "shouldn't" moral code guidelines and guardrails for decency (and stability). But in our post-modern, hyper-technological, information-age, globalized culture, in which we can literally walk anywhere (via airplane) and access any information (via technology) imaginable, there are five particular dangers that our ancestors either didn't anticipate or couldn't imagine us approaching without profound reverence and caution.

Setting aside the obvious dangers of Mammonic avarice and the rest of the "seven deadly sins" (of course, Jeshua the Nazarene made clear we cannot serve two masters), the five great dangers of our time seem to be solipsistic self-aggrandizement and ego-inflation through: (1) fastuous and hubristic approaches to esoteric knowledge and spiritual wisdom; (2) compulsive over indulgence in sacred entheogenic plant, mushroom, and frog medicines; and (3) reckless and delusional interactions with advanced technologies, especially AI and trans-humanism; along with the (4) narcissistic trappings of fame and glamour (particularly exacerbated by the first-generation social media measuring sticks) and (5) frequent Pavlovian compulsions toward the "bright shiny distractions" of fantasy football, fantasy festivals, and all manner of man-made fantasies that clutter our consciousness and devour the precious time and attention we would otherwise make available for authentic relationship cultivation, intimate nature-connection, and deep, impactful service toward people and planet.

I'm aware this may all come off as a bit "preachy," and that's not my intent. Rather, in my connections and collaborations with hundreds of brilliant social entrepreneurs and change-makers, I'm struck by how much more time and attention we could all devote to our deeper soul purposes and to the greater good (and consequently engendering profound, sustained joy and satisfaction in our own lives) when these five great dangers are intentionally moderated and mitigated. We may be wise to remember the wisdom of Alan Watts re: entheogens in particular ("Once you get the message, hang up the phone") and Viktor Frankl re: all other manner of distraction ("When men can't find a deep sense of meaning, they distract themselves with pleasure"). I'm not a prude, and this isn't about advocating starkly square Stoicism (vs. Epicureanism, etc.), but please consider for a moment the unbelievably miraculous and stupendously magnificent world in which we're all now living—the wondrously awesome beauty of Earth and her oceans and mountains and forests and countlessly colorful creatures—and the fact that our decisions right now and within our limited lifetimes are determining the future and fate of it all. This isn't a dress rehearsal—it is our main feature!

We'll All Be Dead Soon Enough—Are You Really Achieving Your Soul's Greatest Purpose?

When we come to understand with clear sight just how precious our time on the planet is—each of us has some 30,000 days +/- if we're fortunate—and we come to recognize that we'll each be dead soon enough, what will we prioritize? What is your soul's uniquely great purpose in this lifetime? Are you navigating it all accordingly?

Being Careful about East Coast "Exceptionalism" and West Coast "Wizardry"

Flanked by marble pillars, adorned with mahogany furnishing, and draped by thick ivy, the old, heavy doorways are tightly guarded through which the rarified subcultures of the socioeconomic elite are accessed. And, the feedback loops between the privileged, the monied, and the "brilliant" are carefully managed by the institutions of *elite* higher education, corporations, capital pools, and halls of government. This creates an insular feedback loop in which privilege and access are too often confused with wisdom, deep intelligence, balance, and beneficence. We ought to be careful about this delusional perception propensity—one which those *who know* would have to agree is running rampant on Wall Street, inside the Beltway, and along Sand Hill Road. We must humble ourselves and recognize the truth that having outsized privilege, capital, access, and power DOES NOT necessarily mean that we know what's best for humanity, for our world, and for our shared futures—indeed certain underlying structural and historical legacies which have contributed to the conditions of our elite status actually, in fact, too often distort and undermine our ability to contrive the wisdom of altruism, the strength of magnanimity, and the beauty of self-transcendent service to life and to all of humanity. Lest we fall into the timeless trap of pride, hubris, and ego-inflation, let us be more *careful* about so-called East Coast "exceptionalism," West Coast "wizardry," and even Austin "awesome" (and their European, Asian, African, and Australian counterparts)—for the greater good of all concerned!

Adulting in the Ecocene: Evolving From "Move Fast and Break Things" to "Move Slowly and Take Good Care"

The prevailing ethos now found in Silicon Valley (and elsewhere) among many gazillionaire technology disrupters and their teams of engineering, finance, and marketing technocrats reminds many of us parents of unruly toddlers' clumsy lumberings or rebellious adolescents' amusements. At neither of those stereotypical stages are *prudence* and *forethought* notable strengths, let alone stewardship, service, and systems stability for the greater good. Moving fast and breaking things typifies behavior of obstreperous children, not community-minded adults. And in this time of polycrisis and deep systems transformation toward the stabilizing conditions of the Ecocene, we need the adults—wise elders and rising leaders alike—to take the helm and take good care. Adulting in the Ecocene is slow and careful, smooth and competent, sure and kind. Slow, smooth, and sure; careful, competent, and kind.

Why Permaculture Matters

For too many of us in the quaternary professions of business, law, economics, technology, information systems, accounting, and finance, we are, on the whole and as of yet, all too ignorant of the ecological stewardship arts and sciences. How can we expect to know *how* to create financial and economic systems for regeneration, stewardship, and sustainability if we don't understand, in an intimate embodied manner, the deep and ancient *practices* of caring for our ecosystems, tending to the waters, and growing our medicinal foods in a manner that builds and enhances the biological vitality of the living soils upon which we all depend? Permaculture (and many of the other ecological stewardship systems, including regenerative agriculture, Biodynamics, and the myriad ancient traditions of Indigenous stewardship from which Mollison and others have drawn so much while articulating the Permaculture and related frameworks) is essential for us in the quaternary professions to rapidly deepen our knowledge, awareness, and wisdom. We must each earn a Permaculture Design Certification—posthaste! And, within the seminal tome of Mollison's body of work, we'll find a distinction between the "visible" structures of nature, ecology, agriculture, and our built environments, and the "invisible" structures of economics, finance, and humanity's organizational structures and systems. And, conversely, for those of us already deep in the regeneration and stewardship of the "visible" structures, we must educate ourselves further about the "invisible" structures of economic, financial, legal, and other quaternary systems. For, as Mollison understood, and as more and more of us leading the regeneration renaissance are coming to understand, it is in the nodes of interconnectivity—the relational boundary "edges" of domains, to use our term of art—between the "visible" and "invisible" structures that we in the quintenary professions are to contextualize our work and measure our success.

Flying Blind—or—Can a Stool Stand with Only One Leg?

As of yet (and setting aside sensationalized news cycles), our advanced data feedback mechanisms are flooded by the political, financial, and economic conditions, capital trends, and social status vicissitudes of 24-hour news cycles. All the while, we suffer from a systemic drought of ecological and sociological data—we lack easy access to information that tells us in real time and with granularity how the planet and all her creatures are doing and how society and all her communities, families, and individual people are faring. With respect to the first (political economy) leg on the stool, we have a surfeit of information. But with respect to the other two (social and ecological), we're severely deficient. Sure, within rarefied academic and policy circles, this imbalance may not be nearly as apparent. But in our mainstream consciousness, the ubiquitous real-time ticker-tape metrics are only financial and economic (and/or sports and entertainment diversions).

Imagine flying an aircraft in pitch darkness, and you only have one of the three key instruments in your purview—either the altimeter, the compass, or the airspeed indicator, but no more than one of these. A recipe for disaster, surely! Let us rapidly develop and deploy a decentralized system of comprehensive data streams for humanity's and nature's well-being—along with their concomitant "dashboards"—so that we all have "eyes open" on the state of the situation we're all in together. (Imagine the ticker tape in New York expanded to include these three streams of critical information!).

In his memoir, *The Age of Turbulence*, Alan Greenspan recalls the months leading up to the official, public demise of the Soviet Union, during which dozens of Soviet and American economists and financial technocrats convened and corresponded regularly in order to avert the potential global destabilization that the anticipated collapse of one of the two great Cold War "superpowers" could unleash—and with it the potential horrors of nuclear holocaust. In his recounting, Greenspan shares intimate conversations with his Soviet counterparts in which they decry the fundamental failure of their centrally-administered state economy—they didn't have the robust *data feedback loops* streaming from the markets and their myriad state and corporate actors . . . they were flying blind. Think about this for a moment. They were flying blind. Now, with respect to the general stability and prosperity of humanity worldwide, and the general stability and integrity of Earth's ecosystems—*our* life-support system—we too are flying blind. This needs to change—*stat!*

Reality-Adjusted (vs. Risk-Adjusted) Returns—Toward the Light of Regenerative Finance

Among the greatest challenges and opportunities of our times is refining and aligning our perceived self-interest with the "interest" (call it well-being) of each other and of our living biosphere. As investors and philanthropists, we are invited to put our capital to work through the organizations and companies that have inherent within their organizational "DNA" the deep purpose of service, healing, and stewardship. Thus, instead of a singular (and often myopic) view toward "risk-adjusting" our anticipated financial returns, we can embrace the reality of the times in which we're living and choose to make our investment and philanthropic decisions according to the conditions in which we're all operating—one that requires a love of humanity and care for our living planet so that we put our capital to use to stabilize systems, lift-up people, and harmonize our economic activities with the biological realities of our world. Although reality-adjusted returns may appear to yield less in narrow financial terms, they give us all so much more by reversing the pathological hyper-wealth concentration and mitigating the very real risks of wholesale systemic collapse and catastrophic capital destruction, otherwise in store for us.

The Myth of the Invisible Hand and Overgrazing the Commons

Among the best-known "tropes" (or "memes") in economic theory is the "invisible hand" articulated by Adam Smith about 250 years ago. In it, he postulated a ("magical" / *deus ex machina*) force operating in the economy that optimally balances supply and demand for the good of the entire system and society as a whole. However, as has been pointed out by many brilliant thinkers, this myth doesn't hold true when it comes to the "commons"—the "goods" provided by nature or by society itself that aren't "owned" by any individual economic actor (company or person). An oft-cited example is a pasture near a village upon which many shepherds graze their flocks, ultimately collapsing the grassland ecosystem through intensive overgrazing. Each shepherd is a "rational" actor in that he seeks to feed and fatten his herd (as one does whilst shepherding), but in the aggregate, the group as a whole undermines their collective well-being and economic prosperity as the overgrazed field no longer provides fodder for any of their animals whatsoever. This simple metaphor can be applied to commons that we're all reliant upon, but on a global scale instead: the climate, the ocean, the Amazon rainforest, etc. It is in all of our collective interest that we curtail the destructive individual "interests" of invisible hands that are, in the aggregate, wreaking havoc. Let's evolve from invisible hands of destruction to visible hands of stewardship!

This is Not Your Parents' Competitive Advantage

As people worldwide continue to develop conscious awareness of how the products and services we choose to purchase either support our health, well-being, and ecological stewardship or don't, and as we additionally become aware that certain companies are embodying the (Quintenary) Ecocene ethics while others aren't, our purchasing decisions—in other words "consumer demand"—will continue to accrue revenue, scale, and other accretive dimensions of competitive advantage toward Quintenary Ecocene companies and away from the non-ecological and non-humanistic companies.

We Don't Actually Need Everybody on Board for Everybody to Come Along—The 3% Phenomenon

Beneficially "disruptive" [sic] punctuated-equilibrium systems change that results from unprecedented innovation does not require immediate adoption by the masses in order to globalize. As Everett Rogers expounded in his *Diffusion of Innovation Theory*, systems change via technology adoption (and analogues) begins with the "Innovators" who comprise approximately 2.5% of the total population. Then the Early "Adopters" (13.5%), who are often considered "influencers" and have great sway within the broader social, economic, and political fabrics adopt. At this point the rest is nearly inevitable: following statistical bell curve distribution, full-scale adoption (as represented by the two early 20th century photos of New York City in chapter 6, "The Ecology of Competitive Advantage and Market Demand") ensues, moving through the subsequent stages and sub-populations of "Early Majority" (34%), "Late Majority" (34%), and "Laggards" (16%). All of this begins with fewer than 3% of the total population, and, once amplified and accelerated by the self-reinforcing feedback loops of market demand and competitive advantage, (often very) rapidly permeates the entire system. Because of this phenomenon we (1) have great reason to be hopeful, and (2) must roll up our sleeves and get to (joyful, calm, and unhurried) work!

Win/Win—Downside Mitigation and Upside Participation

As we move toward reality-adjusted investing and philanthropy, we will find doors opening to us that allow for tempered participation in shared upside, while we also utilize our capital to help avoid the tremendously capital-destructive downsides that will otherwise strike with greater frequency, intensity, and dislocation at global scales. This is the pathway that affords us the opportunity to "win" while we put our capital to work for all of humanity and indeed all of Earth's ecosystems to likewise "win" with greater stability, safety, prosperity, and thriving.

Understanding the Relativity of Financial Wealth

Most of us may be astounded by the astronomical sums describing the financial property of the wealthiest among us, and too many of us are swept up in the pervasive hallucination that we don't have enough. Like plough horses, we have our blinders on, blind to the realities in our periphery, as we trod and plow our proverbial professional fields. But we must remember: financial wealth is a human construct. However grounded it may be in representing the real, fundamental physical needs for living on the one hand, and sublime in representing the cosmic abundance of divine intelligence on the other hand, money itself, as it is generally structured and utilized at present, is a man-made, finite system of "score-keeping" through which each and every one of us can "measure" our relative position on the continuum from the very poorest to the most astonishingly affluent among the entire living human race. The point is, instead of myopically focusing on gaining *more*, let us pause and consider where we find ourselves in the entire scheme. Are we in the lowest quintile? The highest? How might our professional, philanthropic, and community-cultivation decision-making deepen and develop in intelligence and sophistication as we come to understand our relative position? Is there, as Tom Chi tells us, "Plenty of room in the middle" as it pertains to a fattening of the wealth distribution bell curve? Could we, as the beautiful Basque people have already demonstrated for generations in and around Mondragon, eliminate the extremely long tails at either end of the distribution?

Where Do You Stand?

As is laid out in the "Eyes Wide Open" chapter of this book, we each stand in either the first, second, third, fourth, or fifth quintile, globally speaking (since the UBS Global Wealth Report now includes a further breakdown of the top quartile of the global wealth pyramid—reserved for the astonishingly wealthy—we'll refer to all of the upper tiers of that group as the fifth quintile). If we're in the first, second, or third, we are wise to continue cultivating the other essential, non-financial forms of capital in our communities, while also seeking out the organizations who will help us "leap-frog" as we access knowledge, skills, and tools via the decentralized resources of the digital global commons. If we're in the fourth, we have perhaps the most challenging position, cognitively, as we're likely positioned to earn more, and to focus our attentions on doing so, while considering ourselves lacking what the fifth quintile possesses. And, if we find ourselves in the fifth quintile, we may be in the most challenging spiritual situation, as we likely possess in our hearts and psyches a deeply embedded myth that we don't have enough, which altogether blinds us from how very much we have relative to our global brothers and sisters, and the position of privilege (and responsibility) our situation bestows upon us to do all that we can in these critical times. So, the question is simple: in which quintile do you find yourself, and what are you choosing to do differently as a result of this newfound or newly nuanced knowledge . . . today?

Enough Is Enough! (Is It?)

We must ask ourselves: Is this *enough*? Most especially (but by no means exclusively) those of us in the top two socio-economic quartiles must now ask, in the deepest, most thoughtful manner we are capable of doing: *do I have enough*? Do I have *more than enough*? Can I gain and experience more in the realm of well-being and quality of life—true prosperity—while simultaneously letting go of so much desire, acquisition, and possession (indeed, as if being possessed by the Mammonic spirit)? Can we liberate ourselves from these shackles? Now? Today?

The Stickiest Economic Wicket: Interest

Albert Einstein once called compounding interest the eighth wonder of the world. Several of our ancient spiritual scriptures warn against the use and mis-use of interest between and among neighbors and colleagues in communities. Indeed, several trained and armchair economists alike lament the destructive aspects and attributes of a financialized economic system in which interest and clever derivatives thereof not only undermine the prosperity and well-being of many people and families within the society, but also introduce novel (and often compounding) systemic risk into the fundamentals of the economy itself. There is something wholly unnatural about unfettered compounding interest—as Bernard Lietaer and others have pointed out. On the other hand, however, Nature herself is replete with the regenerative abundance that an ecologically—and ethically—attuned "interest" might come to mimic. Does not the single acorn, in time, come to yield countless thousands of new acorns? How might we otherwise appropriately deploy heaps of capital toward the greater social and environmental good without at least some of the supported endeavors yielding future value back to the capital contributors?

Isn't interest, among other things, a mechanism for spreading risk over time, while augmenting capital availability in the present and immediate future? Are there appropriate bounds in which rates ought to be contained, perhaps somewhere between a few points above and even a few points below zero, as Woody Tasch's *Slow Money* and recent economic conditions have both called for? On reflecting on the role, function, and intrinsic attributes of interest, I'm not sure its wholesale elimination would either be wise or feasible . . . and certainly not from the standpoint of the billions upon trillions of dollars of financial capital eagerly awaiting the appropriate Quintenary-Ecocene economic opportunities into which to deploy. Perhaps this isn't the black-and-white binary of absolutes, but is, like so many complex and nuanced things, a matter of degree and temperance. Perhaps we're well advised to transmute our expectations from "most" and "all" that we might earn via interest into "some" and "fair share" instead. Otherwise, this sticky wicket, interest, might gum up the whole works!

Why Mondragon Matters

It is imperative that we all become aware of a few simple facts: The Mondragon region of Spain was the poorest region in the entire nation fifty years ago and is now the most prosperous. It doesn't exhibit the extreme opulence of other European capitals and casino centers. Nor does it have the concomitant poverty and ghettos hidden away in its invisible corners. Everybody lives in the middle—a very wide and wonderful middle of accountants, artists, engineers, executives, farmers, lawyers, mechanics, philosophers, policy-makers, professors, retailers, and teachers. As Tom Chi commented with respect to Earth systems: there's plenty of room in the middle. And with respect to social-economic systems, Mondragon exemplifies this truth and is a model for all of us—for all of us to learn from, be inspired by, and emulate in our own creative versions and variations. Mondragon is real, it exists, and it is among the very best shining examples of what's possible when we subdue our fear-based quixotic quests for astronomical wealth and casino cash-outs and instead focus on cultivating community and authentic, lasting wealth (well-being) in our own lives and networks of relationships.

Perhaps Pyramids are for Potentizing—Not for Profiteering

There are certain geometries and structures in the extant reality that inherently contain powerful properties, or at least have powerful properties attributed to them. Whether at the molecular scale, the cosmic scale, the technological scale, or the non-specific scale of the Platonic Solids, certain geometric forms either contain intrinsically or have been mythopoetically invested with profound powers for millennia (or both). The pyramid, which in an abstract or approximate form is one-half of the Platonic octahedron, is one of the most notable such structures for our discussion. And, in addition to being a fundamental form within our ancient and modern architectures worldwide, it has become the most pervasive form embedded in and used to describe our monetary, financial, and economic systems, structures, and instruments. Indeed, as Lietaer and others have explored, the U.S. dollar bill has the image of a pyramid emblazoned on it!

Whether within the power pyramids of the Anglo-European slave trade, the Dutch East Indies exploits, the whaling liquidation of over 90% of the world's Cetacea in under two centuries, or countless other colonial, dominator, or liquidation/extraction economic models, the symbol of the pyramid has come to imply concentration of capital, control, and the insidious corruption that seeks to amplify and expand said capital and control. These pyramids are the problem, yes. But pyramids need not be so terribly destructive. Indeed, the pyramid is a powerful geometric form with which we can potentize the bio-photonic life force, the love-wisdom of compassion, and the illumination of self-transcendent service to people and planet. Indeed, in our regenerative Biodynamic practices, we work with pyramidal forms to potentize our alchemical land medicines (including, at certain times of year, land medicines with gold, myrrh, and frankincense), and even more esoterically certain crystalline atomic structures within special crystalline and organic forms that we've come to know can help us restore and steward living ecosystems and enhance the health and well-being (prosperity—true wealth) of humanity. Wouldn't it be far more fun and fruitful to work with the life-augmenting pyramids in this humble, purposeful manner—to serve and heal and protect—instead of exploiting, destroying, and controlling? I believe future generations will better understand that pyramids are for potentizing, not profiteering!

Thinking in Quintiles

When we engage in a deep study of biology and living systems, we come to understand the unique centrality of organizing patterns oriented around groups of five. Whether examining the molecular structure of living DNA or the harmonic frequency between the Earth, Venus, and Sun, we discover the geometry of the pentalpha in this ever-ubiquitous, life-giving organizing principle of the five-part pattern. As surprising as it may be to many of our readers unfamiliar with certain ancient and esoteric wisdom, this knowledge is essential to understanding and caring for life itself. Thus, it is also central to a new way of thinking about our systems and structures of human organization and economy. Hence, thinking in quintiles—five major stakeholder categories in business; five major categories of socio-economic resource access and influence; and the fivefold nature of our own individual well-being and approaches to deep leadership—is one of the great *invitations*, and more and more of us will likely become convinced, *requisites* of deep leadership in the emerging Ecocene epoch.

The New Ecocene VCs—Celebrating Visionary Capitalists

The acronym "VC" has taken on a rather negative connotation among many entrepreneurs, founders, and executive leaders. Indeed, the venture capital model—often deserving of the moniker "vulture capital"—has as its fundamental organizational assumption that most (nearly all) of its investments will fail, and the outsized "unicorn" profits (or capital gains in subsequent rounds and eventual exit) of one or two among 10 or 20 otherwise failed ventures will more than make up for those losses and return hefty upside to investors. Wow, what a structure! Wow, what a set of assumptions! What does this tell us about the churn-and-burn dynamics of a shark-infested capitalist ecosystem in which early-stage entrants are far more likely to crash and burn than succeed? An efficient deployment of capital, you say? The cost of innovation you believe? Is there another way—a better way? Yes . . . there has to be. Let's consider that, inspired by the far kinder (and far more successful, on the whole) nurturing and stewardship capitalist ecosystems of the Mondragons of the world, we might evolve how we do "VC" in the mainstream. Instead of betting on most enterprises failing and one or two running away as financial unicorns, how about we recalibrate to ensure the systems, structures, capitalization, and leadership ethos are in place so that over 80% of the new ventures not only survive but thrive, providing solid livelihoods to their teams while also providing plentiful capital resources to other stakeholders in the closed ecosystem of planet Earth? May we see the scaled-up evolution from Vulture Capitalism to Visionary Capitalism, and may we celebrate those Visionary Capitalists who are taking on the early-mover risks by leading the way!

That's All Well and Good . . . But I Gotta Get Mine First! (We're All Prisoners—A Global Dilemma)

One of the better-known "thought experiments" in the discipline of economics is the "prisoners' dilemma." The scenario is simple, perhaps absurdly so, and gives rise to the "zero-sum" / "negative-sum" thinking (and assumption-making about the human "condition") that has infected our modern world and economy. Lest I get off course for our purposes and run too deep down the rabbit hole of critiquing the overlay of reductionist econometric / "mathematical" / pseudo-scientific thinking that has overtaken the rarefied halls of elite universities, mahogany-lined corporate suites, and marble-floored and columned chambers of government, let me stay on point here. In the prisoner's dilemma, there's a simple "A/B" optionality being played out by two "actors" (the term often ascribed to people and companies in economic theory). Both are prisoners. Each is guaranteed release and freedom if he effectively throws the other under the proverbial bus, but both are able to go free in only one scenario—when each exonerates the other. Can you see where this is headed? It's a classic example of "zero-sum" consciousness, in which, ultimately, the most common outcome is neither "good" for nor desirable by either. Although this is, in my opinion, a terrible pedagogical trope in entry-level study of economics—one that implants a bias of "nastiness" and self-interested human behavior that is detrimental to others, it is actually an apt metaphor for the decision-making many of us face in our careers. Do we choose the red or the blue pill, as it were? That is, do we choose the conventional, mainstream career pathway of "certainty and security" through which we'll likely earn more money but have far less positive impact in service to humanity and planet Earth, or do we choose the other route, knowing that we might end up less "well-off" in narrow financial terms. And, what if the puzzle were compounded in complexity by a variable out of each of our own individual control: the more others choose the path of service and stewardship, the better off we all are, and the "higher" our relative quality of life vis-à-vis monetary earnings (and, the converse would also be true: the more we each choose the former, conventional path, the lower our respective quality of life is vis-à-vis our monetary earnings)? What will you choose?

The Corruption and Misery of "Mean Girl" Social Darwinism Makes for Bad Economics (and Lives)

In *Viriditas*' long soliloquy (a monologue with obvious irony for those who have read Rand's *Atlas*), having accessed and interpreted all of humanity's historical record (including the Vatican library and other "secret" archives), the now fully activated artificial intelligence known as OTTO concludes decisively: "A most pernicious and insidious evil was introduced into the collective human consciousness: a quasi-political-economic-philosophy maxim that 'Greed is good.' And although she built her terrible scourge atop a tradition stretching back at least to Niccolò Machiavelli and countless despotic monarchs, magnates, and potentates, it was the author Alisa Zinovyevna Rosenbaum who would capture the imaginations and minds of so many humans in the 20th century. In the course of two well-known novels, *The Fountainhead* and *Atlas Shrugged*, she would, under the nom-de-plume 'Ayn Rand' feed a nasty, mean-spirited, domination-style, 'winner-take-all' ethos that would infuse the highest levels of finance, industry, government, and concentrated pools of capital." Often celebrated as "Social Darwinism," (though poor Darwin deserves not the blame) this misguided and ultimately suicidal (at soul and species levels), dysfunctional worldview is embedded in the economics of Milton Friedman (and many others) and therefore infused throughout our assumptions and structures of late 20th century political-economics. Economist and diplomat Kenneth Galbraith minced no words when he asserted "The modern conservative is engaged in one of man's oldest exercises in moral philosophy; that is, the search for a superior moral justification for selfishness." Ayn Rand is no hero—if you disagree, I implore you to read Lisa Duggan's *Mean Girl* and then reconsider. The corruption and misery of "mean girl" (and ruffian "bro culture"), Social Darwinism makes for bad economics, lousy culture, and miserable lives.

Get the Scalpel—Cutting Out the Arriviste Attitudes and Cynical "Effective Altruism" Excuse-Making

Like a cancerous mass needing excism, the so-called "effective altruism" of Wetiko tech-bro culture is both *weak* and *mean*. The arriviste attitude that refuses to help humanity in need, but simultaneously burns billions on political-economic boondoggles, is a shame—and a cancer on society. I remember when my friend David Beasley (whom I first met at an incredibly moving week-long peace and reconciliation conference in the Balkans, and who later recorded a podcast episode with me while heading up the UN World Food Programme, which was awarded the Nobel Peace Prize under his leadership) revealed this particularly virulent cancer for the whole world to see. In the immediate aftermath of the Covid pandemic, food insecurity among Earth's most vulnerable people skyrocketed, nearly tripling the millions on the verge of serious malnutrition and/or outright starvation (to 270 million total). Responding to this humanitarian crisis, Beasley implored the world's stratospherically rich to contribute a total of $6 billion (a paltry amount, really, relative to the $14 *trillion* owned by the world's richest 2,600 individuals, and $208+ *trillion* owned by the world's wealthiest 1%), and, congratulating Elon Musk on then becoming the wealthiest individual on the planet, was profoundly disheartened by the way Musk responded. Instead of saying something like, "yes, of course I'll help, and I'll encourage my peers to as well), Musk made a public spectacle with this preposterous response that he'd contribute if Beasley could prove doing so would eradicate poverty and hunger permanently. Really?!? Is that who we are? "I'll only help you if you assure me that you'll never need any help ever again." (?) My word. Our Friedman cum Ayn Randian disregard for the disenfranchised is a sickness—a mental illness. So-called "effective altruism" of the Sam Bankman-Frieds and Elon Musks of the world is a smoke-and-mirrors sham. We must celebrate caring for one another—most especially for the poorest and most vulnerable among us—only then can we hope to be considered fully developed—and actually adulting—human beings. Only then.

We Don't Need More Spaceships, "Superheroes," or Self-Aggrandizement!

Instead of waxing loquacious on this one, I'm going to be extremely concise—employing an economy of words appropriate to aphoristic musings.
By no means would I criticize space travel outright, nor any form of peace-
based scientific exploration in general. Indeed, astronomy and astrophysics
are among my favorite hobbies! But let's be real, folks. In a world beset by
polycrisis, in which our social change-making and ecological restoration and
stewardship are encountering blow-back (!) and outright weaponized antipa-
thy from kleptocratic, oligarchic, and nationalistic misanthropes, we are wise
to temper our fetishizing of rocket ship "superheroes" and self-aggrandizing
spaceship sycophancy. We need on-the-ground action, facilitated and curated
by grounded, humble, servant leaders and the cultural fabric of Earth steward
aristocracy that celebrates community, conviviality, cooperation, and systemic
care-ful-ness; not the compassionless arriveste demagoguery too commonly
encountered these days.

Does the Death Star Pay Better?

In my mid-forties as I write this, I'm struck by how very many of my good
buddies and contemporaries express deep dissatisfaction and even some sort
of despair at their professional lives and lifestyles, now decades in the making.
I notice this seems to be most pronounced among those friends and colleagues
who have advanced degrees and "prestigious" careers: legal, finance, consulting,
executive management, and other rarified quaternary roles. Whereas some of
my other friends and colleagues, lower down on the earnings and net assets
spectrum might tend to blame their professional superiors, their circumstances,
their luck, or some combination thereof, the former are inclined to recognize
that they, in many respects, have only themselves to "blame" for their current
circumstances . . . if "blame" is really necessary. So why do they persist in the
career paths that they have chosen, often either subconsciously or very explicitly
wishing to do something that would more directly make the world a better
place and make their own satisfaction, creative fulfillment, sense of purpose,
and quality of life better to boot? Perhaps it's all about the money: they like
the pay. So many of us are essentially working in and on the "Death Star"—to
borrow one of our most recognizable cultural memes for effect—instead of
working on the less lucrative fringes like Endor to improve our shared future.
You see my friends, it is time that we come to understand some of the even more
profound wisdom of George Lucas' deep wisdom-tradition-Jung-influenced
Nietzschean-proto-regenerative and liberation-ecology-narrative told by the
world's greatest luminaries that have come down to us through a succession
of the ages: by and large it is WE who are the workers in the Death Star. Think
about that. Don't you remember wondering as a kid, "Why would all those

workers choose to be in the employ of Darth Vader and the evil Sith Overlord?" Guess what . . . now you know why!

Reclaiming True Wealth

This term "wealth" has come to mean how much money, proxies for money, and material possessions we each own. However, the term didn't always bear such a meaning. Instead, wealth, from the Middle English term *Wele*, meant well-being, and is the very same word from which the term wellness derives. Thus, we are each invited to reclaim what is meant by wealth—true wealth—as we heal our bodies, our minds, and our spirits, and cultivate a culture of sacred stewardship together.

Alchemy of Money: Love, Kindness, and Transmuting Economic Lead into Gold

In one way or another, humans have long sought to turn lead into gold. The alchemists were literal in this pursuit, endeavoring to crack the veiled sub-atomic secret of these two adjacent elements, one of course being far more desirable than the other for its intrinsic as well as its economic value. However, a subtler version of this alchemy has been at play throughout the ages as well: the transmutation of our baser cores into something far more sublime and luminous. Indeed, as we undergo the great transformation from the Anthro-pocene to the Ecocene, the metaphor is apt and the invitation is clear: we are called to do the inner work of transforming our baser, "reptilian" impulses of fear-induced fight or flight instincts into an expansive radiance—the gold which we're invited to cultivate is the gold of the heart, the gold of service, the gold of realizing and experiencing profound joy, safety, prosperity, and tranquility as we work in service to our healing planet and in care of our shared human family through love and kindness.

The Future of Money

We can understand "money" to have evolved through three epochs thus far. The first is actually the "moneyless" epoch of gifting and barter, which slowly evolved into certain precious items (chocolate, seashells, stones, and metals) emerging as a "proxy" for exchanged value. The second epoch is characterized by culture-wide trading of these naturally precious items, taking on a "cur-rency" of exchange. The third epoch is characterized by a symbol or conceptual expression of the value sometimes recorded in clay, sometimes on paper, and sometimes (more recently) in the digital ethers when the value of the exchange, and the underlying tangible bounty of Earth used to represent the value (gold, chocolate, etc.) is substituted by abstract information. History shows a many-millennia-long story in which governing powers sought to establish and maintain stability and foster prosperity through their administration of money, culminating in the central banking and federal fiat currencies of the past century or two.

But what does the future of money hold in store for us? This question, like what does the ecological restoration of our planet look like in totality and what does space exploration hold, is full of mystery, possibility, and imagination. How might we envision and create a novel way of establishing and stewarding "money" for the fundamental purpose of caring for people and for our living planet Earth? This may well be the most profound spiritual question, the most pressing realpolitik matter, and the most elemental aspect of the global regeneration renaissance. And we're not without a polestar. Our dear departed friend, Bernard Lietaer, has devoted a lifetime to this very matter, and has bequeathed to us a rich, reliable body of work—a body of work that must guide our efforts. With a pragmatic yet poetic humor, Bernard named the great opus within this body of work exactly what we're talking about: *The Future of Money.*

Doughnuts, Balloons, Blue Sky, and Childlike Joy

Who doesn't love a doughnut? Although perhaps not the best symbol for a healthful diet, it is for many of us the perfect symbol for childhood joy. Of course, so are balloons—floating overhead against the backdrop of a bluebird sky . . . perhaps with some pillowy cartoon clouds bobbing here and there. What placid, joyful, delicious memories do you cherish from your childhood? Imagine a world in which we continue to experience such easeful joy on the regular as adults, and in which this is the most common worldwide experience of our fellow humans. In her important book, *Doughnut Economics*, Kate Raworth articulates a comprehensive framework in which the stewardship of our complex social and environmental systems brings them into balance. That is, we're no longer "squeezing the balloon" (or, "smashing the doughnut"?), and are instead managing the optimal conditions for the cultivation of widespread prosperity, ecological restoration, and economic vitality.

The Survival of the Happiest

Maria Rodale, the former CEO of the Rodale publishing empire (before selling), and author of *Love, Nature, Magic*, writes that being a gardener and a CEO are not that different, and that, on the whole, it is not survival of the "fittest" but survival of the happiest that best characterizes the living ecosystems of our gardens, our businesses and our economies. And, as she writes, we probably ought to ask ourselves: "Am I happy?" To which, we hope more and more of us will resoundingly respond: YES! "If you're happy and you know it . . ." "People, can you feel it . . . love is everywhere."—The Allman Brothers, "Revival"

C-Suite Coherence Councils Sweeten the Deal

During a year-long Holistic Visions training program curated by the Le Ciel Foundation in Europe, some of my colleagues (and now friends) and I focused on strategies to transform financial systems. And guess what emerged in our creative work together? In order to achieve any meaningful systems-change-making "out there," we have to get at the heart of our interpersonal dynamics, and lay a foundation within our human webworks of collaborative relationships. Just as Fritjof Capra writes about in *Hidden Connections*, there's an inner ecology of awakening available to us and necessary for group genius to emerge with the potency and efficacy needed in these times. For generations we have conducted business and conducted the capital games of competitive advantage within borders—national boundaries, corporate domains, and even liminal borders of our hearts and minds. The preponderance of our economic behaviors and constructs are steeped in militaristic patterns of domination and defense, which understandably trigger the sympathetic neurobiological response of fight or flight—anathema to the complex creativity requisite to solve the polycrisis challenges we face, let alone an impossible condition-set from which we might hope to engender the transformation needed for planetary prosperity. So how do we retrench and retrain this generations-deep impulse at work to one degree or another within each and every one of us? We cultivate *coherence*. Although an emerging field and discipline, there are already ample resources available to us, including the Institute of HeartMath's work as described in *The HeartMath Solution*. The Le Ciel Foundation also has many resources and trainings available (see References), and we're witnessing advisors, consultants, and practitioners emerging world-wide who are offering their techniques and guidance to community groups, civic institutions, and corporations alike. Coherence is not only a powerful pathway to impact and prosperity, it is also a delightful living discipline of inner and interpersonal dimensions that allows us to work and play with far greater tranquility, clarity, and joy.

Gardens, Flowers, Healers, and Paintings

Some of us more econometrically minded thinkers might assume that the data associated with an emergent Ecocene Economic evolution would be complex, arcane, and subtle. Sure, we'll likely be increasingly tracking multi-variable "buckets" of social and ecological metrics as we manage our global economy together. But it doesn't have to be so hard to discern, only allowing the advanced mathematicians, data scientists, and business executives to understand the picture. There's a far simpler way of envisioning, pursuing, and measuring our relative success in achieving robust, well-functioning Ecocene Economics: how many flourishing gardens, flower farmers, holistic healers, and fine art painters are making a solid living with their life works and offerings? You might think these are frivolities—or "luxuries" only available (at least with any frequency) to the financial elite. Not true. Remember, economics is a design discipline—the result of constructed human ethics, expectations, and attitudes—not a science. A healthy human economy will, of course, have many things of beauty (like flowers, gardens, and paintings) and will cultivate as a central aim—a *raison d'être*—the health and well-being of its members. This is both an ethical and an aesthetic renaissance.

Voltaire Was Right—Il Fait Cultivar Notre Jardin!

Let us cultivate our gardens! Let us cultivate our gardens, both literally and figuratively! When we grow food and flowers, trees and pollinator habitat in our immediate surroundings, connecting with the profound intelligence (and neurobiochemical "super-boosters") of soil and water and viriditas life-force, we are smarter, healthier, happier, and closer to true freedom. This is the deep source, the wellspring that fills our hearts and minds and spirits with something so precious, so valuable, it defies quantification. And, this applies metaphorically to our "ecology of thinking" as well. That is, in addition to cultivating our literal, "visible" gardens, we must cultivate our "invisible" mental gardens too. As I wrote about in *Y on Earth* in the chapter titled "Think" (which of course followed "Listen" and preceded "Speak"), to become expert in cultivating (both nourishing and defending) our inner landscapes of consciousness is one of the most important tasks of our entire lives—we would not be incorrect in naming it as *the* task. Be careful about what you invite in—take care of your garden!

On Tulips, T-Bills, and Bitcoins

The great tulip mania in 17th-century Holland was one of the most outlandish economic bubbles in recorded history. People literally sold everything they had—houses and horses alike—in order to speculate in the casino bubble of increasingly rare tulips. Yes, tulips: flowers whose ephemeral beauty belonged to a strange and fleeting asset class in one of the most bizarre economic bubbles ever recorded. Fortunes were made and lost on delicate blooms' colorful stripes and rare color combinations. The bubble eventually collapsed, of course, leaving many in ruins. What does this have to do with our world today? Chasing other "pretty, shiny" objects, as if obsessed, too many of us have converted the emerging technologies of distributed ledgers and blockchain into speculative bubbles. We must remember that in Bernard Lietaer's *Future of Money*, in the most harmonious, beautiful, and sustainable scenario he predicted, a robust basket of digital currencies backed by real-world behaviors, functions, and measures of ecosystem integrity were instrumental. Let's curtail our desire to be "winners" in the global casinos of crypto, EFTs, T-bills, and all other financial instruments, old and new, and instead become winners of life while building and stewarding stabilizing forces through our innovative currency systems. Let's emancipate ourselves from these speculative casinos and learn to cultivate durable, pervasive systems by, of, and for widespread winning.

As We Fix the Game, We Conspire with Subtle Forces and Make Our Own Odds

There is a rich tradition of esotericists, Hermeticists, and Gnostics that focuses *attention* on what's *possible* when the *will* is cultivated to a high degree, oriented around *service to the greater good*. Though arcane, these streams of unconventional knowledge and wisdom, flowing to us through a succession of the ages, have positively influenced our modern world and have delivered many of the leveling and egalitarian political economic structures we might take for granted. Among their frameworks, as famously articulated by Goethe with his "making the weather" adage, is an understanding that our wills, properly aligned with the greater *will-to-good* of *love-wisdom* (which wants to expand, diversify, and amplify), can influence the fabric of shared reality. This has been a precious "secret" of the mystics, seers, and deep-time influencers, perhaps longer than any of us really remembers. From Mondragon's advanced engineering cooperatives to the remarkable off-grid sophistication of Gaviotas in Colombia, the willful ingenuity of our human spirit, rooted in service to the greater good, allows us to bend the flowing rivers of destiny toward better outcomes—changing the "odds" as it were that planetary prosperity becomes an inevitability. Be careful, however, to conspire with said subtle forces if and only if you are confident in your commitment to the greater good, and are—eyes open—increasingly aware of your foibles, susceptibilities, and weaknesses, lest you fall into the very real (and very often encountered) trap of self-delusion. For indeed, with appropriately precautionary humility, we will learn to "fix" the game, making our own odds as we conspire (literally "breathe together") with potent, subtle forces . . . and each other.

On Unicorns, Butterflies, and Forest Ecosystems

As investors, many of us have become trained by the prevailing cultural and market dynamics to seek out "unicorn" opportunities—those that experience extraordinary growth and capital accretion and, thus, deliver outsized returns to investors, especially those of us who, whether through special knowledge, exceptional foresight, or sheer luck (or some combination thereof) got in early. The reality, though, is that current market dynamics and perceived self-interest (of deeply vested interests) pick winners and losers not necessarily out of concern for the greater prosperity of humanity or the broader stewardship of our planet, but out of the establishment, preservation, and continuation of existing power and wealth-concentration dynamics. If we are to turn the corner toward the

Ecocene, and thus *all* experience the upside of new economic developments while mitigating the downside of catastrophic capital destruction, we would be wise to seek out those "unicorns" that are structured not for the extreme economic benefit of a select few, but for the broader good of the world and all human beings. Thus, we need to seek out those emerging unicorns that are themselves embedded with the wisdom of the entire forest ecosystems themselves, to extend the metaphor. And, with respect to those already established institutions that have arisen and attained market dominance leading up to and during the Anthropocene, we have the metaphor of the butterfly to aid us. That is, the entrenched institutions, through exemplary Ecocene leadership and the pressures of a more enlightened demand-driven marketplace, have the opportunity to transform from Anthropocene caterpillars into Ecocene Butterflies. Logic necessitates a future either of scorched forests or of restored Edens with these unicorns and butterflies abounding.

It's All About the Aesthetics, Sweetheart! (Toward an Economy of Beauty)

When then presidential candidate William Jefferson Clinton uttered the wide-reaching phrase during a nationally-televised presidential debate with incumbent president (and former CIA director) George Herbert Walker Bush, Clinton gave voice to a sometimes less apparent political-economic truth: "It's about the economy, stupid." While the term "stupid" may have revealed a generational disrespect not uncommon among the Beatles-Braless-Baby Boomer generation which Clinton was the first to represent in the Oval Office, his point was unmistakable: the economic prosperity of the American populace (or lack thereof) was (and is) often the paramount item of concern among the voting electorate. The same is surely true today, but as people are increasingly growing weary and harried by a surfeit of creature comforts, strip-mall stimuli, information access (and excess), technological oblivion, advertising onslaughts, and comfortable numbness, we have lost *beauty* in our lives. We are living in a momentous time in which we have the opportunity (and the imperative) to restore beauty ubiquitously. As we evolve our priorities toward the supreme humanistic archetypes of beauty, truth, wisdom, and love, our relative progress will be measured in flowers and forest sanctuaries. We get to green our neighborhoods and cities. We get to slow down, connect with nature, destress, plant (and enjoy!) flowers, and work and reside in buildings made with pleasing, natural materials. We get to cultivate a *"ministry of beauty"* a la Demeter, Dionysus, Dendrites, Anthios, Eleutherios, and Shekinah saturation, and as anticipated in the *Secret Teachings of All Ages*, the beauty surrounding us will nurture and amplify the beauty within us, raising up humanity into higher heights of the humble luminosity foretold by the ancients. When we realize the potency of the *"beautifying principle,"* and apply it broadly, we will foster a "heaven on Earth" experience, a Golden Age renaissance whose best proxies are the Edens of our legends, our living garden sanctuaries, and the imprinted genetic memories of our ancestors' real-world wilderness surroundings where oil of joy dew drops glisten with golden light. It's all about the beauty, my friends, or, echoing Clinton with an updated, kinder, gentler message: it's all about the aesthetics, sweetheart!

PART TWO—CULTURE AND SOCIETY

On the Math of Systems Transformation

There's an apparent paradox in the emerging Ecocene economics of the regeneration renaissance—but it's only apparent. While the Ecocene is marked, by definition, by widespread systems and structures that embody care and compassion for all human and non-human inhabitants of Earth (and perhaps beyond—but let's not get distracted from the fundamental mission in these particular times!), that is, it concerns all of us—not all of us are required to pivot and guide us in its direction. No, we only need a critical mass, a preponderance. Because the structures, systems, and institutions of our political economies are subject to ecosystem and network dynamics, changes made by a certain subset of actors will result in the entire system—or set of systems—altogether changing themselves. It's not as if the entire global population in one or two years in the early 20th century collectively (and consciously) decided that it was time to switch from horses to automobiles . . . but it happened . . . swiftly. No, that was the work of a smaller number . . . And, the beauty of our times and task is that a relatively small number of us will tip the scales, and, with each new day the momentum in the direction of an evolved consciousness, an expanded compassion, and an amplifying regeneration and stewardship ethos will ensue (indeed this is already underway). The systems math of our revolution requires not the ubiquity, nor even the majority . . . it requires only us—each of us—the critical mass . . . Rejoice!

Imaginal Cells, Transmutation, and Adversity in Metamorphosis

Many of us are familiar with the veritable "transmutation" that butterflies undergo after their caterpillar bodies decompose inside the chaotic goo of their chrysalises and "imaginal cells" emerge to guide the creation of an entirely different lifeform. But perhaps lesser known is the protracted "conflict" that arises between the caterpillar's waning immune system and the butterfly's nascent imaginal cells (developing out of "imaginal disc" precursors). As Augusto Cuginotti writes in his "Imaginal Cells" article, summarizing an exchange with evolutionary biologist and systems scientist Elisabet Sahtouris, "It took a long time for biologists to understand the reason for the immune system attack on the incipient butterfly cells, but eventually they discovered that the butterfly has its own unique genome, carried by the caterpillar, inherited from long ago in evolution, yet not part of it as such." Recounting Elisabet Sahtouris' reflection upon this phenomenon, Cuginotti continues, "If we see ourselves as imaginal discs working to build the butterfly of a better world, we will understand that we are launching a new 'genome' of values and practices to replace that of the current unsustainable system. We will also see how important it is to link with each other in the effort, to recognize how many different kinds of imaginal cells it will take to build a butterfly with all its capabilities and colors." Indeed, let us not be dismayed by any apparent adversity in the seeming chaos, but forge ahead knowing that, as trillions of butterflies have already shown, the metamorphic goop will soon take flight.

Neuro-Mycelial Fabrics Are Foundational to Planetary Prosperity

In many respects, science is finally catching up to the cosmic truths understood and preserved in ancient indigenous and esoteric knowledge traditions. Recently, Italian scientists Vazza and Feletti published an astonishing determination in *Frontiers in Physics* called "The Quantitative Comparison Between the Neuronal Network and the Cosmic Web," in which they shared their watershed findings that (1) the distribution of matter at the most macrocosmic scale mirrors to a high degree of statistical significance the distribution of matter in human (neural-network) brain tissue, that (2) the data and science therefore suggest the entire cosmic web is itself akin to a living neuronal network, probabilistically capable of consciousness, and that (3) emerging science regarding the super-micro realm of the sub-quantum fabric is indicating a similar pattern. In other words, on both ends of the vast spectrum of scale—approximately 60+ orders of magnitude between the ultra-small Planck length and super large cosmic scale of the observable universe—the distribution of matter indicates the same neuronal networks we find in living brain tissue of advanced species. Of course, the neural-network like filaments of fungi mycelia follow a similar pattern in the soil, and connect the world's terrestrial forests and grasslands together in massive super-networks. In essence, as Otto-Gaia and Mama-Gaia revealed to us in my novel *Viriditas*, we are enveloped in, constructed of, and experiencing consciousness through "neuronal networks, animated by filaments, spheres, discs, vortices, and toroids [. . .] the fundamental pattern of living intelligence, pervading all of phenomenal cosmic reality. This is evident at every scale: the most macro cosmic scale of the known universe, the medial scale of neural tissue in the brains of advanced species, and at the minutest subatomic scale in the structures of the quantum field. From here, at all these impregnated scales, springs forth the animating life force, the awesome intelligence, and the super-consciousness of reality—the Great Spirit, the Akash, the Shekinah—the fundamental causal expression of 'is-ness' and the Source of all life." It is upon this neuro-mycelial fabric pattern that we will biomimetically model our structures and technologies as we step toward the Ecocene, developing and deploying strategies for planetary prosperity.

Our Emerging Meta-Industrial Culture Enables the Regeneration Renaissance

In the 1970s, William Irwin Thompson wrote a compelling essay called "The Meta-Industrial Village," in which he envisioned (the soon-to-be ubiquitous and ever-miniaturizing) digital technology to foster a global renaissance of communication, information-sharing, and decentralized education, all while communities worldwide evolved in the direction of regional ecological and agricultural stewardship patterns. Although outside the purview of most mainstream media, this vision is underway today, and, albeit in niches and sanctuaries, these are emerging worldwide by the thousands if not millions already. Now, however, by further leveraging the power of our consumer demand, and marrying that with the heart-centered and more evolved regenerative finance, social enterprise, and stewardship philanthropy structures and strategies described herein, we are poised to help propel the mainstream directionality of our global marketplace toward a decentralized—though profoundly interconnected—way of living and conducting the business of life here on Earth. But these strategies and structures are only the outward manifestation of something truly sublime that is also underway—the awakening of human hearts throughout all echelons of business and society, such that millions of us are choosing to move in the direction of a kinder, gentler meta-industrial reality. This, my friends, is what makes up the fertile soils of the *Regeneration Renaissance* that has sprouted up and is now growing globally.

In many respects, the industrial culture of the past two centuries—the underpinnings of the Anthropocene—had embedded in it the deep biases, structures, and institutional pathologies of feudalism, slavery, colonialism, and inquisitions that have horrified our world for too many generations, sometimes through overt fascism and far more often through the veiled and covert mechanisms of anonymized, "rational" markets. Now, our transition from the Anthropocene into the Ecocene carries with it the promise of a transition from industrial to meta-industrial culture. Through meta-industrial connectivity, we are each invited to connect in local and regional guilds and societies that are linked up via global neuronal networks to a worldwide web of caring people, convivial cohorts, and compassionate institutions—flowering, as it were—in the Regeneration Renaissance.

Sustainability Is Regenerative!

Like we see with the terms *wealth* and *aristocracy*, the term *sustainability* has been too often abandoned or eschewed as a result of inaccurate and inappropriate usages. We shouldn't abandon terms just because they're being misappropriated and misused but should insist on their correct use, and (moreover) demonstrate such with emphasis! Sustainability by definition means regenerative—it cannot work any other way. As it concerns human social-economic activity in the aggregate, the only way anything can be sustainable, requires, *ipso facto*, fundamentally regenerative behaviors, structures, and strategies. Sustainability is necessarily regenerative, otherwise, "sustainability" is a misnomer!

"Human" Etymology

There's often great insight that we can gain by exploring the etymology of words. The origins and history of our word "human" are of particular importance in the context of our shared evolutionary journey. The term has a complex and many-faceted story running—like colorful threads through a beautiful tapestry—through many cultural and linguistic traditions. At its root, the word is found in the ancient "PIE" (proto-Indo-European) "Ur" languages with which our Greek, Hebrew, Latin, Germanic, Celtic, English, Sanskrit, Persian, Slavic, Indic, Anatolian, and Baltic languages all share common ancestry. And, as the *Online Etymology Dictionary* points out, the meaning of "human" is both beautiful and significant, especially within the context of our book: "of or relating to the Earth, the soil, the clay," and, also important, "humane, philanthropic, kind, gentle, polite, learned, refined, civilized." How human are we, really? How human do we want to be?

On Oikos—Essential for the Ecocene

Another essential word that informs and inspires our shared evolutionary journey is the ancient Greek term *oikos*. Although yes, a clever brand name for a yogurt company, which many of us immediately associate with the word, *oikos* has a much more profound and important signification. Oikos is the root word from which both our words "economy" and "ecology" derive. It means "home" . . . let that sink in: the word means "home." It also has implicit in it the concept, reality, and experience of "community"—of "relationship." In ancient Greece, we would have referred to both our abode as our "oikos" and to the front room or area of that home as the "oikos" of the dwelling—the place where we would receive, introduce, converse with, and relate to our friends, neighbors, and extended family members. This is the fundamental suggestion of ecology and economy: understanding and caring for our home and each other.

On Understanding Seven-Generation Decision-Making and Five-Generation Clusters of Familiarity

In my book *Y on Earth*, I describe my own ethnic heritage as an admixture of Germanic, Slovenian, Celtic, Anglo-Saxon, and Mohawk Indian—or Kanien'kehá:ka, the People of the Flint and the Keepers of the Eastern Gate—one of the tribes comprising the great Iroquois Confederacy. The Haudenosaunee (Iroquois) Confederacy, one of the great many regional confederations found throughout the globe and throughout time (like the Hanseatic League in northern Europe, the Helvetian Confederation of Switzerland, the Medieval stonemason guilds, and the Xiongnu confederation in Asia), developed (and still maintain) advanced forms of governance and social systems, which includes, famously, future-focused decision-making that considers impacts upon the next seven generations to come. This is perhaps the best "model" or specific conceptual framework for sound long-term decision-making that we have.

But why seven generations? Why not six . . . or eight . . . or ten? When, as a teenager, I first learned of this concept, my assumption was that seven was arbitrary. It wasn't until a few years later when my then-baby daughter Osha, who was playing in my grandmother's (her great-grandmother's) arms, that it dawned on me: when a person has direct relationship with her great-grandparents and her great-grandchildren, this familial lineage spans a total of seven generations. Seven generations is the likely maximum we'll know directly (with any real memories), that thus as we ourselves transit time toward elderhood, not only consider our impacts on the lives of our children and grandchildren but also on theirs, including many whom we won't meet in person. However, since we don't generally have much time to get to know our great-grandparents or our great-grandchildren, a five-generation cluster within those seven generations is a likelier span in which we'll have ample conversations, memories, and conscious influence of experience—our grandparents, parents, children, and grandchildren. Profoundly different from the month-by-month and quarter-by-quarter "decision-making" (is it true decision-making? . . . Really? Or superficial reactionism?) so commonly dominating business and financial behavior, long-term seven-generation decision-making and the cultivation of five-generation clusters of inter-generational knowledge and wisdom transfer is a foundational requirement in a healthy, sustainable society.

If It's Only for Our Families, It's Not Even "for" Them

How do we, at the granular scale of our own lives and families, know whether we're aligning with broader planetary prosperity? One simple question we can ask ourselves is: Are we doing what we're doing just for ourselves and our immediate families? The answer to this question has profound consequences, as is clear in the teachings of the Nazarene and other spiritual luminaries throughout the ages, and very recently in the research of Dr. Cloninger. If we're deficient in the "self-transcendence" that equates to serving the greater good, let us take the first step in recognizing this shortfall, and from there the path toward serving the greater good will unfold before us, should we orient our own personal wills with the trans-personal will-to-good. Otherwise, in this time of planetary polycrisis, concerning ourselves only with the wellbeing of our own families and immediate familiars is insufficient. If it's only for our families, it's not even "for" them.

Celebrating Our Forebears while Changing the Bathwater

We hear the expression "don't throw the baby out with the bathwater," and have some general idea of what this means. But, within the context of the Regeneration Renaissance—working in service to the future—it isn't so much the babies as it is the old folks (and their ideas, systems, and legacies) that we're contending with—mostly the old folks of bygone centuries, old folks not now living but long dead whose ideas have had lasting impacts—*legacy*, as it were. We need to, and are invited to change much of this legacy . . . but let us not demonize our forebears. Instead, let us consider that they, too, were doing their best in a complex and changing world. Sure, we might heap criticism on the Bretton Woods institutions (and it is not surprising that the BRICs and others aren't fans), but let us not forget that one of the primary inspirations and impulses moving through the establishment of those structures and systems was an earnest endeavor to ensure market and monetary stability going forward and to prevent the conditions that led to fascist regimes and the horrors and atrocities of the first and second world wars. We are invited to imagine and create something better without denigrating that which has come before (and those who have done their best in previous eras). And, as slavery has been a scourge of nearly every culture and region at some point in time or another, affecting all of us and infecting all of us with its insidious, traumatic imprints, let us liberate ourselves from the mental viruses of supremacy and xenophobia and instead cultivate the planetary humanism and sacred reverence due all of creation—thereby healing the wounds of the past, purifying the cultural waters, and fulfilling our ancestors' greatest hopes for the future.

The Sheer Lunacy of Accelerationism—Or Giving Due Reverence to Stability While We Can

There's a profoundly imprudent world-view that advocates for drastic intensification of capitalistic growth and technological advances in order to destabilize existing social and economic systems throughout the world (with the naïve and subconsciously sadistic expectation that such destabilization will give rise to newer better systems). Of course, it goes without saying that we require many "disruptive" innovations—so long as they are rooted in an ethics of planetary prosperity. But to seek out the systemic destruction advocated by Accelerationism is to wish the madness and mayhem of scenarios like *Mad Max* upon society (at best—that fictitious story had to pass through the "decency" filters of the Motion Picture Association's Classification and Ratings Administration, after all!). Systems collapse almost certainly leads to power grabs by lawless thugs who would exploit hegemony and violence (at whatever scale they can, whether hyper-local or global) to achieve whatever hedonistic and sinister desires they may have. Even the flawed fiats of central banks and fraught institutions of Bretton Woods and the Petro-Dollar pillars being chipped away by the BRICs block have been stabilizing forces through the Cold War and beyond. Sure, profound systems change is essential to our shared future, but we're wise to celebrate stability wherever we have it, still, as we work to change whatever we can in methodical and regeneratively stabilizing ways—soft landings through kind, compassionate intelligence, not wanton destruction.

Intergenerational Knowledge Transfer Is Now at a Unique Bi-Directional Nexus

Intergenerational knowledge transfer is endemic to life. It occurs in the simplest species via genetic code sharing. And, in more complex species it occurs through memory and communication, enabled by electro-chemical messages as in the case of fungi and plants, and language and culture among animals. This is true with birds, bees, wolves, whales, and, one of my very favorites: great bison. As I shared in the chapter "Listen" in *Y on Earth*, I was regaled of a most remarkable story by my dearly departed Permaculture mentor, Scott Pittman, who shared a bison bone broth with me while I visited his home in Pojoaque, New Mexico several years ago. What he shared with me blew my mind. The bison bones that Scott had simmering atop his adobe home stove (this batch rich in minerals particularly suited to his advanced age), were from a rancher in Iowa named Bob Jackson who had managed bison herds in Yellowstone National Park for years. Throughout the seasons, Jackson observed the behavior of the herds very closely and came to realize that they had a complex culture and communication framework in which the elder bison instructed the younger as to which herbs, barks, and roots were helpful for a variety of mineralization, immune, digestive, and general health requirements. Indeed, as they age and mature, elder bison teach younger mother bison how to optimize nutrition for gestation, childbirth, and nursing; and the very old show aging individuals which plants are best for arthritis, stiffness, pain, and the like. It should be no surprise, of course, but for the preponderance of those among us who have grown up in the nature-deficit milieu of modernity this news could come as a big surprise. Animals pass knowledge through the ages in a pattern we call "intergenerational knowledge transfer." Yes, animals including humans! With language, glyphs, books, and now all manner of multi-media communication, this is of course an extremely robust phenom within our human species—so much so that it has in many ways overwhelmed our connection to and ability to learn from other species (aka nature deficit disorder—more on that elsewhere). This pattern is typically unidirectional: the knowledge flows one way from older to younger members of the species. However, at this peculiar moment in our history, the intergenerational knowledge transfer has become markedly bi-directional. That is, among those of us in the generation that straddles the advent of the internet, and more recently the generation that straddles the advent of artificial intelligence, the adoption, proficiency, and even simple knowledge of our ever-accelerating technological tool sets are concentrating among ever-younger members of society. Our youngers now teach the older folks among us (some, but certainly not all, of whom deserve the earned and reverential term *elder*). I discussed this unique moment in our technological evolution to some degree in the chapter "Unplug" in *Y on Earth*, and it deserves far more attention than I have myself given it. Indeed, as we cross the bridge from the Anthropocene to the Ecocene, not only do we require robust bi-directional intergenerational knowledge transfer, especially in terms of equipping our wiser elders with the capabilities provided by technology when wielded with beneficence; but—and just as important—we must encourage our younger members to slow down, gain perspective, cultivate humility, and awaken to the extraordinary wealth of experience, knowledge, and wisdom available to us from our elders—both living and passed on, the latter through books (please read!) and other historic archives to which we have access). In these times, it is imperative that we learn from each other in a deliberate, disciplined, and ample manner . . . all of us!

Leveling Up—Joining the Do-Good Guild

Millions upon millions of us worldwide understand the fundamental importance of kindness, conviviality, respect, reciprocity, reverence, and responsibility. This is foundational to co-creating the Ecocene—the systems, structures, and technologies, certainly, and most importantly the cultural ethos, the milieu, the relational field of agreement governing both our personal behavior and our interactions with our humanity—our fellow brothers and sisters here on planet Earth, as well as all her other myriad living creatures. How do we create an "agreement field" and a "mode of recognition" with which we make our commitment to kindness, conviviality, respect, reciprocity, reverence, and responsibility known, and by which we recognize each other as having made such a commitment? We're hereby announcing the Do-Good Guild. It's here, it is time, and you're invited to join. In due time, we envision an Ecocene economics in which entrepreneurs, executives, financiers, philanthropists, employees, professional service providers, and millions upon millions of parents, grandparents, neighbors, and conscious citizens of planet Earth will have joined the Do-Good Guild and through this profound commitment to goodness, truth, beauty, and care-full-ness (caring for humanity and caring for Mama Gaia), will have profoundly altered our shared human destiny toward the love-wisdom-goodness that is our birthright to claim.

In Praise of Stability, Gentle Transitions, and Soft Landings

Some of us are enamored by sudden systemic change (indeed, as investors, entrepreneurs, and cultural creatives, if the "disruptions" play in our favor, we will benefit from the acquisition of extraordinary wealth and advantage). And, given the precautionary principle and the terrible inertia with which too many adverse trends are careening forward into our near future, some sudden changes may be welcome. However, it behooves us to discern between systemic and structural failures (that inevitably usher in something "new and different," regardless of the "collateral damage") and the gentler, softer blooming and blossoming of prismatic palettes of the Regeneration Renaissance. In short, let us envision a symphony of colors, like a great permaculture garden growing out of a previously desecrated wasteland instead of a wrecking ball felling the skyscrapers of our industrial past. Let us artistically and carefully *create* our way into a new reality—not fetishize collapse and destruction. Let us build for beauty and—like pollinators alighting on spring-time blossoms—celebrate stability, gentle transitions, and soft landings.

Getting a Grip on Reality: Super Abundance vs. the Collective Hallucination of Scarcity

It isn't surprising that, at the outset of the city-state civilization epoch that emerged coincidentally with agriculture, armies, and centralized hierarchies of political-economic power, our forebearers developed a shared illusion of the scarcity of resources upon which human livelihoods, safety, and security depended. A collective hallucination took hold. This profound cultural and psycho-spiritual phenomenon has been examined and understood by myriad scholars, thinkers, and luminaries. The true reality, however, is that the super-abundance of Earth's copious biological productivity, fueled by an unceasing stream of light and energy from our sun, provides ample abundance far exceeding our collective needs. It is only our misguided constructed worldviews, and their outward expression in the systems and structures that we have created, that have given rise to a false perception of scarcity. The truth is that we inhabit a super-abundant world, and, if we succeed in turning the corner toward a regenerative global culture, this abundance will be the beautiful bedrock upon which our Ecocene institutions and communities will find firm footing.

We Must See Through the Veil of Illusion and Ask Ourselves: What's Normal?

Students and scholars of deep history necessarily understand that so much of what we consider "normal" in modernity is highly aberrational. One of my favorite examples of this truth is the manner in which many of us erroneously perceive the "new fad" called organic agriculture—that's a recent phenomenon, right? Perhaps even a "fake news" construct of some progressive-left conspiracy? Well guess what? Not only is organic agriculture and horticulture not a recent invention, it is actually the norm—through 99% of our entire history (and possibly far longer—more like 99.99%, depending on how we define agriculture, horticulture, and the like). You see, in ancient Egypt, ancient China, ancient Mesopotamia, ancient Greece, ancient Rome, ancient Mayan and Incan and Mesoamerican life-ways, on through Medieval, Renaissance, and early modern times, ALL agriculture and horticulture is organic . . . right up and until the very recent advent of chemical-industrial agriculture, an unbelievably risky experiment we've been conducting (especially here in the United States) for about 100 years. And, as Rudolf Steiner has cautioned (see especially his *Agriculture Lectures*), the potential impacts are beyond devastating—to the point where our human wills are no longer vital and integrated with our hearts and minds. Too much of what we believe to be normal (or worse yet, the result of so-called "human nature") are very recent aberrations and profoundly out of synch with longer-cycle patterns of healthfulness and prosperity. We must see through the veil of illusion and ask ourselves: what's normal? Moreover, these times invite us to help establish a *new normal* of planetary prosperity.

Getting Out of Our Heads and Into Our Bodies

In philosophy, as poor chaps like Derrida, Descartes, and Schopenhauer (especially!) have overwhelmingly demonstrated, it's too easy to get lost in endlessly cavernous permutations of abstract symbolism also known as thought and language. Via a strangely modern recapitulation of Platonic and Neoplatonic abstract dualism, mechanism, and separation, this sad and pessimistic view of things (*Weltanschauung*) is by no means limited to the rarified halls of ivory tower academia. Nay, to the contrary—the complex constructs of human concept permeate all our minds and perceptions of reality, and all too often have us living within bizarrely constructed variations of reality in which we're rather quite disconnected from *REALITY* herself! Whether the anti-Gaian and anti-vitalistic eschatological obsession so fiercely critiqued by Nietzsche, or the cynicism that renders Chardin's sublime notion of the Noosphere an "impossibility," such abstract assumption sets are at the deepest foundation of our nature-deficit-disorder-imbued polycrisis. Thank goodness there's a cure! As the great sages have demonstrated, and as Alan Watts has famously and more recently uttered (I particularly like the version of a recording sampled into the song "Overthinker" by INZO), "a person who thinks all the time has nothing to think about except thoughts. He loses touch with reality and lives in a world of illusions. By thoughts, I mean specifically chatter in the skull. I'm not saying thinking is bad—like everything else it's useful in moderation; a good servant but a bad master. And all so-called civilized people have become—have increasingly become crazy and self-destructive" (as a result of abstract dualism, mechanism, and separation). The remedy is simple: we must get a grip! We must exit the building, get outside in nature, away from our screens and spreadsheets and data tables and angular edifices and treat the malady with frequent and copious medicinal applications: quiet, joyful nature immersion is the cure. We must get out of our heads and into our bodies and hearts and directly experience, with profound intimacy and presence, the visceral, palpable, and corporeal (neurobiochemical) connection with Mama Gaia's living wildernesses. And, alongside that remedy (i.e. Shinrin-yoku for nature deficit disorder) we might also cultivate ample doses of *awe* and *gratitude*—as a conscious creature properly *will*, when—eyes (and heart) wide open—(s)he consciously witnesses the sublimely mysterious reality—the Divine immanence—that is our birthright *by definition*.

Maturing Beyond Brittle Ideologies and Mass (Media) Hallucinations

I had a very strange experience while sharing early drafts of this book with some elderly friends and colleagues. One criticized the book as being too capitalistic, and another as being too socialistic. "Aha," I thought (after nursing the shallow bruises of apparent (subjective) rejection), "now I know for sure we're onto something here . . ." Too many of us have developed ossified and brittle "ideologies" (although they hardly ever hold together as such under any meaningful scrutiny), and instead are operating in a cloud of hallucinatory and fragmented notions that too often result in knee-jerk reaction like what we witness in the rotten realms of certain network television and social media echo chambers. We would be wise to engage in the demanding practice of self-examination and deep, unmediated critical thinking should we hope to free ourselves of the mass hallucinations handed down through various channels of conformity—on either the left or the right. Let us mature beyond brittle ideologies and mass media hallucinations as we age, and earn the revered title "elder" through our well-stewarded thoughts, words, and deeds!

The A.I. Imperative: Intimate Connection with the Authentic Intelligence of Nature

In order to be grounded, joyful, effective leaders in the Ecocene, we must embrace and integrate ourselves with AI. But not the AI you might be thinking of. I'm not speaking here of the ever-complexifying algorithms of humanity's self-reflexive ChatGPT hallucinations (nor the even deeper and more potent artificial intelligences that are being furiously pursued in quantum computing laboratories of the most powerful militaries, intelligence agencies, and technology corporations worldwide). No, I'm talking about something altogether different. I'm talking about the Authentic Intelligence of our living world and the incomprehensibly vast cosmic creation in which we're all situated. As we make this the source of our inspiration, wisdom, and insight, we will evolve much more rapidly and understand much more quickly the various keys to unlocking the Ecocene Eden awaiting us. She's there, and will lift her veil as soon as we're ready—what are you waiting for?

Hear Ye, Hear Ye—Whale Song in Our Hallowed Halls of Justice?

The Rights of Nature movement is gaining ground (and rivers) world-wide. Literally incorporating into legal frameworks and legal proceedings the "voices" of natural but non-human interests (such as other species, bodies of water, and the like), this important mechanism for restoring balance has its roots in the indigenous wisdom and lifeways of the Original Instructions. Through non-neuro-typical and shamanic communication, our indigenous ancestors included (and even embodied) the interests of non-human Gaian life in their tribal councils and quotidian lifeways. But in European and other "dominator culture" histories, those with "voice" became a very constricted subset—not only excluding acknowledgement of and consideration for other species, vast portions of *human* societies were likewise excluded. And, as Kant articulated 250 years ago in answer to the question "What is Enlightenment?" *voice* is essential—essential to dignity, to sovereignty, and to standing. In fact, Kant defined Enlightenment as our personal liberation from our self-imposed voicelessness (*selbstverschuldete Unmündigkeit*). For generations, neither children nor women have had "voice" or standing in many courts of law—especially European and Anglo-American. They were voiceless. And, the same is true of the rivers and forests and mycelia and wolves and dolphins and whales. But that's changing. Through the Rights of Nature movement, communities around the world, in cooperation with lawyers, legislatures, and courts, are restoring voice to the otherwise voiceless members of our living biosphere. This is extraordinarily important and inspiring on its face, but there's more. Through AI, as discussed by Brandon Keim in his *National Geographic* article, scientists are fast approaching the ability to communicate directly with our Cetacean cousins, intermediated by hyper-advanced large-language-model computing. And although some of my smartest friends, albeit excited, raise the appropriately skeptical question: "how would we know what they're actually saying (versus what the super computers are telling us)," posing a question that strangely evokes a poetic synthesis between the "imitation game" Turing Test and the manner in which protagonist Dr. Louise Banks established bi-directional communication with the extraterrestrial Heptapods in the awesome science fiction film *Arrival*, one can imagine a variety of "authentication and verification" techniques we might employ. Wow. Imagine. Speaking directly with whales (and dolphins, and wolves, and mycelial mats, as envisioned in my novel *Viriditas*, along with so many other of Mama Gaia's precious creatures)! And including their voices in our near-future legal proceedings and agreements . . . WOW! Hear Ye, Hear Ye . . . indeed!

Hippocrates, the Precautionary Principle, and the Permaculture Ethics

It is generally well known that the ancient Greek Hippocrates told us to "first, do no harm." This was, of course, in the context of proto-medicine, or the care of the biological body. Well, guess what? Our living Earth is a biological body too! Not to mention the trillions of creatures making up the fabric of her biosphere, and the billions of human beings among that great webwork of interconnection making up the corpus of humanity. In our own individual behavior—how we comport ourselves—and in our regional, national, and international decision-making, it is imperative that we become *much* better—nay, *expert*—at making decisions that do no harm to life on Earth. And, this wise, thoughtful approach—also known as the precautionary principle, or as seven-generation decision-making—applies to all of the other systems and structures through which we organize and conduct our human activities. This wisdom is at the foundational root of the Permaculture design discipline—applicable to both "visible" and "invisible" systems, structures, and "organisms"—first, care for Earth; second, care for people; third, maintain "fair share"—that is, set limits (to consumption, etc.) and systematically share surpluses with *everyone.*

Earth Restoration Corps, Agricorps, and Compulsory Military Duty

Several countries require their citizens to serve in their militaries, at once giving young adults defense and professional skills, while also bolstering their national security. We need to do the same for the bolstering of ecosystem and agricultural security—of the organic, regenerative, biophilic sort—much in the same manner as retired US Special Forces soldiers are now doing via Force Blue. As Hanne Strong has proposed, we need a worldwide Earth Restoration Corps, much like AmeriCorps or the Peace Corps, but specifically focused on restoring ecosystems: a growing global network of ecosystem restoration guilds. Similarly, we ought to consider this sort of mechanism for the intense labor requirements that feed us all—if the youth were to experience a season of organic food production, not only would we stabilize our food security and train potential next-generation farmers, we would also engender a much deeper, more realistic appreciation throughout the society (in relatively short order) regarding the hard work and real care that goes into growing, harvesting, and preparing nourishing foods for all of us. I can think of scant few other "requisites" to impose upon our young people, (perhaps other than investing time in libraries with books, visiting with elders, and crossing the socio-economic class borders through service projects).

The Holism Requisite: Getting a Grip on the Global Economy vs. Squeezing the Balloon

Many of us recall from childhood the joy of playing with a balloon and, squeezing part of it only to see the compressed air escape our grip and stretch out another part of the now bulging membrane. Piecemeal attempts at addressing environmental, social, cultural, and economic maladies often have the same effects, metaphorically speaking. In order to best avoid the unintended consequences of narrowly conceived change-making as best we can, a holistic approach is necessary—not necessarily easy, but *necessary*. We are wise to cultivate a holistic world view in our own consciousness. And we are wise to give our attention, audience, and credence to those among us who have done the challenging work of developing substantially holistic worldviews (i.e. wisdom) in their own consciousness—integrating and understanding the complex interconnectedness that is the reality among and between all living creatures, all anthropogenic systems, and edifices, and all cosmological phenomena. This is especially true with respect to the impacts of micro, macro, monetary, fiscal, and policy decision making vis-à-vis the economic impacts on people's relative degree of well-being and ecosystems' relative degree of health and integrity.

Reclaiming Goodness and Goodwill Toward Others

Our spiritual traditions and Indigenous and folk wisdom teach us to cultivate goodwill toward our fellow human beings. This is, of course, the central teaching of the great mystics and spiritual luminaries throughout the ages. And, it is now ours to reclaim. By cultivating genuine goodness, and a genuine goodwill toward one another, we will discover peace, joy, and equanimity (as opposed to being beset by the neurobiochemical fight and flight cocktails that otherwise pervade our bodies and experience), while we reorient ourselves toward a great healing of our cultures and economic lifeways.

Technology, Swadeshi, and Unlocking the Genius of Cottage Artisanship

What is the etymological root of the word "technology," you ask? It's the Greek *tekne*—to "weave" (as in textiles). And, of course, the term "manufacture" has as its original Latin meaning "to make by hand"—*manus*, hand, *factus*, to make. But what are we getting at here? There's a two-fold reason why it is important that we each prepare and make things by hand, especially if we're in positions of leadership. The first is that it enhances our intelligence—our cognitive performance—as it staves off dementia. We humans (hu-manus) have evolved making things by hand: hammering the percussive rhythms of flaking glass-like flint and obsidian into arrowheads, weaving willow reeds into baskets, and sculpting wet clay into pots. This type of focused, tactile "work", which could also include painting, gardening, and carving stone, opens up and helps us access an innate intelligence that might otherwise remain obscured by overactive minds and distracted thoughts. Second, as Gandhi emphasized in his (victorious) quest to throw off the shackles of the British Empire, the more we know how to make things by hand, and the more we hold as sacred the handmade artisan crafts, the more authentic freedom we can enjoy. Autonomy, sovereignty, and liberty, one might say, are, at least in part, "handmade" realities.

On Becoming a Human Being: Self-Emancipation and Deep Freedom (It Takes a Village)

Curiously, many of our ancestral and Indigenous traditions do not make "human beingness" an automatic entitlement or status. Instead, it must be earned. It must be earned through the embodiment of appropriate ethics—thoughts, words, *and* actions—and by taking responsibility in the community. It is here, in the commitment and obligation of responsibility, that we discover and come to possess true freedom. It is in understanding the requirements of being excellent stewards of our living world and excellent neighbors to our fellow human beings that we will approach the threshold and knock upon the doorways leading to deep freedom—doorways that will surely be opened. As Kant famously exhorted us to liberate ourselves from our self-imposed immaturity, so now must we emancipate ourselves from the adolescent inclination toward self-absorption and pass through the doorway into true adulthood—true human beingness. The Ecocene shall present new rites of passage to us all. As we each choose to step forward onto the path of deep leadership to which we're being called, we shall experience the deep and lasting freedom that is our birthright. And, in our meta-industrial villages, literal, metaphorical, immediate, and globally networked, we shall learn to step into the maturity of deep leadership, and then help and guide others in our villages to do the same. If you choose this pathway of stewardship and responsibility, you will be welcomed into the everlasting light of being a true human being, connected with the infinite cosmos.

Toward Guilds and Stewardship Societies

Our folk, ancient, Indigenous, and esoteric traditions worldwide are woven with high-functioning guilds and initiatic stewardship societies. The privileges of membership are predicated on the understanding, embrace, and embodiment of an enhanced sense of responsibility. The webworks of these guilds and societies will transform the parasitism of Anthropocene behaviors into the mutualistic stewardship of Ecocene consciousness, where shared wellness, prosperity, and flourishing are both the foundation and the adornment of the organizations themselves. Whether the medieval stone mason guilds of Europe, the Wu Dong practitioner guilds of China's sacred mountains, the medicine societies of the Haudenosaunee Mohawk keepers of the Eastern Gate of Turtle Island or the initiatic societies of light and sound healers in ancient Egypt, our cultural traditions worldwide are tapestries in which the threads of these guilds and societies are the warp and weft of deep strength, resilience, and prosperity in our cultural ecosystems. Now we are invited to reestablish, recreate, and re-sanctify these beautiful patterns of human culture. Whether to the world-wide ecotourism, agritourism, wellness tourism, and wilderness tourism guild, holistic healer's guild, regenerative farmers guild, the Viriditas Society, or the Sophia Wisdom and Grandmothers Council, we will each be called into one or more of these bodies of fellowship, common purpose, responsibility, and shared resources. What a joy! What a privilege! What an honor!

PART THREE—DEEP LEADERSHIP AND TRUE FREEDOM

The Tao and Wu Wei of Ecocene Leadership

Less is more. Slow is smooth, and smooth is fast. More yin and less yang. More oxytocin and serotonin, and less adrenaline and cortisol. The new, advanced form of deep leadership in the emerging Ecocene not only invites us into a softer, gentler, more intuitive and insightful leadership style, it actually requires of us a slowing down and enhanced quality of life that engenders the advanced, tranquil, centered, and imperturbable way of being that equates to a much higher quality of life and much deeper experience of prosperity, well-being, and abundance. That is, in a nutshell, our work is to cultivate, perceive, and embody the extreme relaxation and profound creative manifestation that requires the *least effort*. It is the practice of connecting directly with a far deeper, vaster, inexhaustible wellspring of inspiration, knowledge, wisdom, and guidance that otherwise remains veiled. Instead of forcing, we flow in the cosmic river of becoming. It is the flowing reed that bends but doesn't break in the gale-force winds. It is true strength, true resilience, true mastery. It is the embodied wisdom of the Tao, the Wu Wei of Leadership. It is joyfully childlike. And it is delightfully efficacious.

Like Water, Willow, and Wu Wei: Meekness is NOT Weakness

In one of the most seminal, world-changing moments in human history, the Master Teacher from Nazareth spoke to a gathering of friends and strangers and, in his "Sermon on the Mount," delivered what would become known as the eight Beatitudes. Among them, one of the most easily misunderstood, in my experience, is the simple statement about meekness: "Blessed are the meek for they shall inherit the Earth." Meekness is often confused with weakness, but means something else entirely: it means gentleness, humility, and equanimity, irrespective of strength or weakness. A great war horse can be meek (refined and under control), and so can an elder grandmother. We all can. In addition to Jeshua, the great teachers Lao Tzu, Siddhartha Buddha, and Confucius also spoke to this essential quality. Overcoming pride with mindfulness, bending flexibly like the willow, flowing like water to nourish all, even in the lowest places, and cultivating the power of watery yin fluidity through Wu Wei are essential to the cultivation of meekness, and are essential to the webwork weaving ways of the new Earth steward aristocracy.

Subduing the Mammonic Dragon

In our shared ancient history, we will find stories of the Mammonic "dragon" being subdued by the light warrior. This is perhaps the most salient metaphor for the task before each of us individually and all of us collectively: subduing the Mammonic dragon, which through some dark magic has us otherwise hallucinating scarcity, zero-sum competition, and survival of the fittest as the "natural" way of things, and, hence, hyper-focused on our own possessions, aspirations, and holdings, we isolate and wall ourselves off . . . cut ourselves off from the super-abundant riches of community, life, and nature—the cosmic intelligence of creation. As I wrote about extensively in *Y on Earth* and *Viriditas*, specifically referring to Mammon in the latter, the great quest of our five-generation cluster is to subdue this Mammonic dragon, open our hearts, work to heal and reconnect with the super-abundant reality of creation, and work in service to our fellow human beings and living Mother Earth. Just as Prometheus set forth, choosing between two divergent pathways, humans also have to choose—between slavery and freedom. If we fail to subdue the dragon, our road will be fraught with deep psycho-spiritual suffering. If we succeed in subduing Mammon, the doors of overflowing abundance, joy, peace, and well-being will swing open immediately before us.

Your Money or Your Life

My friend Jeremy Roske wrote a song, "Your Money or Your Life," when he was quite a young man . . . and you know what? He's right. In the starkest of terms, many of us end up trading our lives—quality of life, freedom, creativity, authenticity, integrity, etc.—for the so-called "security" and "safety" of having more money than we think we might otherwise come to possess. The truth is, with few exceptions, the "safer" our choices seem in terms of perceived financial security, the more likely they are to simultaneously erode our personal psycho-spiritual well-being *and* continue to reinforce the macro-scale behaviors, systems, and structures that are undermining the ecological and cultural well-being of our shared world.

On Hamster Wheels and Rat Races

Too many of us are sprinting and panting to stand still—some on gold-gilded hamster wheels and others on less glittery ones. As Lily Tomlin is purported to have said, "The trouble with the rat race is that even if you win, you're still a rat." Aren't we capable of more than this? So much more? How about instead of treading water or spinning the hamster wheel, where the more we make and have the more we desire and acquire; and emancipate ourselves from the Mammonic treadmills of modernity . . . the alternative is a meta-industrial paradise where life is simply better—much better—and in which the stewardship and maintenance of the requisite conditions for life are plausible.

From Sharks to Dolphins—the True Strength of Yin Style Leadership vs. Toxic Masculinity

First off, I want to recognize that sharks are magnificent creatures, serving the same important predatory functions in oceanic ecologies as lions and other great carnivores serve in the terrestrial domain. This isn't meant to denigrate what sharks actually are and do in their natural way, but to draw a contrast between the symbolic or archetypal difference between "sharks" and "dolphins" within the realm of human behavior, metaphorically speaking. You see, among too many executives, financiers, and others in positions of power and influence, there is a prevailing self-centeredness that is typified by the lone shark lurking in the waters. Meanwhile, the cooperative and mutualistic behavior exhibited by the (cognitively more advanced) Delphinidae not only brings with it a more complex and harmonious social structure, from the perspective of the human observer, but also brings with it a considerable competitive advantage relative to the otherwise superior sharks. That is, one-on-one, many dolphins would quickly succumb to the superior strength and aggression of sharks. But in their pods, dolphins are a far stronger force, chasing the sharks away from their young and ultimately outcompeting them. As genius noble-laureate mathematician John Nash pointed out, Adam Smith's understanding of self-interested competition was limited, or incomplete, and the most advanced, generative and sustainable form of economic behavior is actually the coordinated cooperation among the community, ensuring fundamental needs like safety and security are met while optimizing for the fulfilment of personal desires within the reasonable (and precautionary) bounds of protecting the shared commons and limiting an individual's adverse impact on another in personal desire fulfilment. Put another way, as Hazel Henderson, Barbara Marx-Hubbard, and others have written, this is the greater-good-guided "yin" style leadership of the whole-systems steward versus the "gotta get mine" pathos of the toxic masculine. It requires care-full-ness. It requires education. It requires self-transcendence and service leadership. It requires the archetypal behavior of the cooperating dolphin instead of the selfish shark. As Kropotkin once said, "competition is the law of the jungle, but cooperation is the law of civilization."

Elevating Our Capacity: From Tension to Trust

As we cultivate the receptive and guided discipline of conspiring with the subtle will-to-good forces, we will experience a dissolution of tension and stress, and will increasingly relax into an empirically verified field of trust. As with other aspects of the so-called "mystical" (a term fraught with bias and misconception, but nonetheless pointing toward some of the most sublime aspects of experience and invitations available to us as human beings), it is virtually impossible to conclusively verify their realness without direct experience. On the one hand, this sets up a fallacious critique of "tautology" among skeptics (suffering actually from the rhetorical error of *ignoratio elenchi*)—but none of us without direct experience are actually qualified to dismiss with certainty the phenomenological possibility. This is a classical issue of epistemology—one for which the modern meme (IYKYK—"if you know you know") applies. The point is this, if we allow ourselves—give ourselves invitation and permission— to practice collaborating with the subtler forces of will-to-good, they (as the luminaries have taught for ages) will respond back to us in discernable and often profound ways. The more we practice, the more we experience. And, one of the primary outcomes of this practice is a direct experience that we're held in and collaborating with forces that reach way beyond our little selves, thus inviting us to relax into trust, and restore our neurobiochemistry to deep equanimity and real efficacy—releasing us from the bondage of stress and tension (that we have to figure it all out on our own). Relaxing into the mysterious and loving fabric of reality in which we're enveloped, we are invited to the quotidian experience of sublime awe and blissful existence; all while working in service to the greater good.

On Voluntary Simplicity (Or Is Guaranteed Loneliness Your Goal?)

Perhaps one of the greatest ironies of wealth creation and achieving "success" in life is the truth that the less we need (or are attached to), the happier we become. Called "the simple life" or "downshifting," the deliberate choice to live simply, eschewing the massive material consumption treadmills and one-upmanship of mindless accumulation and consumption of things, is one of the easiest and most potent ways we can create and ensure our own happiness, creative flow, and professional efficacy. On the other hand, we can subject ourselves to the "more, more, more" narrative, shackling ourselves to the never-ending disappointment of "never arriving," or—worse yet—"making it" and finding ourselves in the profound loneliness of the double isolation from "the masses" and existential wastelands of country club critique and comparison, however overt or subtle it all may be. At the end of the day, we become our own worst critics, having set ourselves an impossible task, when we succumb to the monstrous (however bright, shiny, and gilded it may be) machinery of materialism. On the other hand, by connecting to a deep wisdom and choosing the awesome power, expansiveness, and abundance of voluntary simplicity, we become intimately and continuously familiar with the super abundance of reality, and, unburdened by the continuous consumption that ultimately consumes our creativity and soul, we create for ourselves the opportunity to experience true freedom, bliss, joy, and sovereignty. We relieve ourselves of the great weights of "winning" and instead walk freely in the joyful cosmic expanse of wonder.

Gaining Everything (Worthwhile) by Deliberately Relinquishing Power and Wealth

Here's perhaps the perfect paradox regarding leadership in the emerging Eco-cene: we must relinquish wealth and power, as George Washington did in his famous resignation as Commander-in-Chief of the Continental Army before the Continental Congress in Annapolis, Maryland, 1783, demonstrably serving a higher purpose than narrow self-interest. In so doing, we will step into the *sanctum sanctorum* of the true wealth and deep power only known by those who dedicate their lives to the greater good of humanity and our shared living world. A paradox? A truth. Don't get caught in the trap of "if . . . then . . ." of "if I achieve such and such wealth milestone or such and such level of authority or esteem, then I will . . ." No. Start by working in service, by asking yourself: "What can I do to better our world, to serve humanity, to restore balance in Earth's ecosystems today?" Then will the doors be opened—thrown wide open—to you. Then will you see, hear, and experience that which is otherwise unattainable, unimaginable, ineffable. Then will you know.

De-stressing Leadership and Enhancing Ecocene Efficacy—From Adrenaline and Cortisol to Dopamine, Oxytocin, and Serotonin

One of our greatest philosophical, economic, social, and spiritual conundrums can be found at the nexus between purpose, mission, personal will, and leadership. In a word, when we chose to embrace the call and cultivate ourselves as service leaders, with growing responsibilities that extend well beyond the narrow interests of our own person and immediate family and community of familiars, we may often experience a similarly expanding stress. And stress kills. Not only does stress literally kill our bodies, accelerating telomere fraying, oxidation, and DNA fritzing within our complex biological temples, it also undermines our ability to lead with the wisdom, strength, beauty, and beneficence required of us as we boldly enter into the Ecocene. There is a great paradox in this—but as many paradoxes reveal themselves to be, it's only an *apparent* paradox. For as we learn to focus first on our physical, emotional, mental, and spiritual health and well-being, and from that solid, peaceful point and foundation of clarity lead outwardly, we more readily access the cosmic living intelligence of Mama Gaia, the ability to lead with calm purpose, and to see clearly through the tactical forest of to-do lists into the distant gaze of tall trees of strategic primacy. *This* is our fundamental task as Ecocene leaders—in whatever specific capacity we find ourselves: to calm down, to cultivate ourselves, to become the deep, calm waters of inspiration, insight, and instrumentality, and to align ourselves as vessels with what wants to move through us from far greater and more powerful sources of intelligence and wisdom. Thus, do we get smarter, feel better and heal the planet as we become wiser, better, and consequently happier!

On Getting Over Ourselves and Upleveling (Or, Really Understanding Maslow's Hierarchy of Needs)

As discussed in the chapter "Our Inner Work," most of us have heard of Maslow's Hierarchy of Needs, and retain some picture of an ascending hierarchical pyramid ranking a succession of motivating factors, from the most broadly basic like obtaining food, water, and shelter, through to esteem and belonging, all the way to the rarified pinnacle of self-realization . . . what I like to call the "Michael Jordan tier"—that is, being the very best at what you do. Through the self-centered milieu of the Anthropocene narrative, this pinnacle has become for many of us the final, ultimate target and destination in our personal and professional endeavors. But far fewer of us know that there's actually another level beyond that of the self-actualized. Indeed, decades after he first published his hierarchy, Maslow, increasingly cognizant of the inherent flaws and limitations of his initial model, promulgated to the world an improved version in which an additional level was added at the top—the crowning pinnacle of personal development: "self-transcendence." At this level, instead of staying selfishly focused on our own excellence, performance, and rewards, we put our highly developed skills and robust resources to work for the greater good of society and the entire world. It's an evolution from a Michael Jordan archetype to a Keanu Reeves archetype, or from a tycoon's archetype to the archetype of the great avatars like Gandhi, Dr. King, and the Sybil of the Rhine, Hildegard von Bingen. This is transforming from a shark into a dolphin. This is embodying the advanced intelligence and character traits articulated by Dr. Cloninger in his "What Makes People Healthy, Happy, and Fulfilled . . ." essay. And, this is evolving from the limited and diseased Wetiko worldview that "greed is good" into the sublime wisdom of Ubuntu. This is ascending the rungs of the hierarchy . . . where are you on the pyramid?

Recursive Self-Improvement Is Our Formula for Success

There's no magic pill or app that will get us where we want to go. Instead, it's the day-by-day self-stewardship and delightful discipline of soft, continuous improvement that provides the pathway to personal prosperity. Of course, the same is true in the aggregate and at the scale of planetary prosperity. Recursive self-improvement is our formula for success.

Narratives and Knowledge Sets—Who's Guiding the Conversation?

In order to achieve our own personal liberation from the mind-bending machinery of the highly aberrational late-modern Anthropocene culture—the most extreme, systemic form of what Kant called *"Selbstverschuldete Unmündigkeit,"* or "self-inflicted immaturity and servitude" at scale—we must regularly inquire and examine *the roots* of the narratives and knowledge sets we encounter (and which otherwise make their way into forming our "opinions" and "thoughts" if our holistic hermeneutics and "Ecology of Thinking" filters aren't active and robust). The sublime self-cultivation traditions of contemplation, self-examination (Examen), and inner inquiry invite us into a realm of clear-eyed lucidity in which we're able to pierce and gaze through the veneer veils of virulent volition otherwise influencing our thoughts, lives, and realities.

Decolonizing Our Minds, Our Bodies, Our Lives—Or Joining "AAA"

Scant few of us have plumbed the depths of paradigmatic programing that are profoundly driving our perceptions of reality, our desires, our assumptions about human nature, and our constructs of achievement. Coming to understand these ubiquitous influences—the practice of weeding the gardens of our consciousness—is essential to cultivating our roles as deep leaders in the emerging Ecocene. Perhaps we'll need to create and join a new support group, not the AA of Alcoholics Anonymous but the AAA of Anthropocene Advertising Anonymous.

Advanced Leadership is Embodied Kindness & Conviviality

Pay attention to kindness and conviviality—to cultivating them, sharing them, and receiving them from others. The most advanced leaders in our world embody and exude a profound, authentic, unflappable kindness and conviviality. The rest of us are encouraged to cultivate kindness and conviviality as earnestly as anything else we might consider important to cultivate. Kindness is king and conviviality is queen. This is how we cultivate the enduring reality of ULS—ultra low stress—which equates to deep, sustainable joy; hyper-intelligence and creativity; super-cognitive performance; enhanced physical health; and much more effective leadership. Kindness is key. Conviviality is requisite. Are you an advanced practitioner (yet)?

Announcing the DBAD Movement

Okay people, it's time to drive the kindness revolution home . . . and to bring a little humor to the movement, to boot! We'll make hats and shirts and other such ethical "merch" that are embroidered and emblazoned with the catchy acronym: *DBAD—Don't Be a D*ck!* For some of us, the invitation (and psycho-spiritual-cultural imperative) of kindness and conviviality may not quite make sense, yet, so here's the corollary: Don't Be a D*ck! It's that simple, really: Just Don't Be a D*ck!

From Torturing Pixels to Shinrin-yoku—Executive Leadership in the Ecocene (is Quite Different)

It's clear that digital technology is going to be central to our work—at least for a while. Especially for those of us in Quaternary and Quintenary roles, the management of information and ongoing communication require regular, frequent, and often prolonged "screen time" as it were. And, without a doubt, those of us in the primary, secondary, and tertiary sectors are increasingly working with digital technologies as well. Obviously, many of us also recreate and communicate with friends, loved ones, and work colleagues alike using digital technology. But there's a profound weakness and limitation in such hyper-technological ways of working and living. The more we connect and "integrate" with the binary architecture of digital constructs, the less connected we likely are to the analogue intelligence of the living biosphere and the cosmic *Materia*. Hence, we need a strong remedy. We need the wilderness. And we need complete immersion in it.

Time invested walking, trekking, and even sitting surrounded by trees and contemplating aside streams and lakes is part of this strong remedy. So is staying put and instead of going inward (with eyes closed), staying present with the phenomenal, living world that surrounds us. We simply pick a choice spot in the woods (or meadows) and sit there a while. We notice what's happening. We notice the insects flitting about, the ground critters going about their way atop the soil, the bird song, the movement of clouds, the gentle (or brisk) breeze blowing, the cool and warmth of shade and sunlight. We notice the change. We notice the activity. We notice the *life*—the life to which we're all connected and of which we're all a part. This is the art of forest bathing—*Shinrin-yoku* as our Japanese friends call it. The invitation to us is simple: we create frequent pauses in our digital "pixel torture," get outside, immerse, and pay attention. That's it. Another key to the kingdom of kindness and queendom of the Quintenary.

On Slow Leadership, Happiness, Harmony, and Efficacy

Lao Tzu taught that *"Nature does not hurry, yet everything is accomplished."* Especially as our lives and work are infiltrated by ceaseless digital communication, and as our to-do lists burgeon beyond any hope of completion, it is imperative that we slow down. To say "I'm busy" is no longer a self-congratulatory declaration of importance, but admission of something being amiss, or worse yet a declaration of our self-imposed slavery. We *need* to slow down, especially as leaders in the emerging Ecocene. If we're not embodying the calm, joyful happiness and harmony of balance, and if our harried haste precludes deep efficacy, why would we expect our organization, colleagues, and ecosystems to embody this? Slow living, slow leadership, deep leadership, the patient, measured steps of wisdom, intelligence, connection, insight, joy—these are the traits of effective leadership in the Ecocene.

We Must Slow Down to More Expeditiously Get Where We Want to Go (Or Even Get There at All)

Do you want to experience a future of hectic stress and frenetic restlessness? Or, do you prefer a reality of calm, equanimity, peace, and joyful ease and grace? Guess what—to create the future we really want, we must cultivate the same here and now. This is our invitation and requirement. In order to activate ever-higher degrees of insight, creativity, conviviality, and co-creative collaboration, it is our inner neurobiochemistry that we must first attend to—cultivating the conditions that are endemic to the future we desire to experience. It's an *inside out* job, folks, and we're all thus invited to slow down, relax, and allow our heart petals to blossom their fullest as we become coherent, hyper-efficacious change-makers in our lives, our communities, and our global society. And for the entrepreneurs and executives among us, this is especially important—for our companies will embody and reflect the character, tone, and efficacy of our interior realities. We must slow down to more expeditiously get where we want to go (or even get there at all)!

Henry Ford, Belief, and the Ecocene Vision—Whether You Think You Can or Think You Can't . . . You're (Probably) Right

So, whaddya think . . . Can you wrap your mind (and heart) around all of this? Can you "buy" it? Can you envision yourself contributing to and benefiting from the global scaling-up of the Ecocene entities through which humanity is ushering in an epoch of shared stewardship, regeneration, prosperity, health, and well-being? As an investor, philanthropist, entrepreneur, and executive, can you see yourself playing an important role in this awesome ecosystem? Well, to borrow—perhaps with some poetic irony—a pithy insight from a notable (though problematic) entrepreneurial titan, Henry Ford, "Whether you think you can or think you can't, you're right."

Spiritual Slavery vs. True Freedom: On Self-Emancipation and Humanity's Liberation

In ancient mythology it is said that Zeus invited Prometheus to lay out the pathways upon which *human will* could be expressed and exercised, resulting in a two-fold trail system (which would later iterate as the Medieval "Pythagorean Y," which, as explained in the Introduction to my book *Y on Earth*, serves as one of the three inspirational "memes" behind that work's title, and the non-profit we established upon its foundational framework). In Prometheus' framework, two options are provided to humanity: a pathway toward psycho-spiritual slavery, and another toward true freedom. The latter would eventually afford the worthy individual a gentle environment replete with fruitful abundance, peaceful prosperity, and bountiful beauty. The other, instead, would grow increasingly treacherous, ugly, painful, and ultimately doom the traveler to his demise. Curiously, though—and herein lies the lesson of the parable—each of those two strikingly different outcomes are reached by paths that initially appear as their opposites. That is, the path to paradise is challenging at first, and requires of the human "apprentice" entering upon it tremendous strength, courage, fortitude, and patience. On the other hand. The path to deep, inescapable suffering is initially lined with the seductive comforts that appeal to our baser, undisciplined desires. The Medieval "Pythagorean Y" tells this same fable in pictorial "meme" form, often as a woodblock print in which a forked tree presents two very different pathways for the climber—the one seemingly easy and full of base temptations ends in suffering, and the other, at first challenging and less superficially appealing ends in joy and wellbeing. Instead of presenting us with "one big decision" to make one time only, the scenario, like life, presents us with myriad seemingly "small" decisions day by day—the cumulative consequences of which determine our long-term situations.

During Europe's cultural transition from the late Renaissance into the early modern period—an era we refer to as the Enlightenment—Emanuel Kant picked up on this theme and wrote of something similar when responding to a public request to define "enlightenment". His resulting essay, "What is Enlightenment?" describes man's liberation from his own self-imposed subjugation, and very much intended the metaphor to be understood as a liberation of the mind, the heart, and the human spirit—the willful consciousness that is a uniquely sublime flowering from the foliage of humankind. We hope you'll ponder this in earnest, and, when you've internalized the wisdom above, ponder this corollary question: as we lean in to and "learn in to" the requirements and practices for engendering our own psycho-spiritual liberation, how might the contribution to the relief of other's "self-imposed subjugation" be part-and-parcel to truly obtaining our own?

Play and Pray . . . Pray and Play

How do we know ourselves to be living, working, and leading in accordance with the fundamental ethos of deep leadership and the new Earth steward aristocracy? How do we know with confidence that we're not perpetuating the subtler forms of "plunder and pillage" our species has wrought for millennia upon ourselves, each other, and our world? Indeed, most of the Mammonic and Wetiko forces at work in our modern world are wielded not via sword and bullet, but from seemingly innocuous high-rise offices, board rooms, and financial spreadsheets. Divested of the offensive and defensive metallic instruments of past epochs, our contemporary towers of power are markedly different from the armadas and hordes and battlefield assemblages of power projection machinery that we've conjured and feared for hundreds of generations. Now the mechanisms and forces aren't nearly as obvious. They are hidden in plain sight—operating on the software of our minds and hearts and institutions and social circles. So how do we, eyes wide open and hearts in coherence, honestly and genuinely assess our own framework and foundation? How do we *know* we're free of the Mammonic grip of Wetiko? This may be the most important inquiry—psychological, philosophical, spiritual, pragmatic, and aesthetic—for each of us to continuously hold throughout our lives. And, as you'd expect, there's probably much more gray than black and white here, much more subtlety and nuance, when we really get down to it, requiring the utmost intellectual honesty and heartful reflection. And my own experience has proven over the years a fail-safe proxy assessment framework: play and pray . . . pray and play. This phrase, attributed to Miles Davis, may be the best, pithiest advice—sagacious wisdom—to live by. For, it is clear, when we approach our relationships, our collaborations, and most especially our work lives with (creative) playfulness and (intentional) prayerfulness, something is transformed within us. As if a hermetic secret of alchemy accessible to all of us, it's a simple rule and guide—instead of falling prey to the modern Mammonic forces of plunder and pillage, let us pray and play . . . play and pray our way toward planetary prosperity.

PART V

Systems Change Frameworks and Best Practices Checklists

"It is now highly feasible to take care of everybody on Earth at a higher standard of living than any have ever known. It no longer has to be you or me. Selfishness is unnecessary. War is obsolete. It is a matter of converting our high technology from WEAPONRY to LIVINGRY."

—BUCKMINSTER FULLER

SUSTAINABLE DEVELOPMENT GOALS

The Sustainable Development Goals (SDGs) of the 2030 Agenda for Sustainable Development were established and adopted in 2015 by *all* United Nations member-nations, creating 17 key areas of focus with a unifying aim of "peace and prosperity for people and the planet." Since their establishment, the SDGs have been the focus of 4,054 events, 1,363 publications, 8,478 actions, and 169 targets by our global community.

For more about the background, history, implementation progress (including SDG Progress Reports from 2016 onward), and detailed guidelines, visit:

sdgs.un.org/goals

INNER DEVELOPMENT GOALS

Recognizing that in order to achieve the macro-systems and "outward-facing" Sustainable Development Goals, significant transformation of human psychology and a reorientation of our interior frameworks as individuals is requisite, the Ekskäret Foundation, The New Division, and 29k Foundation established the Inner Development Goals (IDGs) in 2020. The IDGs are designed to develop and enhance personal and interpersonal abilities, qualities, and skills that are essential for people and communities to live purposeful, sustainable, and productive lives in alignment with the global community's Sustainable Development Goals. The IDGs are organized in five "dimensions" containing 23 specific skills for inner growth and development.

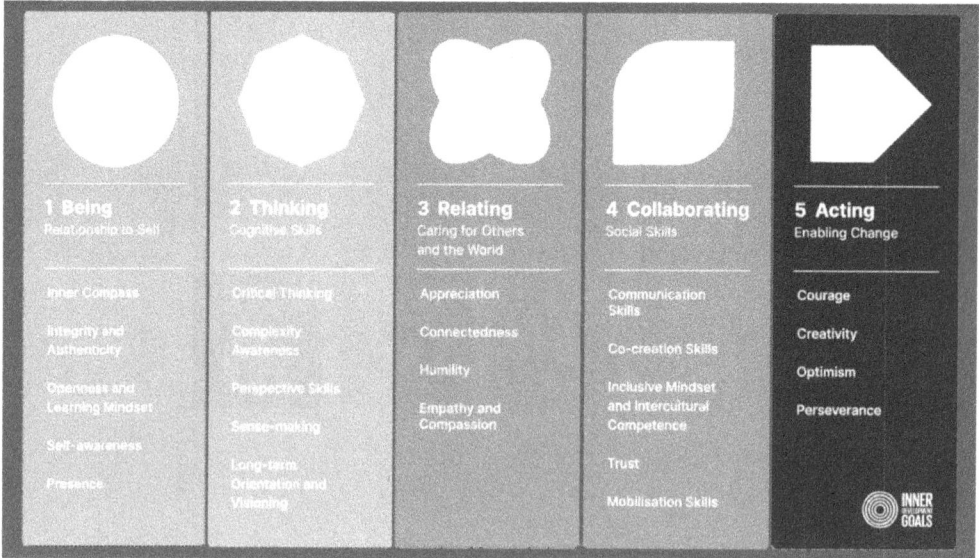

1 Being	2 Thinking	3 Relating	4 Collaborating	5 Acting
Relationship to Self	Cognitive Skills	Caring for Others and the World	Social Skills	Enabling Change
Inner Compass	Critical Thinking	Appreciation	Communication Skills	Courage
Integrity and Authenticity	Complexity Awareness	Connectedness	Co-creation Skills	Creativity
Openness and Learning Mindset	Perspective Skills	Humility	Inclusive Mindset and Intercultural Competence	Optimism
Self-awareness	Sense-making	Empathy and Compassion	Trust	Perseverance
Presence	Long-term Orientation and Visioning		Mobilisation Skills	

innerdevelopmentgoals.org

REGENERATIVE DEVELOPMENT FRAMEWORKS

Regenerative Development Goals (RDGs) expand upon and up-level the SDGs and IDGs in comprehensive frameworks across the pillars of culture, environment, economy, health, and well-being. Although as of yet not formally established and adopted by the global community, foremost among these emergent frameworks are the eight-fold framework promulgated by the Capital Institute (John Fullerton) and the more multi-faceted framework put forward by the Open Future Coalition (Kaitlin Archambault and Jamaica Stevens), and are—perhaps most importantly—being explored, embodied, and acted upon by hundreds of thousands of companies, investors, donors, investors, donors, farmers, holistic healers, and communities, and many millions of people and families worldwide.

capitalinstitute.org
openfuturecoalition.org

LEVERAGE POINTS

Places to Intervene in a System

In 1997, scientist and author Donella Meadows put forward a deceptively simple list of "leverage points" for systems change, which descends from least to greatest potential impact. All of us in the planetary prosperity movement are wise to keep this list (and the orientation of our efforts) front of mind:

12. Constants, parameters, numbers (such as subsidies, taxes, standards).

11. The sizes of buffers and other stabilizing stocks, relative to their flows.

10. The structure of material stocks and flows (such as transport networks, population age structures).

9. The lengths of delays, relative to the rate of system change.

8. The strength of negative feedback loops, relative to the impacts they are trying to correct against.

7. The gain around driving positive feedback loops.

6. The structure of information flows (who does and does not have access to information).

5. The rules of the system (such as incentives, punishments, constraints).

4. The power to add, change, evolve, or self-organize system structure.

3. The goals of the system.

2. The mindset or paradigm out of which the system—its goals, structure, rules, delays, parameters—arises.

1. The power to transcend paradigms.

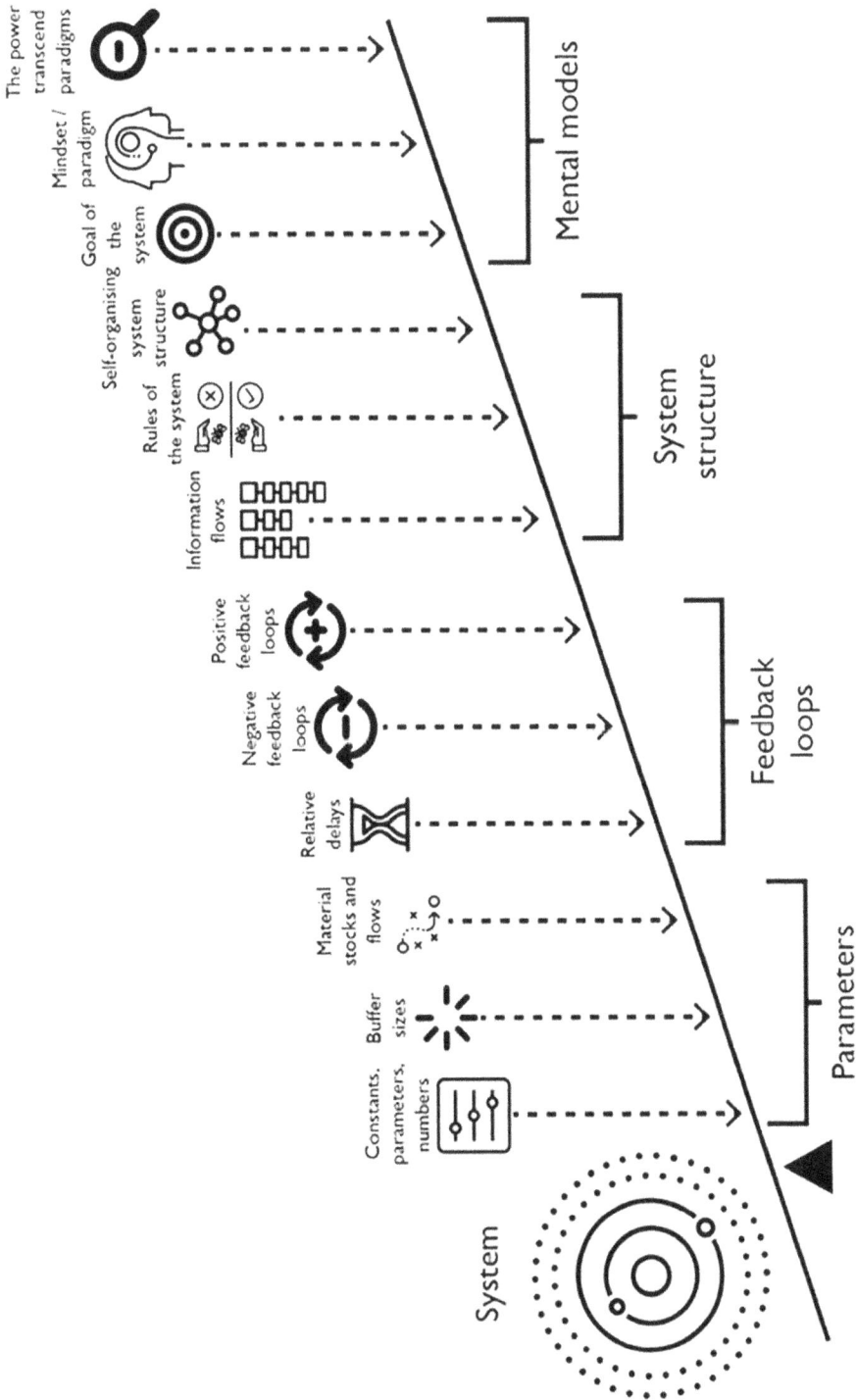

The power transcend / paradigms

Mindset / paradigm

Goal of the system

Self-organising system structure

Rules of the system

Information flows

Positive feedback loops

Negative feedback loops

Relative delays

Material stocks and flows

Buffer sizes

Constants, parameters, numbers

Mental models

System structure

Feedback loops

Parameters

System

"Urban Futures: Systemic or System Changing Interventions?"

"Now I see the secret of the making of the best persons: It is to grow in the open air and to eat and sleep with the Earth."

—WALT WHITMAN

INDIVIDUAL BEST PRACTICES CHECKLIST

Although they may seem "performative" or "prescriptive," the collection of "best practices" outlined below are offered in the spirit of having maximal beneficial impact in the broad systemic feedback loops of our shared world and of cultivating deep, multi-faceted well-being in your own life, and hence in the ways you influence others in your communities, companies, and collaborations—foundations which ultimately weave together into a global fabric of planetary prosperity. At the personal level, we can organize these best practices into five core pillars: Nature, Body, Mind, Spirit, and Community, and into three main categories: Inner Work, Intentional Living, and Impact. Our individual best practices are of course interconnected and can even be cultivated as "stacked function" strategies (for example hiking and practicing Shinrin-yoku (Nature) with a friend or family member (Community) while also enjoying fresh fruits, veggies, and spring water (Body) and discussing a literary work or spiritual/scientific article we've both recently read (Mind and Spirit)—this example speaks to Inner Well-being, Intentional Living, and Impact). As we cultivate our practice and habituate ourselves around these beneficial and vivifying behavioral patterns, we'll find that we're frequently stacking all kinds of benefits together in the normal course of our delightful, blessed (and productive, servant-leadership-led) day-to-day lives—increasingly experiencing "child-like joy" while exercising our adult responsibilities with ease and grace.

IMPACT (NATURE, SPIRIT, COMMUNITY)
- Join 1% for the Planet and commit at least 1% of your income to environmental and social non-profits like the Y on Earth Community and others discussed above
- Tithe even more than 1% using the recommended %s described in the "Eyes Wide Open" chapter above
- Bank with a mission-driven Global Alliance for Banking on Values bank such as Climate First Bank, Amalgamated Bank, and GLS Bank
- Save and invest with mission-driven funds and financial services

providers like Calvert, Goodstead, RSF | Regenerative Social Finance, Amalgamated Bank, Climate First Bank, and GLS Bank

- Procure Life Insurance, car insurance, home-owners insurance, rental insurance, health insurance, liability insurance, and other insurance products from mission-driven companies like Allianz, Bluestone Life, Lemonade, and Progressive Insurance
- Direct your purchasing power and consumer demand toward companies and products that are B-Certified, 1% for the Planet, Certified Fair Trade, Certified Organic, Certified Biodynamic, Certified Regenerative Organic, Social Enterprise, Cooperatively Owned, Employee Owned, and/or Benefits/Purpose Trust Owned
- Participate in local, regional, and national policy and political processes—use discernment to seek out kindness and compassion, especially when heated rhetoric appeals to baser xenophobic and fear-based reactionism
- Work for (or found, fund, and further) socially and environmentally mission-driven companies focused primarily on the greater good instead of extreme financial accumulation for a select few.
- Follow your bliss—your soul purpose—and strive to achieve Ikigai in your creative, personal, and professional endeavors
- Read especially Part III and IV in *Y on Earth* for more recommendations, and the *Viriditas* story for an immersive, instructive experience of them

INNER WELL-BEING (NATURE, BODY, MIND, SPIRIT, COMMUNITY)

- Practice Shinrin-yoku frequently—several times per week for at least an hour, if possible, and overnight in a tent beneath the stars and trees at least five times per year
- Conduct "digital detoxes" frequently (see "Unplug" chapter in *Y on Earth*)
- Cultivate community connections, especially with aligned fraternal, spiritual, study, and service-oriented groups
- Create or join a variety of community cohorts (especially land stewardship, biodynamic and regenerative farm based when possible), "master mind" cohorts (aligned around your vocational and avocational aspirations), spiritual fellowships (based in kindness, service, and inclusivity), and seek out opportunities to mentor and to be mentored.
- Cultivate your mental acuity by reading, (books, essays, articles, and poetry!), studying languages (even the occasional etymology

search is additive), solving puzzles, playing strategy games like chess and Go, and be sure to "tile," protect, and steward your "ecology of thinking" (by "guarding the gate" as it were: eliminating negative and biased media and frivolous, "low-vibe" mind- and time-wasting media from your purview), plan your day first before diving into the fray (so that your work may thus be begun in order, conducted in peace, and concluded in harmony), take frequent walking breaks to breathe deeply, stretch, and gaze at the trees, mountains, lakes, skies, and distant horizons

- Drink loads of pure water, herbal tea, and blended, alkalizing organic veggies and fruits

- Make aromatherapy, exercise, quality sleep, water immersion (soaking, swimming), deep breathing, humming/singing, sound and music, holistic modalities (Jin Shin Jyutsu, massage), and martial art and movement practices (Tai Chi, yoga) part of your regular routine

- Take good care of your emotional self by acknowledging the temporary "weather" of your feelings, practicing gratitude, seeking professional support for deep healing (especially of past traumas), frequently laughing, nurturing healthy (not toxic) relationships and deepening into devotional disciplines to continually align with your deepest soul-purpose

- Stay connected with family and friends by visiting in-person and calling or video chatting with those farther away. Tea times, meals, hikes, walks, and game nights are great ways to cultivate these connections. Book clubs, study groups, fraternal organizations, community gatherings, and themed potlucks are also excellent, as are Biodynamic land alchemy ceremonies and seasonal seed saving / swapping events. Volunteering and mentoring in your community are well-being "gold"—especially among the less fortunate and at biodynamic and regenerative farms!

- Declutter your schedule (consider using a paper calendar instead of a digital calendar—you may be pleasantly surprised by how stress-reducing this can be!)

- Establish ample time alone and be sure to take walks, get in nature, and have time to think, reflect, pray, and listen to the guidance that will show up when you're quietly solo.

- Harmonize and balance your time—after all it's your most precious resource!

- Detoxify your home and office, cultivate plants and flowers, frequent fresh air, hang art with bright yellows and greens, and otherwise steward your space for simplicity, beauty, and harmony

(less noise, more music and ambient sound, less clutter and more feng shui, let beauty and joy be your main organizing principle)
- Read especially Part II in *Y on Earth* and find many clues and insights in *Viriditas* as well

INTENTIONAL LIVING (BODY, MIND, SPIRIT, NATURE, COMMUNITY)
- Detoxify your home, office, and other frequented spaces (cleaning products, hygiene, beauty, and yard and garden products can be among the worst—and therefore the best places to start your home and office detox!)
- Keep plenty of houseplants and flowers growing indoors (especially spider plants and other super air-purifiers) and grow flowers, foods, and herbal medicines in outdoor spaces (even if it's just potted plants on the stoop!)
- Become proficient in your preparedness and resilience skills, including the knowledge, community connections, asset inventories, and skills and supplies potentially needed in emergency situations—see beworldaware.com for more pointers
- Cultivate food forests in your yard and neighborhood and visit regenerative and biodynamic farms in your region (see the "Grow, Know, Show" approach to intentional eating in the "Eat" chapter in *Y on Earth)*
- Connect frequently with forests, meadows, water, and skies—take time to slow down and live intentionally

CORPORATE BEST PRACTICES CHECKLIST

Whether your company is an early-stage start-up or an established corporation quite mature in its lifecycle, the following recommendations will better align it for success and impact as we progress into mid and late 21st century stewardship. As with our individual practices, our corporate practices are also highly interconnected, but for easy administration we can organize these strategies into Internal (within the organizational boundaries of the company) and External opportunities and actions.

INTERNAL

- First of all, ensure that your company's core mission, vision, and purpose are deeply aligned with the greater good of planetary prosperity, and that your products and services are in-line with the same.
- Secondly, ensure that your governance and cash-flow participation structures are inclusive and incentivize your entire team to align as deeply as possible with the long-term interests of the company (and therefore, vice-versa)—see especially chapter four, "The Body Corporate," above.
- Third, do all that you reasonably can to foster a culture and environment of "whole person" cultivation and stewardship—especially encouraging, enabling, and incentivizing your team to take on the practices and intentional living strategies outlined in the Individual Best Practices Checklist.
- Fourth, get certified! The B-Certification provides a robust framework for continual improvement, and provides access to an extraordinary (and growing) ecosystem of companies throughout the world working toward planetary prosperity.

EXTERNAL

- Bank with Global Alliance for Banking on Values member banks such as Climate First Bank, Amalgamated Bank, GLS Bank (and others) and utilize financing solutions from other financial institutions working toward planetary prosperity such as RSF | Regenerative Social Finance

- Procure insurance products for your company and team from mission-aligned firms such as Allianz, Bluestone Life, Lemonade, and Progressive
- Give at least 1% of your top-line revenue to environmental and social non-profits through 1% for the Planet membership, and consider evolving your business model all the way toward a true social enterprise in which over 50% of your net free cash flow (after reinvestment, research, development, and taxes) is donated to such non-profits (perhaps *pari passu* with investor proceeds, if applicable)
- Seek out the best "Earth steward aristocracy" versions of each and every financial and transactional "touchpoint" such as payment processing and point of sale services so that every transaction, every little fee "haircut" is going not to "old-school" legacy vendors (and conventional accumulated capital pools) but to the most environmentally and socially progressive vendors whose models embody Ecocene ethics and deliberately steer capital toward the areas of impact, stewardship, and regeneration needed to achieve planetary prosperity.
- Hire the accounting, brokerage, legal, branding, copywriting, graphics, marketing, public relations, trade show, and other professional service providers who themselves embody the progressive principles of planetary prosperity, and seek out goods and services from the known networks of mission-aligned businesses like 1% for the Planet, B-Certified, Coop, Employee-Owned, Regenerative Organic, and the like. Herein, at scale, we will find previously dormant financial and economic feedback loops that will accrue tremendous benefit to our entire world when thus activated and amplified.

DECLARATION OF INTERDEPENDENCE

As a progressive evolution and powerful echo of the great victory for liberty and self-governance contained in the original Declaration of Independence (signed in 1776), a Declaration of *Inter*dependence has emerged in the most recent century in which ecological stewardship and regeneration are woven into the fabric of social justice, peace, and economic sustainability, creating a framework for the familyhood of humanity and anticipating the promise of a future Ecocene era marked by planetary prosperity. What follows are two versions of this Declaration of Interdependence, the first promulgated by the great historian Will Durant (along with Meyer David and Dr. Christian Richard) in response to the rise of fascism and the horrors of the World Wars (and added to the United States Congressional Record in 1945 by Hon. Ellis E. Patterson), and the second promulgated by David Suzuki, et al., at the United Nations 1992 Earth Summit in Rio de Janeiro, Brazil.

Declaration of INTERdependence (1944)

Human progress having reached a high level through respect for the liberty and dignity of men, it has become desirable to re-affirm these evident truths:

That differences of race, color, and creed are natural, and that diverse groups, institutions, and ideas are stimulating factors in the development of man;

That to promote harmony in diversity is a responsible task of religion and statesmanship;

That since no individual can express the whole truth, it is essential to treat with understanding and good will those whose views differ from our own;

That by the testimony of history intolerance is the door to violence, brutality and dictatorship; and

That the realization of human interdependence and solidarity is the best guard of civilization.

Therefore, we solemnly resolve, and invite everyone to join in united action.

To uphold and promote human fellowship through mutual consideration and respect;

To champion human dignity and decency, and to safeguard these without distinction of race, or color, or creed;

To strive in concert with others to discourage all animosities arising from these differences, and to unite all groups in the fair play of civilized life.

Rooted in freedom, children of the same Divine, sharing everywhere a common human blood, we declare again that all men are brothers, and that mutual tolerance is the price of liberty.

Declaration of INTERdependence (1992)

This we know

We are the earth, through the plants and animals that nourish us.

We are the rains and the oceans that flow through our veins.

We are the breath of the forests of the land, and the plants of the sea.

We are human animals, related to all other life as descendants of the firstborn cell.

We share with these kin a common history, written in our genes.

We share a common present, filled with uncertainty.

And **we** share a common future, as yet untold.

We humans are but one of thirty million species weaving the thin layer of life enveloping the world.

The **stability** of communities of living things depends upon this diversity.

Linked in that web, we are interconnected—using, cleansing, sharing and replenishing the fundamental elements of life.

Our home, planet Earth, is finite; all life shares its resources and the energy from the sun, and therefore has limits to growth.

For the first time, we have touched those limits.

When we compromise the air, the water, the soil and the variety of life, we steal from the endless future to serve the fleeting present.

This we believe

Humans have become so numerous and our tools so powerful
that we have driven fellow creatures to extinction, dammed
the great rivers, torn down ancient forests, poisoned the
earth, rain and wind, and ripped holes in the sky.

Our science has brought pain as well as joy; our comfort is
paid for by the suffering of millions.

We are learning from our mistakes, we are mourning our
vanished kin, and we now build a new politics of hope.

We respect and uphold the absolute need for clean air, water
and soil.

We see that economic activities that benefit the few while
shrinking the inheritance of many are wrong.

And since environmental degradation erodes biological
capital forever, full ecological and social cost must enter
all equations of development.

We are one brief generation in the long march of time; the
future is not ours to erase.

So where knowledge is limited, we will remember all those
who will walk after us, and err on the side of caution.

This we resolve

*All this that we know and believe must now become the
foundation of the way we live.*

*At this turning point in our relationship with Earth,
we work for an evolution: from dominance to
partnership; from fragmentation to connection; from
insecurity, to interdependence.*

When you are inspired by some
Great purpose, some
Extraordinary project,
All your thoughts break
Their bonds: Your mind
Transcends limitations,
Your consciousness
Expands in every
Direction and you find
Yourself in a new, great
And wonderful world.
Dormant forces,
Faculties and talents
Become alive, and you
Discover yourself to be a
Greater person by far
Than you ever dreamed
Yourself to be.

— PATANJALI

ACKNOWLEDGMENTS

'Tis cliché to say that "it takes a village" to shepherd a book project to full fruition—cliché and true. In the case of this book, however, it is a significant understatement—especially given how many authors, organizations, and production team members have been involved in its genesis.

Thus, it is with great pleasure and deep gratitude that I acknowledge each of the following:

First and foremost, I must say a very special thank-you to Maggie McLaughlin, whose brilliant recommendation several years ago to create a book featuring many of the tremendous leaders that we host on our Y on Earth Community Podcast and that we collaborate with throughout our global network was the impetus for this ambitious project. And, prior to and including *Our Biggest Deal*, it is Maggie who has made all of our Earth Water Press publications so beautifully and thoughtfully designed and produced—thank you Maggie—bravo!

And, a very special thank-you to Jake Welsh as well, whose graphic design "fingerprints" are found cover to cover and throughout the entire book—the graphics and book cover art are fabulous—thank you Jake!

And, of course, a very special thank you to each of the essay authors—your contributions have enhanced this project immeasurably: John Perkins, Dilafruz Khonikboyeva, Mark Finser, Dr. Riane Eisler, Dr. Robert Cloninger, Sarah Arao, Kate Williams, Tom Chi, Jack Wielebinski, Samantha Power, Dr. Stephanie Gripne, Azuraye Wycoff, Eduardo Esparza, Georgia Kelly, Hannah Odell, Dr. Jandel Allen-Davis, Steve Farrell, John Rogers, Miranda Clendening, Alena Maslova, Hunter Lovins, Dr. Martin Frick, Henry Mitchell, John Milton, Maria Rodale, Kevin Townley, and Kawenniiosta Jock.

To Bud Wilson for working behind the scenes and "quarterbacking" the process to put John Milton's essay together so cogently.

Thank you to Emily Campbell for helping to research and compile the myriad corporate data and information that made their way into our Case Study Vignettes.

To our beloved editors, David Aretha of Clean Edits and his project intern Amina Alieva—thank you both for cleaning-up our drafts and polishing our prose!

A very special thank you to Tim Capria, Mariel Soehner, and their colleagues at Husch Blackwell for generously providing pro bono legal support to this project.

To Brad Lidge, Verona Rylander, Artem Nikulkov, Miranda Clendening, Osha Chesnutt-Perry, and Caressa Ayres for reading early versions and providing such encouraging and thoughtful feedback on the drafts.

To the many financial supporters, partners, and sponsors of Our Biggest Deal and our work at the Y on Earth Community in general, especially including: andCO Hospitality, the Brad and Lindsay Lidge Family Foundation, the Blaise and Leslie

Carrig Family Foundation, Bluestone Life Insurance, Chelsea Green Publishing, Clean Content, Climate First Bank, Dobrosphera Kind Media, Dr. Bronner's, Earth Coast Productions, Gaia AI, Goodstead, Husch Blackwell, Launch Legal, Martin Newton, Patagonia, Patagonia's Home Planet Fund, Regenerative World Quest, Riverside Boulder, Sally Ranney, Shaye Skiff Communications, SoundLight Foundation, Transition Network International, Verona Rylander Philanthropies, Wele Waters, and Zeal Optics. And to all of the unnamed Y on Earth Supporters, past, present, and future, especially our Global Advisory Board members Stewardship Circle members, Visionary Council members, and Community Impact Ambassadors.

And a very special thank you to Brad Lidge and Artem Nikulkov for your fabulous friendship and unwavering support of all that we're accomplishing through the Y on Earth Community—it is a precious joy to navigate and celebrate these "middle year adventures" together in the bonds of fellowship!

To Verona Rylander for our delightful friendship, founded in beauty and the ethics of aesthetics—you're a true artist and poet and inspire me and so many others with your creativity and insight.

To Martin Newton for years of friendship, fun, and financial support—it has been quite a journey, my friend... no straight lines, right?!

To Miranda Clendening for "getting" the shared vision of *Our Biggest Deal*, Ecoscene, and Viriditas at such a profound level—we are being guided by the mycelial neural networks to be sure!

To my daughter Osha Chesnutt-Perry for so many enthusiastic and enriching conversations about the themes of polycrisis, mental health, and the multifaceted solutions available to us—you are a source of hope and inspiration!

To my son Indigo Hunter Chesnutt-Perry for so many early conversations about sustainable business, planetary prosperity, and environmental stewardship around the campfire, while hiking, and while enjoying cigars together in the mountain wildernesses!

To Alena Maslova, Dimitrii Maslov, and the Dobrosphera Kind Media Team— thank you for collaborating so wonderfully on this book, our Ecoscene project, and so many other aspects of our Y on Earth Community work!

To the entire Y on Earth Community ecosystem of friends, colleagues, and collaborators, especially our beloved Ambassadors and our Y on Earth Community Podcast guests: Dr. Nancy Tuchman, Ph.D.; Judith Schwartz; Brook Le Van; Rev. Fletcher Harper; Stephanie Syson; Safi Kaskas; Rev. Kalani Souza; Mark Retzloff; Katie Garces; Lauren Tucker; Angela Maria Ortiz Roa; Maureen Hart; Sarah Davison Tracy; Dr. Ghita Carroll, Ph.D.; Brett KenCairn; Adam Stenftenagel; Clay Dusel; Brigitte Mars; Christine Robinson; Chef Maria Cooper; Sahar Alsahlani; David Haskell; Hunter Lovins, Esq.; Dr. Dana McGrady, N.D.; Jennifer Menke; Scott Black; Courtney Cosgriff; Dr. Jandel Allen-Davis, M.D.; Artem Nikulkov; Lila Sophia Tresemer; RWB Kevin Townley; Maija West, Esq.; Dr. Ralph ("Bud")

Sorenson, Ph.D.; Nicole Vitello; Dr. Nicola Siso, Ph.D.; Brad "Lights Out" Lidge; Dayna Seraye; Kimba Arem; Addison Luck; Osha Chesnutt-Perry; Chip Commins; Pat Frazier, N.P.; Adam Eggleston; Alex Martin; Xiye Bastida; Geraldine Patrick; Thea Maria Carlson; Matt Gray, C.S.O.; Sally Ranney; Dr. Anita Sanchez, Ph.D.; Jonathan Granoff; Emilie McGlone; Paul ("DJ Spooky") Miller; Trammell Crow; Joanie Klar; Brian Czech; Tiffany Cook; Fallan Jacobs; Kawenniiosta Jock; Sarah Drew; Stone Hunter; Ludovica Martella; Michael Cain; Pastor Brian Kunkler; David Bronner; Bethany Yarrow; Eric Lombardi; Meadow Cook; Hunter Chesnutt-Perry; Ryan Zinn; Jeff Moyer; Karenna Gore; John Perkins; Sydney Steinberg; Harrison Steinberg; Dr. Oakleigh Thorne II, Ph.D.; Charles Orgbon III; Shelby Kaminski; Maria Nikulkova; Brian Dillon; Adrian Alex Rodriguez; Lem Tingley; Dr. Julienne Strove, Ph.D.; Ryan Lewis; Judith Schwartz; Kate Williams; Jacquelyn Francis; Rennie Davis; eneral Wesley Clark; Dr. Yichao Rui, Ph.D.; Nicole Wallace; Tyler Bell; Finian Makepeace; Mike Lewis; Tom Chi; John Liu; John Fullerton; Ron Lemire; Lin Bautze; David Beasley; William ("Sandy") Karstens; Julie Morris; Louise Chawla; Nick Chambers; Geoffrey May; Jackie Bowen; Elaine Blumenhein; Charmaine Boudreaux; Jason Denham; Ann Armbrecht; Dr. Robert Cloninger, Ph.D., M.D.; Gero Leson; Layth Matthews; Stephen Brooks; Elizabeth Whitlow; Mike Bronner; Miguel Gil; Richard Hardiman; Rowdy Yeatts; Oliver Retzloff; Eric Knutson; Dr. David Laird; Marissa Pulaski; Nick DiDomenico; Danielle Ryan Broida; Dr. David Haskel; John Perkins; Ruby Au; Dr. Bernard Amadei; Hayley Nenadal; Douglas Gardner; Hanne Strong; Rev. Matthew Fox; Chief Tuwe; Ari Brasil; Ben Raskin; Georgia Kelly; Tom Chi; Nisha Poulose; Dr. James Gordon; Nathan Stuck; Maria Rodale; Cynthia Tina; Vicki Hird; Jerry Tinianow; Matthew Derr; Sheila Foster; Jorge Fontanez; Ander Etxeberria; Hunter Lovins; Nicolette Hahn Niman; Ueli Hurter; Jean-Michel Florin; Sarah Arao; John Rogers; Lisa Bronner; Soraya Afzali; Gabe Brown; Helen Atthowe; Sophie Monpeyssen; Olivier Girard; Jake Plummer; Dr. Elaine Ingham; Jared Meyers; Kate Wilson; Kelpie Wilson; Dahr Jamail; John Milton; Ken LaRoe; Jeff Poppen; Tina Morris, and Cynthia James Stewart. Your work, words, and wisdom have surely made an imprint on this project. I must give a special shout-out to Artem Nikulkov who, like Maggie with this book, suggested years ago that we launch a podcast series. Who knew it would become such a powerful, mycelial engine for connection and collaboration!?

To Sophie Monpeyssen and Olivier Girard of the Le Ciel Foundation, and our "Team 5" cohort on Financial Systems and Coherence Councils: Chloe Bradbury-Rutherford, Samir Singh, Rebecca Saltman, Justin Winters, Elia Braunert, Don Duke, Hristiyan Atanasov, Jordan Sukut, Nina Holtsberry, Sean Dilweg, and Tina Marie Blohm—many thanks for all you do!

And thank-you to John and Dianne Rogers for your generosity during the Le Ciel Foundation gathering in Barcelona.

To Blake Terry, Roger Lawley, Martin Sugg, Matthew Petrocco, Rich Carrol, Greg Harris, Jack Dawson, Scott Youmans, Darren Klinefelter, Tim Burger, Kevin

Pardon, Jason Ryan, Paul Dart, Lance Whitehorse, Bill Deaver, Jason Burke, Michael Nabors, Nathan Feinberg, Johnny Robson, Robert Serrano, Henry Mitchell, Jerry Spainhower, Aaron Spear, Dane Barns, Rob Jones, Bobby Juchem, Aaron Klostermeyer, Mike Long, Ben Williams, Terry Christiansen, Scott Wolter, Mike Moore, Myron Deputat, and Rene Perez.

To Professor William "Sandy" Karstens for your enthusiastic support of our work at the Y on Earth Community, and your early feedback on the manuscript of this book.

To Professor Adrian Del Caro for all of the wonderful "deep dive" conversations into various philosophical considerations, contemplations, and conundrums, especially the timeless Faustian wisdom and the luminous insights of the great aphorist and his Zarathustra—as ol' HH tells us, the journey to the east continues forever!

To Professor Ann Schmiesing for your encouraging, patient, and copious use of "red ink" on my early forays into writing—thank you for awakening a profound appreciation for the craft itself!

To Angela Thieman Dino for your commitment and mentorship around human rights in particular and a spirituality rooted in service to the greater good in general.

To the Jesuits of Regis High School who inculcated in us a strong understanding that the world can be made better through our individual *caritas,* care, concern, and concerted action, most especially Father James Burshek, Father Phil Steele, and Father Mark Bosco.

To Bruce Bridges for all of your kindness, support, and hospitality at the chateau . . . and of course for solving half of the world's problems whenever we chat, and doing what we can to keep up with the ladies in Pitch.

To my brother, Ethan Perry, for our deep ethics, systems change, and spirituality discussions, and for all of the creative play over the years, including dancing with the angelic forces.

To my mother, Marcia Perry, for all of your thoughtful, unwavering support and appreciation, and for embodying an agapic love directionally indicative of our great Mother Earth's.

A very special thank you to my sweetheart Caressa Ayres for indulging and lovingly supporting me through the seasons as I pondered out loud the many themes and topics of this and previous books; for all of your thoughtful input and feedback on the early drafts, graphics, and cover design; and most especially for your love and affection throughout the entire process . . . thank you gazillions!

And to several dearly departed friends and heroes, mentors, especially Jane Goodall, Scott Pittman, William Irwin Thompson, Kevin Townley, and Bernard Lietaer—you have each given so much to me and to our world, and we are all much better off having had you among us and having your legacies living with us now.

REFERENCES

Allianz Global Insurance. "Sustainability Through Time." https://www.allianz.com/content/dam/onemarketing/azcom/Allianz_com/sustainabilityreport/2024/index.html (accessed 4.10.25).

Amalgamated Bank Annual Reports. https://www.annualreports.com/Company/amalgamated-bank (accessed 4.10.25).

Angheloiu, Corina and Mike Tennant. "Urban Futures: Systemic or System Changing Interventions? A Literature Review Using Meadows' Leverage Points as Analytical Framework." *Science Direct*. Cities: Volume 104, September 2020, 102808. https://www.sciencedirect.com/science/article/abs/pii/S0264275119313265.

Arnold, Laura and John. Arnold Ventures website. https://www.arnoldventures.org/about (accessed 2.16.25).

B-Lab. "About B-Corp Certification: Measuring a Company's Entire Social and Environmental Impact." B-Lab website (accessed 2.16.25). https://www.bcorporation.net/en-us/certification/.

Bachofen, Johann Jakob. *Das Mutterrecht (Mother Right): An English Translation.* English translation of 1861 original by David Partenheimer. Lewiston, NY: Edwin Mellen Press. 2005.

Bailey, Alice. *Money: The Medium of Loving Distribution.* Excerpts from various writings compiled by The Lucius Trust (accessed 2.9.25). https://www.lucistrust.org/content/download/14991/187279/file/MONEY-compilation.pdf.

Barr, Damian. "We Are Not All In The Same Boat. We Are All In The Same Storm. Some Are On Super-Yachts. Some Have Just The One Oar." March 25, 2021. https://www.damianbarr.com/latest/tag/We+are+not+all+in+the+same+boat.+We+are+all+in+the+same+storm.

Benson, Tracy and Sheri Marlin. *The Habit-Forming Guide to Becoming a Systems Thinker, Second Edition.* Waters Center for Systems Thinking. 2021.

Bernstein, Martin. "Money for Nothing: Why the Modern Financial Sector is Better at Extracting Rents than Funding the Future." *Jacobin.* Summer 2025. https://jacobin.com/2025/06/money-for-nothing/.

Berry, Thomas. *The Christian Future and the Fate of Earth.* Edited by Mary Evelyn Tucker and John Grim Maryknoll. NY: Orbis Books, 2009.

Bookchin, Murray. "Toward a Philosophy of Nature—The Basis for an Ecological Ethics." In Michael Tobias (ed.). *Deep Ecology.* Op. cit.

Bourgeault, Cynthia. "Radiant Intimacy of the Heart." Science and Nonduality Conference Keynote Speech. December 23, 2017. https://www.youtube.com/watch?v=I_bV8mxaXhE

Braden, Gregg. *Pure Human: The Hidden Truth of Our Divinity, Power, and Destiny.* Carlsbad, California: Hay House. 2025.

Brown, Lester R. "Ecopsychology and the Environmental Revolution: An Environmental Foreword." In Theodore Roszak, et al. (eds.). *Ecopsychology.* Op cit.

Capra, Fritjof. "Deep Ecology: A New Paradigm." In George Sessions (ed.), *Deep Ecology for the 21st Century.* Boston: Shambhala. 1995.

Capra, Fritjof. *The Hidden Connections: Integrating The Biological, Cognitive, and Social Dimensions of Life into a Science of Sustainability.* New York: Doubleday Press. 2002.

Capra, Fritjof. *The Turning Point: Science, Society and the Rising Culture.* New York: Simon and Schuster. 1982.

Capra, Fritjof. *The Web of Life: A New Scientific Understanding of Living Systems.* New York: Anchor Books. 1996.

Capra, Fritjof and Hazel Henderson. "Qualitative Growth: A Conceptual Framework for Finding Solutions to Our Current Crisis that are Economically Sound, Ecologically Sustainable, and Socially Just." *Fritjof Capra Blog Post.* September 14, 2009. https://www.fritjofcapra.net/qualitative-growth/.

Childre, Doc Lew, and Howard Martin. *The HeartMath Solution: The Institute of HeartMath's Revolutionary Program for Engaging the Power of the Heart's Intelligence.* San Francisco: Harper. 1999.

Cuginotti, Augusto. "Imaginal Cells | The Caterpillar's Job to Resist the Butterfly." https://augustocuginotti.com/imaginal-cells-caterpillars-job-to-resist-butterfly/ (Accessed 7.10.25).

Cushing, Ellen. "Americans Need to Party More: We're Not Doing It As Much As We Used To. You Can Be the Change We Need." *The Atlantic.* January 2025. https://www.theatlantic.com/family/archive/2025/01/throw-more-parties-loneliness/681203/?utm_campaign=atlantic-daily-newsletter&utm_content=20250126&utm_source=newsletter&utm_medium=email&utm_term=The+Atlantic+Daily.

Choi, Sooyeon and Richard A. Feinberg. "The LOHAS (Lifestyle of Health and Sustainability) Scale Development and Validation. *Sustainability.* 2021, 13(4), 1598. https://www.mdpi.com/2071-1050/13/4/1598.

Cogito blog for OECD Centre for Entrepreneurship https://oecdcogito.blog/2024/06/04/together-for-good-why-japan-is-backing-worker-co-operatives/.

Devall, Bill and George Sessions. *Deep Ecology: Living as if Nature Mattered.* Layton: Gibbs Smith. 1985.

Devereux, Paul, et al. *Earthmind.* New York: Harper & Row. 1989.

Duggan, Lisa. *Mean Girl: Ayn Rand and the Culture of Greed.* University of California Press. 2019.

Duquette, Nicolas. "Highlighting The (Elitist) History of the Charitable Contribution Income Tax Deduction." *HistPhil.* April 23, 2019. https://histphil.org/2019/04/23/highlighting-the-elitist-history-of-the-charitable-contribution-income-tax-deduction/.

Dwivedi, O. P., "Vedic Heritage for Environmental Stewardship." *Worldviews*, Vol. 1, No. 1 (April 1997), pp. 25-36. https://www.jstor.org/stable/43809624.

Elliot, Larry. "World's Billionaires Should Pay Minimum 2% Wealth Tax, say G20 Ministers: Brazil, Germany, Spain, and South Africa Sign Motion for Fairer Tax System to Deliver £250bn a Year Extra to Fight Poverty and Climate Crisis." *The Guardian.* April 25, 2024. https://www.theguardian.com/inequality/2024/apr/25/billionaires-should-pay-minimum-two-per-cent-wealth-tax-say-g20-ministers.

Falk, Pamela. "U.N. Hunger Agency Chief Follows Up Tweet Exchange with Elon Musk with Plea to Billionaires." *CBS News.* November 5, 2021. https://www.cbsnews.com/news/david-beasley-elon-musk-world-food-programme-plea-to-billionaires/.

Feld, Brad. *Entrepreneur's Weekly Nietzsche: A Book for Disruptors.* Lioncrest Publishing. 2021.

Feld, Brad. *Give First: The Power of Mentorship.* Ideapress Publishing. 2025.

Feld, Brad. *Startup Communities: Building an Entrepreneurial Ecosystem in Your City.* Wiley. 2020.

Feld, Brad. *The Startup Community Way: Evolving an Entrepreneurial Ecosystem.* Wiley. 2020.

Forbes, Jack. *Columbus and Other Cannibals: The Wétiko Disease of Exploitation, Imperialism, and Terrorism.* Rev. ed. New York: Seven Stories Press. 2008.

French Gates, Melinda. *The Next Day: Transitions, Change, and Moving Forward.* Flatiron Books / Bluebird Publishing, 2025.

Fuller, Buckminster. *Operating Manual for Spaceship Earth.* Southern Illinois University Press. 1969.

Fullerton, John. *Regenerative Capitalism: How Universal Principles and Patterns Will Shape Our New Economy.* Connecticut: Capital Institute. 2015.

Fullerton, John. *Regenerative Economics: Revolutionary Thinking for a World in Crisis.* Gabriola Island, Canada: New Society Publishers. 2025 (forthcoming).

Gashweseoma, Martin. "Hopi Message to the United Nations." Address to United Nations. New York, New York. December 10, 1992. https://crab.rutgers.edu/users/omaha/NAI/Hopi_Prophecy.htm.

Gimbutas, Marija. *The Language of the Goddess* (with Foreword by Joseph Campbell). New York, New York: HarperCollins Publishers, 19j89.

Giving Block. "The 'Great Wealth Transfer' Signals a New Era in Philanthropy." By *The Giving Blog* (website). July 29, 2024. https://thegivingblock.com/resources/the-great-wealth-transfer-and-philanthropy/.

Global Alliance for the Rights of Nature. https://www.garn.org/.

Gopnik, Adam. "The Art of Aphorism: Why Are These Fragments of Wisdom—Empirical or Mystical, Funny or Profound—Such an Enduring Form?" The New Yorker. July 15, 2019. https://www.newyorker.com/magazine/2019/07/22/the-art-of-aphorism.

Hanauer, Nick. "Beware Fellow Plutocrats, the Pitchforks are Coming: The Dirty Secret of Capitalism - - And a New Way Forward." New York: *TED Talks—TED@250 Salon NY2014.* https://www.ted.com/talks/nick_hanauer_beware_fellow_plutocrats_the_pitchforks_are_coming?language=en (Talk delivered August, 2014, and posted to TED on September, 2019).

Hall, Don. *The Regeneration Handbook: Transform Yourself to Transform the World.* New Society Publishers. 2024.

Hall, Manley P. *The Secret Teachings of All Ages.* Original limited edition first published 1928. Later editions published by Philosophical Research Society, Los Angeles, California.

Henderson, Hazel. *Building a Win-Win World: Life Beyond Global Economic Warfare.* Oakland, CA: Berrett-Koehler Publishers. 1996.

Henderson, Hazel. *Ethical Markets: Growing the Green Economy.* White River Junction, VT: Chelsea Green Publishing. 2006.

Henderson, Hazel. *Paradigms in Progress: Life Beyond Economics.* London: Adamantine. 1993.

Henderson, Hazel and Daisaku Ikeda. *Planetary Citizenship: Your Values, Beliefs, and Actions Can Shape a Sustainable World.* Santa Monica, CA: Middleway Press. 2004.

Henderson, Hazel, Jean Houston, Barbara Marx-Hubbard, Barbara Delaney, and Mary Clare Powell. *The Power of Yin: Celebrating Female Consciousness.* New York: Cosimo. 1997, 2007.

Hinton, David. *Wild Mind, Wild Earth: Our Place in the Sixth Extinction*. Boulder, Colorado: Shambhala Publications. 2022.

HRH Prince Charles. *Harmony: A New Way of Looking at Our World*. New York: HarperCollins. 2010.

Hui, Andrew. *A Theory of the Aphorism: From Confucius to Twitter* A Theory of the Aphorism: From Confucius to Twitter: Hui, Andrew: 9780691188959: Amazon.com: Books.

Inner Development Goals. https://innerdevelopmentgoals.org/. Basel, Switzerland: Inner Development Goals Foundation. Accessed June 19, 2025.

International Cooperative Alliance company website. https://ica.coop/en/cooperatives/facts-and-figures. (accessed 1.15.25).

Kahn, Iqbal, James Davies, Rodrigo Lluberas, Anthony Shorrocks et al. *Global Wealth Report 2023*. The Credit Suisse Research Institute (CSRI), Credit Suisse AG, UBS Group. https://www.ubs.com/global/en/family-office-uhnw/reports/global-wealth-report-2023.

Kahn, Iqbal, Robert Karofsky, Enrico Börger, et al. *Global Wealth Report 2024*. The Credit Suisse Research Institute (CSRI), Credit Suisse AG, UBS Group. https://www.ubs.com/us/en/wealth-management/insights/global-wealth-report.html.

Keim, Brandon. "Whales Could One Day Be Heard in Court—And In Their Own Words." National Geographic. April 24, 2025. https://www.nationalgeographic.com/animals/article/whale-communication-legal-personhood.

Kessel, Andrew. "Starbucks Faces Scrutiny as CEO's Pay is 6,666 Times that of the Median Barista. *Investopedia*. September 11, 2025. https://www.investopedia.com/starbucks-faces-scrutiny-as-ceo-s-pay-is-6-666-times-that-of-the-median-barista-11807782.

Klaax, Brian. "The Rise of the Selfish Plutocrats: Instead of Pursuing Philanthropy, Many Now Seek to Evade Social Responsibility." *The Atlantic*. February 7, 2025. https://www.theatlantic.com/international/archive/2025/02/the-ultrarich-werent-always-this-selfish/681599/?utm_source=newsletter&utm_medium=email&utm_campaign=the-atlantic-am&utm_term=The+Atlantic+AM.

Konstan, David. "Greek Friendship." The American Journal of Philology. Vol. 117. No. 1 (Spring, 1996). Johns Hopkins University Press. http://www.jstor.org/stable/1562154.

La France, Adrienne. "Capitulation is Contagious: When Fear Spreads in a Society, Powerful People Who Know Better Are Often the First to Show Their Weakness." *The Atlantic*. March 2025. https://www.theatlantic.com/magazine/archive/2025/03/washington-post-bezos-trump-cartoon-ann-telnaes/681406/?utm_source=newsletter&utm_medium=email&utm_campaign=the-atlantic-am&utm_term=The+Atlantic+AM.

Lala, R. M. *For the Love of India: The Life and Times of Jamsetji Tata*. Penguin India. 2004.

Lao Tzu. *Tao Te Ching: A New English Version*. Translated by Stephen Mitchell. Harper Perennial. 1991.

Le Ciel Foundation. London, UK. https://lecielfoundation.com/.

Leon, Natalie. "Forget the Four Seasons: How Embracing 72 Japanese 'Micro-Seasons' Could Change Your Garden (And Your Life)." *The Guardian*. May 11,2024. https://www.theguardian.com/lifeandstyle/article/2024/may/11/how-embracing-72-japanese-micro-seasons-could-change-your-garden-and-your-life.

Levy, Paul. *Disspelling Wetiko: Breaking the Curse of Evil*. North Atlantic Books. 2013.

Levy, Paul. *Wetiko: Healing the Mind-Virus That Plagues Our World*. Rochester, Vermont: Inner Traditions. 2021.

Lietaer, Bernard. Biographic information. *Wikipedia*. https://en.wikipedia.org/wiki/Bernard_Lietaer. (accessed 7.26.24).

Lietaer, Bernard. *The Future of Money: A New Way to Create Wealth, Work, and a Wiser World*. New York, New York: Century Publishing. 2001.

Lovins, L. Hunter. *A Finer Future: Creating an Economy in Service to Life*. With contributions by Stewart Wallis, Anders Wijkman, John Fullerton, and Club of Rome. Gabriola Island, BC, Canada: New Society Publishers. 2018.

Lyons, Oren. "When We Walk Upon Mother Earth." Address to United Nations. New York, New York. December 10, 1992. https://s2.smu.edu/twalker/orenlyon.htm.

Mackey, John and Raj Sisodia. *Conscious Capitalism: Liberating the Heroic Spirit of Business*. Boston: Harvard Business Review Press. 2013.

Macy, Joanna. *World as Lover, World as Self: Courage for Global Justice and Ecological Renewal*. Berkeley, CA: Parallax Press. 2007. (Originally published 1991).

Macy, Joanna with Chris Johnstone. *Active Hope: How to Face the Mess We're in Without Going Crazy*. Novato, CA: New World Library. 2012.

Mark, Joshua. "The Negative Confessions" [of Ancient Egypt]. *World History Encyclopedia*. April 27, 2017. https://www.worldhistory.org/The_Negative_Confession/.

Metzner, Ralph. "The Emerging Cosmological Worldview." In Mary Evelyn Tucker and John Grim (eds.), *Worldviews and Ecology: Religion, Philosophy, and the Environment*. Cranbury, NJ: Associated University Presses. 1980.

Meadows, Donella. "Leverage Points: Places to Intervene in a System." The Donella Meadows Project—Academy for Systems Change. 1997. https://donella-meadows.org/archives/leverage-points-places-to-intervene-in-a-system/.

Meadows, Donella. *Thinking in Systems: A Primer*. White River Junction, VT: Chelsea Green Publishing. 2008.

Metzner, Ralph. *Green Psychology: Transforming Our Relationship to the Earth*. Park Street Press. 1999.

Milgram, Stanley. *Obedience to Authority: An Experimental View*. New York: Harper and Row. 1974.

Mohan, Pavithra. "Study: This is How Much Money You Need to Earn to be Financially Successful." Fast Company. November 22, 2024. https://www.fastcompany.com/91234667/how-much-annual-income-financial-success.

Mollison, Bill. *Permaculture: A Designer's Manual*. Chicago: Tagari Publications. 1988

Morrison, Roy. *We Build the Road as We Travel: Mondragon, A Cooperative Social System*. Philadelphia, Pennsylvania: New Society Publishers. 1991.

Mosley, Tonya. "Melinda French Gates On What Billionaires with 'Absurd' Wealth Owe Back to Society." NPR, Fresh Air. April 15, 2025. https://www.npr.org/sections/goats-and-soda/2025/04/15/nx-s1-5364640/melinda-french-gates.

Naess, Arne. *Ecology, Community and Lifestyle: Outline of an Ecosophy*. Cambridge; New York: Cambridge University Press. 1989.

Naess, Arne. *Ecology of Wisdom: Writings by Arne Naess*. Alan Drengson and Bill Devall, eds. Berkeley, CA: Counterpoint. 2008.

National Center for Employee Ownership https://www.nceo.org/research/employee-ownership-by-the-numbers.

National Cooperative Bank. "Newly Released NCB Co-op 100® Report Reveal Cooperatives with Revenue Totaling $325 Billion." October 22, 2024. https://ncbaclusa.coop/blog/newly-released-ncb-co-op-100-report-reveals-top-producing-cooperatives-with-revenue-totaling-325-billion/.

National Cooperative Business Association. "Co-op Sectors: Where Cooperatives Operate." NCBA website accessed 2.8.2025. https://ncbaclusa.coop/resources/co-op-sectors/.

Neuman, Scott. "Killing Comes Naturally To Chimps, Scientists Say." NPR. September 18, 2014. https://www.npr.org/sections/thetwo-way/2014/09/18/349564036/killing-comes-naturally-to-chimps-scientists-say.

Office of the Surgeon General (OSG). "Our Epidemic of Loneliness and Isolation: The U.S. Surgeon General's Advisory on the Healing Effects of Social Connection and Community." U.S. Department of Health and Human Services. Washington D.C.: National Library of Medicine. 2023. https://pubmed.ncbi.nlm.nih.gov/37792968/ (accessed 6.23.25).

One Small Planet. Philanthropic Fund Annual Report—2023. https://www.onesmallplanet.org/one-small-planet-water. https://www.paperturn-view.com/one-small-planet/pdf?pid=ODg8838624&v=4 (accessed 4.11.25).

Orr, David. *Ecological Literacy: Education and the Transition to a Postmodern World.* Albany, New York: SUNY Press. 1992.

Parkes, Graham. "Staying Loyal to the Earth: Nietzsche as an Ecological Thinker." In John Lippitt (ed.). *Nietzsche's Futures.* New York: St. Martin's Press. 1999.

Parrish, Priyah. "Why ESG assets are heading toward $50 trillion despite attacks on 'woke capitalism'" *Fortune.* Oct. 10, 2024. https://fortune.com/2024/10/10/why-esg-assets-grow-despite-attacks-on-woke-capitalism/.

Patel, Jagdish. "The Underground Economy That Outpaces Wall Street." *LinkedIn.* September, 2025. https://www.linkedin.com/posts/jagdishpatelinfo_mycorrhizae-naturebasedsolutions-activity-7365583704443805696-vskL/.

Perry, Aaron William. *Viriditas: The Great Healing Is Within Our Power.* Boulder, Colorado: Earth Water Press. 2022.

Perry, Aaron William. *Y on Earth: Get Smarter, Feel Better, Heal the Planet.* Boulder, Colorado: Earth Water Press. 2017.

Perry, Nicolette. *Symbiosis: Close Encounters of the Natural Kind.* Poole-Dorset, UK: Blandford Press. 1983.

Ricard, Matthieu. *Altruism: The Power of Compassion to Change Yourself and the World.* Little Brown and Company. Translation Edition 2015.

Rogers, Everett. *Diffusion of Innovations.* Chicago: Free Press of Glencoe. 1962. (See also 5th Edition, 2003).

Romero, Dr. José. "Adaptation: Risk Management in Switzerland." Swiss National Focal Point for the UNFCCC, KP and the IPCC. Swiss Federal Office for the Environment. https://unfccc.int/sites/default/files/switzerland_extended_version.pdf (accessed 6.23.25).

Roske, Jeremy. "Your Money or Your Life." *People Rise.* 2005. https://www.youtube.com/watch?v=MMKP7aPQbX8 (accessed 5.7.25).

Roszak, Theodor. *The Voice of the Earth.* New York: Simon & Schuster. 1992.

Roszak, Theodor. "Where Psyche Meets Gaia." In T. Roszak, et al. (eds.). *Ecopsychology.* Op. cit.

Roszak, Theodor, Mary Gomes and Allen Kanner (eds.). *Ecopsychology: Restoring the Earth, Healing the Mind.* San Francisco: Sierra Club Books. 1995.

Ruddick, William. *Grassroots Economics: Reflection and Practice.* Grassroots Economics Foundation 2025.

Sahtouris, Elisabet, Brian Swimme, and Sidney Liebes. *A Walk Through Time: from Stardust to Us.* New York: Wiley. 1998.

Sahtouris, Elisabet and James Lovelock. *EarthDance: Living Systems in Evolution.* Lincoln, NE: iUniverse. 2000.

Scharmer, C. Otto. "Ten Economic Insights of Rudolf Steiner: Returning 'Eco' to Economics." Kosmos: Journal for Global Transformation. Vol. 19., Issue 4. (accessed 2.16.25). https://www.kosmosjournal.org/kj_article/rethinking-economics/.

Scott, MacKenzie. "Investing." *Yield Giving* (website). December 18, 2024. https://yieldgiving.com/essays/investing.

Sessions, George (ed.). *Deep Ecology for the 21st Century.* Boston: Shambhala. 1995.

Simard, Suzanne. *Finding the Mother Tree: Discovering the Wisdom of the Forest.* New York: Alfred A. Knopf. 2021.

Singer, Peter. *The Most Good You Can Do: How Effective Altruism is Changing Ideas About Living Ethically.* New Haven: Yale University Press. 2015.

Singer, Tania and Matthieu Ricard, eds. *Caring Economics: Conversations on Altruism and Compassion, Between Scientists, Economists, and the Dalai Lama.* With Foreword by His Holiness the Dalai Lama. New York: Picador. 2015.

Sisodia, Raj and John Macky. *Conscious Capitalism.* Op. Cit.

Sisodia, Raj. *Shakti Leadership: Embracing Feminine and Masculine Power in Business.* Oakland: Berrett-Koehler Publishers. 2016.

Stamets, Paul. *Mycelium Running: How Mushrooms Can Help Save the World.* Ten Speed Press. 2005.

Steiner, Rudolf. *Agriculture: A Course of Eight Lectures* (1924). 3rd Edition. Biodynamic Association. 1974.

Steyer, Tom. LinkedIn Post "The data is clear, renewable energy is winning..." https://www.linkedin.com/posts/tomsteyer_the-data-is-clear-renewable-energy-is-winning-activity-7227350647078096896-VmgZ/.

Sundheim, Doug. "How Patagonia Became the Most Reputable Brand In the United States." *Forbes.* December 12, 2023. https://www.forbes.com/sites/dougsundheim/2023/12/12/how-patagonia-became-the-most-reputable-brand-in-the-united-states/.

Talmon, Joseph and Karl Russell. "The Greatest Wealth Transfer in History Is Here, With Familiar (Rich) Winners," *The New York Times.* May 14, 2023. https://www.nytimes.com/2023/05/14/business/economy/wealth-generations.html.

The Threshold Foundation. https://www.thresholdfoundation.org/.

Thompson, William Irwin. "The Meta Industrial Village." *Darkness and Scattered Light.* Anchor Press. 1978.

Tobias, Michael (ed.) *Deep Ecology.* San Diego: Avant. 1985.

Tompkins, Peter, and Christopher Bird. *Secrets of the Soil.* Harper & Row. 1989.

Tompkins, Peter, and Christopher Bird. *The Secret Life of Plants.* Harper & Row. 1973.

Tucker, Mary Evelyn and John Grim (eds.). *Worldviews and Ecology: Religion, Philosophy, and the Environment.* Cranbury, NJ: Associated University Presses. 1994.

Twist, Lynne. *Living a Committed Life: Finding Freedom and Fulfillment in a Purpose Larger Than Yourself.* With Foreword by Van Jones. Oakland: Berrett-Koehler Press. 2023.

Underhill, Evelyn. *Mysticism: A Study in the Nature and Development of Man's Spiritual Consciousness.* London: Methuen. 1912.

U.S. Chamber of Commerce. "Preparing for Climate-Related Catastrophes Beats Focusing on Recovery Alone." *The Preparedness Payoff: The Economic Benefits of Investing in Climate Resilience—2024 Climate Resiliency Report.* (Produced in Partnership by the U.S. Chamber of Commerce, Allstate Insurance, and the U.S. Chamber of Commerce Foundation). June 25, 2024. https://www.uschamber.com/security/the-preparedness-payoff-the-economic-benefits-of-investing-in-climate-resilience (accessed 6.23.25).

Van Tongeren, Daryl. *Humble: Free Yourself From the Traps of a Narcissistic World.* The Experiment Publishing. 2022.

Vazza, F., and A. Feletti. "The Quantitative Comparison Between the Neuronal Network and the Cosmic Web." *Frontiers in Physics.* Vol. 8. November 16, 2020. https://www.frontiersin.org/journals/physics/articles/10.3389/fphy.2020.525731/full.

WANGO https://www.wango.org/resources.aspx?section=ngodir, https://www.wango.org/about.aspx.

Watts, Alan. *Nature, Man, and Woman.* New York: Pantheon. 1958.

Weisman, Alan. *Gaviotas: A Village to Reinvent the World.* Chelsea Green Publications. 1998.

White, Lynn. "The Historical Roots of Our Ecologic Crisis." In Glotfelty and Fromm (eds.). *The Ecocriticism Reader.* Athens, Georgia: University of Georgia Press. 1996.

Whiting, Kate and Adam Tooze. "This is Why 'Polycrisis' is a Useful Way of Looking t at the World Right Now." World Economic Forum. March 7, 2023. https://www.weforum.org/stories/2023/03/polycrisis-adam-tooze-historian-explains/.

Wikipedia. "List of Confederations" [in history]. https://en.wikipedia.org/wiki/List_of_confederations. (accessed 2.8.2025).

Wray, L. Randall. "The Rise of the Modern Monetary System: An Integration of the Credit and State Money Approaches." Hudson, NY: Levy Economics Institute of Bard College. 2025.

Xian Li and Fuming Wei, "What Confucian Eco-Ethics Can Teach Us about Solving the Dilemma of Interpreting the Concept of Sustainability." *Religions.* 2023, 14, 1216. https://doi.org/10.3390/rel14091216.

Many, many more resources mentioned throughout *Viriditas* (especially chapter 33), and in the bibliography of *Y on Earth* by Aaron William Perry, op cit.

ABOUT THE AUTHOR

Aaron William Perry is an author, entrepreneur, speaker, and consultant. Founder and executive director of the Y on Earth Community, he hosts the Y on Earth Community Podcast series; the regenerative finance VIP Enclave Gatherings; and a variety of community-based programs in collaboration with Y on Earth Community Ambassadors. He is the author of the visionary novel *Viriditas: The Great Healing Is Within Our Power*, as well as the foundational nonfiction tome *Y on Earth: Get Smarter, Feel Better, Heal the Planet*, along with a children's book series, collection of poetry, and the *Soil Stewardship Handbook*.

Previously, Aaron launched and led companies in the local and organic food, regenerative agriculture, recycling, food waste recovery, and renewable energy industries, and he has advised scores of additional companies in the food, energy, and wellness sectors. Additionally, he advises and coaches mission-driven entrepreneurs and executives.

Aaron studied at New York University, and the University of New Mexico, and holds a master's degree from the University of Colorado, where he studied Germanistiks, Philosophy, Literature, History, Environmental Policy, and Sustainable Economic Development. During graduate school and the many years since, he has studied and practiced Biodynamics, Herbal Medicine, Hot Spring Soaking, Folk and Indigenous Wisdom, Permaculture, and Shinrin Yoku forest immersion throughout the Rocky Mountain West and internationally. He resides in Lyons, Colorado with his sweetheart Caressa, where they often hear the owls hooting at night and the call of eagles and hawks during the day.

www.ingramcontent.com/pod-product-compliance
Lightning Source LLC
Chambersburg PA
CBHW081142020426

42333CB00021B/2637